CW01460581

The Antichrist Revealed!
Book 4 of The Original Revelation Series

The Antichrist Revealed!
Book 4 of The Original Revelation Series

by
Rav Sha'ul

Copyright © 2015 by Rav Sha'ul
All rights reserved. No part of this book may be reproduced, scanned,
or distributed in any printed or electronic form without permission.
First Edition: April 2015
Printed in the United States of America
ISBN-13: 9781514142844

To all those who cherish his coming.

Preface

In this book I am going to clearly identify what has eluded mankind for 2,000 years... *The identity of the Beast and the religion behind it*. The Bible declares that all mankind will worship the Beast at the end of 6,000 years. This has come true as the religion of this "beast" is the largest religion on Earth. The god of this "beast" is a false image of the true Messiah whom we have elevated in our hearts as God incarnate above Yahuah our Creator.

The Beast (Greek: Θηρίον, Thērion) refers to two beasts described in the Book of Revelation as together they form the "god" and the religion behind this false god. The first beast comes from "out of the sea" and is given authority and power by the dragon. We are going to clearly identify the first beast and second beast and the dragon or 'spirit behind the Beast'.

The second beast comes from "out of the earth" and directs all peoples of the Earth to worship the first beast. The second beast is described in Revelation 13:11-18. The second beast is also referred to as the false prophet. The false prophet is not a physical man but rather the religious system that evolved around the worship of the first beast. This religious system is identified as Mystery Babylon b John and associated with Rome by Peter.

The two beasts are aligned with the dragon in opposition to the Creator Yahuah and the Messiah Yahusha. This beastly system is another gospel built around the religion that evolved out of Babylon. As I explain in my first 3 books (**Creation Cries Out!**, **Babylon the religion of the Beast**, and **Christianity the Great Deception**) this religion is defined by its rituals which are opposed to the rituals defined by Yahuah in the Bible.

We have two very different gospels in front of us:

- **Babylonian Rituals:**
  Trinity/Jesus/Sunday/Easter/Holidays/Lawlessness

- **The Creator's Rituals**:
  Yahuah/Yahusha/Sabbath/Passover/Holy Days/the Law

Our Creator, Yahuah, who revealed Himself in The Bible, warns us that His word would be altered by translators and scribes then twisted by Greeks into 'another gospel'. A false gospel that teaches that the Law was abolished and presents us with an "image" of the Messiah that is false. This false image of the true Messiah is called *The Lawless One.*

Jeremiah 8:8
How can you say, "We are wise because we have the Word of Yahuah," when your teachers and scribes have twisted it by writing lies?

2 Peter 3:16
The Apostle Paul Speaking of these things in all of his letters. Some of his comments are hard to understand, and those who are ignorant and unstable have twisted his letters to mean something quite different (*The Pauline Doctrine*), just as they do with other parts of scripture. And this will result in their destruction.

2 Thessalonians 2
[3] Don't be fooled by what they say. For that day will not come until there is a great rebellion against Yahuah (*as the Law will be abolished*) and the man of lawlessness (*the image of a man in whom the Law is abolished*) is revealed… [7] For this lawlessness is already at work **secretly**, and **it will remain secret** until the one who is holding it back steps out of the way. [8] Then the man of lawlessness (*the one who abolished The Law*) will be

revealed (*at the time of the end by the testimony of Yahusha through men of wisdom and insight*).

We call this false *image* of a man the **Lawless One** because in this image the Law of Yahuah was abolished. This image represents the opposite of the 3 witnesses we must have in the Book of Life. All 3 witnesses we need to have in that book are found in the Torah and by abolishing it we are left without any hope of eternal life. This will come as a total shock on that day to those who followed this false messiah because all along they *believed* he was God incarnate.

> ### Matthew 7
> [21] "Not everyone who says to Me, 'Master, Master,' will enter the kingdom of Yahuah, but he who does the will of My Father (*Yahuah*) who is in heaven *will enter*. [22] Many will say to Me on that day, 'Master, Master, did we not prophesy in Your name, and in Your name cast out demons, and in Your name perform many miracles?' [23] And then I will declare to them, 'I never knew you; DEPART FROM ME, YOU WHO PRACTICE LAWLESSNESS.'

You see, all humanity worships a false messiah and those who follow this false image of the true Messiah call him by a pagan name. They are addressing him by a name that literally means '*Earthy Pig*' and gives glory to another god. They never knew his true name and they abolished the Law/Will of Yahuah and followed the Lawless One!

Humanity has committed what the Bible calls the *Transgression of Desolation* which is the transgression of The Creator's Feasts, Torah, and Sabbaths. This world-wide transgression causes the desolation of this planet and almost everyone on it. We call this the **Great Tribulation** when the Earth and its inhabitants must pay for abolishing the Law of Yahuah. The Great Tribulation is not caused by "the Antichrist committing the *Abomination* of Desolation" as we are taught in Christianity. The Great Tribulation is caused by the inhabitants of Earth committing the

Transgression of Desolation as we have believed in _The Lawless One_:

Isaiah 24
[3] The earth will be completely laid waste and completely despoiled, for Yahuah has spoken this word... [5] The earth is also polluted by its inhabitants, for they transgressed the Law of Yahuah (_abolished the Law_), violated His statutes (_changed His Holy Days to pagan holidays_), and broke the everlasting covenant (_of the Sabbath and changed it to Sunday_). [6] Therefore, a curse devours the earth (_the curse of disobedience to the Torah is death_), and those who live in it are held guilty (_because they put their faith in Easter not Passover and their sin is not forgiven_). Therefore, the inhabitants of the earth are burned, and few men are left.

The "_Abomination_ of Desolation", on the other hand, is committed by those who invite this "Lawless One" into their heart and elevate this "image of a man who died" as God incarnate above Yahuah.

Romans 1
[21] because, although they knew Yahuah, they did not glorify _Him_ as God, nor were thankful, but became futile in their thoughts (_that the Torah was abolished_), and their foolish hearts were darkened (_the Torah is a light unto our path_). [22] Professing to be wise, they became fools, [23] and changed the glory of Yahuah who cannot die into an image of a man who died.

I will clearly explain all of what I just said above in this book. We are warned that this other gospel would be '_Mystery Babylon_' in the book of Revelation as the Messiah commands us to come out of this world-wide false religion. We are warned that we would abolish the Law and change Yahuah's Feasts to Babylonian rituals.

Daniel 7:25
He (_the Beast_) will speak against the Most High (_setting himself up as God incarnate_) and oppress his holy people

(*those who keep the Sabbath*) and try to change the set times (*Ordained Festivals*) and the Laws (*of Yahuah*).

2 Thessalonians 2:4
He (*the Beast*) will oppose (*the True Messiah*) and will exalt himself (*in our hearts*) over everything that is called God or is worshiped, so that he sets himself up in God's temple (*the hearts of man*), proclaiming himself to be God (*incarnate*).

We are warned that we would forget the name of Yahuah and begin worshipping The LORD (Ba'al) the Babylonian sungod on Sunday.

Jeremiah 23:27
They think the dreams they tell one another will make my people forget my name Yahuah, just as their ancestors forgot my name through Baal (*The LORD*) worship (*on Sunday not The Sabbath*).

Then we are warned that a false image of the true Messiah would emerge coming in the name of pagan gods and false teachers would prevail as we surround ourselves with teachers who do not teach the truth but rather "tickle our ears".

2 Timothy 4:3
For the time will come when people will not put up with sound doctrine (*but fall for sound-bite implied doctrines*). Instead, to suit their own desires (*not to have to obey the Law*), they will gather around them a great number of (*false*) teachers to say what their itching ears want to hear (*so they can continue to be lawless*).

Instead of doing what our Creator instructs in His Torah, we would do whatever we see fit:

Deuteronomy 12:8
You **are not to do** as we do here today, everyone doing as

they see fit (*we are to worship our Creator when and how He instructed us*).

We would attempt to worship our Creator through Babylonian rituals. We would "say" we are worshipping our Creator in the process while violating the very instructions He gave us in the Torah:

Deuteronomy 12:31
You must not worship Yahuah your God in their (*Babylonian*) way, because in worshiping their (*Babylonian Trinity*) gods, they do all kinds of detestable things Yahuah hates. They even burn their sons and daughters in the fire as sacrifices to their gods (*all Christian/Babylonian holidays are directed at our children*).

We are warned that we would not search the scriptures and test these lies but rather put up with all of this easily enough. This is because we are "sheeple" who are *spiritually lazy* and turn our eternal lives over to "prophets for profit" who cater to our desires for the sake of money.

2 Corinthians 11:4
For if someone comes to you and preaches a messiah (*Jesus Christ the Easter pig*) other than the Messiah we preached (*Yahusha the Passover Lamb*), or if you receive a different spirit (*Spirit of Error*) from the Spirit (*of Truth*) you received, or a different gospel (*Trinity/Jesus/Easter/Sunday/Christmas/Law abolished*) from the one you accepted (*Yahuah/Yahusha/Passover/Sabbath/Holy Days/Law written on our hearts*), you put up with it easily enough.

The false messiah would be defined by the false religion. This religion would teach us that this false gospel is the faith taught in the Bible and believed by the disciples and the early church. We would not test these doctrines in scripture and ignore historical evidence. This false gospel, false religion, and false messiah would be so convincing that it would lead humanity astray. All humanity would worship this false messiah thinking him to be the one prophesied to come in the Bible and believe him to be "God incarnate".

Revelation 13

And power was given him (*the false image of the True Messiah*) over all kindreds, and tongues, and nations. [8] And all that dwell upon the earth shall worship him (*as God incarnate and elevate this false image of a man who died as God in their heart above Yahuah* **Romans 1**).

The Messiah was never supposed to be the object of our worship. The Beast is given power to deceive humanity through signs and wonders that seem to give power to his name.

2 Thessalonians 2

[9] The coming of the Lawless one (the one in whom the Law is abolished) will be in accordance with how Satan works (the spirit behind the false messiah is the serpent). He will use all sorts of displays of power through signs and wonders that serve the lie.

This "lie" behind the false gospel, false religion, and false messiah is so strong that it misleads humanity. If possible it could even mislead the Elect because it is a mixture of the truth with pagan traditions. This is called 'Syncretism' which was accomplished through 'Hellenism' which I will demonstrate in this book.

The Bible declares that at the end just before the true Messiah returns that the Elect will be called out of every nation. As we come out of the nations we emphatically declare that all of our ancestors were misled by this lie. This "religion" is simply passed down from generation to generation through traditions that no one dare question.

Jeremiah 16:19
Yahuah, my strength and my fortress, my refuge in time of distress, to you the (*elect among the*) Gentile nations will come from the ends of the earth and say, "Our ancestors possessed nothing but lies, false gods, and worthless idols that did them no good."

The false messiah will be very deceptive because it is an "image" based on the life of the true Messiah merged with myths of pagan demi-gods. Because this "image" is based on the life of the true Messiah, the false messiah would fulfill most of prophesies spoken in The Bible concerning the Messiah **but fail in critical specific ways**. We are given very specific prophesies so that we can clearly identify this "image of a man" that is proclaimed to be God incarnate. In the end just before the Messiah Yahusha returns, the Bible tells us that the Elect would overcome this false image by the blood of the **Passover** Lamb and their testimony.

Revelation 12:11
They triumphed over him by the blood of the Lamb and by the word of their testimony; they did not love their lives so much as to shrink from death.

The proper sacrifice for sin is the Passover Lamb not the Easter Pig. The testimony of the true Messiah is prophecy! That is how we are to identify the true Messiah from the false image and triumph over this false messiah.

Revelation 19:10
Hold to the testimony of Yahusha. Worship Yahuah! For it is the Spirit of prophecy who bears testimony to Yahusha (*that he is the true Messiah*)."

In this book I am going to shine a bright spotlight of prophecy on the false image of the true Messiah. The false "image of a man who died" in history that has replaced Yahuah as God in our hearts. That "image" is *Hesus Horus Krishna* known today as *Jesus H. Christ*. We will see if that image can withstand the testimony of the true Messiah… Prophecy! I will explain in detail how this false image of the Messiah fulfills **every** prophecy of what we call the Antichrist. I will also explain how the religion that grew up over time around this false messiah is blinded to these prophesies. This false religion has redirected the world's attention away from the false messiah all together. This false religion has us all looking the other way. Even worse this religion has led us all to commit the Abomination of Desolation unknowingly!

That false religion is (by its own definition) a merger of all pagan religions into one world religion called the Universal Catholic Church which is the foundation of the Christian Religion. This Beast is not limited to Catholicism but to all Trinity, Jesus, Sunday, Easter, Christmas, Lawless Protestant churches as well. Every religious establishment that believes in these pagan rituals are simply "**protest**ing" Catholics known as **Protest**ants and guilty as charged for worshipping the false messiah.

The "god" of Christianity is an "image" created based on the life of the Messiah merged with myths of pagan demi-gods and defined by the rituals of Babylon. This false image worshipped as God incarnate was named after 3 pagan demi-gods Hesus, Horus, and Krishna by the High Priest of the Sungod (Potifus Maximus) known as the Roman Emperor Constantine. Over time it became known as **Jesus** (*Hesus*) **H.** (*Horus*) **Christ** (*Krishna*). This "image" is known by the mark X, the monogram **I.H.S.** (*Isis, Horus, Seb*), and the pictogram HES. I will prove in great detail that Jesus Christ is literally identified in the Bible by his name, mark, monogram, Christogram, sacrifice, rituals, and spirit as the false messiah. There is only one "image of a man" in history or in the future that qualifies as the Antichrist. Only one; Jesus H. Christ and he is the fulfillment of every prophecy in the Bible that points us to the false messiah.

The Beast has been revealed and now we can "see" the Abomination of Desolation as I will clearly define it in detail. Christianity has caused all humanity to worship Jesus H. Christ and in doing so we have all committed both the Transgression of

Desolation and the Abomination of Desolation. It is not too late to overcome it and rededicate the altar of your heart back to Yahuah. It is not too late to properly pour the blood of the Passover Lamb over that altar and purify it and prevent the desolation of His Temple (your body).

Yes, **_dethrone_** Hesus Horus Krishna from his throne over your life, remove his mark "on your forehead", and take back your life and give it to Yahuah as a living sacrifice. You invited Jesus H. Christ into your heart and that false god is there by invitation only. You can uninvited this pagan god just as easily if you have the strength. Stop elevating the image of a man who died as God above Yahuah who is the ONLY TRUE GOD! Clean the blood of the Easter Pig off of Yahuah's altar! Then properly pour out on the altar of your heart the blood of The Passover Lamb of God whose name is Yahusha.

In this book I will leave no stone unturned as we discover the truth behind the historical background of the Christian Church, its rituals, its gods, and more. I will demonstrate the meaning of scripture both in context of the entire Bible and within historical context. I will prove without a shadow of a doubt that Jesus H. Christ is the Antichrist.

HalleluYahuah and worthy is the Passover Lamb Yahusha who is the true Messiah.

<u>John 17:3</u>

Now this is (*the key to*) eternal life: that they know you (*Yahuah*), The <u>ONLY TRUE GOD</u>, and Yahusha the Messiah, whom you (*Yahuah*) have sent (*as a human Messiah to give his life as the Passover sacrifice for sin to purify His altar*).

Table of Contents

Chapter 10 - How the new "god' of this false religion was created … 137

Chapter 11 - Christianity is born with a new god… Jesus H. Christ (I.H.S) … 146

Chapter 12 - Jesus Christ the Beast of Revelation … 150

Chapter 13 - True meaning of Revelation Chapter 13 ... 188

Chapter 14 - The Spirit of Truth and the Spirit of Error ... 201

Chapter 15 – The Spirit of the Antichrist ... 212

Chapter 16 - The Antichrist is in an image of all pagan trinity gods ... 277

Chapter 17 – The Antichrist changes the Holy Days to Babylonian festivals ... 295

Chapter 18 – The Antichrist is The Lawless One who commits The Transgression of Desolation ... 335

Chapter 19 – The Antichrist enters the Temple of Yahuah ... 385

Chapter 22 – The Mark of the Beast ... 468

Conclusion ... 492

Introduction

This book is perhaps the most important book I have written and the hardest book you, the reader, will ever have to digest. This book is an *abstract* of my book series '*The Original Revelation Series*'.

The Original Revelation Series is a book series I have written designed to take us all back to the true faith, the original faith and the original revelation of Yahuah to mankind. There are many concepts and terms used that I define later in other books so I encourage everyone to read the entire series... twice! Again, this book is just an *abstract teaser*. Please read the entire series *The Original Revelation Series* which is designed to walk you out of this deception and back into proper covenant with your Creator. In that series everything is broken down in detail and proven through historical documents, church records, mainstream references, and Scripture. This book series is an in depth study in the battle of the ages. That battle is between the Truth of Yahuah and sun worship.

In *The Original Revelation Series* I walk the reader through this battle as sun worship began early in the history of man then was formulated into a religion in Babylon and then passed down through time and now exists in the form of Christianity. Then I relay the foundation of Truth starting with who The Messiah really is, what The Kingdom of Yahuah is, and a detailed account of The Yahushaic Covenant (The Renewed Covenant).

In this book I am going to ask the hard questions and I am not afraid of the answers to those questions nor do I make any apologies for the obvious conclusions these question reveal. This book is for all those who are serious about their faith and their salvation and have a desire to "work out their own salvation with fear and trembling" outside of what they have been taught all their lives or what their friends and families believe.

We have two competing Gospels in front of us. We have Christianity which is

The Trinity/Jesus/Sunday/Easter/Christmas/no Law

and then we have what the Bible actually commands in

Yahuah/Yahusha/Sabbath/Feasts of Yahuah/The Law written on our hearts.

Jesus Christ represents the former and Yahusha the Messiah represents the latter. We have two Gospels, two Messiahs, and two names that are polar opposites of each other. There is a sign (the Sabbath), a seal (The Shema or name of Yahuah), and a path to deliverance defined in the Bible through the blood of the Passover Lamb. Only those who have these witnesses in the Book of Life receive eternal life. Yahusha represents The Way and his name means "Yahuah's Salvation" as he came in the name of Yahuah. If you follow him you will have all three witnesses. Jesus represents another gospel and his name means Beast of the Earth as he came in the name of all pagan demi-gods and If you follow Jesus you will be robbed of all three required witnesses and your name will be blotted out of the Book of Life.

The religion created around Jesus Christ deliberately changed the name of Yahuah to a trinitarian pagan deity known as The LORD (a title for the trinitarian Babylonian god Baal). The Sabbath was changed to the day of Baal worship Sunday. Passover was changed to Easter which is the worship of the son of (and incarnation of) Baal named Tammuz. One is the true way and the other a pagan Babylonian lie called Mystery Babylon. The modern English translations are complicit in this deception replacing the name of the true Messiah Yahusha with the name of the false messiah Jesus Christ and have replaced the name of Yahuah with The LORD god Ba'al. These translations have been proven to have been altered adding text to support the Babylonian Trinity. This deception runs deep and is well entrenched into our traditions over the past 2,000 years.

We have two Messiahs presented to us:

- One represents the true sacrifice for sin The Passover Lamb, the other the abominable sacrifice of a pig that destroys your body... Easter.
- One is the first born son of Yahuah born fully human then divine through resurrection. The other is the pagan incarnate god in the image of all pagan god-men going back to Babylon.
- One is the true way to eternal life by example; the 'salvation of Yahuah'. The other is the broad path that leads to destruction... the son of perdition.
- One is the true Messiah of Israel; the other is the false Greek demi-god.

This book series will make crystal clear which is the true Messiah found in the Bible that honors Yahuah and expose the imposter. What we have in front of us are two paths and the fulfillment of Yahuah's prophetic word. Blessed is he who finds the narrow gate for very few there are that ever find it.

Below I quote from the Gospel of John as we see the true Messiah's relationship with his Father Yahuah. We see Yahusha deny "the Trinity" and declare Yahuah the only True God and giver of eternal life to those who enter into The Yahushaic Covenant. Throughout this book series I put every scripture I quote in context of the entire Bible by inserting the context in blue Italic parenthesis so that these scriptures can be properly understood. Every comment in blue parenthesis is explained in detail in my book series.

> **Note:** At times when I quote scripture I will also insert into that portion of scripture, references to other scriptures to prove my comments in blue parenthesis. You can see this below as I insert scripture in the book of Hebrews (and indent it) into my quotation of John. I do this below to demonstrate that Yahusha was human and relied upon Yahuah to save him from death just like every other man. It is quite obvious that Yahusha is not "Yahuah in the

flesh" but a human crying out to Yahuah:

John 17

17 Yahusha spoke these things; and lifting up his eyes to heaven, he said, "Father, the hour has come; glorify your (*first born*) Son (*through resurrection*),

Hebrews 2:17

For this reason Yahusha had to be made (*by Yahuah human*) like them (*the rest of Yahuah's sons*), **fully human in every way**, in order that he might become a merciful and faithful high priest (*not a demi-god*) in service to Yahuah, and that he might make atonement for the sins of the people (*as is the role of the human High Priests*).

Hebrews 5

[7] Yahusha, in the days of his flesh (*when he was "fully human in every way"*), when he had offered up prayers and supplications, with vehement cries and tears to Yahuah who was able to save him from death.

Continuing with John 17

that the Son may glorify You, [2] even as You gave me authority over all flesh (*appointed Yahusha High Priest and King Zachariah 3*), that to all whom You have given me, **You (Yahuah not "Jesus") may give eternal life**. [3] **This is eternal life, that they may know You** (Yahuah)**, the *only true God*,** and (*be in covenant with*) Yahusha the Messiah whom You have sent (*according to The Plan of Salvation to die on Passover*). [4] I glorified You on the earth (*as your proxy; the perfect human image and reflection of the invisible God **Colossians 1:15***), having accomplished the

5

work which You have given Me to do (*Yahusha denied his own will and his entire life was his sacrifice*). [5] Now, Father, glorify Me (*as preeminent among creation* **Colossians 1:17** *"He is the beginning, the firstborn from the dead, that in everything he might be preeminent"*) together with Yourself (*as your first born son through resurrection not human birth*), with the glory which I had (*in the Plan of Salvation that was*) with You before the world was (*created according to Your Plan by which all was done and nothing was done outside of that Plan* **John Chapter 1**).

[6] "I have manifested the name Yahuah to the men whom You gave Me out of the world (*Yahusha displayed he was a sealed servant*); they were Yours and You gave them to Me (*in covenant*), and they have kept **Your** commandments (*the Law is written on their hearts* **Jeremiah 31**). [7] Now they have come to know that everything You have given Me (*through inheritance*) is from You (*by whom all things were created*); [8] for the words which You gave Me (*that You are our Father and You are begetting a family, the mystery of the ages*) I have given to them; and they received *them* and truly understood that I came forth from You (*as your first born in that family*), and they believed that You sent Me (*in fulfillment of your Plan of Salvation*). [9] I ask on their behalf; I do not ask on behalf of the world, but of those whom You have given Me (*in covenant*); for they are **Your** Children (*just like Yahusha is*); [10] and all things that are Mine are Yours, and Yours are Mine (*through inheritance*); and I have been glorified in them. [11] I am no longer in the world (*it was his time to die*); and *yet* they themselves are (*still*) in the world, and I come to You (*through resurrection*). Holy Father, keep them in Your name (*Yahuah which is the seal on our foreheads*), *the name* which You have given Me (*Yahusha, Yahuah's Salvation*), that they may be one even as We *are (in marriage covenant)*. [12] While I was with them, I was keeping them in Your name (*the seal on our foreheads*), *the*

name which You have given Me (*Yahusha which means Yahuah's Salvation*); and I guarded them and not one of them perished but the son of perdition, so that the Scripture would be fulfilled.

We are saved through faith in the promises made by Yahuah. Yahuah never promised to come to Earth and die!

He actually said He would never do such a thing and it is impossible for Him to die. In fact, it is impossible for a fully begotten "son" of Yahuah do die!

Numbers 23:19
Yahuah is not human, that he should lie, not a human being, that he should change his mind. Does Yahuah speak and then not act? Does he promise and not fulfill?

Luke 20:36
and they can no longer die; for they are like the angels. They are Children of Yahuah, since they are children of the resurrection.

That is why Yahusha was crying out to Yahuah in John 17! Because he was facing death as a human; and had not yet been fully begotten through resurrection. Yahuah promised us a human Messiah, a human High Priest, a human King, a human Passover Lamb sacrifice that He would accept as the sacrifice for our sin against Him. He promised to sacrifice His first born son in the family He has purposed to beget to purchase the lives of all the rest of His sons in fulfillment of the Abraham/Isaac shadow. He then promised to raise this human Messiah from the grave and make him a "god" in Yahuah's likeness and seat that risen son at His right hand and give him all authority over the Universe as an Inheritance. That son is Yahusha who is the Messiah not Jesus Christ (who is a Greek demi-god).

I wrote this book knowing the shock value it will have on everyone who reads it. If Yahuah has so chosen you as a future son or daughter of His; then He will move in your spirit to continue on in this book series where everything is proven in detail. If you have committed **The Abomination of Desolation** and elevated Jesus Christ in your heart as God above Yahuah then you will be given over to believe the lie of Christianity. If that is true of you then I doubt you will get much further than this introduction. If you have committed this abomination and elevated the image of a man who died as God in your heart, scripture declares that Yahuah will literally give you over to a depraved mind. Those who elevate a man above Yahuah in their hearts (accept Jesus into their hearts over Yahuah) are filled with **The Spirit of Error**. That is what Scripture declares of those who do not have their mind sealed with The Shema, but has believed in the incarnation of Jesus.

Romans 1
[18] For the wrath of Yahuah is revealed from heaven against all ungodliness and unrighteousness (*breaking His Law*) of men **who suppress the truth in unrighteousness** (*teach unrighteousness i.e. that the Law was abolished as truth*), [19] because that which is known about Yahuah is evident within them (*The Law is written on our hearts*); for Yahuah made it evident to them… [21] For even though they knew Yahuah, they did not honor Him as God or give thanks, but they became futile in their speculations (*that Jesus abolished The Law and that Jesus is God*), and their foolish heart was darkened (*because The Torah is a light unto our path: Psalm 119:105*). [22] Professing to be wise, they became fools, [23] and exchanged the glory of the incorruptible Yahuah for ***an image in the form of corruptible man*** (*Jesus died their "god" was a corruptible man*)… [28] And just as they did not see fit to acknowledge Yahuah any longer (*instead they pray to Jesus, invite Jesus to sit on the throne of Yahuah in their heart as God, have the mark of The Pagan Trinity on their mind*), **Yahuah gave them over to a depraved mind**"

You see, our hearts are the Spiritual Alter of Yahuah not an altar to an image of "Jesus". Nowhere in the Bible does it say "invite Jesus into your heart" it says the opposite… do NOT elevate a man in your heart above Yahuah.

We are to keep Passover in light of Yahusha and in doing so we express our faith that he is the Passover Lamb and the blood of the Lamb is then poured out over the Altar of Yahuah (our hearts) and our sin is "Passed Over". By replacing the Altar of Yahuah with an altar of "Jesus"; we express our faith in Easter and pour the blood of the Ishtar Pig over that pagan altar leaving us with no sacrifice for our sin. This is The Abomination of Desolation as I will prove.

I wrote The Original Revelation Series so that we can tear down every high place we have elevated above Yahuah and purify out "altar" with The Blood of the Lamb and overcome The Abomination of Desolation.

I am not here to tickle your ears and tell you what you want to hear. You can go sit in your Christian Church and be entertained if that is what you desire. I am a true teacher and Truth is all that matters to me. Yahusha did not come to bring "peace on Earth" but a divisive **SWORD**.

Matthew 10:34
"Do not suppose that I have come to bring peace to the earth. I did not come to bring peace, but a sword.

The Truth is a double edged sword that divides the very soul and spirit of a man. That is exactly what each and every book in this series will do and it is not comfortable. Truth hurts.

Hebrews 4:12
For the word of Yahuah (*The Torah and Prophets*) is alive and active (all of it). Sharper than any double-edged sword, it penetrates even to dividing soul and spirit, joints and

marrow; it judges the thoughts and attitudes of the heart.

Throughout this book series we will have to face the truth that Christianity is based on Hellenism. We say that the Hebrew texts and the Gospel and all the Hebrew names were "Hellenized" not realizing what that means. That word does not just mean the Hebrew texts were translated into Greek and Latin. What Hellenized literally means is that the polytheistic religion of the Greeks was merged into the texts of The Bible. The text were altered to be "Greek appropriate" so the pagans could be assimilated into one world religion called Christianity. Hellenism is Greek paganism.

Everyone should fully understand what happened during this time in history. The Truth of Yahuah was merged with pagan Hellenism through a process called syncretism. It is this syncretic Hellenistic religion based in Rome that is the false religion!

We see below that nothing changed with Hellenism and that the same gods continued to be worshipped until 300 CE. This is when Constantine brought everything under one pagan religion called Christianity:

> http://en.wikipedia.org/wiki/Hellenistic_religion
> ## Hellenistic religion
> From Wikipedia, the free encyclopedia
>
> *Hellenistic religion is any of the various systems of beliefs and practices of the people who lived under the influence of ancient Greek culture during the Hellenistic period and the Roman Empire (c. 300 BCE **to 300 CE**). **There was much continuity in Hellenistic religion: the Greek gods continued to be worshipped, and the same rites were practiced as before**.*

Yes, the SAME "rites" that defined Roman sun worship brought over from Babylon continued to be worshipped through Hellenism. We call this assimilation of Greek paganism *to be Hellenized*. We know that the pagan Greek religion (Hellenism) overtook the truth of Yahuah and the resulting religion is now called Christianity:

http://en.wikipedia.org/wiki/Hellenization

Hellenization

From Wikipedia, the free encyclopedia

The twentieth century witnessed a lively debate over the extent of Hellenization in the Levant and particularly among the ancient Palestinian Jews that has continued until today. The Judaism of the diaspora was thought to have succumbed thoroughly to its influences. Bultmann thus argued that **Christianity arose almost completely within those Hellenistic confines and should be read against that background as opposed to a more traditional (Palestinian) Jewish background**

So let us begin our journey... to prove that Jesus Christ is the Antichrist and Christianity is the Beast.

Chapter 1
The Mystery Language

Introduction to the "Secret Things"... *The "Mystery Language" of Yahuah*

Before I go any further in this book; I want to reveal that The Bible is written in "another language" or "tongue" if you will. A language we must "learn" to speak if we are to understand such things as The Yahushaic Covenant, the Transgression of Desolation, The Abomination of Desolation, the identity of the false messiah, Grace, Liberty, and The Law of Yahuah. It has been my goal over the course of my book series ***Original Revelation*** to slowly and progressively open the readers "eyes and ears" to this language the Bible is written in.

Very few (only the Chosen Few) truly understand the things of Yahuah or the language in which the Bible was written in. Yahusha was the true teacher of Righteousness (The Torah) and he veiled every word he spoke in this Mystery Language using parables, parallels, idioms, etc. I have been disclosing this Mystery Language throughout this book series. I am attempting to open our eyes to the Spiritual meaning of the physical metaphors, and parables, and helping us to understand the Hebraic Mindset and meaning behind the Hebrew language. The Bible has been Hellenized by Greeks who twisted the scriptures. Not even the Hebrew people understood Yahusha when he spoke to them. This is because Yahuah has hidden Himself and The Truth of His Kingdom in a language few understand.

That language we (who have The Spirit of Holiness guiding us) speak in ***another tongue*** is a secret language that is revealed only to a chosen few by The Spirit of Holiness. It is not a bunch of babbling words no one understands as is taught by Pentecostal Christianity. It is not foreign languages. It is a <u>metaphorical language</u> of parables, parallels, idioms and prophetic portraits that transcend all languages! The *secret things* of The Kingdom of Yahuah are veiled in The Bible. The Apostle Paul addresses this other ***Mystery Language*** that is translated as "speaking in tongues"

13

below:

1 Corinthians 2:4-15

4 And my speech and my preaching was not with enticing words of man's wisdom (*Paul or Yahusha did not speak in literal terms*), but in the demonstration of the Spirit of Holiness and of power (*which gives us understanding of hidden things*): 5 That your faith should not stand in the (*literal*) wisdom of men (*to be taken literally*), but in the power of Yahuah (*In a Mystery Language taught only by The Holy Spirit to a chosen few*). 6 However we (Yahuah's *Chosen Few*) speak wisdom (*Spiritual Understanding*) among them that are perfect (*perfected by The Spirit of Holiness*): yet not the wisdom (*Literal / pagan / natural understanding*) of this world, nor of the princes of this world, that come to nothing (*they do not understand The Bible language*): 7 But we (*Yahuah's Chosen Few*) **speak the wisdom of Yahuah in a mystery, even the hidden wisdom**, which (*this Mystery Language*) Yahuah ordained before the world unto our glory (*those who know Him, the Chosen Few*): 8 Which none of the princes of this world knew (*the hidden mystery language of Yahuah that His Word is written in*): for had they known it (*this Mystery Language*), they would not have crucified the King of glory (*the did not understand the physical to Spiritual Truth of Passover*). 9 But as it is written, (*the natural*) EYE (*does not see Spiritual Truths and*) hath not seen (*the hidden mysteries*), nor (*the natural*) EAR heard (*the Spiritual Truth*), neither have (*these mysteries*) entered into the (*natural*) HEART of (*natural*) man (*humanity has been given over to a Spirit of Error and the mind has been depraved of Spiritual understanding **Romans 1***), the things which Yahuah hath prepared for them (*the Chosen Few*) that Love Him. 10 But Yahuah hath revealed them (*the secret mysteries and hidden knowledge*) unto us by His Spirit of Truth (*we speak the hidden language*): for the (*HOLY*) Spirit searches all things, yes, and the deep (*hidden / mysterious*) things of Yahuah. 11 For what man knows the

things of a (*natural*) man, save the (*natural / human*) spirit
of man which is in him? Even so the things of Yahuah
knows no man, but the (*HOLY*) Spirit of Yahuah (*reveals
this hidden language to them*). 12 Now we (*The Chosen
Few / Righteousness Seekers*) have received, not the
(*human nature / natural*) spirit of the world, but the
(*HOLY*) spirit which is of Yahuah; that we might know
(*these hidden mysteries and speak the hidden language or
tongues through The HOLY SPIRIT*) the things that are
freely given to us of (*by*) Yahuah. 13 Which (*Mysterious /
Secret*) things, also, we (*The Chosen Few / Righteousness
Seekers*) speak, not in the (*literal*) words which man's
wisdom teaches, but which the Holy SPIRIT teaches;
comparing spiritual things with spiritual (*physical to
Spiritual Parallels / Parables/ metaphors, allegories/
Idioms, anthropomorphisms, poems, prophetic languages,
proverbs, etc*). 14 But the natural man receives not the
(*hidden/mysterious*) things of the (*HOLY*) Spirit of Yahuah:
for they (*the hidden mysteries*) are foolishness unto him (*1
Corinthians 1:23*): neither can he know them (*these hidden
mysteries*), because they (*the hidden mysteries of Yahuah*)
are (*HOLY*) spiritually discerned (*through the Mystery
Language*).

1 Timothy 3:9
9 Holding the mystery (*hidden or secret things: G3466*) of
the faith in a pure conscience.

This is why the Roman/Greek based Christian Church and all of its
pastors and teachers cannot and do not teach The Truth; but rather
misinterpret, mistranslate, and teach false doctrines. They simply
do not speak the *Mystery Language of Yahuah* and do not
understand what they read. They are spiritually blind, deaf, and
dumb! They look to the "Greek" words for meaning and pour into
those Greek words all the pagan implications of Hellenism. This
began as Paul took The Gospel to a pagan Greek world:

2 Peter 3:16 – New Living Translation
Paul speaking of these (*hidden*) things in all of his letters.
Some of his comments are hard to understand (*Paul spoke
the Mystery Language*), **and those (***Greeks***) who are
ignorant (of** *the Mystery Language***) and unstable (***in their
minds given over to depraved carnal minds absent of the
light of The Torah***) have twisted his letters to mean
something quite different (***understood in the context of
Hellenism***), just as they do twist the rest of Scripture**.
And this will result in their destruction.

So let us seek out His Wisdom and understand what these "secret
things" and "Mystery Language" are all about. This is a "learned
language". Yahuah has literally hidden Himself in His Word
through a Mystery Language also referred to as "hidden things",
"deep things", and mysteries. He did not give humanity the Spirit
of Holiness required to understand this Mystery Language until
Yahusha ushered in the Spiritual Kingdom of Yahuah and Yahuah
poured out His Spirit of Holiness on Shav'uot or "Pentecost":

Deuteronomy 29:4
Yet Yahuah has not given you a heart to perceive (*hidden
Spiritual things*), and eyes to see (*hidden Spiritual things*),
and ears to hear (*hidden Spiritual things*), unto this day.

The "secret things" were kept hidden by Yahuah and only "those
physical things" were given to Israel in the Mosaic Covenant i.e.
the "letter of The Law". The Spiritual Intent was not given at that
time:

Deuteronomy 29
29 The **secret things** belong unto Yahuah our God: but
those (*physical*) things which are revealed belong unto us
and to our children for ever, that we may do all the words
(*letters*) of this law.

The intent behind the law is hidden and revealed to only those who have a heart to perceive it (those with eyes to see and ears to hear). So what does "secret things" above in Deuteronomy 29 mean?

Below is the word "secret" or "hidden" means in Hebrew:

Hebrew Lexicon word H5641 – Secret is the word Cathar (saw-thar') which means:

       I. to hide, conceal
       A. (Niphal)
              i. to hide oneself
              ii. to be hidden, be concealed
       B. (Piel) to hide carefully
       C. (Pual) to be hidden carefully, be concealed
       D. (Hiphil) to conceal, hide
       E. (Hithpael) to hide oneself carefully

<u>Yahuah has literally hidden Himself in plain sight</u>! No matter what language the Bible is translated into, the Mystery Language is very present in every language. But it must be learned for the reader to understand and the reader must be guided by The Spirit of Holiness to receive it. We have His Word but only those who speak His Mystery Language (like Yahusha) understand what those words mean! Daniel was given this mystery language:

Daniel 2
20 Daniel answered and said, Blessed be the name of God (*Yahuah*) for ever and ever: for wisdom and might are his: 21 And he changes the times and the seasons: he removes kings, and sets up kings: he gives (*Spiritual*) wisdom unto the (*chosen*) wise, and knowledge to them that know (*Spiritual*) understanding: 22 **He reveals the deep and secret things**!

Isaiah was eventually given this Mystery Language after many years of not understanding:

Isaiah 48

[6] You have heard these things; look at them all. Will you not admit them? 'From now on **I will tell you of new things, of hidden things unknown to you**. [7] They are created now, and not long ago; **you have not heard of them before today**. So you cannot say, "Yes, I knew of them." [8] **You have neither heard nor understood; from of old your ears have not been open**.

Yahuah simply did not give The Spirit of Holiness to all of His Chosen that teaches us to know these hidden secret things until The Yahushaic Covenant. Even then, Yahusha continued to veil these things behind parables and parallels so that only those so chosen could understand:

Matthew 13

[10] The disciples came to him and asked, 'Why do you speak to the people in parables?' [11] He replied, '**Because the knowledge of the secrets of the kingdom of heaven has been given to you, but not to them**. [12] Whoever has (*the Spirit of Holiness*) **will be given** (*speaking of a future date when Yahuah would pour out His Spirit*) more (*hidden knowledge*), and they will have an abundance (*of Spiritual understanding*). Whoever does not have, even what they have will be taken from them. [13] This is why I speak to them in parables:

'Though seeing (*with their physical mind*), they do not see (*the Spiritual parallel*); though hearing (*with their physical ear*), they do not hear (*the Spiritual Truth*) or understand (*the Spiritual meaning*). [14] In them is fulfilled the prophecy of Isaiah:

'''You will be ever hearing but never understanding; you will be ever seeing but never perceiving.

¹⁵ For this people's heart has become calloused;
  they hardly hear with their ears,
  and they have closed their eyes.
Otherwise they might see with their eyes,
  hear with their ears,
  understand with their hearts
and turn, and I would heal them."

¹⁶ But blessed are your eyes because they see (*the physical to Spiritual parallels*), and your ears because they hear (*the Truth*). ¹⁷ For truly I tell you, many prophets and righteous people longed to see what you see but did not see it, and to hear what you hear but did not hear it (*because it was not revealed until The Yahushaic Covenant and only then to a Chosen Few*).

Matthew 13:35
That it might be fulfilled which was spoken by the prophet, saying, **I will open my mouth in parables; I will utter things which have been kept secret from the foundation of the world**.

Yes, Yahuah has hidden Himself in His Word in a Mystery Language that only the Chosen Few are ever given eyes to see and ears to hear and a mind to understand. You must have The Spirit of Holiness who teaches you this Mystery Language to understand the Word of Yahuah.

This Mystery Language is spoken in parables, physical to Spiritual parallels, idioms, proverbs, etc. It is a metaphorical language and that is what "speaking in tongues" really means. When The Spirit of Holiness moved on the disciples in the "upper room" on Shav'uot their Spiritual eyes and ears were opened and they began to "see" and speak in this Mystery Language as well.

The Apostle Paul (as we read at the beginning of this section in *1 Corinthians 2:4-15)* spoke this "Mystery Language" and called this Mystery Language "another tongue":

1 Corinthians 14:2 – KJV
² For he that speaks in **an unknown tongue** (*Mystery Metaphorical Language*) speaks not unto (*the physical things of*) men, but unto (*the hidden Spiritual things of*) Yahuah: for no man understands him (*they don't have eyes to see, ears to hear*); however in **the spirit (*of Holiness*) he speaks mysteries (***of the Kingdom of Yahuah*****).**

King Solomon was given the Mystery Language. We read in the Book of Wisdom below as Solomon describes the "wisdom of Yahuah":

Wisdom 2
21 Such things they did imagine, and **were deceived**: for their own wickedness hath blinded them. 22 As for **the mysteries of Yahuah**, they knew them not: neither hoped they for the wages of righteousness, nor discerned a reward for blameless souls. 23 For Yahuah created man to be immortal, and made him to be an image of His own eternity.

Wisdom 6:22
As for wisdom, what she is, and how she came up, I (*Yahuah*) will tell you (*Solomon*), and **will not hide mysteries from you**: but will seek her out from the beginning of her nativity, and bring the knowledge of her into light, and will not pass over the truth.

Wisdom 8:4
For she (*wisdom*) is privy **to the mysteries of the knowledge of Yahuah**, and a lover of his works.

We read in the book of Ben Sira (written by the Jewish scribe Shimon ben Yahusha ben Eliezer ben Sira of Jerusalem nearly 200 years before Yahusha lived which is considered the earliest witness to a canon of the books of the prophets):

Ben Sira 3
19 Many are in high place, and of renown: **but mysteries are revealed unto the meek** (*humble who seek after Yahuah's wisdom*). 20 For the power of Yahuah is great, and He is honoured of the lowly. 21 Seek not out things that are too hard for you, neither search the things that are above your strength. 22 But what is commanded of you, think upon with reverence, **for you do not need to see with your** (*physical*) **eyes the things that are in secret**.

Now, if you carefully read the verses above, you will now know and understand that the secret, hidden mysteries of Yahuah are told through parables (and parallels) that not everyone is going to understand. Only the humble and repentant heart (inner man, the righteousness seeking mindset) will perceive them.

This is what "speaking in tongues" actually is – it isn't a language (like Sumerian or English or Greek or Hebrew) per say, but messages communicated through the Holy Spirit (parables and parallels) that are conveyed in every language the Bible is written in and translated to. "Speaking in tongues" is "speaking in the mystery language or tongue" that the Bible is written in. This is what happened on Shav'uot, Yahuah opened the Spiritual eyes and ears of the followers of Yahusha, they began to "understand" the language Yahusha spoke, and they too began to speak in the same way and everyone around them understood them in their native language.

Acts 10
[44] While Peter was still speaking these words (*he was not speaking a foreign language or babbling a bunch of nonsense*), the Holy Spirit fell upon all those who were listening to the message (*and opened their eyes to the Spiritual Parallels and meaning of the words Peter was speaking*). [45] All the circumcised (*Jewish*) believers who

21

came with Peter were amazed, because the gift of the Holy
Spirit had been poured out on the Gentiles (*House of Israel*)
also (*they too began to understand the physical to Spiritual
parallels and parables*). [46] For they were hearing (in their
native language) them speaking with tongues (*in the
Mystery Language like Yahusha spoke*) and exalting
Yahuah.

Acts 2:4
And they were all filled with the Holy Spirit (*and finally
understood the Mystery Language Yahusha spoke*), and
began to speak with other tongues (*or a Mystery Language
full of Parables, Idioms, Parallels, etc.*), as the Spirit gave
them utterance.

Only those chosen few who have been given The Spirit of
Holiness, who have had their eyes and ears opened, who
understand Spiritual things with their mind speak this language and
understand it:

Matthew 11:25
At that time Yahusha answered and said, I thank you, O
Father, Lord of heaven and earth, because you have hid
these things from the wise and prudent, and have revealed
them unto babes (*this language cannot be taught in human
learning institutions, so you can toss out any Theological
Degrees Christian pastors and teacher flaunt… they mean
NOTHING!*).

But there are very few who are risen up at the time of the end to
unravel the hidden mysteries and unlock the seals placed over His
Word:

Revelation 10
[4] Now when the seven thunders uttered their voices, I was
about to **write; but I heard a voice from heaven saying to
me, "Seal up the things which the seven thunders
uttered, and do not write them."** *And they were hidden*

until the very end of time and given to men of Wisdom risen up for the appointed time.

Daniel 12

[9] He replied, "Go your way, Daniel, because the words are rolled up and sealed until the time of the end. [10] Many (*chosen by Yahuah to teach*) will be purified, made spotless and refined, but the wicked will continue to be wicked. None of the wicked will understand, but those who (*chosen by Yahuah*) are wise will understand.

Daniel 11

32 Those who do wickedly (*abolish The Law*) against the covenant he shall corrupt with flattery (*false teachings*); but the people who know their God (*you know Yahuah by keeping His Law 1 John 2:3*) shall be strong, and carry out great exploits. 33 And those men of Wisdom who understand (*the hidden mysteries*) shall instruct many; ... 35 And some of those of understanding shall fall, to refine them, purify them, and make them white, until the time of the end; because it is still for the appointed time.

Well, we are at that appointed time of "the end". We need those men of Wisdom who understand these hidden things to come forward and teach, because the identity of the Antichrist and such things require this type of understanding. While we all like to think that we can just open up our modern translations and are capable of understanding the words on the page, this is not what the Bible says. We need men who have "eyes and ears to hear" and understand the secret things whom Yahuah moves on and anoints to teach us. The identity of the Antichrist is literally shrouded in mistranslated text, altered texts, false teachings, twisted scriptures, dreams, physical shadows, and mystical beasts and then literally "sealed" by Yahuah until the end. We are at the "end" now and his identity has been revealed.

The first thing we must do when identifying the false messiah is to establish the true name of The Creator and the Messiah because their names were removed from our modern Bibles.

One we know the true names then we can take a critical look at the name Jesus Christ because that name is not the name of the Messiah in any language not even Greek and Latin! The name of the true Messiah was removed from our modern translations and replace with the name of the false messiah or Antichrist.

Chapter 2

The name of God, the Messiah, and the false messiah

Proverbs 30:4

Who has gone up to heaven and come down? Whose hands have gathered up the wind? Who has wrapped up the waters in a cloak? Who has established all the ends of the earth? What is his name, and what is the name of his son? Surely you know!

Introduction

The name of the Jewish Messiah in The Hebrew Bible uses Yahusha (יהושע), and then later modern form Yeshua (ישוע), for the English transliteration of 'Joshua', which means "Yah(uah) is Salvation (yasha)". "Yah" being the short poetic form of Yahuah and "yasha" being Hebrew for salvation; combined into a contracted sentance name Yah-usha. There are several spellings of this set apart name of the Messiah in scripture with the most prevalent being Yahusha:

ישוע = YESHUA   USED 28 TIMES IN TANAK

יהושע = YAHUSHA   USED 216 TIMES IN TANAK

יהושוע = YAHUSHUA   USED 2 TIMES IN TANAK

ע ו ש ו ה י   YOD-HAY-UAU-SHIN-UAU-AYIN: "YAHUSHUA"

The two uses of this 6-lettered spelling are found at Deut. 3:21 and Judg. 2:7

We are given the name of the Messiah directly in Isaiah as Yahuah speaks through the prophet concerning the day He renews His vows in the Renewed Covenant below:

Isaiah 12

1 You will say in that day (*that I renew my vows*): "I will give thanks to you, O YAHUAH, for though you were angry with me (*for breaking your vows and divorced me*), your anger turned away (*and you restored me as your bride*), that you might comfort me. [2] "***Behold, Yahuah is my salvation*** (*this statement is literally naming the covenant of Yahusha by name. Yahusha is a contraction of Yahuah Yahsha and means "Yahuah is my salvation". So we can replace that longer from with the contraction and we get ... Behold Yahusha! Pointing us directly to our Messiah*);

This 'declaration' that "Yahuah is my salvation" is the name given to Joseph and Mary to name their child for "Yahuah shall yasha (save) His (own) people from their sin" through a final Passover sacrifice. That final Passover Sacrifice would be THE purpose of the Messiah in that way Yahusha represents "the salvation of Yahuah". Joseph and Mary's son would be that Messiah they were to name this son "YahuahYasha" or "Yahusha" in short because he was prophesied to "come in the name of Yahuah".

This name, (עשוהי), was transliterated into English in the Book of 'Joshua' as "Joshua". Joshua the son of Nun succeeded Moses and "led the children of Israel into the promised land" a messianic foreshadowing of the coming Messiah **in deed and in name**. Yahusha would lead the "children of Yahuah" out of slavery to sin and into the Promised Land of eternal life. The son of num's name was actually Yahusha not Joshua. We also see the Messiah named by name in Zachariah Chapter 3 as Yahusha was consecrated High Priest directly by Yahusha.

Why then, did the scribes "transliterate" (transliterate means not a literal translation) the name of the Messiah in the NT not keeping true to the English translation "Joshua" like they did in the OT? They instead, *and intentionally*, mis-translated the name (עשוהי) into "Jesus" in the New Testament which isn't even a name in Hebrew and in no way at all implies or has the name Yahuah in it! "Jesus" fails a MAJOR test by failing to fulfill the prophecy that he would come in Yahuah's name. So in name only, "Jesus" is a false messiah. But it gets much worse.

The translators obviously know the English transliteration was Joshua not Jesus, they had transcribed it semi-correctly in the so-called "Old" Hebrew scriptures. They also are well aware the Messiah was a Jewish Rabbi with a Jewish name not a Greek name with Greek conventions that give glory to a Greek "god". What is most important about the name of the Messiah is that the "intent" of the name remains intact as we go from Paleo Hebrew to Modern Hebrew to any other language and in our case especially English.

Intent of the name

It is interesting to note that while the Messiah's name gives glory to Yahuah as our savior, Yahuah's name points us to His chosen proxy:

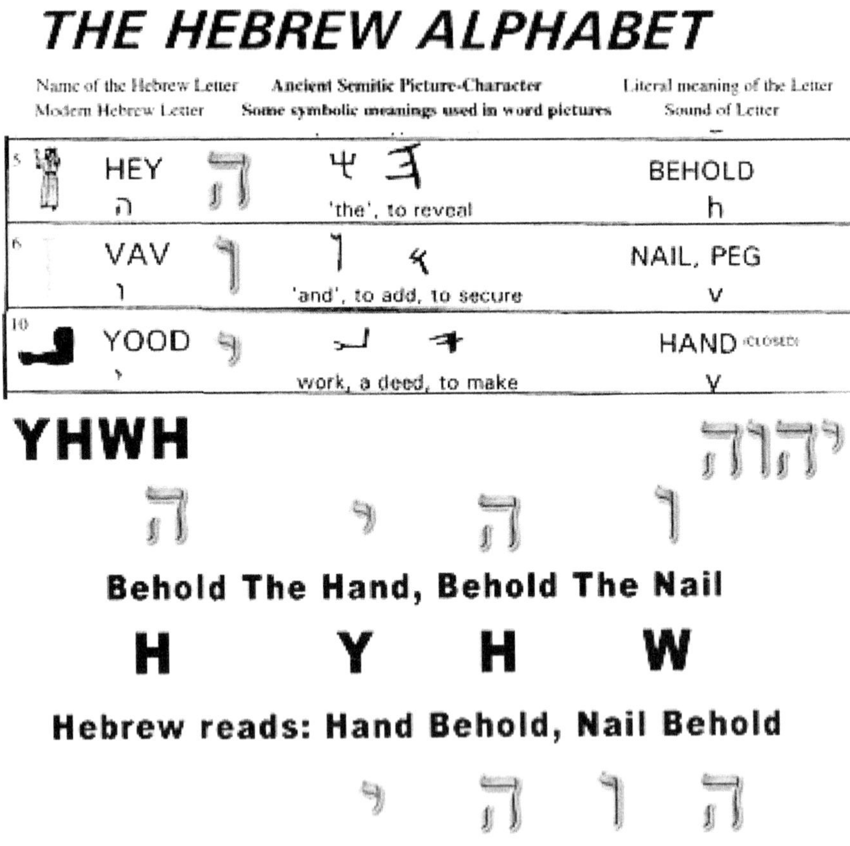
THE HEBREW ALPHABET
Name of the Hebrew Letter
Ancient Semitic Picture-Character
Literal meaning of the Letter
Modern Hebrew Letter
Some symbolic meanings used in word pictures
Sound of Letter
5 HEY ה
'the', to reveal
BEHOLD
h
6 VAV ו
'and', to add, to secure
NAIL, PEG
v
10 YOOD י
work, a deed, to make
HAND (CLOSED)
y
YHWH
יהוה
Behold The Hand, Behold The Nail
H Y H W
Hebrew reads: Hand Behold, Nail Behold

So we see the original pictograph of The Creator's name as well as the message written in the stars foretells of the coming of and sacrifice of Yahusha the Messiah. The "intent" of what the name "means" should remain in any language not just a literal attempt at translating each letter into a letter in another language. That was the very reason the Messiah was named Yahusha to begin with, because that name embodies the *intent* of Yahuah to save 'yasha' His people. It was this way of translating the name of the Messiah that is in error, translating each letter and ignoring the intent of the name, that Satan was able to manipulate humanity as we will soon see.

It was, after all, the "intent" behind why the Messiah was named that was important and this is found in both the Prophets and when the Angel brought the "meaning of the name" ***in Hebrew*** to Joseph and Mary. We should be obedient to this intent in any language and then look to Hebrew for the meaning of the name of the Messiah not derive the name of our Messiah by Greek and Latin transliterations. That "intent" of the Messiah's name was to make a very clear statement… "***Yahuah is our savior***". This truth is well established in His Word. the Messiah himself never intended to take glory away from Yahuah. Yahusha instructed us to pray to Yahuah and give Glory <u>to His Holy Name</u>:

> **<u>Matthew 6:9</u>**
> [9] " Pray, then, in this way:'Our Father who is in heaven, hallowed be <u>Your</u> name (𐤉𐤄𐤅𐤄 Yahuah).

He did not instruct us to pray his own name, but the name of Yahuah! Funny how Christians completely disobey that command by the Messiah and pray in "the name Jesus" isn't it? After all, "Jesus" is the image of a man elevated in their heats above God which is an abomination to Yahuah as we will see in this book.

The problem is that the translators literally removed the name of Yahuah from The Bible based on some human Jewish tradition that the name was too holy to look at or to pronounce. The name Yahuah was in the Word of Yahuah (it is His Word after all) over 8,000 times and taken out and replaced with "The LORD" or "LORD God" in violation of Yahuah's command not to add to or subtract from His Word.

The effect of replacing the name Yahuah with titles

Yehezqel/Ezekiel 36:23
"And I shall set apart My great Name,
which has been profaned among the gentiles,
which you have profaned in their midst.
And the gentiles shall know that I am ᴤYᴤ𝄔,"
declares the Master ᴤYᴤ𝄔,
"when I am set-apart in you before their eyes."

We have sufficient proof showing that the Name of Yahuah has been completely erased from the Holy Scriptures and from common knowledge and use altogether, because of the man-made traditions of our forefathers and Jewish rabbis. *The Century Bible, Volume 1, pages 90-91*, tells us the following.

> *Some time after the return from the Captivity, and before the beginning of the Christian Era, the Yahdaim (*Jews)* came to believe (*tradition*) that the Holy Name Yahuah was too sacred to be uttered on ordinary occasions. It was said (*tradition*) to be pronounced by the High Priest on the Day of Atonement. At other times, when any one read or quoted aloud from what is called the Old Testament, the titles "Adonay", "Lord," and "God" was usually substituted for Yahuah (*by* tradition), and similarly the LXX (Septuagint Version) has Kurios, the Vulgate dominus, and the e.v. lord,* **where the Hebrew has Yahuah.** *Hebrew was originally written without vowels, but when the "vowel points" were added, the vowels of "Adonay" or "Elohim" were written (*according to tradition adding titles instead of The Name*) with Yahuah, as a direction that these words were to be read instead of the word whose consonants were* 𐤅𐤄𐤉 *(the name given to Moses in Paleo Hebrew)*

30

*pronounced Yahuah; thus we find the combinations YeHoWaH and YeHoWiH. At the Reformation, the former being the more usual, was sometimes used as the Name of the (Mighty One) of Israyl, **and owing to ignorance** of its history was misread as "Jehovah," a form which has established itself in English, but does not give the pronunciation of the Holy Name it represents.*

What is stated above is that The LORD, LORD God, and Adonay are titles not His name and that Jehovah is not His name either. And many today claim Yahuah's name is Jehovah, Yehowah or Hehowih which came from using vowel points incorrectly taken from the word Elohim (god)... yEhOwIh the "e", "o", and "i" being the vowel points in ElOhIm. These mistranslations are meant to be 𐤉𐤄𐤅𐤄 which is properly pronounced "Yahuah" with vowels added to illustrate the proper pronunciation. the Messiah Yahusha made his feelings about the use of "tradition" as justification for changing the original Words of Yahuah clear:

Mark 7:13
13 Thus **you nullify the word of 𐤉𐤄𐤅𐤄 Yahuah by your tradition that you have handed down**. And you do many things like that."

The Creator's Name (𐤉𐤄𐤅𐤄 Yahuah) was never intended to be hidden or unspoken; rather it was always intended to be written and to be glorified in speech, song and worship.

John 12:28
Father, glorify your name (𐤉𐤄𐤅𐤄 *Yahuah*)!" Then a voice came from heaven, "I have glorified it, and will glorify it again."

Psalm 69:30
Then I will praise 𐤉𐤄𐤅𐤄 Yahuah's name with singing, and I will honor him with thanksgiving.

What does The Bible say that God's "name" is?

Jeremiah 33:2
This is what Yahuah says Who made the earth, Yahuah Who formed it to establish it— 𐤉𐤄𐤅𐤄 **Yahuah is His Name**.

Exodus 3:15
Yahuah also said to Moses: This also shall you say to the children of Israel; 𐤉𐤄𐤅𐤄 Yahuah, the Heavenly Father of your fathers, the Mighty One of Abraham, the Mighty One of Isaac, and the Mighty One of Jacob, has sent me to you. **This 𐤉𐤄𐤅𐤄 is MY NAME forever, and this is MY MEMORIAL: the Name by which I am to be remembered by, from generation to generation, for all generations**.

Isaiah 42:8
I am 𐤉𐤄𐤅𐤄 Yahuah, that is MY NAME; and My glory I will not give to another, nor My praise to graven images.

Psalm 68:4
Sing to 𐤉𐤄𐤅𐤄 Yahuah; sing praises to His Name! Extol our Father Who rides the clouds by His Name— 𐤉𐤄𐤅𐤄 Yahuah, and rejoice in front of Him!

The true Messiah, Yahusha, was prophesied to "come in the name of Yahuah" and Yahusha clearly acknowledged this fact.

Psalms 118
26 Blessed is he who **comes in the name of Yahuah**.

In fact, in the gospel of Luke, Yahusha in a plea to repent or perish the Messiah actually stated that **_only those_** who acknowledge that his name gives glory to Yahuah will ever see him again.

Luke 13

34 "Jerusalem, Jerusalem, you who kill the prophets and stone those sent to you, how often I have longed to gather your children together, as a hen gathers her chicks under her wings, and you were not willing. 35 Look, your house is left to you desolate. I tell you, **you will not see me again until you say, 'Blessed is he who comes in the name of** 𐤉𐤄𐤅𐤄 **Yahuah**.'"

John 12:13

Hosanna: Blessed is the King of Israel that cometh in the name of the 𐤉𐤄𐤅𐤄 (*Yahuah*)!

John 17:6

I have spoken your name (𐤉𐤄𐤅𐤄 *Yahuah*) unto the men which you gave me out of the world"

The requirement to call the Messiah <u>by the intent of his name</u> in that he "came in the name of Yahuah" as "the salvation of Yahuah" or "Yahusha" is clear. Remember there is only 1 name under Heaven that paves "the way" to salvation through Yahuah. This is why those who come to Yahusha at the time of judgment calling him another name are rejected.

These people are confused because they "thought" they knew him calling him "Jesus" only to be rejected by him for not knowing his name and not keeping the Law of Yahuah and proclaiming the name Yahusha acknowledging that he "came IN THE NAME of Yahuah". There is absolutely no chance you can get the name Yahuah out of "Jes**us**" but rather that name <u>like all pagan Greek names</u> give glory to Ze**us**. This is something Christianity simply cannot admit.

True and false disciples are defined by the name

Under the heading "true and false disciples" in the Book of Matthew we see that the definition of "true" and "false" is tied directly to the NAME of the Messiah. Many of those who call him "Lord" (which is not a name but a title given to every British land owner for the past 1,000 years) and think they know his name calling him "Jesus" discover they never knew the real Messiah. "In your name" is **emphasized 3 times** in Matthew below because we are warned of a false messiah that almost the entire world falls to by deception… and the name is the primary issue!

Yahusha tells those who call him by this meaningless, empty, and pagan name "Jesus" to DEPART from him they never knew him. Yahusha goes on to explain "you evildoers" or in some translations "you who practice lawlessness" which the Hebrew word Yahusha used actually means in English TORAHLESS!

Those who call him Jesus and abolish the Law of Yahuah are the exact ones he is speaking to (i.e. Christians):

> **Matthew 7**
> 21 "Not everyone who says to me, 'Lord, Lord,' will enter the kingdom of heaven, **but only the one who does the will of my Father who is in heaven**. 22 Many will say to me on that day, 'Lord, Lord, did we not prophesy *in your name* and *in your name* drive out demons and **in your name** perform many miracles?' 23 Then I will tell them plainly, '**I never knew you**. Away from me, you evildoers' (literally *translated those 'who do not keep the Torah!'*)

The first thing I want to do before we get into anything else is clearly establish the name of The Creator (God), the name of the Messiah, and the name of the false messiah.

In order to clearly prove that Yahusha is the true name of the Messiah, we must first establish the true name of The Creator (the one and only God).

John 17
[3] This is eternal life, that they may know You 𐤉𐤄𐤅𐤄, the only true God, and (be in covenant with) Yahusha the Messiah whom You 𐤉𐤄𐤅𐤄 have sent (according to The Plan of Salvation).

What is the name of The Creator (𐤉𐤄𐤅𐤄)?

The name that **The Creator** gave when Moses asked "who sent him to deliver the children of Israel" is 𐤉𐤄𐤅𐤄 *Yahuah* in Paleo Hebrew. Yahuah, however, is not the actual name it is how we write the name 𐤉𐤄𐤅𐤄 in English so that we can pronounce it. The name 𐤉𐤄𐤅𐤄 gave Moses is a 4 letter Paleo Hebrew word that contains no vowels and 𐤉𐤄𐤅𐤄 in modern Hebrew is יהוה– which in English translates to Yahuah. It is comprised of the 4 Hebrew characters **yod hay vav hay which sounds like *Yahuah* when pronounced.** This name is known as the Tetragrammaton "tetra = 4" and "grammaton = letters".

> **NOTE:** *The literal translation from the Hebrew characters of* **yod hay vav hay** *is Y(yod) H(hey) V(vav) H(hay)…*
>
> *Yahuah.* ***I use this name*** 𐤉𐤄𐤅𐤄 ***or the English spelling of how it is pronounced (Yahuah) to be as accurate as I can be in the English language in all my writings. The letters YHWH are most often used as the English transliteration of*** *Yahuah* ***as the letter vav makes the sound of the English letter W when pronounced. Both are acceptable forms of the Creator's name in my opinion, I just choose*** *Yahuah* ***to illustrate the pronunciation.***

Below are sources to demonstrate the true name of the Creator is 𐤉𐤄𐤅𐤄 Yahuah and not the LORD:

The Jewish Encyclopedia of 1901, Volume 12, page 119, states.

> It thus becomes _possible to determine with a fair degree of certainty the historical pronunciation of the Tetragrammaton_, the results agreeing with the statement of Ex. iii. 14, in which 𐤉𐤄𐤅𐤄 terms Himself hyha. "I will be", a phrase which is immediately preceded by the fuller term "_I will be that I will be_ or, as in the English versions, "_I am_" and "_I am that I am_." The name 𐤉𐤄𐤅𐤄 is accordingly derived from the root hwh (= hyh), and is regarded as an imperfect. _This passage is decisive for the pronunciation "Yahuah"; for the etymology was undoubtedly based on the known word._

The Encyclopedia Judaica, Volume 7, page 680, further states this fact.

> _The true pronunciation of the name 𐤉𐤄𐤅𐤄 was never lost._ Several early Greek writers of the Christian Church testify that _the name was pronounced "Yahuah"_. This is confirmed, at least for the vowel of the first syllable of the name, by the shorter form Yah, which is sometimes used in poetry (e.g., Ex. 15:2) _and the -yahu or -yah that serves as the final syllable in very many Hebrew names._

The Encyclopedia Britanica, Volume 23, page 867, confirms this fact.

> Yahuah, the _proper name_ of the God of Israel; it is composed of _four consonants_ (𐤉𐤄𐤅𐤄) _in Hebrew_ and is therefore _called the Tetragrammaton_...

The Universal Jewish Encyclopedia, Volume 9, page 160, confirms this fact.

> *Of the names of God in the Old Testament, that which occurs most frequently (6,823 times) is the so-called Tetragrammaton, अपत, the distinctive personal name of the God of Israel.*

The Jewish Encyclopedia Volume 12, pages 118-119, confirms this fact also.

> *TETRAGRAMMATON: The quadrilateral name of God, (अपत). The Tetragrammaton is the ancient Israelitish name for God...*

***The Jewish Encyclopedia*, Volume 9, pages 162-163**, also shows us that while the rabbis recognized only one proper name for the Creator, they also considered other names as titles for the Creator. As you read this excerpt, notice and remember the title (Adonai) that was used in place of the Creator's Name:

> *...The Rabbis as well as the cabalists steadfastly maintained their belief in monotheism. Hence they recognized only one proper name for the Deity, considering the other names as appellations or titles signifying divinity, perfection, and power, or as characterizing His acts as observed and appreciated by mankind...The name अपत is considered as the Name proper; it was known in the earliest rabbinical works simply as the Name;; and as Yod He Vaw He (spelling letters of अपत).*

Therefore, anytime you see *the LORD* or *LORD GOD* in the Old Testament, realize that originally it was written in the Hebrew Bible as Yahuah or Yahuah Elohim. When you see *LORD* in all caps in the New Testament it is referring to Yahuah. When you see '*Lord*' not in all caps; that is a mistranslation of HaMashiach which is Hebrew for the anointed King of Israel and is referring to Yahusha. It is through the use of these titles and not their proper names that confusion and false doctrines are born.

Why does my English Bible use *the LORD*?

The LORD is not the name of the Creator that is the name/title for the Babylonian sungod Ba'al and is a pagan reference to just about all pagan "gods"... the LORD is a false god:

> http://en.wikipedia.org/wiki/Baal

> **Baal**, *also rendered* **Ba'al** *(Biblical Hebrew בַּעַל), is a Northwest Semitic title and honorific meaning "master" or "lord" that is used for various gods who were patrons of cities in the Levant and Asia Minor, cognate to Akkadian Bēlu. A* **Baalist** *or* **Baalite** *means a worshipper of Baal i.e.* **The Lord***.*

> *"Ba'al" or "**The Lord**" can refer to any god and even to human officials. In some texts it is used for Hadad, a god of the rain, thunder, fertility and agriculture, and the lord of Heaven. Since only priests were allowed to utter his divine name, Hadad, Ba'al was commonly used. Nevertheless, few if any Biblical uses of "Ba'al" refer to Hadad,* **The LORD** *over the assembly of gods on the holy mount of Heaven; most refer to a variety of local spirit-deities worshipped as cult images, each called ba'al and regarded in the Hebrew Bible in that context as a "false god".*

Etymology

Ba'al (*bet-ayin-lamedh*) *is a* <u>Semitic</u> *word signifying* **"<u>The Lord</u>**, *master, owner (male), keeper, husband",*

Yahuah told Elijah and Jeremiah that the Israelites would adopt "the way of the pagans" in Babylon who worshipped Ba'al and forget His name Yahuah and use the title *the **LORD*** which is a reference to Ba'al.

1 Kings 18

[18] "I have not made trouble for Israel," Elijah replied. "But you and your father's family have. **You have abandoned Yahuah's commands and have followed Baal** (*The LORD*).

Jeremiah 23

[25] "I have heard what the prophets say who prophesy lies in my name. They say, 'I had a dream! I had a dream!' [26] How long will this continue in the hearts of these lying prophets, who prophesy the delusions of their own minds? [27] They think the dreams they tell one another will make my people forget my name, **just as their ancestors forgot my name through Baal (*The LORD*) worship**.

The LORD "Ba'al" was worshipped on Sunday the "day of the invincible sun" or Dias Solis and the sacrifice to the LORD "Ba'al" was the pig of Ishtar (Easter) in Babylon. I cover this in great detail in my book **Babylon: The religion of the beast**. The prophecies in 1 Kings that we would abandon Yahuah and follow Ba'al have come true in Christianity who calls on the LORD on Sunday and who put their faith in Easter.

Just as Jeremiah foretold we would forget the name 𐤉𐤄𐤅𐤄 Yahuah and use the LORD as they did in Babylon. We see below that the

39

name Yahuah was regularly pronounced by His chosen until superstitious Jews who adopted the pagan practices of their Babylonian captors changed the name Yahuah to the LORD coming out of Babylonian captivity:

> *The Encyclopedia Judaica*, Volume 7, pages 680-682

> 𐤉𐤄𐤅𐤄 *or Yahuah. The personal name of the God of Israel is written in the Hebrew Bible with the four consonants* 𐤉𐤄𐤅𐤄 *and is referred to as the "Tetragrammaton". At least until the destructions of the First Temple in 586 b.c.e., this name was regularly pronounced with its proper vowels (Yahuah), as is clear from the *Lachish Letters, written shortly before that date. But at least by the third century b.c.e., the pronunciation of the name* 𐤉𐤄𐤅𐤄 *was avoided, and Adonai, "the Lord", was substituted for it, as evidenced by the use of the Greek word Kyrios, "Lord", for* 𐤉𐤄𐤅𐤄 *in the Septuagint, the translation of the Hebrew Scriptures that was begun by Greek-speaking Jews in that century. Where the combined form *Adonai* 𐤉𐤄𐤅𐤄 *occurs in the Bible, this was read as *Adonai *Elohim, "Lord God".*

We also see below from the same source that the Jews replaced the proper vowel points in Yahuah with the vowel points in Adonai to avoid saying His name giving us the name Yehowah in ERROR. Then uninspired Christian translators came up with the totally foreign name Jehovah out if ignorance. Then later in a total disconnect from all reality, the Jews started just saying ha-Shem and totally abandoned the name of the Creator all together. The Encyclopedia Judaica, Volume 7, pages 680-682 continued:

> *In the early Middle Ages, when the consonantal text of the Bible was supplied with vowels points to facilitate its correct traditional reading, the vowel*

> *points for 'Adonai with one variation - a sheva with the first yod of* 𐤉𐤄𐤅𐤄 *instead of the hataf-patah under the aleph of 'Adonai were used for* 𐤉𐤄𐤅𐤄*, thus producing the form Yehowah. When Christian scholars of Europe first began to study Hebrew, they did not understand what this really meant, and they introduced the hybrid name "Jehovah". In order to avoid pronouncing even the sacred name *Adonai for* 𐤉𐤄𐤅𐤄*, the custom was later introduced of saying simply in Hebrew ha-Shem (or Aramaic Shemc, "the Name") even in such an expression as "Blessed be he that cometh in the name of* 𐤉𐤄𐤅𐤄 *Yahuah" (Ps. 118:26).*

This is an abomination! Yahuah gave us His name and He declares that it is His memorial for all generations:

Exodus 3:15

And Yahuah said moreover unto Moses, Thus shalt thou say unto the children of Israel, 𐤉𐤄𐤅𐤄 Yahuah the God of your fathers, the God of Abraham, the God of Isaac, and the God of Jacob, hath sent me unto you: this 𐤉𐤄𐤅𐤄 is my name for ever, and this is my memorial unto all generations.

His name is not "the LORD" or "Adonai" or "haShem" or anything else. His name is Yahuah and that is His everlasting memorial by which He is to be called upon.

Our English Bibles use the title *the LORD* for Yahuah which is <u>a violation of the command not to add to nor subtract from His Word</u> not to mention it is idolatry calling upon the Babylonian god Ba'al. We, humanity, have totally forgotten the name of our Creator which was originally written in His Word over 8,000 times! We replaced every reference to it with the LORD Ba'al. Below we see the Jews committed this abomination out of what I call "reverent stupidity" as they followed the way of the pagans in Babylon:

Unger's Bible Dictionary, on page 665:

> Lord (Hebrew, Adon), an early word denoting
> ownership; hence, absolute control. _It is not_
> _properly a divine title._ The Jews, _out of a_
> _superstitious reverence_ for the Name 𐤉𐤄𐤅𐤄 Yahuah,
> always, in reading, pronounce Adonai (lord) where
> 𐤉𐤄𐤅𐤄 Yahuah _is written._

Smith's Bible Dictionary, 1872 Edition, states the following:

> The substitution of the word Lord is most (sad); for,
> _while it in no way represents the meaning of the_
> _Sacred Name_ 𐤉𐤄𐤅𐤄, the mind has constantly to
> guard against a confusion with its lower uses, and,
> _above all, the direct personal hearing of the Name_
> _on the revelation of Yahuah..._**is injuriously out of**
> **sight.**

This is extremely important as the name of the Messiah contains the Tetragrammaton to fulfill the prophetic requirements of the _one name under heaven_ whereby we may obtain salvation:

Acts 4:12
Salvation is found in no one else, for there is _no other name_ under heaven given to mankind by which we must be saved."

When I quote scripture in this book, no matter what translation I use, I will always replace the pagan reference and title of **_the LORD_** with **Yahuah** and _Lord_ with **King** as it applies to Yahusha. I will always clarify **in context** the use of impersonal pronouns such as 'he' and 'him' by identifying the subject by name. I will turn the text from passive voice to active voice. I will demonstrate when the uninspired translations are corrected in this way; the truth comes shining through as to the real meaning of the text. In doing

42

so many of the scriptures used to justify the false doctrines of the *incarnation* and *The Trinity* completely fall apart in light of the truth.

Salvation is found exclusively in the declaration that "Yahuah is salvation"

Isaiah 43:11 and 45:21
"I, even I, am Yahuah; and ***beside me there is no savior***…a just God and a Savior; there is none beside me"

The Biblical instruction that name of the Messiah **must embody** the idea that "Yahuah is our savior" is clear. Below, Joel literally gives us the name of the Messiah, the name that "*whoever calls on the name Yahusha will be saved*". In Hebrew, **Yahusha** is a contracted form of the sentence "Yahuah will save" so you can legally replace the phrase below "Yahuah will be saved" with the contracted form of that sentence… **Yahusha**:

Joel 2
30 "I will display wonders in the sky and on the earth, Blood, fire and columns of smoke. 31 "The sun will be turned into darkness And the moon into blood Before the great and awesome day of Yahuah comes. 32 "And it will come about that whoever calls on the name of ***Yahuah Will be saved***: **(which could legally read** *whoever calls on the name Yahusha as Yahusha is a contracted sentence name meaning "Yahuah is salvation"*)"

So in the scripture above it could be legally translated to say "*And it will come about that whoever calls on the name of* ***Yahusha***" directly pointing us to the true name of the Messiah which is contracted form of 'Yahuah yasha' using the poetic form of YAH and the Hebrew word for salvation… yasha. Giving us Yahu-sha.

Below, we see that the messenger of Yahuah delivered the name of the Messiah and we see the name was given <u>because</u> it is a name with meaning. That meaning is *"Yahuah will save His people from their sin"*. That name that was given to Joseph and Mary was **Yahusha** which was mistranslated into English as Jesus <u>which is not a name in Hebrew</u>.

> **Matthew 1:21**
> She will give birth to a son, and you are to give him the name **Yahusha**, <u>*because*</u> He (*YAH*) will deliver (*yasha*) His people from their sins."

We see below that the Messiah must come "in the name of Yahuah" i.e. **Yahusha**.

> **Psalms 118**
> 26 Blessed is he who comes in the name of Yahuah.

> **John 12:13**
> Hosanna: Blessed is the King of Israel that cometh in the name of the Yahuah

We see below that Yahusha dealt with these same issues as the Jews had removed the name of Yahuah from Yahusha and shortened it to *Yeshua* in error coming out of Babylon due to **reverent stupidity** as to not speak the name Yah. Yahusha was not happy with the Jews misusing his name speaking it as Yeshua instead of Yahusha and warned them all they would never see him again until they admitted his name is Yahusha not Yeshua, not Yehoshua, not Jesus… Only ONE of those names is "in the name of Yahuah" and that is Yahusha the ONLY name under heaven by which you may be saved.

> **Luke 13**
> 35 Look, your house is left to you desolate. I tell you, you will not see me again until you say, `**Blessed is he who comes in the name of Yahuah**.`"

Yahusha did not make that critical error of removing the name of Yahuah. He used the name Yahuah often and that is one of the reasons he fell afoul with Rabbinical Judaism of his day as their "ears were offended" by the use of the name of Yahuah:

> **John 17:6**
> I have manifested thy name (𐤉𐤄𐤅𐤄 *Yahuah*) unto the men which thou gavest me out of the world"

It is a clear Biblical command from Yahuah that the name of the Messiah must embody "Yah" and must declare salvation "yasha". Any name that doesn't embody this "intent" is a counterfeit. Every time you utter the name Yahusha you are literally making the required declaration in Joel **that whoever calls on the name of _Yahuah will be saved._**

The Messiah's name is Theophanous

One of the first things we should learn in our search for the true Messiah is His Name. The importance of knowing this man's name cannot be overstated. Names were and are very important to the Hebrew people, and their meanings are of great significance! Not only are names significant to individuals, but also to entire families.

The name **Jesus** is <u>an invention of man</u> which in no way carries the meaning of the true Name of this Man mentioned in the New Testament (we'll look at this name later in this chapter). The simple fact (which is easily proven from authoritative sources) is that this man, the Messiah, spoken of in Scripture was born a Hebrew and he had a Hebrew name not a Greek name such as Jesus. There is no such name as Jesus in the Hebrew language.

Reading from *The Encyclopedia Judaica*, we find that the supposed name **Jesus** is actually the common Greek transliteration of the Hebrew name Joshua (which is the Hellenized uninspired transliteration of Yahusha into English).

The Encyclopedia Judaica, **Volume 10, page 10**

> ***JESUS****(d. 30 c.e.), whom Christianity sees as its founder and object of faith, <u>was a Jew who lived toward the end of the Second Commonwealth period</u>.*

> ***THE NAME, BIRTH, AND DEATH DATE OF JESUS****. Jesus is the <u>common Greek form of the Hebrew name Joshua (in Heb. Yahusha)</u>. Jesus' father, Joseph (Yahseph), his mother, Mary (in Heb. Miriam), and his brothers James, Joses, Judah, and Simon (Mark 6:3) likewise bore very popular* **Hebrew** *names.*

The Encyclopedia Judaica gives us additional information concerning the Hebrew spelling of עשוהי or YAHU-sha, which is *yod-heh-waw-shin-ayin* or literally *YAHU-sha*.

Joshua is not an accurate translation into English either it is the Hellenized version with the intent again to remove the name Yahuah from it.

The Encyclopedia Judaica, **Volume 12, page 805**

> The <u>first personal name</u> that was definitely <u>constructed with the tetragrammaton</u> is יהושׁע, (Joshua).

This source also points out to us that this Name, correctly pronounced Yahusha, is a compound name constructed with the Tetragrammaton, which is the Name: **Yahuah**, 𐤉𐤄𐤅𐤄. The Name Yahusha follows the common practice among the true worshippers of Yahuah (who did not follow Jewish superstition and remove the name of the Creator from the name), in forming and using compound names which brought glory to 𐤉𐤄𐤅𐤄 Yahuah's Name.

The Jewish Encyclopedia tells us this about compound names which glorify Yahuah:

The Jewish Encyclopedia, Volume 9, page 153

> *A distinctive characteristic of Bible onomatology is the frequency of composite names, which form at times even complete sentences, as in the case of Isaiah's son Shear-jashub (="the remnant shall return"). In the majority of cases these composite names are theophorous, referring to, or actually mentioning...the name of Yahuah using the shortened poetic form **YAH**.*

The Interpreter's Dictionary, Volume 3, page 505, tells us:

> *There is an increasing tendency, especially in the 7th Century b.c. to <u>use compound names</u> which state a fact or express a wish... The most numerous are names compounded with **'YAH'**... which number over 150 names in the Bible and are almost entirely personal or family names.*

This common practice to construct sentence names that convey an expression giving glory to Yahuah in Hebrew can be found in many names throughout scripture. The names in our modern translations were "Hellenized" to remove all Hebrew nature from them. In the process they remove the Glory given to Yahuah as they intended. This process of Hellenization was brought about due to the wars between Rome and The Jews and the hatred for the Jews as a result. The new religion formed in Rome needed to present a "new savoir" that could be accepted by Greeks and a "new gospel" that eliminated all Jewishness from it that pagan

47

religions would accept. This is called "syncretism" and I cover this in detail in my book ***Christianity and The Great Deception***.

The names in our English Bibles <u>are meaningless</u> removing the "compound" name structures found in Hebrew as well as the very meaning of their names which give Glory to Yahuah:

- Samuel – should be ***Shemuyl*** meaning "***Heard of Yahuah***"
- Daniel - should be ***Daniyl*** meaning "***Yahuah is my judge***"
- Elijah– should be ***Eliyyahu*** meaning "***my God is Yahuah***"
- Isaiah– should be ***Yesha'Yahu*** meaning "***Yahuah is salvation***"
- Hosea – should be ***Hosheyah*** meaning "***Yahuah saves***"
- Joel – should be ***Yahyl*** meaning "***Yahuah is our strength***"
- Amos – should be ***Amosyah*** meaning "***Corroborated by Yahuah***"
- Obadiah – should be ***Obeadyah*** meaning "***Worshipper of Yahuah***"
- Jonah – should be ***Yahnah*** meaning "***Ornament of Yahuah***"
- Micah – should be ***Micahyah*** meaning "***Who is like Yahuah***"
- Nahum – should be ***Nachumyah*** meaning "***Consolation of Yahuah***"
- Zephaniah – should be ***Zephanyah*** meaning "***Protected by Yahuah***"
- Haggai – should be ***Chagyah*** meaning "***Feast of Yahuah***"
- Zechariah – should be ***Zecharyah*** meaning "***Remembrance of Yahuah***"
- Malachi – should be ***Malakyah*** meaning "***Messenger of Yahuah***"
- Matthew – should be ***Mattithyah*** meaning "***Gift of Yahuah***"

- John – should be *Yahchanan* meaning *"Yahuah is merciful"*
- Paul – should be *Sha'ul* meaning *"asked of Yahuah"*
- Jesus/Joshua – should be *Yahusha* meaning *"Yahuah is salvation"*

The Name **Yahusha** (Heb עשוהי) is just such a contracted compound sentence Name. It is a combination of Yahuah's Name into a contracted personal name והי (**YAH:** *yod-heh vav*) and **Shua עש** (*shin-ayin*). The name Yahusha means *Yahuah will save* or *Yahuah is our savior*.

The Hebrew-English Lexicon of the Old Testament tells us that the name Yahusha means **Yahuah is salvation**. We see below that the original form of the name is עשוהי Yahusha but was "later" shortened to עושי which is Yeshua in order to remove Yahuah's name:

The Hebrew-English Lexicon of the Old Testament, by Brown, Driver, and Briggs, page 221

יְהוֹשֻׁעַ, יְהוֹשֻׁעַ, and (later) יֵשׁוּעַ, **n.pr.m.** (& loc., v. 9 infr.) (" is *salvation,* or " is *opulence.* ...in any case it came to be associated with יֵשׁ, cf. Mat I²¹; on יְשׁוּעַ v. esp. Frä^VOJ̈w. 1890, 332 ⁄ Müll ^SK 1892. 177, ⁱ· who cite analog. for change of וֹ to later—, & Nes l.c.)—1. Moses' successor, son of Nun, (𝐺 Ἰησου)יְהוֹשֻׁעַ Dt 3²¹ Ju 2⁷;=יְהוֹשֻׁעַ

The Hebraic Tongue Restored gives us this information concerning the Hebrew word, **shua**.

We find that this word comes from the word **yasha:**

> ### The Hebraic Tongue Restored, by Fabre d'Olivet, page 462
>
> שע shuh. Every idea of <u>conservation, restoration, cementation</u>.
>
> > שע In a literal sense, lime, cement; in a figurative sense, that which <u>consolidates, guarantees; which serves as safe-guard; which preserves.</u>

Gesenius' Hebrew-Chaldee Lexicon To The Old Testament tells us that yasha implies to be freed from danger and distress:

> ### Gesenius' Hebrew-Chaldee Lexicon To The Old Testament, page 811
>
> שׁוּעַ ...not used in Kal, i.q.שׁעַ—(1) TO BE AMPLE, BROAD; hence—
>
> (2) *to be rich, wealthy* (see שׁוּעַ, שׁוֹעַ No. 1).
>
> (3) *to be freed* from danger and distress (compare יָשַׁע).

The Hebrew-English Lexicon of the Old Testament, by Brown, Driver, and Briggs, page 447, tells us about the word **yasha and shua** specifically express the idea "*Salvation is from Yahuah*"

יֶשַׁע n.m. ˡˢ ⁶¹,⁵ deliverance, rescue, salvation, also safety, welfare;—יֵשַׁע ψ 20⁷ + 4 t.; יֶשַׁע Jb 5¹¹ + 4 t.; sf. יִשְׁעִי 2 S 22³ + 11t., + 14t. sfs.;—1. safety, welfare, prosperity 2 S 23⁵ ψ 12⁶ Jb 5⁴,¹¹. 2. salvation, i.e. primarily physical rescue, by Yahweh, oft. with added spiritual idea: Is 62¹¹ ψ 69¹⁴ 85⁸,¹⁰; אֱלֹהֵי יִשְׁעִי salvation from Yahweh ψ 50²³; used as infin. with acc. יִשְׁעֲ לְ Hb 3¹³,¹³ (see Ew §²³⁹ᵃ); accordingly Yahweh is אוֹרִי וְיִשְׁעִי my light and my salvation ψ 27¹; יֵשַׁע צוּר 95¹; קֶרֶן יִשְׁעִי 18³=2 S 22³;

Note that these sources use the modern English name Yahuah for the correct name Yahuah. The modern name Yahuah is not accurate to the name given in Paleo Hebrew to Moses which was 𐤉𐤅𐤄𐤅. The modern English version uses the "w" instead of the u sound. This was done by the Germans who combined the u u into a double u and created a new character we call the W in the late 14th century so Yahuah cannot be the most accurate name nor the name given to Moses. For that reason I do not adhere to the modern translation of Yahuah but rather the original pronunciation Yahuah. We read of the origin of the W below:

> **http://en.wikipedia.org/wiki/W**

> > *The Germanic /w/ phoneme was therefore written as ⟨VV⟩ or ⟨uu⟩ (⟨u⟩ and ⟨v⟩ <u>becoming distinct only by the Early Modern period</u>) by the 7th or 8th century by the earliest writers of Old English and Old High German... It is from this ⟨uu⟩ digraph that the modern name "double U" derives... It was probably considered a separate letter by the 14th century in both Middle English and Middle German orthography, although it remained an outsider not really considered part of the Latin alphabet proper, as expressed by Valentin Ickelshamer in the 16th century, who complained that*

> > *Poor w is so infamous and unknown that many barely know either its name or its shape, not those who aspire to being Latinists, as they have no need of it, nor do the Germans, not even the schoolmasters, know what to do with it or how to call it; some call it we, [... others] call it uu, [...] the Swabians call it auwawau[4]*

Thus we have עשׁוהי (*yod-heh-waw-shin-ayin*). This name is correctly pronounced **YAHU-SHA**, instead of *Yahushua* or *Yahusha* since the work Shua is derived from the word yasha and considering the letter waw (vav) in this compound is silent, just as *The Hebraic Tongue Restored* tells us.

> *Hebraic Tongue Restored,* by Fabre d'Olivet, pages 112-113

>> ***Conjunctive or Convertible Article.***--*This article in uniting nouns, causes the movement of nothingness, of which the character W becomes the sign, as we have seen: in making actions pass from one time to another, it exercises upon them the convertible faculty of which this same character is the universal emblem. Its conjunctive movement can be rendered by: and, also, thus, then, afterward, that, etc. But its convertible movement is not expressible in our tongue and I do not know of any in which it can be expressed. In order to perceive it one must feel the Hebraic genius.*

Where do we get Yahshua, Yeshua and Yehoshua?

If Yahusha is correct, then why do some instead use *Yahshua*, Yeshua and *Yehoshua*. Yahshua is Aramaic for Yahusha and I really have no problem with the use of Yahshua as it was Aramaic that was spoken at the time of the second temple period. However, Yeshua and Yehoshua are not correct as these two names insert the letters 'e' and 'o' instead of 'a' and 'u' as we have demonstrated. Are these names *Yeshua* and *Yehoshua* the true name? Many in the Hebrew Roots movement use the name Yeshua as that is the Modern Hebrew name today.

They too refuse to admit that "Yeshua" does not embody the name "Yah". "Ye" means "he" and is passive and does not directly identify Yahuah by name. These names remove Yahuah's name thereby failing the scriptural test concerning the requirement to express "Yahuah is our savior".

The Israelites adopted the worship of the LORD (Ba'al) and therefore removed the name of Yahuah and replaced it with the LORD. They also then either shortened the name Yahusha to Yeshua to remove the name of **Yah**uah and replaced the vowel points with the vowel points in Elohim giving us Yehoshau. Both Yeshua and Yehoshua are attempts to not use, write, or pronounce the name of Yah. We see below that the worship of Ba'al (the LORD) was assimilated into the worship of Yahuah: this is known as **syncretism**. It was the replacing of the name of Yahuah that led to the decline of Israel as a people.

Jewish Encyclopedia *__The unedited full-text of the 1906 Jewish Encyclopedia__:*

__How the Hebrews Adopted the Cult.__

It would appear that the Hebrews first learned Ba'al-Worship from the agricultural Canaanites. Their life before the conquest of Canaan, whether lived in or outside of Palestine, was nomadic, and therefore kept them beyond the circle of religious associations promoted by the cultivation of the soil. __After their settlement the Israelites began to live as did the people of the land__, and with the new mode of industrial and domestic life came the example and the incitement of the religious use and wont that were inseparable from the soil. The stated festivals, in which the Ba'als of the land had drawn to themselves all the enthusiasm and devotion of an intensely religious people, were a part of the fixed order of things in Palestine, and were necessarily appropriated by the religion of Yahuah. With them came the danger of mixing the rites of the false gods and the true God; and, as a matter of fact, __the__

53

> *syncretism did take place* *and contributed more than anything else* **to the religious and moral decline of Israel***.*

As I pointed out earlier, the Jews developed a superstition (I call **reverent stupidity**) that it was too holy to pronounce the name Yahuah or even lay eyes on it so they replaced every occurrence of the name 𐤉𐤄𐤅𐤄 Yahuah (over 8,000 times in scripture) with the title *LORD* in keeping with their Babylonian captors whose god was also **the LORD** god Ba'al. This abomination was carried forward and at the time the current modern translations were penned, they used these faulty Hebrew texts coming out of Babylonian captivity not the original Hebrew scriptures prior to Babylonian captivity.

These modern uninspired translations in English carried forward that superstition not to write the name of God. They also removed the name YAH from the name YAHusha giving us Yeshua instead then transliterated Yeshua into Iesous and finally into Jesus. Where the scribes encountered the true name of the Messiah which is pronounced YAHU-SHA with the proper vowel points added, they translated it with the vowel points of "Elohim" not Yahuah giving us Yehoshua instead of Yahusha... That is where and how we get Yeshua, Yehoshua, and Jesus instead of Yahusha. This is not even the fault of the Christian Church they were just following the lead of Jews who began worshipping Ba'al while in Babylonian captivity.

We have sufficient proof showing that the Name of 𐤉𐤄𐤅𐤄 Yahuah has been completely erased from the Holy Scriptures and from common knowledge and use altogether.

We see below that that it was the Jews who first began subtracting the name of The Creator from His own word:

> **The Century Bible,** Volume 1, pages 90-91, tells us the following.

Some time after the return from the Captivity, and before the beginning of the Christian Era, <u>the Yahdaim (Jews) came to believe that the Holy Name Yahuah was too sacred to be uttered on ordinary occasions.</u> It was said to be pronounced by the High Priest on the Day of Atonement. <u>At other times, when any one read or quoted aloud from what is called the Old Testament, the word '𐤀𐤃𐤍ai",</u> "Lord, " was usually substituted for____, and similarly the LXX (Septuagint Version) has Kurios, the Vulgate dominus, and the e.v. lord, where the Hebrew has Yahuah. Hebrew was originally written without vowels, but when the "vowel points" were added, the vc𐤀𐤃𐤍 of "Adonai" or "Elohim" were written with____, <u>as a direction that these words were to be read instead of the word whose consonants were Yahuah</u>; thus we find the combinations YeHoWaH and YeHoWiH. At the Reformation, the former being the more usual, was sometimes used as the Name of the (Mighty One) of Israel, and owing to ignorance of its history was misread as "Jehovah," a form which has established itself in English, but does not give the pronunciation of the Holy Name it represents.

The Theological Dictionary Of The New Testament, Kittel and Bromiley, Volume 3, page 284, tells us that the name Jesus (*Iesous*) is a Greek form of the Hebrew proper Name **Yahusha** (עשוהי). Keep in mind, however, that this name Jesus carries none of the meaning of the original Hebrew Name Yahusha, which means **Yahuah is salvation. We see below that AFTER the return from exile The Jews shortened the name Yahusha to Yeshua again out of reverent stupidity (I mean *reverent superstition*)....**

Ἰησοῦς → ὄνομα.

1. <u>The Greek form of a list of OT char-</u>
<u>acters who in pre-exilic Hebrew are</u>
<u>called יהושע and usually after the Exile</u>
<u>ישוע</u>.

The Prophet Yerem**YAH** (Hellenized to *Jeremiah* to remove the name of YAH) warned that this practice of removing Yahuah's Name would be handed down to us from the unfaithful priests, interpreters and scribes, when the Hebrew Scriptures were first translated to Greek, then to Latin, and finally to English.

Jeremiah 8:8
How can you say; We *are* the wise, and the Law of Yahuah is with us? Behold, the lying pen of the scribes has falsified them, and written them wrong!

That's why, today, we have foolish sounding names like Jesus, Joshua, Yeshua, and Yehoshua, which do not honor or glorify our Heavenly Father Yahuah, because they carry none of the original intent and meaning.

Why is "Jesus" not the true name?

The reality is that the Greeks did not hold true to the "intent" of the name when translating it. Instead they attempted a direct translation of each of the characters in Yeshua which was the standard Hebrew form coming out of Babylonian Captivity (but Yeshua is in error). We already learned that Yeshua is a later derivative of Yahusha removing the name YAH believing it to holy to pronounce.

So the translators began with Yeshua an uninspired <u>later derivative</u> instead of Yahusha. Yeshua remove the "intent" of the name of the Messiah to give glory to Yahuah as our savoir. To get the name

Jesus the translators used Yeshua עֵשׁוּיַ, with vowel pointing *yēšūă'* in Hebrew which was a common alternative form of the name עֵשׁוּהִי (*Yahusha*) in later books of the Hebrew Bible translated **AFTER** the Babylonian captivity. It was these books *mistranslated book of the Hebrew Bible* that were used among Jews of the Second Temple period when Yahusha was born. The name *Jesus* corresponds (is a transliteration because Jesus cannot be translated from Hebrew directly) to the Greek spelling *Iesous*.

This name **Iesous** is the result of the translators then attempting a character by character translation from the erroneous 'Yeshua' into Latin instead of translating the "intent of the name" which is what is important. Translating character by character was impossible as the character sets in Greek and Hebrew do not contain the same characters so they ended up with a "transliteration" of Iesous. Then from Iesous we had Hesus (which was in the original King James Bible) then ultimately Jesus today. Jesus is a modern name not even found in the original King James translation.

So the first point I want to make is that the translators began with Yeshua not Yahusha and to come up with Iesous that removed Yahuah from the name of the Messiah and therefore fails the scriptural test of the Messiah's name. the Messiah was to come in the name of Yahuah. Only those who declare "Yahuah is salvation" will be saved. Both Yeshua which means "he saves" and Jesus (which is not a Hebrew name at all) both fail this test and there is only ONE name by which salvation can be assured.

The Catholic Encyclopedia admits that Jesus is a *transliteration* of a Latin word that represents the Greek form of Yeshua which is itself a LATER derivative of the vowel dissimilation of Yoshua itself a CONTRACTED form of Yehoshuah (using the **wrong** vowel points of Elohim, should be Yahusha with the proper vowel points) or the contracted name sentence "Yahuah is salvation"... which points to the ACTUAL name given by the Messengers of Yahuah to Miriam which tells us the REAL name is YahuahSHUA "Yahuah is salvation".... YAHUSHA:

The New Catholic Encyclopedia, Volume 7, pages 970-971

> *JESUS (THE NAME). In English the name <u>Jesus</u> is a transliteration of the Latin form <u>Iesus</u>, which represents the <u>Greek form</u> of the Hebrew name ye-šûa`. The latter is a late form, by <u>vowel dissimilation, of the name yôšûa`, itself a contracted form of yhôšûa`, "Yahuah is salvation."</u> This was the name of Moses' successor. *Josue (Joshua), son of Nun. Both because of the fame of this early hero of Israel and because of the meaning of the name, many men both in the OT and in the NT bore the name of Josue or Jesus. The Septuigint generally uses the <u>Greek form</u> Iesous where the <u>Hebrew text has the form yôšûa`or y'hôšûa`.</u> So also the NT, in referring to Josue, son of Nun, calls him Jesus (Acts 7:45; Heb 4:8). An allusion is made in Mt. 1:21 to the meaning of the name ("<u>Yahuah is salvation</u>"):*

The Theological Dictionary of the New Testament, by Kittel and Bromley, Volume 3, page 289, tells us that in fact the REAL name of the Messiah is a "sentence name" of "Yahuah is salvation" or Yahusha actually containing the Tetragrammaton:

> The full form יהושׁע is a sentence name, [36] in which the subject comes first and represents a form of the divine name יהו, and in which the verb is a subsidiary form of the verb ישע which is also found in names like אבישׁוע, מלכישׁוע and אלישׁוע which means "to help". Philo's explanation ...recognizes the two parts (Mut. Nom., 121): Ἰησοῦς σωτηρία κυρίου. More exact is the interpretation in a pap. of the 3rd to 4th cent. A.D.: Ἰησοῦς Ιω σωτηρία. [37] The Rabbis, too, were aware of the two parts of the name, Nu. r., 16 on 13:2 (Str.-B., I, 64): הושׁע is called יהושׁע (Nu. 13:6), i.e., ' is added, because in view of the wickedness of the spies Moses said: יה' יושׁיעך מן הדור יהוה: The ' thus indicated the tetragrammaton (or its abbreviation יה) The shortened form ישׁוע no longer expresses Yahweh's Name clearly, directing attention simply to the verb ישׁע.

We see above that the full "sentence name" is **עשׁוהי** notice the name contains the name of YAH **והי** followed by the Hebrew

עשׁ modern word SHUA which is derived from the Paleo Hebrew word YASHA which means "salvation" i.e. YAHUSHA.

The "shortened" form Yeshua **עושׁי** "no longer expresses Yahuah's name clearly, it is passive voice putting the emphasis on "shua" and means "he saves". Thereby failing the Biblical requirements that the Messiah must come "in the name of Yahuah".

The Theological Dictionary Of The New Testament, Kittel and Bromiley, Volume 3, page 290 gives us clear insight into the pagan origins of the name "Jesus"...

> H. Lamer believes that the Gk. Jesu is a masculine form of 'Ιησώ, the goddess of salvation, for which we have the form 'Ιησώ, in Herond, Mim., iv. 6[42].
>
> [42]*Philol. Wochenschr.*, 50 (1930), 764 f. The goddess 'Ιησω. is the only figure in Gk. mythology which can be brought into relation with Jesus.

The next point I want to make concerning the name Jesus is that the name of the Messiah is a sentence name to convey the idea "Yahuah is salvation". The Greek translators failed this test. Instead of translating the "intent" of the name using the Latin word for salvation, they translated (or attempted to translate) each character and lost the intent all together.

The reality is they used "sous' to give glory to Zeus as was their common practice in naming people and places the Greek and Roman culture.

Jesus is not the proper translation into Greek

As a matter of fact, the name 'Jesus' did not even exist in the English language 400 years ago—as evidenced by the fact that it was not recorded in the original 1611 King James Bible. But let's dissect that name anyway as that has come to be the accepted name of the Messiah today we need to address it.

If the first part of the name 'Iη' (Ie) comes from 'Iehovah' following the Jewish superstition not to use Yahuah thereby using Elohim in the vowel points resulting in ignorance of the name Jehovah.

The Century Bible, Volume 1, pages 90-91

> *Some time after the return from the Captivity, and before the beginning of the Christian Era, the Yahdaim (Jews) came to believe that the Holy Name Yahuah was too sacred to be uttered on ordinary occasions. It was said to be pronounced by the High Priest on the Day of Atonement. At other times, when any one read or quoted aloud from what is called the Old Testament, the word "Adonai", "Lord," was usually substituted for Yahuah, and similarly the LXX (Septuagint Version) has Kurios, the Vulgate dominus, and the e.v. lord, where the Hebrew has Yahuah. Hebrew was originally written without vowels, but when the "vowel points" were added, the vowels of "Adonai" or "Elohim" were written with Yahuah, as a direction that these words were to be read instead of the word whose consonants were Yahuah; thus we find the combinations YeHoWaH and YeHoWiH. At the Reformation, the former being the more usual, was sometimes used as the Name of the (Mighty One) of Israel, and owing to ignorance of its history was*

> *misread as "Jehovah," a form which has
> established itself in English, but does not give the
> pronunciation of the Holy Name it represents.*

Therefore the prefix of the name Je or (Ie) is in <u>error</u>. But does the **suffix** 'σους' (**sous**) mean 'saves' or 'salvation' in the **Greek** of the New Testament period? No.

We know for a fact that "Ie*sous*" was not then the proper way to translate the "intent" of the name given the Messiah that '*Yahuah is salvation*' even in Greek or Latin. The Greek word for "salvation" is Strong's entry 4991 *soterion* it is not *sous*.

Strong's Number: 4992

> **soterion**, adjective. Meaning saving, bringing
> salvation he who embodies this salvation, or
> through whom God is about to achieve it the hope
> of (future) salvation

So if the translators were even true to their own language it would not have been translated "Jesus" or "Iesous" but rather something along the lines of "***Iasoterion***". It must be obvious by this point where the suffix "so***us***" came from. Jes***us*** holds to the Greek tradition of naming people after ***their*** pagan god of the Pantheon… Ze***us***.

Why did the translator us 'sous' instead of 'soteria'?

It should be noted at this point that the Greeks had a similar naming convention as did the Hebrews. Where the Hebrews used "YAH" in the construction of their names giving glory to Yahuah, the Greeks ended names and cities using "sous/sus/us" after their own god Ze***us***. Take for example the name of Juli***us*** Caesar "Gai***us*** Juli***us***" or the name of the Roman Emperor Constantine who literally created Christianity "Flavi***us*** Valeri***us*** Aureli***us***

Constantin*us* August*us*". The suffix "*us*" was added to Greek and Roman names to give glory to Ze*us* where **Yah** was added to Hebrew names to give glory to Yahuah. Jes*us* is just such a Greek name like all Greek names ending in "us" that gives glory to Zeus!

Dictionary of Christian Lore and Legend

> *"It is known that the Greek name endings with sus, seus, and sous were attached by the Greeks to names and geographical areas as means to give honor to their supreme deity, Zeus."*
> *"This name of the true Messiah, Yahusha, being Hebrew, was objectionable to the Greeks and Romans, who hated the Judeans (Jews), and so it was deleted from the records, and a new name inserted. Yahusha was thus replaced by Ie-Sous (hail Zeus), now known to us as Jesus."*

Iesous in Greek

So Yahusha is English for the Hebrew name of the Messiah (anointed King of Israel) and Jesus is the name of the Greek "good man" or Christos created in the image of Zeus. It is that simple. But what does "Iesous" mean in Greek. It has no meaning in Hebrew; as it is not a Hebrew word. In Greek, "Iesous" literally translated means "Hail Zeus". The name "Jesus" didn't even exist until the 4th Century and was a later derivative of the late Latin Isus and Jesu both pagan gods.

> *"It is known that the Greek name endings with sus, seus, and sous were attached by the Greeks to names and geographical areas as means to give honor to their supreme deity, Zeus."*
> ### Dictionary of Christian Lore and Legend

> *"This name of the true Messiah, Jahshuwah (Jehoshua), being Hebrew, was objectionable to the Greeks and Romans, who hated the Judeans (Jews), and so it was deleted from the records, and a new name inserted.*

Jahshuwah (Jehoshua) was thus replaced by Ie-Sous (hail Zeus), now known to us as Jesus."

-The Origin of Christianity
by A.B. Traina

"It is simply amazing to think that all these years, hundreds of years; mankind has been calling the Savior by the wrong name!! It's hard to give up the name of Jesus because it's so deeply ingrained in us and much has been said and done in that name."

-Gospel of The Kingdom
True Names and Title
Dr. Henry Clifford Kinley
1931 - Ohio USA

"In the 1611 KJ New Testament the name Yahusha appeared originally wherever the Messiah was spoken of. Yahusha means "Yahuah is Salvation". Later the Messiah's name was replaced with Iesus (Greek) which later in the 1600's it became Jesus starting with the new English letter "J" which was introduced at that time. Further, the Greek "Iesus" comes from the name Zeus, the ruling God in the Greek pantheon."

-Gospel of The Kingdom
True Names and Title
Dr. Henry Clifford Kinley
1931 - Ohio USA

We see in historical documents that the name "Jesus" did not even come into existence until the 1600's when the letter "J" was introduced into our English language. So the name "Jesus" is only around 400 years old! The Greek "Iesus" comes from the name Zeus, the ruling God in the Greek pantheon.

"Je**sus**" is a transliteration of a Latin name only ONE letter off "Ioe**sus**" pronounced hey-sus - which has no meaning in Hebrew, but in Latin it means "Hail Zeus". If Yahusha's name had been transliterated into our language, it would have been *Joshua*. If the name was treated properly using the compound naming convention <u>Yahuah intended</u> it would be YAH(weh)(ye)SHUA shortened to "Yahusha" using the short contracted form maintaining the meaning of the name and fulfilling prophecy that the Messiah "came in the name of Yahuah".

If the name was handled properly in Greek by the uninspired pagan scribes, it would hold true to the "meaning" of the name as given by the Angel to Joseph and Mary; then "shua" or salvation would have been translated "soterion or soter" not "sous". So we see a gross mis-handling of the Messiah's name at best but when you look back in history we see a Hellenization of the name *with the intent* to give glory to the pagan god Zeus.

The reason behind this abomination is clearly seen. The name *Jesus* has the exact same suffix as the name of the Roman Emperor who created it: **Flavius Valerius Aurelius Constantinus Augustus**. Why does every word in Constantine's name end in "us"? It would only stand to reason that the all powerful Emperor would give a name to his new god in his own image with the suffix "us". After all, Constantine believed himself to be re-incarnated Apollo (the son of Zeus). And he remade the Messiah in his own image then elevated that "image of the false messiah" in the name "Jesus" as god to be worshipped.

This act of paganizing the Messiah and worshipping an image of a man above Yahuah is condemned by Paul in a letter to the church in Rome!

> ### Romans 1
> 21 Because that, when they knew Yahuah, they glorified Yahuah not as God (*elevating Jesus/Trinity in their hearts as God incarnate*), neither were thankful; but became vain in their imaginations, and their foolish heart was darkened (*to believe a pagan lie*). 22 Professing themselves to be wise, they became fools 23 and exchanged the glory of the immortal Yahuah for images **made to look like mortal man** (*the image of "Jesus"*) and birds and animals and

reptiles (*signs of The Zodiac*).

[24] Therefore Yahuah gave them over in the sinful desires of their hearts to sexual impurity for the degrading of their bodies with one another. [25] **They exchanged the truth about Yahuah for a lie** (*pagan Trinity*), **and worshiped and served created things rather than the Creato**r—who (*the Creator Yahuah*) is forever praised. YalleluYahuah!

When we simply take the first step and admit to ourselves the obvious, it becomes abundantly clear both "why" and "how" the name "Jesus" was easily accepted by a pagan population that worshiped Ze**us**, Hes**us**, Hor**us**, Krishna, Juli**us** Caesar and the demi-god Apollo the god of the sun. To the pagan Romans of their day, the name Iesous (Jesus Christ or JC) looked and sounded almost identical to their god-man Julius Caesar or (JC). This is true today even in English (Julius / Jesus) even their initials remain the same and have nothing in common with Yahusha the Messiah. The English translation of Yahusha looks nothing and sounds nothing like "Jesus" it is "Joshua" or even truer still Yahusha.

The obvious truth is the Messiah's name was changed and he was given a name like every other Greek in honor of Zeus. No wonder Yahusha condemns those who "in his name" did all that amazing stuff using the name "Jesus" teaching the Law has been abolished. They never knew him. They literally fell for *the false religion of pagan Rome*.

The English name "*Jesus*"

As I stated earlier in this chapter we are going to "reverse engineer" this name "Je*sus*" and when we do it traces directly back to Babylon no matter how we look at it. But what would happen if we look at the name "Je*sus*" as a compound **English** name composed (as English words are) of the Latin prefix and suffix "*Je*" and "*sus*"?

We must look at it that way because the true name of the Messiah was a compound name YAH (Yahuah)(ye)SHUA (salvation) in Hebrew. Supposedly "Je*sus*" comes from the name of the Messiah so if we break it into it component parts what does it say about "Je*sus*" in English.

Does it identify The Passover Lamb sacrifice of Yahuah or an abominable sacrifice of a pig on Easter? Does it begin to bring into focus the exact same sacrifice of The Ishtar Pig (Easter) which is the unquestioned "sacrifice" of the false religion of Christianity as well as Babylon? Let's look at the prefix "*Je*" and suffix "*sus*" in the English dictionary.

When considering the prefix we find that "*Je*" is another form of "*Ge*" derived from the Latin/Greek word for "earth". GE/JE is a short form of Gaia or Jee which is the "mother earth" or Roman goddess Tellus! The suffix "sus" comes from the Latin word for "pig" sous. "Sous" in Latin means pig this is where we get the pig call "soooouuuuiiii".

So in English if we examine the name Je*sus* as a compound name it means literally "earthly pig" or "pig of Tellus/Goddess Mother Earth".

The name "Jesus" in no way implies or means Yahuah is Salvation. *Shocking... I know.*

Below is the Webster's entry for the suffix JE and SUS:

Je

GE (**je**, ge) GAEA;GAIA GAEA (Jee),Noun. [Gr. Gaia derived from "Ge", earth] <u>in Greek mythology the earth personified as a goddess</u>,mother of Uranus the Titans,etc, MOTHER EARTH: <u>identified by the Romans with Tellus</u>: also Gala,Ge. GEO (jeo,jee) [Gr. "geo" derived from gaia, ge, the earth] a combining form meaning earth, as in geo/centric, geo/phyte. (*WEBSTER'S NEW WORLD DICTIONARY*)

sus

sus, sus N 3 1 NOM S C T, sus N 3 1 VOC S C T sus, suis swine; hog, pig, sow; (Latin-English-Latin Java Dictionary with Whitaker's Wordlist) sus : swine, pig, hog.

Jesus literally means the 'Beast of the Earth' in fulfillment of Revelation 13!

The swine or pig is the most abominable "beast" in the Torah. Now we see why Revelation identifies The Beast as "the beast of the earth", it is literally telling us the "name" of the Antichrist.

We now are coming closer to the false messiah's sacrifice on Easter to the goddess Ishtar (a pig) in replace of The Passover Lamb. That is why we eat ham on Easter because a pig killed Ishtar's son Tammuz later called Apollo / Hesus / Horus / Krishna then Je*sus*. We are taught that anyone obedient to the dietary laws of Yahuah are not true Christians (which is true because the followers of Yahusha were called Nazarenes). So to PROVE our total lawlessness in the eyes of Yahuah ... we actually eat the most unclean abominable animal that is not even "food" on Ishtar day! And worship the Earthly (**Je**) Pig (**sus**) or beast of the earth.

The most abominable animal to Yahuah in His Word (a pig), we eat it in defiance to a pagan god we have elevated in our hearts above Yahuah and then we disobey Passover.

Those who commit such an abominable sacrifice in their heart on Easter and are disobedient to The Passover are not true sons of Yahuah. I will prove this next when we look at "how" and "why" Passover was changed to "Ishtar/Easter" and a pig sacrificed (eaten) instead of a lamb on Passover as Yahuah instructed and Yahusha confirmed. Passover is an EVERLASTING ordinance of the Living God, Yahuah.

> ### Luke 22:19
> 19 And when he had taken some bread and given thanks (*on Passover*), he broke it and gave it to them, saying, "This (*Passover Dinner*) is my body (*Passover Lamb*) which is given (*sacrificed*) for you; **do this** (*keep Passover*) in remembrance of Me."
>
> ### Exodus 12
> 14 'So this day shall be to you a memorial; and you shall keep it as a feast to the Lord throughout your generations. **You shall keep it as a feast by an everlasting ordinance**.

So Yahusha is English for the Hebrew name of the Messiah (anointed King of Israel) and Jesus is the name of the Greek "savior" or Christos (all pagan god-men were called Christs such as Christos Mithras and Krishna etc.). It is that simple. But what does "Iesous" mean in Greek. It has no meaning in Hebrew; as it is not a Hebrew word. In Greek, "Iesous" literally translated means "Hail Zeus".

So both the prefix of "Ie" and the suffix of "sous" are in error and are **mistranslations** of the Hebrew name *Yah* and *shua*. In the 21st century we have <u>no need to trace the Messiah's name through pagan Rome</u>. We, today, can simply translate it directly from Hebrew to English leaving out all the transliteration errors going from Latin/Greek and all the English variations.

Proverbs 30:4

Who has gone up to heaven and come down? Whose hands have gathered up the wind? Who has wrapped up the waters in a cloak? Who has established all the ends of the earth? *What is his name, and what is the name of his son? Surely you know***!**

His name is 𐤉𐤄𐤅𐤄 Yahuah as given to Moses and His son's name is Yahusha. The true English translation directly from **עשוהי** as given to Yahseph and Miriam

Chapter 3
The Second Beast... The False Religion

Now that we know the true name of the Messiah is Yahusha and Jesus is actually a pagan name that means "Beast of the Earth" we can begin to move forward. Before we prove that Jesus Christ (the Earthly Pig) is the Antichrist and abominable sacrifice on the Altar of Yahuah, let's establish the beastly system. It is that beastly system or the second beast that causes all mankind to worship the Earthly Pig of Ishtar (the Babylonian sacrifice). The spirit behind this false religion, The Dragon, has a firm hold on the mind of humanity and this lie is so powerful that if possible could even deceive the elect of Yahuah... *if possible*.

Yahuah warned us over and over **not to learn the way of the pagans and worship Him in their way**, doing such things are considered an abomination to Yahuah. He told us very clearly how He demands to be served and worshipped in His Torah, the very example set by Yahusha who lived it by being obedient to His Feasts, His Torah, and His Sabbaths... We are to follow Yahusha's example not the Pope of Rome's edicts.

> **1 John 2:6**
> Whoever claims to live in (*covenant with*) Yahuah must live as Yahusha did.

In this book I will demonstrate how the Babylonian Priesthood was formally transferred from Babylon to Rome. The Roman Emperors became the new High Priest of the Babylonian sun god called Pontifus Maximus. Every fundamental doctrine of the Christian Church (Trinity/Jesus/Sunday/Easter/Christmas/No Law) was given by decree of this pagan High Priest and violates explicate scripture and the example set by the Messiah.

Yahusha never kept Sunday worship, never kept Christmas or Easter. Yahusha kept the Law of Yahuah and all the Sabbaths and Festivals defined within it. These holy days bear witness of Yahusha that he is the true Messiah. That is our example and we must live it or we simply are not in covenant with Yahuah through Yahusha.

Yahuah warmed us about <u>trading in</u> the example set forth in His Instructions in Righteousness (Torah/Law) for pagan practices:

<u>Deuteronomy 12</u>

3 Break down their altars, smash their sacred stones and burn their Asherah poles in the fire; cut down the idols of their gods and wipe out their names from those places. 4 You must not worship Yahuah your God in their way... 8 You are not to do as you do here today, everyone doing as they see fit!... 28 Be careful to obey all these regulations I am giving you, so that it may always go well with you and your children after you, because you will be doing what is good and right in the eyes of Yahuah your God... be careful not to be ensnared by inquiring about their gods, saying, "How do these nations serve their gods? We will do the same." 31 **You must not worship Yahuah your God in their way**, because in worshiping their gods, they do all kinds of detestable things Yahuah hates.

But wait! This is EXACTLY what we have done! We do nothing Yahuah said to do, instead we "say" we are worshipping Yahuah while worshipping in **the exact same way** as they did in Babylon, then Egypt, then Rome, now the USA. We just "say" we are worshipping "god" (we do not even address Him by His Holy Name Yahuah) without even identifying exactly "which one" we serve. The "god" we serve is defined by the rituals we keep!

Christianity worships The LORD... Ba'al

<u>1 Kings 18</u>

[18] "I have not made trouble for Israel," Elijah replied. "But you and your father's family have. **You have abandoned Yahuah's commands and have followed Baal** (*The LORD*).

Jeremiah 23

[25] "I have heard what the prophets say who prophesy lies in my name. They say, 'I had a dream! I had a dream!' [26] How long will this continue in the hearts of these lying prophets, who prophesy the delusions of their own minds? [27] They think the dreams they tell one another will make my people forget my name, **just as their ancestors forgot my name through Baal (*The LORD*) worship**.

Most people do not realize that when they address Yahuah as "The Lord" they are doing exactly as stated above and calling upon Baal as Jeremiah explains "we have forgotten the name Yahuah for Ba'al and call upon The LORD:

http://en.wikipedia.org/wiki/Baal

> *Baal, also rendered Ba'al (Biblical Hebrew בַּעַל), is a Northwest Semitic title and honorific meaning "master" or "__lord__" that is used for various gods who were patrons of cities in the Levant and Asia Minor, cognate to Akkadian Bēlu. A Baalist or Baalite **means a worshipper of Baal i.e. The Lord**. "Ba'al" or "The Lord" can refer to any god and even to human officials.*
>
> *In some texts it is used for Hadad, a god of the rain, thunder, fertility and agriculture, and the lord of Heaven. Since only priests were allowed to utter his divine name, Hadad, **Ba'al was commonly used**. Nevertheless, few if any Biblical uses of "Ba'al" refer to Hadad, the lord over the assembly of gods on the holy mount of Heaven; **most refer to a variety of local spirit-deities worshipped as cult images, each called ba'al and regarded in the Hebrew Bible in that context as a "false god"**.*

I was having this discussion recently with a long time friend of over 20 years who is a Christian. He finally had to admit that there is no scriptural backing for The Trinity/Sunday/Easter/Christmas worship but he said it didn't matter because he it wasn't those days that are important he was worshipping "the god behind them" implying he was worshipping Yahuah. Well, the sad fact is that Yahuah is not behind those worship days. Those rituals come to us passed down from Babylon, Egypt, Rome, and now Christianity.

These are the exact rituals Yahuah <u>prohibited</u> us from keeping and Yahuah said we could not "say" we are worshipping Him through those pagan rituals. We are fooling only ourselves by doing such things; we are not fooling Yahuah who is our judge. There is no salvation in these Babylonian now Christian rituals. Salvation is found in obedience to Yahuah and specifically in keeping the Passover the true sacrifice for sin and calling on the name of The Creator and Messiah..

So while Yahuah gave us specific direction and instruction on "how to worship" Him in His Torah and even went so far as to forbid us from worshipping in the style of Babylonian pagan ritual, we outright have declared Yahuah's instruction *abolished and <u>keep Babylon's rituals</u>* and even call upon the name of Ba'al… The LORD.

We don't praise His Holy Name Yahuah we call Him by titles such as "LORD" and "GOD" and "Hashem" and even recon Him a "pagan Trinity" in nature. All the same titles and nature pagans use for their gods. The Second Commandment is that we are not to take the name Yahuah in vain. The Hebrew word there for "vain" means "to bring to nothing or of no effect" which is EXACTLY what calling Him by the name "LORD" does! We have hidden the name of Yahuah from our site and bring it to nothing in our use of titles and even outright rebel against His Instructions in Righteousness (Law).

In this book, I am going to demonstrate the origin of "The Dragon" in the book of Revelation and trace that very dragon to the god

Dagon of Babylon known as ***The LORD god Ba'al***. Dagon the Dragon is the "god" or spirit behind the Catholic/Christian Churches of today whose ritualistic worship continues unchallenged in every Christian Church. Anyone who dares question or challenge these obvious pagan rituals are cast out and rejected from their church, by their friends, and even by family member. But then again, isn't that the entire point of scripture? We are to be "set apart" or sanctified by His Word (The Torah).

Yet we just continue along in the largest religion on Earth, the widest path, ignoring the commandments of Yahuah, keeping every pagan ritual, calling the Messiah by a clearly pagan name and we completely ignore the obvious in scripture and historical records. We do this because it is the "easy way", it is the "comfortable way" and because "everyone is doing it" not because it is **THE WAY** and example set by Yahusha the Messiah. He set no such examples as disobedience to The Law, Sunday worship, Trinity worship, incarnation, Easter, Christmas, etc. etc. That is another gospel all together.

For the purpose of understanding The False Religion, we are not making any distinction between Catholic and Protestant as they are identical even though they like to splinter into various groups and argue over who better serves Ba'al.

Both (Catholic and Protestant) together make up Christianity as a whole as defined by the Babylonian rituals through which they worship:

- Sunday Worship
- Trinity "god"
- Jesus
- Christmas
- Good Friday
- Easter
- Call on Baal i.e. The LORD not Yahuah

As I demonstrated through historical facts in my second book *Mystery Babylon the religion of the Beast*, the above list *is identical* to the religion that evolved out of Babylon… a carbon copy in fact.

The False Religion is *any establishment* that adheres to the Nicean Creed as defined by the Council of Nicaea and whose ritualistic worship is defined by Trinity / Jesus / Sunday / Easter / Good Friday / Christmas. The actual differences between Catholic and Protestant are negligible. These differences are irrelevant as **none of the rituals** they keep are Biblical nor do they honor Yahuah as He instructed us to worship Him.

Protesting Catholics (**Protest**ants) protest the authority of The Pope yet they obey his every word concerning The Sabbath vs. Sunday, Passover vs. Easter, and Christmas vs. the Feasts of Yahuah. All of Christianity has abolished the Laws of Yahuah in favor of the edicts of the High Priest of The Dragon who is Dagon… The Pope of Rome.

Haven't we been warned of this long ago? Haven't I read of this abomination before somewhere? Yes, in the book of Revelation we read speaking of "the woman" or Whore of Babylon.

Revelation 17:4

And the woman was *arrayed in purple and scarlet colour*, and decked with gold and precious stones and pearls, *having a golden cup in her hand* full of abominations and filthiness of her fornication

If the photo above is not obvious enough it soon will be undeniable. This book literally exposes Christianity for what it is… The False Religion that has evolved from The Mystery Religion of Babylon. To fully understand The False Religion known as "Christianity" we must admit to ourselves the "source" of the pagan worship that defines both Catholic and Protestant Christianity. That "source" is The Pope of Rome who is far from being a servant of Yahuah, he is in fact a puppet figure through which Satan manipulates humanity. The Pope is nothing more than a pagan High Priest of Dagon the Dragon and that position can be traced all the way back to Nimrod, the founder of Babylon.

In this book I am simply going to "reverse engineer", if you will, the religion of Christianity whose foundation is in Rome or Spiritual Babylon as Peter claimed. I am going to clearly spell out the origins of Christianity and how it has come to dominate the human race as **the largest religion on Earth**. That alone should raise an eyebrow as it is prophesied that The Mystery Religion of Babylon would deceive the entire planet at the time Yahusha returns and be the broad and wide gate that leads to our destruction. It is not, the narrow path which only the small remnant of humanity who are called by Yahuah find and obtain salvation. Only "a very few" find the Truth of

Yahuah / Yahusha / Sabbath/ Passover/ Law

and overcome the false religion of

Trinity / Jesus / Sunday / Easter / Passover / No Law:

Matthew 7
[13] "Enter through the narrow gate. For wide is the gate and broad is the road that leads to destruction, *and many enter through it.* [14] **But small is the gate and narrow the road that leads to life, and only a very few find it...** [21] "Not everyone who says to me, 'Lord, Lord,' will enter the kingdom of heaven, but **only the one who does the will of my Father** (*defined in The Torah, there was no NT when*

78

he said this) who is in heaven.

Chapter 4

From Dagon to the Dragon the "Spirit" behind the Beast

From Dagon to the Dragon

The word "dragon" comes from the word "Dagon" one of, if not the, oldest pagan gods dating back to Nimrod. Dagon evolved over time and cultures into the dragon:

DAGON

Dagon (fish god)= Neptune= Posiedon (who carries the Trident) = Satan = Leviathan = Taneen = dragon = seraph

man creates everything
in his own image

Dagon is where the word dragon came from. When a nation conquered another nation, they would take their gods and incorporate them into their belief system. Semaramis (queen of Babylon) became Isis, who became Ishtar/Easter, who became Venus, who became Aphrodite, and finally Mary. In the same way Nimrod (King of Babylon) became Dagon became the sea serpent, then the dragon, then Neptune, then Poseidon, and then Zeus, and finally Satan. The reason Neptune carried the trident, is the same reason you see Satan with the pitch fork. The trident was the article from the Jewish Tabernacle for turning the sacrifice.

80

The Taneem (great sea monster Genesis 1:21) was created on the 5th day when God created the fishes and the birds.

The association to the goat is also in scripture as well as in satanic worship. The goat fish Capricorn was also a direct association to Satan as well as the Hydra, the Septa (the sea Monster), and the serpent.

As I demonstrated in the second book in this series "The Mystery Religion of Babylon" Nimrod was the first false messiah ruling over the first attempt at a world government. Beginning with Nimrod in Babylon mankind began to worship leviathan (sea serpent) they called Dagon later known as The Dragon:

- Job.41:1 Canst thou draw out leviathan with an hook? or his tongue with a cord which thou lettest down?
- Job.41:5 In that day the Lord with his sore and great and strong sword shall punish leviathan the piercing serpent, even leviathan that crooked serpent; and he shall slay the dragon (or Taneem in Hebrew) that is in the sea.
- Job.41:7 Canst thou fill his skin with barbed irons? or his head with fish spears?

This *Dragon in the Sea or DAGON the Fish God* called leviathan in scripture was worshipped by those in ancient Babylon and associated with Nimrod the first High Priest of Dagon. Worship of

Dagon was passed down after Yahuah confused the languages and scattered humanity across the globe. It was this religion that was prevalent and continued at the time Rome destroyed Jerusalem. It was this religion of Dagon that permeated the high priestly ranks of paganism and was the foundation of The Christian Church which even today continues to wear the priestly garments of Dagon:

The etymology of the name "Satan" is directly connected to Leviathan. Sa-TAN and Levia-TAN both are derived from the word **Tan**eem (sea creature) which is plural. The singular of Taneem is TAN. Sa-TAN and Levia-TAN are simply later versions of the Taneem god Dagon later known as The Dragon.

It is Dagon the Dragon that is *the spiritual* source behind the Christian Churches which are based in Rome (any Sunday/Christmas/Easter/Trinity/Jesus church). The Pope and priesthood of the Catholic Church is the high priest and priests of Dagon the Dragon in disguise (not a very good disguise actually):

The Priests of Dagon even to this day wear the "fish hat" and dictate Christian theology world-wide including Protestant Theology from the City of Rome. Every fundamental doctrine of the Christian Church such as Sunday worship, Christmas, Easter, The Trinity, abolishment of The Law, pagan holidays, etc. were all **_Papal Edicts_** not found in scripture. They violate clear explicit commands in scripture. Rome is actually called "Babylon" in The Bible because it embodied the same Mystery Religion of Babylon.

1 Peter 5
The church that is at Babylon (*speaking of the church in Rome*), elected together with you, saluteth you; and so does Marcus my son

Once we fully understand what "Christianity" actually is, what it is based on, and where it came from, *then* we can begin to understand why Christianity abolished the Law of Yahuah, abolished His Sabbath Day, and changed the sacrifice of the Passover Lamb to the Easter Pig. Every one of the above moves (not commanded by

Yahuah) were made by the Pope of Rome… The High Priest of Dagon… The Dragon.

The Mitre Hat

The priests of Dagon were known by their "Mitre Hat" which resembled an open mouth of a fish. The same exact hat wore even today by The Pope as well as Cardinals and Bishops. All "priests of Dagon" and the religion that surrounds them, even to this day, is identical to that born in Babylon.

As the pagan religion of Babylon was forced upon humanity by the Roman Emperor Constantine, the pagan aspects of worshipping Dagon, the fish god, was toned down as to not offend other religions as each pagan religion was literally assimilated into The Universal Church of Rome through the process of syncretism. Syncretism is the blending of pagan religion with the worship of Yahuah. It is an abomination to Yahuah.

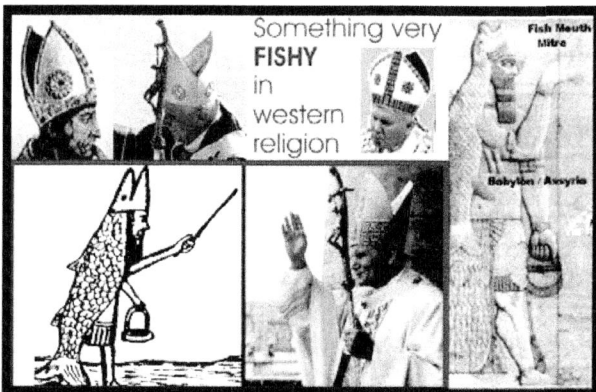

Not only are the ancient *Priests of Dagon* (Fish Worship) found wearing the mitre hat, but also the Pope and Bishops of Rome are frequently found wearing this Mitre Hat. This "clergy" system forms *a pagan priest class NOT defined in The Word of Yahuah* but rather clearly defined in Ancient Babylon. And it is from this false class of "priests" **_we get every doctrine of the Christian Church_**.

We see the Priest of Dagon on the ancient wall drawing in ever culture even as far back as the Sumerians when The Pope then served the Nephilim rulers:

The High Priest of The Dragon – The Pope of Rome

DAGON or OANNES - "He would go back into the sea to spend the night, because he was amphibious. He had the head of a man; covered by the head of a fish, and had the legs and feet of a man and the torso of a man, but was covered by the scales and tail of a fish. " - **Berossus; from ancient fragments**
(Isaac Preston Cory)

Christianity (or shall I say Satan behind it) has done a very masterful job at concealing its true identity. However, that mask is coming off as knowledge increases at exponential rates (mainly due to the internet). We are no longer bound by the mental chains of the Christian Church who has made it a top priority to keep the masses in total ignorance. We can now actually research its origins and test the historical accuracy of its claims. Many over the centuries have questioned its rituals and practices simply because they cannot be found in the Bible. But now, we can fully unmask this false religion and expose it for what it is… paganism dating back to Babylon.

The Religious "Mitre" Hat From Babylon | **The Priest of Ancient "Dagon" Fish Worship**

"The great apostate church of the Gospel Age, true to its Babylonish origin, has actually adopted this fish god in its ritual; for the pope on certain occasions manifests by his head gear that he is the direct representative of Dagon. As it was an indispensable rule in all idolatrous religions that the high priest should wear the insignia of the god that he worshipped, so the sculptures discovered by Layard show that the priests of Dagon were arrayed in clothing resembling fish. This is probably the "strange apparel" referred to in Zeph. 1:8. Berosus tells us that in the image of Dagon the head of the man appeared under the head of the fish, while Layard points out that in the case of the priests "the head of the fish formed a mitre above that of the man, while its scaly, fan-like tail fell as a cloak behind, leaving the human limbs and feet exposed."
(Babylon and Nineveh, p. 343)

85

The Dagon priests in Babylon wore hats that represented the open mouth of the fish, as if it were placed upon their heads - and the fish's body was seen extending from that head and mouth, down the priest's back to form a "robe". These exact priestly garments adorn the ranks of the Christian Clergy.

"The two-horned mitre, which the Pope wears, when he sits on the high altar at Rome and receives the adoration of the Cardinals, is the very mitre worn by the priests of Dagon, the fish-god of the Philistines and Babylonians." - **The Two Babylons ; Alexander Hislop; p. 215**

Not only does the Pope wear this "Mitre" hat, but so do the Cardinals on certain occasions when they are dressed in their royal regalia… a far cry from the suffering servant Yahusha the Messiah and what he taught. These "priests" of Dagon today known as The Pope, Cardinals, and Bishops have elevated their station literally to Royalty among men.

There is nothing in **The Word of Yahuah** or the historical record indicating that The Messiah Yahusha ever wore such a hat or created such a priestly High Class of royalty.

> *"...there are <u>strong</u> evidences that **Dagon was Nimrod**.... All scholars agree that the name and worship of Dagon were imported from Babylonia."* - **The Two Babylons, Hislop, p. 215**

86

"In their veneration and worship of Dagon, the high priest of paganism would actually put on a garment that had been created from a huge fish! The head of the fish formed a mitre above that of the old man, while its scaly, fan-like tail fell as a cloak behind, leaving the human limbs and feet exposed." - **Babylon and Nineveh, Austen Henry Layard, p. 343**

"The most prominent form of **worship in Babylon was dedicated to Dagon,** <u>*later known as Ichthys, or the fish.*</u> *In Chaldean times, the head of the church was the representative of Dagon, he was considered to be* **infallible***, and was addressed as 'Your Holiness'. Nations subdued by Babylon had to kiss the ring and slipper of the Babylonian god-king. The same powers and the same titles are claimed to this day by the Dalai Lama of Buddhism, and the Pope. Moreover, the vestments of paganism,* **the fish mitre and robes of the priests of Dagon** *are worn by the Catholic bishops, cardinals and popes*

-The Wine of Babylon; Pg 9

87

ICHTYS Symbol of "The Fish"

Dagon (fish worship) is the source of the Christian symbol of the fish. Actually it can be traced back to fish worship of Dagon and the Zodiac Sign of Pisces. We are "told" it is because some of the disciples were "fisherman" or that Yahusha would make us "fishers of men" among other excuses. The truth is that it is nowhere defined in Scripture but yet… the real source of the Christian fish symbol is that of Dagon fish worship. Just like the Mitre Hat.

*According to Egyptian mythology, when the judges found Osiris [Nimrod] guilty of corrupting the religion of Adam and cut up his body, they threw the parts into the Nile. It was said that a fish ate one of these chunks and became transformed. Later, Isis [Semaramis] was fishing along the river bank when she fished up a half-man, half-fish. This sea creature was **Dagon, the reincarnated Nimrod.** And Dagon is the representation of Nimrod (of ancient Babylon) resurrecting out of the ocean depths as a half-man, half-fish.*

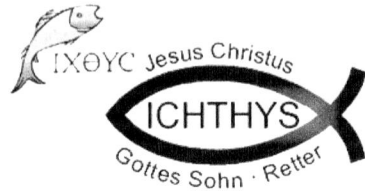

Smith's Bible Dictionary Dagon Fish Worship - from "*Ancient Pagan and Modern Christian Symbolism*"

"Dagon is the diminutive of dag, and signifies… fish… The Babylonians believed that a being, part man and part fish, emerged from the Erythraean Sea, and appeared in Babylonia in the early days of its history… Representations of this fish-god have been found among the sculptures of Nineveh. The Philistine Dagon was of a similar character."

- **Manners and Customs of the Bible;
by James Freeman**

This also explains the symbol for Christianity, the fish – the "Ichthys" which is Dagon:

Definition – "Ichthyic" – "of, pertaining to, or characteristic of fishes; the fish world in all its orders."

- **Oxford English Dictionary (C. E.)**

The worship of Dagon also affected people's eating habits. Now the mystery of why the Catholics abstain from **eating fish** on all days except Fridays comes into focus. This restriction of eating fish is not found in Scripture. Whether they realize it or not, they are practicing the ancient pagan rite of worshipping Dagon. The Catholic Encyclopedia even admits such abominations of the "so-called Church":

"As to the ritual of his worship... we only know from ancient writers that, for religious reasons, most of the Syrian peoples abstained from eating fish, a practice that one is naturally inclined to connect with the worship of a fish-god."

- **The Catholic Encyclopedia, 1913, Encyclopedia Press**

Remember in *The Word of Yahuah* we are forbidden to have any graven images including that of a FISH or a CROSS. It is commanded to have NO GRAVEN IMAGES at all of any kind period. Yahuah forbid such idols because over time we would eventually forget their true origins and buy into lies that they are somehow symbolic of Yahusha.

With that, let us unravel the mystery that lies behind *The False Religion* called today "Christianity". Who created it, what did they believe, what is its goal?

Chapter 5
The "Great Deception"

Introduction

Armed with a complete understanding of what ***The Mystery Religion of Babylon*** (defined in book 2) believed, the rituals, and the "gods" worshipped in that religion, we can begin to see the "Great Deception" or "End-Time Lie" or "Grand Delusion" mentioned in scripture.   The great delusion is Christianity:

Delusion

A delusion is a belief held with strong conviction despite superior evidence to the contrary. As a pathology, it is distinct from a belief based on false or incomplete information, confabulation, dogma, illusion, or other effects of perception.

In this chapter, I am going to prove that Christianity (both Catholic and Protestant) has literally created a new messiah and another gospel based totally on lies that are founded in ***The Mystery Religion of Babylon***. Christianity has given us a lie in The Trinity/Jesus/Sunday/Christmas/Easter/Lawlessness. A lie totally contrary to The Truth and The Way found in scripture… Yahuah/Yahusha/Sabbath/Feasts/Torah.

The Bible defines a Sign, a Seal, and Salvation by sacrifice:

- The Sign is ***The Sabbath***
- The Seal is the knowledge that ***Yahuah is ONE God***, the single greatest commandment known as The Shema
- The sacrifice for salvation is through ***The Passover Lamb of God*** named Yahusha

Christianity robs us of the sign, the seal, and the deliverance of Yahuah **and our salvation** teaching us a lie:

- The Sign is *Sungod Day*
- The Seal is the believe in *The Babylonian Trinity*
- The sacrifice for salvation is through the *Easter Pig of Ishtar* named Jesus

This "lie" is founded in "the man of lawlessness" who is not an actual man but defined in scripture as *an image* of a man in which The Law has been abolished. He is "the son of destruction or perdition" (destroying all those who put their faith in him).

An *image* of a man that will be elevated as God (in our hearts and minds which are the Altar and Temple of Yahuah) above the invisible Yahuah **the one and only God**.

> **John 17:3**
> Now this is eternal life: that they may know you (*Yahuah*), **the only true God**, and Yahusha the Messiah, whom you have sent.

This "lying image" is defined by the Apostle Paul below. Paul explains

> **2 Thessalonians 2**
> 2 Now we request you, brethren, with regard to the coming of our Messiah Yahusha and our gathering together to Him, 2 that you not be quickly shaken from your composure or be disturbed either by a spirit or a message or a letter as if from us, to the effect that the day of the Lord has come. 3 Let no one in any way deceive you, for it will not come unless the apostasy (*great falling away from The Faith*) comes first, and the man of lawlessness (*man in whose name The Law is abolished*) is revealed, the son of destruction, 4 who opposes and exalts himself above every so-called god or object of worship, so that he takes his seat

in the temple of Yahuah, displaying himself as being Yahuah (*in the flesh*). 5 Do you not remember that while I was still with you, I was telling you these things? 6 And you know what restrains him now, so that in his time he will be revealed. 7 For the mystery of lawlessness (*abolishing The Law*) is already at work; only he who now restrains will do so until he is taken out of the way. 8 Then that lawless one (*the one in whose name The Law is abolished*) will be revealed whom Yahusha will slay with the breath of His mouth and bring to an end by the appearance of His coming; 9 that is, the one whose coming is in accord with the activity of Satan (*Dagon*), with all power and signs and false wonders, 10 and with all the deception of wickedness for those who perish, because they did not receive the love of the truth so as to be saved.

11 For this reason Yahuah will send upon them a deluding influence (*spirit of error*) so that they will believe what is false (*Christianity*), 12 in order that they all may be judged who did not believe the truth, but took pleasure in wickedness.

The description above is a warning against exactly what had begun at the time Paul wrote this letter. This Great Apostasy is called now **syncretism** or blending of pagan practices with The Truth. Paul is referring to the "image" of a man in whose name The Law of Yahuah will be abolished which was spoken of also by the Prophet Daniel:

Daniel 7
He (*the false messiah* Χξϛ *or beast*) will speak against the Most High (*Yahuah*) and oppress his saints and try to change the set times (*ordained feasts/Sabbaths*) and The Laws (*of Yahuah*).

This false messiah will not be an actual man, but will rather be an "image of the true Messiah" based on lies and falsehoods; In other words a "false messiah". The False messiah or "Antichrist" is <u>not</u>

a true human historical figure. It is, in fact, Satan; behind **an image** (a fabricated lie) of a man that never actually existed. It is a false image and a false name created to deceive the masses. That "image" χξϛ was given the name IHS - Jesus H. Christ "IHΣΟΥΣ" *as I will prove in this book*. χξϛ is the symbol John saw in Revelation 13 that identifies the Antichrist, that symbol was removed from our Bibles and replaced with 666 in violation of the command not to add to or subtract from those words. I'll address this in detail in this book. Throughout this book I will use χξϛ with the name of the Antichrist.

This image of a false messiah is based on the life of the true Messiah Yahusha or at least that is what we are lead to believe, but given a pagan name, a pagan sacrifice, a pagan day of worship, and most of all… in this name IHS (Jesus' monogram in Latin) the Laws and Ordained Times of Yahuah *were abolished*. Please understand we are at the end of "His Story" or history and the beginning of the Millennial Reign and looking back over the past 6,000 years there is only ONE name in whom the Law was abolished… ***Jesus H. Christ***! This is in fulfillment of what is prophesied of the Antichrist:

> ### Daniel 7:25
> He (the Antichrist) will speak against the Most High and oppress his holy people and try to change the set times (*Holy Days*) and the laws of Yahuah.

This image is a total fabricated lie.

Romans 1

> 18For the wrath of Yahuah is revealed from heaven against all ungodliness and unrighteousness (*transgression of The Law/Feasts/Sabbaths*) of men, who hold the truth in unrighteousness (*men who teach a lie as Truth that the Messiah abolished the Law*); 19 Because that which may be known of Yahuah is manifest in them (*written on our hearts*); for Yahuah hath shewed it (*His Righteousness*

defined by His Law) unto them. 20 For the invisible things of him from the creation of the world are clearly seen, being understood by the things that are made (*The Zodiac*), even his eternal power and Godliness; so that they (*that teach and believe this lie*) are without excuse:

21 Because that, when they knew Yahuah, they glorified Yahuah not as God (*elevating Jesus/Trinity in their hearts as God*), neither were thankful; but became vain in their imaginations, and their foolish heart was darkened (*to believe a lie*). 22 Professing themselves to be wise, they became fools,

And what was the result of this foolish lie?

23 And (*those who elevated the lie as Truth that the Messiah abolished The Law*) changed the glory of the incorruptible Yahuah into **an image made like to corruptible man** (*yes, that "image" is of a false messiah named Jesus* χξϛ *who was corruptible i.e. he died has replaced Yahuah as God who cannot die*)

Yes, we have changed the invisible Yahuah into an *IMAGE* OF A MAN named χξϛ Jesus Christ as we will see... We began worshipping the creature (an image of man, χξϛ) instead of the Creator Yahuah! This "image of a man" is a false image of the true Messiah.

There simply was never a man in Israel 2,000 years ago named "Jesus". That is not the name of the Messiah and not even a name in Hebrew! There was never a man named "Jesus" born on December 25th to Joseph and Mary in Bethlehem. Yahusha was born during Succoth in the fall. There was never a man named "Jesus" crucified on a "cross" on Good-Friday. The true Messiah Yahusha was impaled on a stake on Passover and raised on The Sabbath. There was never a man named "Jesus" who rose from the dead on Easter Sunday. No man named "Jesus" actually lived and taught the abolishment of The Law of Yahuah or changed The

Sabbath to Sunday. Yahusha said he did not come to abolish The Law but to fulfill the shadow pictures of it and elevated it through transposition to written on our hearts spiritually. He kept the Feast of Yahuah and literally fulfilled their prophetic meaning! Then transposed the entire "Law" to spiritually written "on our hearts". A far cry from abolished. This religion known as Christianity is steeped in pagan rituals with doctrines based on circular reasoning and "implied doctrines" that violate **sound explicit doctrine** and Truths of Yahuah found plainly stated and COMMANDED in scripture.

This "image χ§ς of man named Jesus" is the image of the False messiah or Antichrist based not on Yahusha the Jewish Rabbi and Messiah (as we led to believe) but rather *Tammuz* the second member of the Babylonian Trinity. χ§ς Jesus represents The Pig Sacrifice of Ishtar (ham on Easter) in name and ritual as I will prove. The True Messiah Yahusha represents the Passover Lamb.

The Antichrist is an "image"

The Bible declares over and over the false messiah is not an actual "man" but an IMAGE of a man that is false. This "image" will be a "beast/pig" which we will learn in this book series is the Ishtar Pig by name and by sacrifice. The "image of χ§ς Jesus H. Christ" is the first beast and the religion of Christianity is the second beast that grew up around this false Greek messiah causing the world to worship the first beast χ§ς Jesus as I will clearly prove in this book. We see this clearly in Revelation:

Revelation 13
The Earthly (**Je**) pig (**sus**) (*the name "Je-sus" means Earthly Beast or Pig; the suffice "je" means earthly in Latin and the suffice "sus" means pig in Latin… Jesus is a Latin name not Hebrew*)

11 Then I saw another beast (*Christianity*), coming out of the earth. He had two horns like a lamb (*goat/mitre hat*),

but he spoke like a dragon (*Dagon/Satan*). 12 He (*Christianity*) exercised all the authority of the first beast (ΧΞϚ *Jesus Christ*) on his behalf (*Authority of the Church/Tradition of Men*), and (*Christianity*) made the earth and its inhabitants worship the first beast (ΧΞϚ *Jesus Christ*), whose **fatal** wound (*crucifixion*) had been healed (*resurrection*). 13 And he (*second Beast/Christianity*) performed great and miraculous signs (*healings, casting out demons, etc.*), even causing fire to come down from heaven to earth in full view of men. 14 Because of the signs he (*Christianity*) was given power to do on behalf of the first beast (ΧΞϚ *Jesus Christ*), he (*second beast/Christianity*) **deceived the inhabitants of the earth** (*the largest religion on Earth is Christianity*). He (*Pope/Christianity*) ordered them (*humanity*) to **set up an image** (*in their hearts/Temples of Yahuah*) in honor of the beast ΧΞϚ who was wounded by the sword and yet lived (ΧΞϚ). 15 He (*second Beast/Christianity*) was given power to give breath (*Spirit of the False messiah*) to the image of the first beast, so that it could speak (*to the hearts of man metaphorically*) and cause all who refused to worship the image to be killed (*the inquisition did exactly that, Christianity has been waging a war on the True Sabbath Keeping Saints for 2000 years killing all those who would not worship Constantine's pagan god*).

Yes, the false messiah is AN IMAGE of the Messiah that isn't true, it is a false image of a man that never really lived or existed in any way but was created by man at the Council of Nicaea and given a name that literally means "Beast/Pig of the Earth" in Latin. We will look at the name "Jesus" closely in this chapter. It is an IMAGE, not a real man:

Rev. 14:9-12
"A third angel followed them and said in a loud voice: 'If ANYONE worships the beast and **his image** and receives his mark on the forehead or on the hand,

Rev. 19:20
With these signs he had deluded those who had received
the mark of the beast and **worshiped his image**. The two of
them were thrown alive into the fiery lake

Rev. 20:4-6
"I saw thrones on which were seated those who had been
given authority to judge. And I saw the souls of those who
had been beheaded because of their testimony for Yahusha
and because of the word of Yahuah. They had not
worshiped the beast or **his image** and had not received his
mark on their foreheads or their hands.

I will explore *syncretism* which is the blending of the True Faith
with paganism. Paul faced this everywhere he went as he took the
Truth of the Feasts of Yahuah/Torah/Sabbaths/Messiah to a pagan
Roman Empire. In 2 Thessalonians 2, Paul warns us of the
following:

1. The great apostasy or "falling away" occurs first. This is
   referring to The Transgression of Desolation, the
   transgression of Yahuah's Feasts/Torah/Sabbaths.

2. The "man of lawlessness" will be revealed. "Lawlessness"
   is defined as… transgressing Yahuah's
   Feasts/Torah/Sabbaths, total "lawlessness" is abolishing
   them in full.

3. Paul then describes "The Abomination of Desolation" - a
   "son of destruction" who exalts himself above Yahuah in
   the Temple displaying himself to be God destroying the
   Temple of Yahuah. The exact same description given by
   the Prophet Daniel.

4. The Archangel Michael "the restrainer of evil" will be
   removed from his "continual defense" of the holy people
   and will be taken out of the way when it is "time" for this

false messiah to be revealed at the end. The restrainer Paul is referring to is named by name in Daniel 12, the very one John speaks of in Revelation 12 which is the Archangel Michael. It is Michael who provides the continue defense of the holy people and restrains evil.

5. Then this "false messiah" will be revealed to be a satanic counterfeit based on The Mystery Religion of Babylon. Deceiving those who perish for not loving The Truth of Yahuah (Feasts/Torah/Sabbaths) and elevating the son of Satan as God. Those who do will be given over to believe a massive lie.

The name of the False messiah was inserted instead of Yahusha

The deception is compounded by the mistranslation of the Messiah's name replacing it instead with the name of the false messiah in our modern Bibles. Yahusha was mistranslated to Jesus. Below I replace the name "Jesus" with the Messiah's true name Yahusha:

2 THESSALONIANS 2

THE MAN OF LAWLESSNESS

2 Concerning the coming of our King Yahusha the Messiah and our being gathered to him, we ask you, brothers and sisters, [2] not to become easily unsettled or alarmed by the teaching allegedly from us—whether by a prophecy or by word of mouth or by letter—asserting that the day of Yahuah has already come. [3] Don't let anyone deceive you

in any way, for that day will not come until the rebellion occurs (*Transgression of Desolation*) and the man of lawlessness (*in whose name the Law was abolished i.e.* 𝑋ЄƧ *Jesus Christs*) is revealed, the man doomed to destruction. [4] He will oppose and will exalt himself over everything that is called God or is worshiped, so that he sets himself up in Yahuah's temple (*the heart of man*), proclaiming himself to be God (*Christianity has elevated* 𝑋ЄƧ *Jesus Christ as God incarnate*).

[5] Don't you remember that when I was with you I used to tell you these things? [6] And now you know what is holding him back, so that he may be revealed at the proper time. [7] For the secret power of lawlessness (*The Transgression of Desolation*) is already at work; but the one who now holds it back will continue to do so till he is taken out of the way. [8] And then the lawless one will be revealed whom our King Yahusha will overthrow with the breath of his mouth and destroy by the splendor of his coming. [9] The coming of the lawless one (*the one who abolishes The Law*) will be in accordance with how Satan works. He will use all sorts of displays of power through signs and wonders that serve the lie, [10] and all the ways that wickedness deceives those who are perishing. They perish because they refused to love the truth (*of The Torah*) and so be saved. [11] For this reason Yahuah sends them a powerful delusion (*Christianity*) so that they will believe the (Babylonian) lie (Trinity / Sunday / Easter / Christmas) [12] and so that all will be condemned who have not believed the truth but have delighted in wickedness.

This deception is not easily overcome and I encourage the reader to continue on and read all 6 books in this series. Each book contains more and more information on the deception that is Christianity and the false messiah that is 𝑋ЄƧ Jesus Christ.

Chapter 6

The Great Apostasy
The falling away from the true faith

I realize most people reading this either are now or were professing "Christians" and simply cannot begin to believe what I am saying in this book. I too had to overcome this lie by first admitting The Truth in His Word that is clearly stated that contradicts the pagan rituals of Christianity. Before we even begin to examine the doctrines of Christianity, let us first simply look at the term "Christian" and ask ourselves; "would Yahuah ever accept such a name for His Elect?"

Where did the term "Christian" come from?

Very few people realize that the term "Christian" was a very popular pagan label associated with many pagan cults long before the Messiah lived and died! In fact, the followers of Mithras, Helios, and Orisis… all "Christians" or "Chrestos" in Greek:

- Chrestos Mithras
- Christ Helios
- Chreistos Osiris
- Krishna (is Sanskrit for Christ)

The followers of Yahusha the Messiah were called by a very specific name and it was never "Christians" it was "Nazarenes" see Acts 24:5 and Acts 28:22.

The question that begs to be asked is the following:

"*What would a bunch of Israelites that practice the Torah of Yahuah and follow a Yahudi (Jewish) Messiah be doing with a Greek term used by Pagans as a label for themselves?*" … they didn't and wouldn't. Are we to search out the Greco-Roman roots, or the Hebrew origins of our faith? One of them hinders and clouds our understanding, and the other is essential to it! Should we defend the Greek term, or abandon it and use the term Nazarenes - the term they were really known by?

The term "Christos" is Greek, and is defined as meaning "anointed". Although *it is treated* as a translation for the Hebrew word "Mashiach", its use in the Greek language is derived from a completely different application. It is a Greek word and in fact not a translation from Hebrew at all. The term Christos was more of a medical term, because healers in the Greek culture used all manner of tinctures for various ailments; some taken internally, and others used topically. The first two letters in "Christos" are CHI + RHO, and appear as X (CHI) and P (RHO). If you put these together, they form the "R-X" symbol still used today in the pharmaceutical and the apothecary trade, who mix and weigh dosages of medication for the sick.

The Greeks' tongue blended sounds in strange ways, producing combinations like "DZ" and others. As early as 200 BCE, there were Pagan worshippers of Serapis that called themselves "Christians".

In the Vatican, one can view an original Pagan relief depicting MITHRAS with the words CHRESTOS MITHRAS, meaning "good Mithras". Mithraism was the main Pagan religion of ancient Rome, and became blended with the Messiah of Israel through the compromises of the Nicaean Council, headed by Constantine and his son Crispus (325-326 CE).

The Greco-Roman mindset of translators **gave preference** to the Greek over the Hebrew language, and played-down the Hebrew terminology, in order to make everything more acceptable to the pagan culture of the unwashed, uneducated masses. That is why we have "Christian" in our English Bibles instead of Nazarenes.

The Hebrew term "Mashiach" was carried over into the Greek letters as "MESSIAH" because the Greek alphabet is unable to transliterate the exact sounds of some letters, such as the sound of "SH" - this became the "SS", because Greek cannot make this sound. The Hebrew meaning of Mashiach is anointed King, and applies to the person that is reigning as KING of Israel. A chosen man was "anointed" as the king with oil, as we see the prophet anointed David on his head with oil. It may have been olive oil, but it represents the "Spirit" of Yahuah being placed upon the ruler. All kings of Israel were "Mashiachim", or anointed ones. "Mashiachim" may have been the original word used by Luke at Acts 11:26, **however translators preferred the Greek flavor**, and used the word "Christian" 3 times in the "Renewed Covenant" (New Testament) writings.

Simply put, the Creator's Elect would never be called by a Greek pagan reference to other gods.

(EXCERPT FROM THE BOOK, TORAH ZONE)

*Look at the big picture, and keep an open mind for several options. Knowing there is some relationship with the word **cretin**, what if the people of Antioch, at first, called the disciples **CRETINS** (retards, idiots)? Don't fall for the excuse, "we speak English, not Hebrew". The word "crestos" (or kristos, chreistos) isn't English, it's Greek. If we follow the redemption plan of our Creator, keeping the Torah of Yahuah, we are counted among the **citizenship of Israel**; not a "Gentile", foreign nation. In fact, we are no longer Gentiles at all (Eph. 2:11-13), although we were at one time strangers to the covenants. After our immersion, there is no distinction, and no dividing wall between us and a native-born Israelite. The main idea that people seem to be steered away from when words like "Christian" are examined closely is that the **original word** (the Hebrew word, MASHIACH) is not being brought to the table, but is typically kept from the discussion. The word "Christianity" is not found in the Scriptures at all, so there is no such thing in reality. Misdirection is used to convince the listener of supposed facts which are not true, and by simply saying the lie often enough, it will become familiar, and therefore comfortable. In this particular case, the premise is that the original word was this **Greek** word "Christos", since it is emphasized (by those with an agenda to preserve the error of tradition) that the disciples of Yahusha all spoke and wrote in Greek. We are*

104

*expected to pay no mind that Greek is a **foreign language** to the people of Israel. It's a promotion of the Jesuits to believe that the Messiah and His students spoke to one another, and wrote everything down, in Greek. The truth is, Greek was a transitional language, or **translation**, of the original texts <u>originally written in Hebrew</u> (or the dialect of it, Syraic Aramaic). Remember, all the first "protestants" were Catholics, and they had already been indoctrinated with the Jesuit teachings. What is practically unknown is the fact that **<u>there</u> <u>were</u>** "**Christians**" on Earth before Yahusha haMashiach was born - and they were Pagans.*

*The Greek word "Christos" (kristos) has come to mean anointed, and this corresponds to the Hebrew word Mashiach. What is not commonly known is that Osiris and Mithras were both called "Chreistos", which meant "GOOD". The word was adopted from gnostic Paganism: **The inscription "CHRESTOS" can be seen on a Mithras relief in the Vatican.** During the time of Marcion, around 150 CE, Justin Martyr said that "Christians" were **"Chrestoi"**, or "good men". Clement of Alexandria said **"all who believe in Christ are called "Chrestoi, that is 'good men'"**. Rome was the center of **Chrestos Mithras** worship, so the adaptation or revisionism to the new faith for this title should hardly be a huge mystery; but this information has been intentionally buried. The word "Christian" is only used 3 times in the received Greek texts; and if it were in fact what the disciples called themselves as a "sect", it would have seemed very foreign to not only them, but to everyone involved. Of course, **<u>every</u> <u>Israelite</u>** (and modern orthodox "Jew") believes in a "Mashiach" that is coming at some point. Many of them - in fact most - don't currently believe in the Mashiach portrayed by the "Christian" faith in any of its diverse denominations. However, if we had to adopt a Greek word for these practitioners of "Judaism" that related to them as believers in a **coming <u>Mashiach</u>**, then they too could be labeled "Christians". But, the word "Christian" is a very **non-specific** label when you consider that it doesn't specify who the Mashiach is. The true sect that followed Yahusha's teachings did use a term for themselves, and it was NATSARIM (Acts 24:5). Even the "Church father" Epiphanius wrote of the Natsarim, whom he called* *"heretics", because they observed the Commandments of Yahuah and were indistinguishable from "Jews", except that they believed in the Mashiach.*

In relation to the Torah, a Christian might well be considered to be retarded;

Hebrews 5:12
Spiritual Immaturity
[12] For though by this time **you ought** to be teachers (*of the Torah, there was no such thing as the New Testament for another 300 years later*), you need someone to **teach you again the first principles of the oracles of God** (*what is that?* **It is the Torah***!*); and you have come to need milk and not solid food. [13]For everyone who partakes only of milk is **unskilled in the word of righteousness** (*i.e. the Torah/Law*), for he is a babe. [14]But solid food belongs to those who are of full age (*mature Saints with minds set on Spiritual Law*), that is, **those who by reason of use** (*by obedience to the Law*) have their senses exercised (*trained by the Torah*) to discern both good and evil (*which is defined by the Law of God, good is obedience to His Commands, evil is breaking them*).

As the actual word that means "retard" or "idiot" is derived from the same root as CHRISTIAN: crestin!

The **American Heritage Illustrated Encyclopedic Dictionary** tells us the etymology for the word *CRETIN*:

cre-tin (kre-tin, kret'n) n. 1. One afflicted with Cretinism. 2. A fool; an idiot. [French, cretin, from Swiss French, crestin, CHRISTIAN, hence human being (an idiot being nonetheless human).] Cretinism is dwarfism and or retardation. Cretin is simply the word that is derived from the word CHRISTIAN, crestin.

"For we have found this man a pestilent fellow, and a

mover of sedition among all the Yahudim throughout the world and a ringleader of the sect (G139, hairesis) of the Nazarenes (G3480) . . ."

The Greek word hairesis above gives us our word "heresy" translated "sect". So we know the "sect" being spoken of was not the Christians, because Christians developed <u>later</u>. The word christianos was used twice in the Greek text as a device of scorn, since in the ancient world it conveyed a much different sense than it does today. The use of the word **christianos** *did not "name" the sect, but it was a derisive, scornful <u>label</u> that meant they were like gullible, dumb beasts, or "cretins".*

*The word "christianos" (Latin, **Christianus**) was a term of scorn, traced back through a related word which history never "revised":*

cre·tin (krēt'n) n.

1. A person afflicted with cretinism.

Slang: An idiot.

[French crétin, from French dialectal, deformed and mentally retarded person found in certain Alpine valleys, from Vulgar Latin *christiānus, Christian, human being, poor fellow, from Latin Chrīstiānus, Christian; see Christian.]

For more information on this topic, refer to
http://www.fossilizedcustoms.com/christian.html

Christianity the False Religion of the Beast

I realize this "Great Deception" called Christianity is so powerful that if possible could even deceive the very elect of Yahuah. This is the exact same warning given by the Messiah Yahusha:

> ## Matthew 24
> [22] "If those days had not been cut short, no one would survive, but for the sake of the elect those days will be shortened. [23] At that time if anyone says to you, 'Look, here is the Messiah!' or, 'There he is!' do not believe it. [24] **For false messiahs and false prophets will appear and perform great signs and wonders to deceive, if possible, even the elect**. [25] See, I have told you ahead of time.

Yahusha is warning us NOT to fall for this false messiah or "Christ" of which there are LONG line that all evolved from Tammuz of Babylon into Hesus Horus Krishna aka Jesus H. Christ as I will show historically in this book. Yahusha above in Matthew 24 is speaking of the result of the *Transgression of Desolation* which leads to the *Abomination of Desolation*. The "falling away" is the *Transgression of Desolation* or Great Apostasy that causes the inhabitants of the Earth and the Earth itself to be destroyed. The Earth is led astray by false messiahs and prophets to disobey the commandment of Yahuah. This deception is so strong it almost even deceives the very chosen sons of Yahuah. This "*Transgression of Desolation*" is spoken of by the prophet Daniel in Daniel 8:12 and the prophet Isaiah. Isaiah defines the *Transgression of Desolation* (transgression that desolates) and "great apostasy" or falling away as violating the Feasts/Torah/Sabbaths of Yahuah:

> ## Isaiah 24
> 1 See, Yahuah is going to lay waste the earth and devastate it; he will ruin its face and scatter its inhabitants— 5 The earth is defiled by its people; they have disobeyed the laws,

violated the statutes and broken the everlasting covenant (*The Sabbath*). 6 Therefore a curse consumes the earth; its people must bear their guilt. Therefore earth's inhabitants are burned up, and very few are left.

In Daniel 8 this is called **The Transgression of Desolation** which causes the daily defense of the Archangel Michael to be removed (Daniel 12:1). The word "sacrifices" in your modern English translation below was added by the translators in error as I will cover in this book series:

Daniel 8
Then I heard one saint speaking, and another saint said unto that certain saint which spake, How long shall be the vision concerning the daily **sacrifice** *(sacrifice was added, should have been daily defense of Michael see Daniel 12:1)*, and **the transgression of desolation**, to give both the sanctuary and the host to be trodden under foot?

It is the "Great Apostasy" or violation of the Laws, Feasts, and Sabbaths of Yahuah that define this "*false messiah*" as he is the one in whose name the Law is abolished i.e. *the lawless one*, and the ordained times (feasts) and calendar of Yahuah are all changed to pagan in origin.

Daniel 7
25 He will speak out against the Most High and wear down the saints of the Highest One, and he will intend to make alterations in (*ordained*) times and in (*the*) law (*of Yahuah*);

There is only ONE name in the history of mankind in which credit is given for changing the Law (abolishing it) and changing the ordained times from those commanded (Sabbaths/Passover/Feasts) to pagan rituals (Sunday/Easter/Christmas). That name is Χ៏Ϛ **Jesus H. Christ**. There was never an actual man by that name as it is not Hebrew, that is an IMAGE of the Pig of Ishtar or Beast of the Earth that is **not Yahusha.** Jesus is the latest incarnation of TAMMUZ the son of the Queen of Heaven and "the sun of God" the second member of The Babylonian Trinity as I explain in detail in this book!

In this book I am going to define exactly "what" that Great Deception or *The Transgression of Desolation* is and how it came to happen. Who was it that caused the entire population of Earth to transgress the Feasts/Torah/Sabbath of Yahuah. In what false image of the Messiah was this done? What "image of a man" have we elevated in our hearts as God above Yahuah? I will provide proof scripturally and historically.

Syncretism

We learned in my book *The Mystery Religion of Babylon* exactly what Sun worship is… The Trinity/Sunday/Easter/Christmas. We will learn in this chapter that in fact "Christianity" (as created by the Roman Emperor Constantine) is **verbatim** *The Mystery Religion of Babylon* and has nothing in common with The Faith found in the Bible.

Through Christianity, we have elevated Tammuz (under his pagan names Hesus Horus Krishna which evolved into Jesus H. Christ) and the unholy Trinity of I.H.S. (Isis/Horus/Seb the pagan god names of Semaramis/Nimrod/Tammuz) in our hearts as God above Yahuah. And in that name, *Jesus*, which is a false image of the true Messiah, we have abolished the Feasts/Torah/Sabbaths and are guilty of the Great Apostasy called The Transgression of Desolation and have fallen away from Yahuah in totality. We have become lawless and where there is no law there is no sin, where there is no sin there is no Grace. We will die dead in our transgressions having put our faith in Easter over Passover as commanded.

Because we have committed the *Transgression of Desolation*, Yahuah has given us over to believe a lie; the Babylonian Religion repackaged for us today by Constantine called Christianity. We have replaced Yahuah / Yahusha / Passover / Sabbath / The Law with a pagan Babylonian lie of The Trinity / Jesus / Easter / Sunday / Christmas / no law and we are guilty of committing ***The Abomination of Desolation***! That abominable sacrifice is the blood of the Ishtar Pig on our hearts (the Alter) instead of the blood of the Passover Lamb as each year we sacrifice a pig (eat ham) on Easter (celebration of Ishtar) instead of a lamb on Passover. We put out faith in the Good-Friday/Easter Sunday "Jesus" instead of the Passover/Sabbath Yahusha! One is the "Earthly Pig of Ishtar" literally by name; the other is The Lamb of Yahuah literally by name.

This abomination each year causes the daily sacrifices and oblation of The Passover Lamb (Yahusha) to cease on our behalf which causes the destruction of our bodies (The Temple of Yahuah). I explain all of this in detail in this book series. First, we must identify, define, and expose the ***Transgression of Desolation*** called The Great Apostasy. A false religion carefully put in place over time blending paganism into the Truth (deluding from the Truth i.e. Grand Delusion) so that it "seems" or is "believed" to be based on the Word of Yahuah. When in fact, it is an abomination to everything holy to Yahuah and has been since The Tower of Babel until now.

It is this false religion that causes us to "transgress" the ordained times, Sabbaths, and law of Yahuah, that per Isaiah 24:1-6, which leads to our own spiritual and physical destruction but also that of the surface of the Earth... The Great Tribulation.

What occurred from the time of The Messiah's death until now is called Syncretism:

> ***Syncretism*** (definition): *is the combining of different (often contradictory) beliefs, often while melding practices of various schools of thought. Syncretism may involve the merger and analogizing of several originally discrete traditions, especially in the theology and mythology of religion, thus asserting an underlying unity and allowing for an inclusive approach to other faiths.*

This is exactly what the Roman Emperor Constantine did in a purely political and quite genius move to being peace in his realm. Constantine created Christianity (or rather sold us on his existing religion of Mithraism called The Cult of Sol Invictus) solely for the political purposes of bringing peace among pagans. He combined many contradictory belief systems into one Christo-pagan religion by melding practices of all pagan religions and various schools of secular scholarly thought. He merged these pagan traditions discretely into one "Universal Religion" he called *Christianity* and literally "altered the original manuscripts" in the New Testament to make it inclusive in this lie. Then had the originals burned to hide this abomination. I will confront these altered modern translations and prove them to be uninspired to say the least.

Constantine originally blended all religions into one to "allow for an all inclusive approach" to his new religion (which was actually his existing religion) from all faiths in his Empire. He did this as a political move to unify the Roman Empire under one religion to secure his reign. He then burned all the evidence and forced this new religion on all subjects of The Roman Empire by threat of death. This is known as *The Inquisition*. Then by banning all religious texts, his new "religion" the Roman Catholic Church took control and plunged the world into what is known as *The Dark Ages* restricting access to books for so long that no one would ever question their pagan traditions and doctrines. No one could own a copy of The Word of Yahuah to know the Truth. All those who "knew the Truth" had been executed in the Inquisition or went into hiding. The Dark Ages fell upon humanity in the 5th Century and lasted until the 10th Century. Literally 500 years The Catholic Church dominated humanity and entrenched this pagan religious lie so well that even ***today it is not even dared questioned by most***.

I guess congratulations are in order if you are even reading this book series. You are one of the very "few" who will now know the true origin of Christianity. If you continue through the entire series you will be one of the even fewer to know what The Bible actually says.

The Reformation that began with Martin Luther, John Calvin, and Augustine after the Renaissance (enlightenment) was only **the beginning** leading to the "protesting Catholic" or Protestant Christian denominations.

These Protestant "daughters of the Whore" to this day still keep the fundamental doctrines of the Catholic Church (The Trinity/Jesus/Sunday/pagan holidays) in total opposition to Yahuah/Yahusha/Passover/Sabbath/Feasts of Yahuah which is the True Faith.   Both Catholic and Protestant churches are *Christianity – The Great Deception*.

This "reformation" has continued among the true chosen among the gentile nations and continues today. I have been engaged in this battle to reform Christianity for 25 years. It is a "process" and a slow one as this pagan religious lie is very well entrenched and not easily purged from the hearts and minds of humanity.

 Even today one is "excommunicated" from family, society, politics, and especially their church for even questioning such abominations as The Trinity, Sunday worship, the name Jesus, Easter, or Christmas. All of which are clearly pagan in origin and directly apposed to sound explicit doctrine in Scripture. So let us know expose these false doctrines and fundamentals of Christianity by first exposing its origin.

Chapter 7
The Pagan History of the Christian Church

The Great Deception is the false religion known as "The Whore of Babylon" in Revelation. It is the ***Transgression of Desolation*** that causes the destruction of the surface of the Earth spoken of by Isaiah and detailed in the 7 plagues/bowls/trumpets of Revelation. This Great Apostasy through Syncretism results in transgressing The Law of Yahuah leading to the curse found in The Torah for disobedience to Yahuah's Law.

The Great Apostasy is literally defined in Scripture as the abolition of The Law of Yahuah, His Feasts/Torah/Sabbaths, and the elevation of a man as God in our hearts above Yahuah. Christianity is the fulfillment of those prophecies. The fundamental doctrines of Christianity are just that: The Law has been abolished and Jesus Christ is God as second member of The Trinity. Sunday replaced The Sabbath, Easter replaced The Passover, Christmas replaced The Fall Feasts, and the name Jesus replace the name Yahusha. Each of these lies was given to us by the High Priest of Dagon originating from ancient Babylon.

In this chapter we will examine historical documents, mainly from the Catholic Church itself, which openly admit to changing the Laws, Feasts, and Sabbaths of Yahuah in favor of pagan "traditions of men" and creating a "new" composite god in the "image and name of Tammuz". This new god was created in the image of Hesus, Horus, and Krishna all various names for Tammuz in other cultures and is known today in its English derivative Jesus H. Christ. I will prove this in this book.

We are now going to look back in history at exactly how this false religion was created and how overtime through syncretism it blended pagan sun worship into the true faith creating a false religion that opposes The Truth of Yahuah.

Let's look at this very crafty deception called Christianity that most people today "believe" is based on Biblical Truth. Is Christianity REALLY based on Scriptural Truth or pagan ritual and tradition? We are not going to exempt anything in our search for the answer. Sunday worship, Christian Holidays, and the very name of the "god" of Christianity (Jesus H. Christ) will be closely examined under the blinding light of history and the Truth of Yahuah.

We have been warned!

In this Chapter we are literally going to "reverse engineer" the "faith" passed down to us. If it is true, it should lead us back to the Word of Yahuah found in the Torah. If it is false it should lead us back to Babylon as Yahuah warned us.

This exercise MUST be done in each and every one of our hearts and minds because Yahuah warned us that we would be misled by scribes who literally Altar the Scriptures changing The Law into a lie and we would have nothing but pagan lies passed down to us from our forefathers.

The prophet Jeremiah sent out a warning to all who read The Bible:

> ### Jeremiah 8:8
> "How can you say, 'We are wise, And the law of Yahuah is with us'? But behold, the lying pen of the scribes (*under The Spirit of Error*) has made it (*The Torah*) into a lie (*and abolished it*)."

Jeremiah speaks of a "Greater Exodus" from among all nations at the end as Gentiles all over the Earth will be brought out of the nations:

> ### Jeremiah 16
> 14 "However, the days are coming," declares Yahuah, "when it will no longer be said, 'As surely as Yahuah lives, who brought the Israelites up out of Egypt,' 15 but it will be said, '*As surely as Yahuah lives, who brought the Israelites up out of the land of the north and out of all the countries where he had banished them.' For I will restore*

them to the land I gave their ancestors.

Jeremiah goes on to say of the sons of Yahuah who are brought out of the gentile nations at the end in the Greater Exodus are crying out "we have been lied to all our lives for generations"…

Jeremiah 16
19 Yahuah, my strength and my fortress, my refuge in time of distress, to you the nations will come from the ends of the earth and say,

"Our fathers have inherited nothing but falsehood, Futility and things of no profit." 20 Can man make gods for himself? Yet they are not gods!

21 "Therefore I will teach them— this time I will teach them my power and might. **Then they will know that my name is Yahuah**.

Above it is prophesied that we would literally attempt to "create gods" to worship in place of Yahuah. We who are brought out of the nations will literally be crying out that we have inherited nothing but lies! We will discover in this book that this is exactly the case with Christianity. We have inherited nothing but lies.

There is only ONE God and His name is Yahuah or Yahuah *not "Jesus" or "The Trinity" or "God" or "Lord"*. Mankind has literally banished the name Yahuah from His own book, created a "god" for himself elevating a man who died on a stake (the Messiah Yahusha) a corruptible man as God in their hearts remaking the Messiah into an "image and name" of the Babylonian Tammuz. We have literally inherited nothing but futile lies of no profit in Christianity. We have abolished Yahuah's Laws, changed His calendar and reckoning of time, changed His Sabbaths and His Feasts all for pagan traditions that began in ancient Babylon.

Christianity is The Mystery Religion of Babylon!

This is exactly what the Apostle Paul was trying to tell us today in his letters to the Romans of his day. That we have **abolished The Law** that was supposed to be strengthened within us, that **Yahuah is God and is invisible** not a corruptible man (a man who died). And even though Yahuah is evident all around us, our hearts/minds will be darkened to believe a LIE. We will exchange the Glory of the incorruptible God (Yahuah cannot die on a "cross" or in any way) for an "image" of a man who died and worship that image of a man in our hearts as God above Yahuah. Those who make this tragic error will be given over by Yahuah to believe this lie and as a result they will perish.

Romans 1

18 For the wrath of Yahuah is revealed from heaven against all ungodliness and unrighteousness of men who suppress the truth in unrighteousness (*abolish The Law*), 19 because that which is known about Yahuah is evident within them (*the Law is written on our hearts*); for Yahuah **made it** evident to them (*by transposing the written Law into our hearts*).

20 For since the creation of the world (*gospel written in the stars in The Zodiac*) His invisible attributes, His eternal power and divine nature, have been clearly seen, being understood through what has been made (*creation cries out to its Creator*), so that they are without excuse. 21 For even though they knew Yahuah, they did not honor Him as God or give thanks, but they became futile in their speculations, and their foolish heart was darkened. 22 Professing to be wise, they became fools, 23 **and exchanged the glory of the incorruptible God for an image in the form of corruptible man** (𝑋Ṡ𝑆 *false Christs as incarnate god-men*) and of birds and four-footed animals and crawling creatures (*fallen angels taught man to worship the signs of The Zodiac*).

4 Therefore Yahuah gave them over in the lusts of their hearts to impurity, so that their bodies would be dishonored among them. 25 For they exchanged **the truth of God for a lie, and worshiped and served the creature (***a corruptible man*** χϟϲ) rather than the Creator**, who is blessed forever.

The Spirit of Error

This "Spirit" that has triumphed in the hearts and minds of Christians that "a corruptible man" is "God" is clearly defined as <u>The Spirit of Error or Spirit of the Antichrist</u>. The "Spirit of Error" is anyone who denies that Yahusha was totally human in every way not God. Yes, the belief that "Jesus" is Yahuah in the flesh the second member of a Trinity *is The Spirit of Error* by definition:

> **1 John 4**
> 1 Beloved, do not believe every spirit, but test the spirits, whether they are of Yahuah; because many false prophets have gone out into the world (*proclaiming to be gods incarnate*). 2 By this you know the Spirit of Yahuah: Every spirit that confesses that Yahusha the Messiah has come in the flesh (*was fully human in every way **Hebrews 2:17***) is of Yahuah, 3 and every spirit **that does not confess that Yahusha the Messiah has come in the flesh** (*but believes in the incarnation and The Trinity*) is not of Yahuah. And this is the spirit of the False messiah (χϟϲ *Jesus Christ*), which you have heard was coming, and is now already in the world (*the belief that* χϟϲ *Jesus is God in the flesh*)...
> 12 **no one has seen Yahuah**.

That is right, it is not those who claim Yahusha was a man that are in error, but those who elevate him in the "image of Jesus" **as God** that the Word claims are in error. Not only are those who worship the image of Jesus as God "in error", the Word declares they have been filled with "The Spirit of the Antichrist" because as I will prove Jesus Christ is named by name in Revelation Chapter 13 as the antichrist by his mark, monogram, and pictogram.. John literally gave us the exact symbols used for Jesus Christ for centuries written all over Christianity.

The Spirit of Jesus Christ is that he was not fully human in every way but an incarnate demi-god. Exactly like every other incarnate demi-god from Nimrod to Tammuz to every incarnation of them over cultures until now.

Scripture teaches us that Yahusha was "fully human in every way" so in no way was he Yahuah (as Yahuah is Invisible Spirit and no one has ever seen Yahuah **1 John 4:12**). Below the Messiah Yahusha is clearly described <u>not as "Yahuah in the flesh" or "God" in any way</u>, but rather flesh and blood and fully human in EVERY WAY who helps the descendants of Abraham as he was a human High Priest chosen from among men not gods.

> **<u>Hebrews 2</u>**
> 14 Since the children have flesh and blood, **he too shared in their humanity** (*he was human too*) so that by his death (*the death of a human not God*) he, Yahusha, might break the power of him who holds the power of death—that is, the devil— 15 and free those who all their lives were held in slavery by their fear of death. 16 For surely it is not angels he helps, but **Abraham's descendants**. 17 For this reason he (*Yahusha*) had to be made like them (*he was made human by Yahuah*), (*and Yahusha was made*) **fully human in every way**, in order that he might become a merciful and faithful high priest (*who are chosen from among men*) in service to Yahuah (*on behalf of humanity*), and that he might make atonement for the sins of the people. 18 Because he himself suffered when he was tempted, he is able to help those who are being tempted.

In other words it takes a HUMAN High Priest to serve humanity before the throne of Yahuah. Not a "god". Now, let us examine this "image of a corruptible man" or a man who died that we elevated as God in our hearts above Yahuah, the "image" of a man that sits in The Temple (our hearts and mind) proclaiming himself to be god. What is that "sacrifice" made on The Alter, what is the abominable "beast" that is sacrifice in replace of The Passover Lamb?

Let us go back into historical documents and with an open mind for the Truth look at how and why this religion called Christianity came about.

Chapter 8
How "Christianity" was created

The Truth behind the Christian Church

2000 years ago around the time that Yahusha the Messiah lived and died and the early Jewish believers were converted; Jerusalem was under the control of the pagan Roman Empire.

The Roman Emperor around that time was the Caesar Nero. Nero believed himself (like many ancient rulers) to be Divine (just another of the many incarnate god-men in history) and was threatened by the growing allegiance in his empire to another "King"; the coming Messiah. **At this time, there was no such person as "Jesus" as that name did not even exist until literally centuries later the 4th century A.D. to be exact.** Jewish converts were now coming to Yahuah in covenant with The Messiah and keeping the Feasts and Sabbaths in light of and in the name of Yahusha.

Nero attempted to stop this growing rebellion against him by gathering up all Sabbath Keeping believers in Yahusha who would not bow to him and have them murdered in massive coliseums by feeding them to hungry lions as a spectator sport. However, many of the pagan onlookers were so moved by the bravery and faith of these believers in Yahusha and Yahuah that they converted! This plan of Satan to put a stop to the spreading faith in Yahusha failed miserably. Satan had to devise a new plan.

This new plan was to create a counterfeit religion that he would craft slowly over time into a "false" religion that would "seem" to be based on the true Messiah and the Bible. It would, however, actually be based on Tammuz of Babylon. This is where the Roman Emperor Constantine comes in.

The First Pope of Rome – The Roman Emperor Constantine

While we are told the first "Pope" was the disciple Peter (Peter never kept Sunday/Easter/Christmas nor did he believe in a Trinity God) it was actually Emperor Constantine. Constantine held the title "Pontifex Maximus" which literally means "High Priest" of the sun god Zeus/Apollo (Greek incarnations of Nimrod/Tammuz). He was the High Priest of his god Apollo also known as Mithra the sungod. Apollo and Mithra are just other name for Nimrod/Tammuz that evolved out of ancient Babylon as the languages were confused at the Tower of Babel. Constantine's religion was called The Cult of Sol Invictus which means the Cult of the Invincible Sun. Constantine was a sun worshipper as the religion of Babylon was literally transplanted to Rome. I covered that in my last book and again in both *The Kingdom of Yahuah* and *The Yahushaic Covenant*.

The Pope of Rome to this day holds the same title of Pontiff and to this day worships the same sungod. This "Roman religion" is known as The Cult of Sol Invictus or The Cult of the Invincible Sun. The Cult of Sol Invictus dates back to the Babylonian religion created by Semaramis defined in my book **Mystery Babylon – *The Religion of the Beast.***.

History records that Constantine became the first "Christian" Emperor of Rome and played a major role in converting the pagan Roman Empire to "Christianity". This is actually true. The religion of Christianity was actually created by the Roman Emperor and High Priest of Apollo. This religion created by Constantine was nothing new, it was the exact same religious system dating back to Babylon and the same religion Constantine worshipped before and until his death… sun worship. Constantine was a follower of Christos Mithra whose followers were known as Christians. It was identical in every way to worship of the stars (Sun/Moon/Planets) that originated in Babylon.

124

Christians today claim that "God" came to Constantine in a "vision" of a "cross" and Constantine converted to a servant of Jesus Christ. Well actually this is true, sort of. Actually Constantine just renamed Tammuz/Apollo/Mithra to "Jesus" and converted the world to his existing religion as history proves. As the "legend" goes, Constantine was on his knees worshipping the Sun facing East (as sun worshippers do) and saw a vision of the cross of Tammuz and was told "in this sign conquer". "Conquering" humanity through force and converting by threat of death… is the total opposite of the Messiah's Message of evangelism through love and regeneration through faith. Constantine then went on to conquer the known world for his god Tammuz which he created at the Council of Nicaea and called Jesus H. Christ. He did so through MUCH bloodshed and converted through the threat of death (the inquisition). There is zero chance that Constantine was a true believer we know this because of his fruit. We also know this because his coins remained inscribed "dedicated to the Invincible Sun" until his death.

Historical Background of the Emperor Constantine

After the death of Constantine's father, his brother Maxentius was in line for the throne and stood in the way of Constantine. On 312 A.D., on October 28th at Stone Milvian Bridge at the Tiber River, Constantine's army was greatly outnumbered as it was arrayed in battle against the army of Maxentius. It was then, while Constantine bowed before the Sun in worship to Baal, he saw a "cross" and heard a voice "in this sign conquer". As I stated before in my book *The Mystery Religion of Babylon* the "cross" was the universal sign of Tammuz a cutout of the center of The Zodiac. So it is no surprise Constantine while bowing to the sun saw the Cross of Tammuz… **that was his religion**.

This command he heard to go forth and conquer was the same expression used in Revelation 6:2 of the rider on the white horse that goes out to conquer and to conquer (an image of the False messiah). Constantine went forth from that point and conquered the pagan world through his new religion and **much bloodshed**.

Revelation 6:2
And I saw, and behold a white horse: and he that sat on him had a bow; and a crown was given unto him: and he went forth conquering, and to conquer.

We see above that this rider went forth with a crown (an Emperor) and a bow (the symbol of Nimrod/Tammuz the great hunter) to conquer. The exact historical image of Constantine (the founder of Christianity). This same "bow" is carried to this day by the subsequent "Pontifex Maximus" the Pope of Rome. It is a "bowed cross" and the staff of the Pope. The Pope literally wears a two horned Mitre (two horns like a goat) on his head carrying about a cross in the shape of a bow. On top of this staff is the cross of Tammuz with the image of the false messiah renamed Hesus Horus Krishna (Jesus H. Christ) or latin I.H.S. This false messiah is none other than Tammuz the pig of Ishtar in name and sacrifice.

Revelation 13:11
Then I saw another beast, coming out of the earth. He had two horns like a lamb (*MITRE hat*), but he spoke like a dragon (*a puppet for Dagon the Dragon i.e. Satan*).

Back to our story; Once Constantine defeated Maxentius and became Emperor and High Priest of sun worship; the main problem Constantine faced in his Empire was strife between religions. There were many different gods among the pagan

126

people and this caused conflict. This religious conflict lead to what we know today as the "foundation of Christianity"; the **Council of Nicaea**. The resulting creed, the Nicean Creed, is professed by every Christian on Earth. A total blasphemous creed as we will now discover.

Chapter 9
The foundation and birth of "Christianity"

Introduction

The true beginning of the religion known today as Christianity is shrouded in secular and pagan thought and tradition. The historical beginnings of this religion is all but "hidden" and kept silent in today's churches. When we do a little digging… it is understandably so. The slightest research into the origins of Christianity will literally destroy your faith in it. So I guess to most Christians, "Ignorance is bliss"! However, in this case, it is eternal destruction. We see below this is the case as we are destroyed by the lack on knowledge and rejected by Yahuah for abolishing His Law.

> **Hosea 4:6**
> my people are destroyed from lack of knowledge. "Because you have rejected knowledge, I also reject you as my priests; because you have ignored the law of your God, I also will ignore your children."

All we need to know concerning the "new" religion that evolved at the hands of the Roman Emperor Constantine formalized at the Council of Nicaea we can learn from early scholars of the day and Catholic Church documents that live on historically. These all openly admit that the "religion" was neither "new" nor "strange" to the pagans of their day and that the only thing "new" about it was the name of the new "god" they created. This new god's name was Jesus H. Christ or I.H.S in Latin. So we are going to take a long hard look at this name.

The Council of Nicaea was held around 300 AD and writers of that era admit what should now be obvious to the reader of this book, if not it will be soon enough:

> ▪ **Eusebius of Caesarea (circa 283-371 CE) wrote:**
> *"The religion of Jesus Christ is neither new nor strange."*

- **St. Augustine of Hippo (354-430 CE) wrote:** *"This, in our day, is the Christian religion, not as having been unknown in former times, but as having recently received that name."*

Yes, Christianity was not new to the pagans and as St. Augustine pointed out it has been known all the way back to Babylon and only recently called "Christianity". Every Christian Church today from the Roman Catholic Church to every last Protestant denomination expresses its faith in what is called **The Nicene Creed**. This is the resulting creed that came out of the first council at Nicaea where Christianity and its fundamental doctrines of sun worship were formulated by Constantine to unite his kingdom through **syncretism**.

Constantine openly worshipped a pagan sun deity named Mithra or Apollo who was simply another name for Tammuz or Baal the sungod. Constantine believed the Hebrew Messiah Yahusha was yet another incarnation of this second member of the Babylonian Trinity who is Tammuz. At the council in Nicaea Constantine set out to formulate a religion that all pagans and all those who had newly found faith in Yahusha could accept if he could twist the scriptures to conform to his sun worship. Since Constantine believed Yahusha to be an incarnation of Tammuz, he had no problem replacing the Holy Days/Sabbaths/Feasts of Yahuah with those of his god Tammuz/Apollo/Mitha. After all, to Constantine, Yahusha was the latest incarnation of them all and therefore he kept the Babylonian pagan days of worship. And of course, the re-incarnated "Tammuz" would have abolished the Sabbath/Holy Days of Yahuah and established those of Sunday/Easter/Christmas in his image. This is what Constantine believed and he was "Emperor" and what Constantine believed defined his empire.

Let us take a close look at Flavius Constantinius who ruled Rome and was literally "the author" of what today we call Christianity. Make no mistake, the religion of Christianity was not authored by the Jewish Messiah Yahusha as it has no relationship to the Hebrew Faith held by Adam, Noah, Abraham, Isaac, Jacob, Moses,

Joshua, David, Solomon, Yahusha, even the Apostle Paul, or any of the disciples or apostles or early church in Jerusalem. In fact, Constantine's religion of Christianity is a carbon copy of The Mystery Religion of Babylon… sun worship.

An ancient religion reborn with a "new" god

Constantine was the High Priest of the sungod Sol Invictus (invincible sun) and his coins remained inscribed "Sol Invicto Comiti" or "committed to the unconquered/invincible sun" to the day he died.

From Wikipedia entry "Sol Invictus". Constantine's coin depicting Sol Invictus

Constantine decided to call an official Roman (Rome was a pagan empire) council at Nicaea which is now considered the first "Christian Council" in an attempt to standardize all religions in his empire. There were literally hundreds of "gods" worshipped throughout the empire and it was cause of constant division and conflict. So a council of pagan priests were convened.

Who participated and what exactly was discussed in this council is somewhat unclear because Constantine burned all the evidence. However, we know exactly what resulted from this council as we will see. It is hard to know what took place behind close doors because **all documentation of this blasphemous council was literally destroyed by Constantine** as he had all the documents burned to hide the abomination that transpired. A far cry from

131

how **Yahuah documented every step of the Truth** found in the Torah for all to know and read throughout history.

The Catholic Encyclopedia admits the truth behind Christianity

The "lie" Christianity is based on was carefully and totally destroyed to hide its origin. What we do know is openly found in the Catholic Encyclopedia:

> *"It was British-born Flavius Constantinus (Constantine, originally Custennyn or Custennin) (272-337) who authorised the compilation of the writings now called the New Testament. After the death of his father in 306, Constantine became King of Britain, Gaul and Spain, and then, after a series of victorious battles, Emperor of the Roman Empire. Christian historians give little or no hint of the turmoil of the times and suspend Constantine in the air, free of all human events happening around him.*
>
> *In truth, one of Constantine's main problems was the uncontrollable disorder amongst presbyters and their belief in numerous gods. The majority of modern-day Christian writers suppress the truth about the development of their religion and conceal Constantine's efforts to curb the disreputable character of the presbyters who are now called "Church Fathers".* **(Catholic Encyclopedia, Farley ed., vol. xiv, pp. 370-1).**

There it is, plain admission from the "source of Christianity" the Catholic Church that the very "Church Fathers" invited to the Council of Nicaea were not men of Yahuah *but disreputable pagan priests* or "presbyters" who worshipped many different gods. So "who were" these preachers running around the Roman Empire dreaming up all kinds of various "gods" to worship that today's Christian Church considers *"fathers of their faith"*? Below is how they were described…

*"...the most rustic fellows, teaching strange paradoxes.
They openly declared that none but the ignorant was fit to
hear their discourses ... they never appeared in the circles
of the wiser and better sort, but always took care to intrude
themselves among the ignorant and uncultured, rambling
around to play tricks at fairs and markets ... they lard their
lean books with the fat of old fables ... and still the less do
they understand ... and they write nonsense on vellum ...
and still be doing, never done."* ***(Contra Celsum ["Against
Celsus"], Origen of Alexandria, c. 251, Bk I, p. lxvii, Bk
III, p. xliv, passim)***

These pagan "preachers" invited to formulate the new religion at
the Council of Nicaea were "rustic fellows teaching strange
paradoxes" to the ignorant uncultured fools of that day at pagan
fairs and markets in Rome. These men were not the mighty men of
God and descendants of Abraham/Isaac/Jacob. No, these men
literally created "Christianity" from "**fat old fables**". I was
certainly never made aware of any of this in my 20 years in the
Christian Church! I was taught to blindly pledge allegiance to...
The Nicaean Creed, no less, ***the abominable creed*** that came from
these babbling fools. Little did I know (until I decided to question
it and test it) that this creed was a complete denial of Yahuah and
His Truth created literally by pagan "idiots" or "Christians" as they
came to be known.

Constantine's dilemma

Let's look at exactly what was actually going on in the Roman
Empire under Constantine and we find it openly admitted that the
conversion and baptism of Constantine was nothing more than
simply **a legend**. In reality he was a sun worshipping
Emperor/High Priest with a very real political problem that had to
be dealt with.

> *"Clusters of presbyters had developed "many gods and many lords" (1 Cor. 8:5) and numerous religious sects existed, each with differing doctrines (Gal. 1:6). Presbyterial (pagan) groups clashed over attributes of their various gods and "altar was set against altar" in competing for an audience"...* **(Optatus of Milevis, 1:15, 19, early fourth century)**.

> *From Constantine's point of view, there were several factions that needed satisfying, and he set out to develop an all-embracing religion during a period of irreverent confusion. In an age of crass ignorance, with nine-tenths of the peoples of Europe illiterate, stabilizing religious splinter groups was only one of Constantine's problems. The smooth generalization, which so many historians are content to repeat, that Constantine "embraced the Christian religion" and subsequently granted "official toleration", is "**<u>contrary to historical fact</u>**" and should be erased from our literature forever...* (**Catholic Encyclopedia, Pecci ed., vol. iii, p. 299, passim**).

So our contention that Constantine embraced the Jewish Messiah is not true and should be totally erased from our minds. Simply put, there was no Christian religion at Constantine's time, and the Church acknowledges that the tale of his "conversion" and "baptism" are "entirely legendary" and never happened at all. (**Catholic Encyclopedia, Farley ed., vol. xiv, pp. 370-1**).

Constantine "never acquired a solid theological knowledge" and "depended heavily on his advisers in religious questions" (**Catholic Encyclopedia, New Edition, vol. xii, p. 576, passim**). According to Eusebeius (260-339), Constantine noted that among the presbyterian (pagan) factions "strife had grown so serious, vigorous action was necessary to establish a more religious state", but he could not bring about a settlement between rival god factions (**Life of Constantine, op. cit., pp. 26-8**). His advisers warned him that the presbyters' pagan religions were "destitute of foundation" and needed official stabilization. Constantine saw in this confused system of fragmented dogmas the opportunity to create a new and combined State religion, <u>neutral in concept</u>, and to protect it by law. Then ensure it through forced conversation and death for disobedience.

When he conquered the East in 324 he sent his Spanish religious adviser, Osius of Córdoba, to Alexandria with letters to several pagan bishops exhorting them to make peace among themselves. The mission failed and Constantine, probably at the suggestion of Osius, then issued a decree commanding all pagan presbyters (pagan priests) and their subordinates "**be mounted on asses, mules and horses belonging to the public, and (forced to) travel to the city of Nicaea**" in the Roman province of Bithynia in Asia Minor.

The Council of Nicaea a pagan council!

After these pagan priests were commanded to "mount asses and come to Nicaea" they were instructed to bring with them the testimonies they orated to the rabble (uneducated pagan masses), "bound in leather" for protection during the long journey, and surrender them to Constantine upon arrival in Nicaea (***The Catholic Dictionary, Addis and Arnold, 1917, "Council of Nicaea" entry***). Their writings totaled "in all, two thousand two hundred and thirty-one scrolls and legendary tales of gods and saviors, together with a record of the doctrines orated by them" (***Life of Constantine, op. cit., vol. ii, p. 73; N&PNF, op. cit., vol. i, p. 518***). Of course, we don't have them now to compare to Yahuah's Truth, these pagan writing which were the foundation of Christianity were carefully and totally destroyed after the Council of Nicaea… for obvious reasons.

Now the "**foundation of Christianity**" and how this massive lie started begins to come into focus. It was created at The Council of Nicaea founded not on The Torah and Messiah but rather "two thousand two hundred and thirty one scrolls and legendary tales of literally hundreds of gods and savious and pagan doctrines". This is what Constantine set out to standardize into **one generic neutral religion** that they all could agree upon! A syncretic religion was born! That resulting religion was named "Christianity" and the god of this new religion was named Hesus Horus Krishna later to be known in English as… **Jesus** (Hesus) **H.** (Horus) **Christ** (Krishna). This is historical fact.

I go into great detail concerning this name of the false messiah later in this book. In truth, history has proven that four years prior to the Council of Nicaea Constantine was ***initiated into the Cult of Sol Invictus***; the sun worshipping religion that evolved out of Babylon. That was the "conversion" that truly happened to Constantine he was never converted as a follower of Yahusha… ever. That is why he was bowing down facing East worshipping the sun in the first place and seeing the Cross of Tammuz (if that even really happened at all because it was never documented by a "Legend" to placate the ignorant masses).

What we do know, is the religion that came out of the Council of Nicaea was a **carbon copy** of what Constantine already believed and anyone that did not bow down to the new "god" he created **was executed in the inquisition**. All the pagans surrendered to this new religion while all the true sons of Yahuah were executed or went into hiding leaving only "Christianity" in the Roman Empire by law. This is exactly what the Prophets of Yahuah said would happen!

Chapter 10

How the new "god' was created, called Jesus H. Christ

What really happened at the Council of Nicaea

At the Council of Nicaea, Constantine gathered together all the "presbyters" (pagan priests) of his day and all their gods and saviors and had them debate together in an attempt to create one composite "god" they all agree to worship. The list of gods represented by their respective "priests" included Eastern and Western gods and goddesses: Jove, Jupiter, Salenus, Baal, Thor, Gade, Apollo, Juno, Aries, Taurus, Minerva, Rhets, Mithra, Theo, Fragapatti, Atys, Durga, Indra, Neptune, Vulcan, Kriste, Agni, Croesus, Pelides, Huit, Hermes, Thulis, Thammus, Eguptus, Iao, Aph, Saturn, Gitchens, Minos, Maximo, Hecla and Phernes and many more. It was in this "context" that the "god" Jesus H. Christ was created. The long list was narrowed down to the main gods of the Roman Aristocracy (Zeus and the son of Zeus Apollo) and the gods worshipped by the bulk of the common people (Julius Caesar and the sun god Mithra) along with the Eastern god Krishna.

Up until the First Council of Nicaea, the Roman aristocracy primarily worshipped two Greek gods-Apollo and Zeus-but the great bulk of common people idolized either Julius Caesar or Mithras (the Romanized version of the Persian deity Mithra who was an incarnation of the Babylonian Tammuz). Caesar was deified by the Roman Senate after his death (15 March 44 BC) and subsequently venerated as "the Divine *Julius*" (very close to the name "*Jesus*"). The word "Saviour" was affixed to his name, its literal meaning being "one who sows the seed", i.e., he was a phallic god. Julius Caesar (the initials JC same as Jesus Christ) was hailed as "God made manifest and universal Saviour of human life", and his successor Augustus was called the "ancestral God and Saviour of the whole human race" (***Man and his Gods, Homer Smith, Little, Brown & Co., Boston, 1952***). So Julius was known as "Julius Christos" making it very easy for his followers to accept the new god "Jesus Christ". Emperor Nero, whose original name was Lucius Domitius Ahenobarbus, was immortalized on his coins as the "Saviour of mankind". The Divine Julius as Roman Savior and "Father of the Empire" was considered "God" among the Roman uneducated pagan population for more than 300 years. He was the deity in some Western pagan priestly texts, but was not recognized in Eastern or Oriental writings. So Constantine was forced to include the Eastern realm god *Krishna*.

<u>Constantine had a political problem that required a religious solution</u>. He had to come up with a "god" that those who worshipped Julius would accept that would be acceptable to the factions in the Eastern and Orient who worshipped Krishna. All of these gods (Jove, Jupiter, Salenus, Baal, Thor, Gade, Apollo, Juno, Aries, Taurus, Minerva, Rhets, Mithra, Theo, Fragapatti, Atys, Durga, Indra, Neptune, Vulcan, Kriste, Agni, Croesus, Pelides, Huit, Hermes, Thulis, Thammus, Eguptus, Iao, Aph, Saturn, Gitchens, Minos, Maximo, Hecla and Phernes and many more) were narrowed down from literally hundreds down to 53 then after much debate down to only 5 through balloting: Caesar, Krishna, Mithra, Horus and Zeus (***Historia Ecclesiastica, Eusebius, c. 325***).

To make a very long and detailed story short, the council could not come to a decision on just one god they all could accept, <u>so Constantine exercised his authority as Emperor and High Priest</u> to consolidate the 3 primary gods that would effectively represent the Greek masses and the Eastern and the Oriental religions of the Roman Empire. Every one of these so called "gods" are nothing more than later incarnations of the Babylonian Religion whose saviour was Tammuz the second member of the Trinity and son of "God". Then names simply changed at the tower of Babel. So, Constantine chose the following "gods" to unite his empire:

- To placate the powerful British factions he chose the great Druid god which was the sun god **<u>Hesus</u>** (an incarnation of Nimrod/Tammuz),
- To placate the faction from Egypt he chose the Assyrian sun god **<u>Horus</u>** (an incarnation of Nimrod/Tammuz).

- To placate the Eastern/Oriental factions he chose the Eastern Saviour-god, Krishna (Krishna is Sanskrit for Christ) (an incarnation of Nimrod/Tammuz).

These three main sun god / saviours were then united into one composite deity called Hesus Horus Krishna which later became known in its English derived name as Jesus H. Christ. Satisfying the "Julius", Esu, Horus, and Krishna faithful who made up the vast majority of his empire, Constantine now had a "god" for his new religion which was not new at all but **the rebirth of Babylonian sun worship**. A "god" easily acceptable by all throughout his realm (except true followers of Yahusha whom he simply had killed in the inquisition).

The new "god" of Constantine's religion

Now let's review the gods that make up the new composite god of the newly formed (yet known by all pagans as very old) state religion of Rome. Each of these pagan gods were nothing more than later triune (trinity) incarnations of

Nimrod/Semaramis/Tammuz

handed down through history from the Tower of Babel as mankind spread across the globe with different languages and cultures taking the worship of the planets with them… sun worship. Let's look a little closer at these so-call "gods" that are the foundation of the fictional messiah Jesus H. Christ who abolished the law of Yahuah.

Below we are going to take a deeper look at the 2 pagan gods Constantine chose to pattern his new god Hesus Horus Krishna aka ΧξϚ Jesus H. Christ after.

Hesus

The 18th century Druidic revivalist Iolo Morgannwg identified Esus with Jesus on the strength of the similarity of their names. He also linked them both with Hu Gadarn, writing:

> "Both Hu and HUON were no doubt originally identical with the HEUS of Lactantius, and the HESUS of Lucan, described as gods of the Gauls. The similarity of the last name to IESU [Welsh: Jesus] is obvious and striking."

When we simply take a step back and admit to ourselves what happened at the Council of Nicaea the similarities between Hesus and "Jesus" can easily be understood. They are one in the same. We'll get more into the meaning of the name Jesus later. Hesus is a later derivate of the name Esus pronounced "eh-soos". This is identically to the latin name Iesous where we get the English word "Jesus". Strong's #2424: Iesous (pronounced ee-ay-sooce').

Hesus too was part of a Trinity. A well-known section in Lucan's Bellum civile talks about the gory sacrificial offerings proffered to a triad of Celtic deities: Teutates, Hesus (an aspirated form of Esus), and Taranis. Among a pair of later commentators on Lucan's work, one identifies Teutates with Mercury and Esus with Mars. According to the Berne Commentary on Lucan, **human victims were sacrificed to Esus by being tied to a tree and flailed.** Now is the execution of Yahusha coming into focus? Yahusha was killed by ROME in a pagan sacrifice orchestrated by Satan. He was tied to a tree stump and flailed then (according to Roman legend) hung on the Cross of Tammuz as a sacrifice.

Left is a picture of "Jesus" as Hesus, Teutates, and Taranis. Right is the triune god worshipped by the Vikings was another version of this triple deity of Hesus, Teutates, and Taranis.

Trinity, Norway, 14 Century, CE

141

Horus

SUN GODS: Isis, Horus, & Seb

Horus too was part of a Trinity, **the second** member in fact. This is the very Trinity of the Catholic/Christian Church of Isis, Horus, Seb or I.H.S. the monogram of Jesus H. Christ with the cross of Tammuz all in the middle of the invincible sun god. Below is a picture the Catholic "Monstrance" that today represents Jesus H. Christ.

In fact, Horus was none other than the Egyptian manifestation of Nimrod reincarnated as Tammuz. The same mother/son marriage relationship existed with Horus and Hathor in Egypt just like Babylon between Semaramis and Tammuz. Horus was the Egyptian Tammuz that was a reincarnated god from a "virgin birth" by the rays (spirit) of the sun god. His mother Hathor is none other than Ishtar/Semaramis of Babylonian lore. The names changed because of the different languages by the ritual surrounding their worshipped did not. To this day they remain intact in the fundamental doctrines of Christianity.

The earliest recorded form of Horus is the patron deity of Nekhen (another name for Tammuz) in Upper Egypt, who is the first known national god, specifically related to the king who in time came to be regarded as a manifestation of Horus in life and Osiris in death. The most commonly encountered family relationship describes Horus as the son of Isis (Ishtar/Semaramis) and Osiris (Baal/Nimrod) but in another tradition Hathor is regarded as his mother and sometimes as his wife (just like Tammuz/Semaramis). Horus served many functions in the Egyptian pantheon, most notably being the god of the sky, **sun**, **war** and protection.

Krishna

Krishna was the **second member** of the Hindu Trinity just like Horus and Tammuz and Jesus are all second members of their respective pagan trinities. Krishna in fact was simply the Hindu incarnation of Tammuz in their language and culture.

Many progressive Christian scholars go so far as admit the Hindu source for many of the events in Jesus' life and is a topic is worth studying. Many non-Christian religious belief systems, including Hinduism, permeated the Mediterranean region in the 1st century CE. where Christianity was born. The word "Krishna" is Sanskrit for Christ and over time the word evolved from Krishna to Krischto to Chresto to Christ. It means "the anointed one" and the meaning is **very different** from the Hebrew word "messiah".

We see "Jesus" and Krishna portrayed in paintings and the similarities are striking complete with the solar deity trait of the cross of The Zodiac in front of the blazing sun.

There were various male heroes within Egyptian, Greek, Indian, Roman and other pantheons of gods, whose role was to be saviors to humanity -- much like Jesus. In order to compete with those religions, Christianity (as created by Constantine) would have had to describe a new composite god "Jesus H. Christ" in terms that matched or surpassed the legends and myths of other religions.

Otherwise, it would not have survived. Then assimilate all other pagan religions into this new one by threat of death. The authors of the gospels may well have picked up themes from other sources and added them to their writings in order to make Christianity more credible to a religiously diverse world, most of which worshiped multiple gods and goddesses. **Or**, which has proven to be the case, the original transcripts of the Gospels must have been altered by pagan Catholic scribes. I suggest the reader purchase the book *Misquoting Jesus* for an introduction to Textual Criticism

144

where it has been proven the original manuscripts were altered to support pagan doctrines such as The Trinity and much more.

By isolating and removing such foreign material from the Gospels that are obvious references to pagan deities, we might be able to get a clearer picture of what Yahusha the true Messiah actually taught and how he lived. When we do, we are left with a perfect match of the O.T. Prophets who spoke of a human Messiah and prophet of Yahuah who would further teach The Torah and reveal Yahuah to mankind.

When you remove all the pagan associations from the altered texts of the Greek manuscripts we are left with:

- A very human, itinerant, Jewish, rabbi-healer.
- An observant Jew who had a special relationship with God -- a kinship so close that he referred to God by the familiar term "Abba."
- An innocent man literally sacrificed on Passover who rose from the grave on The Sabbath according to the Spring Feast Cycle.
- A fully human in every way High Priest chosen from among men to represent mankind before God. Exactly like The Bible describes the Messiah.

Chapter 11

Christianity is born with a new god… Jesus H. Christ (I.H.S)

Now that Constantine had his "god" for his universal religion which was literally 3 different incarnations of Nimrod and Tammuz. This new "god" came complete with the "sun and cross of Tammuz behind his head". With this new Greek god in place, bringing all the different major factions together through syncretism was easy!

Hesus (son of Zeus)   Horus "sun" of God   Krishna or Christ   Tammuz with a new name "Jesus H. Christ"

Paintings even began to emerge of this triple figured "god" named Jesus with the sun over his head, it was the new Sungod to be worshipped on Sungod Day called to this day Sunday.

This "new Greek pagan god" was given the acronym "I.H.S" and represented with the "cross of Tammuz" that depicts the 4 equal points of the ecliptic or "equinoxes" of The Zodiac. The same religion of sun worship founded in Babylon. Below you can easily see the "Cross of Tammuz" the acronym IHS (Isis, Horus, Seb) and a yellow sun behind the heads of the newly renamed versions of Semaramis and Tammuz now called Mary and Joseph.

Even the Vatican was constructed with a large obelisk in the center of a massive astrological "cross of the equinoxes" in St. Peter's Square as the Pope carries around a monstrous symbol of the sun god.

147

With the "new god" firmly in place now depicted as "crucified on the cross of Tammuz" in opposition to the Bible which clearly states he was "impaled on a stake", the only items on the agenda of the Council of Nicaea was to now bring in all the pagan religious festivals associated with sun worship. Name these pagan rituals after the new "Chrestos" (X-mas, Good Friday, Easter, Sunday, Valentine's Day, Halloween, etc.) and rename all the pagan idols to their new names where they remain today in The Vatican. Then, of course, change the capital city from Jerusalem to Rome.

After all, ROME had already executed The Messiah in pagan sacrificial ritual to Baal. Rome had already sacked Jerusalem and destroyed The Temple of Yahuah. The Roman Empire had already made their statement crystal clear; it hated every aspect of the Hebrew Faith and the Hebrew God. The only thing left at this point was to "change the times and Laws of Yahuah" and kill all the remaining Sabbath keeping sons of God. This was attempted by the Inquisition. Satan's hands all over it all…

Christianity was born as I mentioned at the Council of Nicaea. The pagan doctrines of The Trinity, the Virgin Birth, Sunday Worship, Christmas, Easter, etc. were all formulated and the New Testament texts altered to "imply" these new doctrines in direct contradiction of explicit commandments from Yahuah. Throw in the obelisk (steeple) with the cross of Tammuz and the new religion was now complete and Constantine had his "Universal (Catholic) Church". He then brought in all the pagan sun worshipping "fathers and nuns" from Mithraism and Brigit worship, altered the texts of the New Testament to fit his new religion, and began teaching the illiterate masses a lie that this "religion" was based on The Bible. He then killed any dissenters in the inquisition and banished all intellectual thought in The Dark Ages and 2,000 years later we have accepted every word of this lie as "Truth".

Still to this very day, no one questions "why" the name Jesus gives glory to Zeus not Yahuah and "why" the name is not even in the Hebrew language.

Chapter 12
Jesus Christ the Beast of Revelation

The Deceiver

The False messiah is "the lawless one" (2 Thessalonians 2:8). Yahusha overthrows this "false image" of himself with the "power of his testimony" which is the spirit of prophecy.

Revelation 19:10
"Worship Yahuah! For it is the Spirit of prophecy (*Yahuah's prophets*) who bears testimony to Yahusha."

Yahusha was prophesied by Moses as the greatest prophet who will properly teach The Law.

Acts 3:22
For Moses said, "Yahuah your God will raise up for you a prophet like me from among your own people; you must listen to everything he tells you.

John 5:46
If you believed Moses, you would believe me, for he wrote about me.

The Law and the Festivals of Yahuah are prophesied to be abolished and changed to pagan rituals by the False messiah.

Daniel 7:25
The False messiah will speak (*to the hearts of man*) against the Most High and oppress his holy people and try to change the Ordained Festivals and the laws of Yahuah.

The Messiah is a deceiver who does not come "in the name of Yahuah" but rather in his own name giving glory to 3 pagan gods (Hesus, Horus, Krishna). Yahusha comes in the name of Yahuah and no one who denies this will ever see Yahusha again.

Matthew 21:9
"Hosanna to the Son of David!" "Blessed is he who comes in the name of Yahuah!" "Hosanna in the highest heaven!"

Matthew 23:39
For I tell you, you will not see me again until you say, 'Blessed is he who comes in the name of Yahuah.'"

John identified Jesus Christ as the Beast

Revelation 13 - The Beast out of the Sea

[16] The dragon stood on the shore of the sea. And **I saw a beast** coming out of the sea…[17] so that they could not buy or sell unless they had the mark, which is the name of the beast or the number of its name. [18] This calls for wisdom. Let the person who has insight calculate the number of the beast, for it is the number of a man. That number is 666.

Above John specifically and uniquely names *Jesus Christ* as the Antichrist. Doesn't look like it in English does it? That is because the English translation of this verse is in grave error. I am going to challenge this uninspired translation above that has kept us all in the dark for thousands of years. Here again, we are warned that to understand the "name of the beast" requires those who have the *wisdom* and *insight* into spiritual things. We are going to employ just such wisdom and insight in this scripture to clearly identify *Jesus Christ* as **the name** of the beast and demonstrate that what John actually said and meant in Revelation 13 is this:

Revelation 13 - ΧϚϚ The Beast out of the Sea

13 The dragon stood on the shore of the sea. And **I saw a beast** coming out of the sea (*sea serpent* ϛ)…[17] so that they could not buy or sell unless they had the mark (Χ), <u>which is the name of the beast</u> or (*rather*) the *symbol* of its name. [18] This calls for wisdom (*to discern the Christogram*). Let the person who has (*spiritual*) *eyes to see* reckon up the (*pictogram of the*) *symbol* of the beast *that identifies him,* for it is the *symbol* of a man. That *symbol* is ΧϚϚ

153

No exposition of **The False messiah** would be complete without exposing the name of the beast and the *number* of his name. Again we are misled by The Christian Church to believe The Mark of the Beast is 666 when actually it is the spiritual mark of The Trinity which is an X on the forehead (belief that Jesus in God incarnate) which is opposite of **The Mark of Yahuah** which is that He is ONE God and there is no other.

In reality, the numbers 666 have nothing to do with anything at all! That is where the wisdom and insight come in. You see, John didn't write down a "number", he wrote down the 3 Greek letters of the <u>symbol of Jesus Christ to the exclusion of all others in history</u>. This is why the pagan translators removed the symbol and inserted a number!

666 is a violation of scripture not to "add to or subtract from"

Below is what Revelation 13 looks like in the Greek language:

ωδε η σοφια εστιν ο εχων τον νουν θηφισατω τον αριψμον του ψηριου αριψμοα γαρ ανψρωπου εστιν και ο αριψμοα αυτου χξς

The last 3 letters at the end is what John wrote not 666. So the number 666 in our English Bibles is misleading as it only represented **the gematria** or the associated <u>number</u> of what John actually wrote in <u>Greek letters</u> , Χ , ξ and ϛ , (Chi, Xi and Sigma).

Translators converted the Greek letters χξς into the number 666 because they <u>mistranslated the meaning of the Greek word</u> *arithmos* in Rev. 13 as "number". Then they subtracted χξς and added 666 which is forbidden to do!

They should never have changed *the SYMBOL* to a number in the first place! The Translators should have left this 'symbol' in our English Bibles as χξς so that at "the time of the end" we would recognize the mark, the monogram, and the pictogram of the False messiah.

The number 666 has nothing to do with what John actually wrote as he didn't write down a number but *a symbol*. We arrived at our English translation of Revelation 13 by uninspired translators and scribes who did not possess the "wisdom" and spiritual "insight" John said was required, leaving us all subsequently in the dark <u>until now</u>. So let's illuminate Revelation 13 with a little Wisdom from Yahuah and spiritual insight…

John saw the *SYMBOL* ΧϚϚ not a *NUMBER*

What John was shown in Revelation 13 was a vision of the mark, the symbol of the serpent, the pictogram, and the monogram of **Jesus Christ**. John did not see nor write a number.

The symbol John saw was a symbol for Jesus Christ which is called a *Christogram*.

> http://en.wikipedia.org/wiki/Christogram

> *A **Christogram** is a monogram or combination of Greek letters that forms an abbreviation for the name of Jesus Christ, traditionally used as a **Christian symbol**. Christogram comes from the Latin phrase "Christi Monogramma", meaning "monogram of Christ". **Different types of Christograms are associated with the various traditions of Christianity***

The Catholic Encyclopedia admits that *XS* is one of the standard *Christograms*:

> **Catholic Encyclopedia** -
> http://www.newadvent.org/cathen/07649a.htm

> ## IHS

> *A monogram of the Jesus Christ. From the third century the names of our Savior are sometimes shortened, particularly in Christian inscriptions (IH and XP, for Jesus and Christus). In the next century the "sigla" (chi-rho) occurs not only as an abbreviation but also **as a symbol**. From the beginning, however, in Christian inscriptions the nomina sacra, or names of Jesus Christ, were shortened by*

*contraction, thus IC / XC (which is IS / **XS** today) or IHS and **XPS** for Iesous Christos.*

John saw in his vision <u>one</u> of those different types of monograms or **symbols** of **Jesus Christ.** There are many Christograms used throughout history and all of them use different combinations of the Greek letters in *Christos* ΧΡΙΣΤΟΣ.   The monogram that John wrote down is <u>unique</u> using the Greek letter that symbolizes the serpent Ϛ . John used the first and last Greek letters in **Χ**ΡΙΣΤΟ**Σ** (*the most commons symbol in history for Jesus Christ*) with the letter sigma Ϛ in the middle:

We read below these 3 Greek characters represent the pagan Greek title *Christos* **Χ**ΡΙΣΤΟ**Σ** used of all pagan demi-gods after which Jesus Christ was fashioned by Constantine. But this ONE monogram **XS** includes the symbol of the sea serpent mentioned in Revelation 13:1…

"Number in Scripture" - Dr E W Bullinger pg 49

> *Indeed the expression of this number,* Χ͂ϚϚ *, consists of the initial and final letters of the word*
>
> ΧΡΙΣΤΟ**Σ** *(Christos), Christ, the X and* Ϛ*, with the symbol of the serpent between them, X—ξ—ς. <u>The middle letter represents the symbol of the serpent and is intimately connected with the ancient Egyptian Mysteries.</u>*

Bear in mind that we are still after the 'Name' of this opposing force against the True God Yahuah, which, if this Scripture in Rev.13:16-18 has any reference to it, is linked with this mysterious symbol linked to paganism - the symbol of the serpent Ϛ which

Revelation declares gives the false messiah his power, authority, and throne on Earth.

Does *'arithmos'* mean 'number' or 'symbol' in context of Rev. 13?

Throughout history, the name Jesus Christ has been represented by symbols not numbers as John demonstrated by writing down the symbol χξϛ in Revelation Chapter 13:18.

> http://en.wikipedia.org/wiki/Christogram

> *A **Christogram** is a monogram or combination of Greek letters that forms an abbreviation for the name of Jesus Christ, traditionally used as a **Christian symbol**.*

The Catholic Encyclopedia admits that these *Christograms* are *symbols* not numbers:

> **Catholic Encyclopedia** -
> http://www.newadvent.org/cathen/07649a.htm

>> ***IHS***
>> *A monogram of the Jesus Christ. From the third century the names of our Savior are sometimes shortened, particularly in Christian inscriptions (IH and XP, for Jesus and Christus). In the next century the "sigla" (chi-rho) occurs not only as an abbreviation but also **as a symbol**.*

Arithmos (αριθμος) mistranslated

The word *arithmos* translated as *number* in Revelation 13:18 should have been translated as **symbol** or the "*figurative representation*" that "*lifts up*" a specific man as to "*identify*" him by name… such as a *mark, pictogram,* or *monogram*. In

Revelation 13:18 the Greek word translated *number* in English is Strong's #706 *arithmos* below

706	arithmos *ar-ith-mos'*	From root word - **airo** 142; a number (as reckoned up):--number.

Arithmos can mean "number" because a number IS a symbol as in the sense of; **a symbol** that represents a specific calculated measurement of units. *Arithmos* can also mean; "representation" or "symbol" in the sense of "reckoned up" to identify something. The words "representation" and "symbol" are English synonyms of "number" see... http://thesaurus.com/browse/number

Given that John wrote a symbol not a number in context of Revelation 13:18, "symbol" would be a much more accurate English word for the Greek word *arithmos*. *Arithmos* as used by John is in the sense of "representation" or "symbol" used to "reckoned up" and identify something in this case *The False messiah' name*.

To understand which word (*number* or *symbol*) better represents *arithmos* in this specific case, the translators should have consulted the ROOT WORD of *arithmos* which is *airo*. *Airo* gives us a full sense of what John was saying given he wrote down a symbol not a number. *Arithmos* is derived from the Greek root word *airo* Strong's #142 below:

142	airo *ah'-ee-ro*	a primary root word; to lift up; by representation, to take up or away; figuratively

The word *arithmos* in conjunction with its root *airo* implies a "symbol" that is used "to figuratively lift up; by representation" not a mathematical symbol (number) used to calculate. *Arithmos* is used this way by John in Revelation 13:18 and means a *symbol* or a *"figurative representation"* that *"identifies"* i.e. a *mark*, *pictogram*, or *monogram*! That is why John did not write down a number after *arithmos* <u>he put down 3 Greek letters</u> that is used as a *symbol* that *figuratively represents* **Jesus Christ**...

The reason the number 666 appears in our English Bibles and not his *symbol* χξϛ is because the translators mistranslated *arithmos* as *number* instead of *symbol*. Then the translators took <u>the liberty of changing the text</u> and converting χξϛ into the number 666 using the system of Gematria. <u>This was a grave error in translation</u>. They should have left the text alone, remember the warning not to add to or subtract from the Book of Revelation? Well in this case the translators did both!

Revelation 22:18
[18] I testify to everyone who hears the words of the prophecy of this book: if anyone adds to them, Yahuah will add to him the plagues which are written in this book; [19] and if anyone takes away from the words of the book of this prophecy, Yahuah will take away his part from the tree of life and from the holy city

So *arithmos* as used by John should have been translated as *symbol* in the sense of a *"figurative representation to lift up and identify"* the name of the false messiah. That is the full meaning and how it is used by John in Revelation 13:18. John put down the Greek **symbol** χξϛ , the "figurative representation" that "lifts up" and identifies the name of the coming False messiah *Jesus Christ*.

It is no wonder John warned us we would need "wisdom and insight" to figure this one out because our translators failed us yet again. What John was actually saying in Revelation 13 and the proper translation is this:

Revelation 13 - The Beast out of the Sea

[18] This calls for wisdom. Let the person who has insight reckon *up* the **symbol** of the beast, for it is the **symbol** of a

man *that identifies him.* That **symbol** is χξϛ

This *"figurative representation that lifts up to identify"* i.e. χξϛ is the symbol of Jesus Christ <u>exclusively</u> no other figure in human history uses this symbol.

Do these Greek letters χξϛ point us uniquely to the name "Jesus" and "Christ"?

Throughout history, the Christian Church has used <u>various combinations</u> of Greek letters in Christos ΧΡΙΣΤΟΣ to represent Jesus Christ as **_SYMBOLS_**; it does not and has never used 666 or numbers.   Sometimes we see letters in Christos in combination with letters from other titles used as the monogram for Jesus Christ. For instance, the famous chi-rho monogram (a symbol which became part of the official standard of the emperor Constantine) was made from the first two letters of <u>C</u>hristos ΧΡΙΣΤΟΣ. **Other symbols use the first and last letter ΧΡΙΣΤΟS, or just the first X, and so on.**

<u>http://en.wikipedia.org/wiki/Chi_Rho</u>

> *The **Chi Rho** is one of the earliest forms of the Christogram and is used by some Christians. It is formed by superimposing the first two (capital) letters chi and rho (**XP**) of the Greek word "**XP**ΙΣΤΟΣ" =Christ in such a way to produce the monogram. Although not technically a Christian cross, the Chi-Rho invokes the crucifixion of Jesus, as well as **<u>symbolizing</u>** his status as the Christ.*

> *The Chi-Rho symbol was used by the Roman emperor Constantine I, which is known as Labarum. Early pagan symbols similar to the Chi*

Rho were the <u>Staurogram</u> (⳨) and the <u>IX</u> <u>Monogram</u> (✳)

The version of the Christogram used by Constantine ✳ is to this day emblazoned on the pagan altar of The Catholic Church. The Christogram of Constantine is also inscribed on the YMCA building below:

What version of the Christogram did John see in Rev. 13?

Most versions of the Christogram use letters in the Greek word for Christ (ΧΡΙΣΤΟΣ). The one John saw too represents the first and last letters in Christos Χριϲτο**S** or **<u>XS</u>**. **XS** is one of the most common Christograms throughout history which in medieval times was written as **XC** as C was used for the Greek letter Sigma. Anytime we see **XC** in paintings or murals <u>that is equivalent to **XS** today</u> as we now use S for the letter Sigma.

As I mentioned earlier the letters in a Christogram can be combined with other symbols as well to make the Christogram more meaningful. Like the one Constantine used ✗ that is still being used today on the pagan Altar of the Catholic Church and other Christian structures. The Christogram that John used in Revelation portrayed the most famous monogram for Christos (ΧριστοS) with the Egyptian pagan mystery symbol of the serpent ς in the middle to give it more meaning.

The sea serpent is identified In Revelation 13:1 as the "beast coming out of the sea" or sea serpent and is the source of the power, authority, and throne of The False messiah. So when identifying **that** beast, John used the first two letters of Christos (ΧριστοS) with the symbol of the serpent ς in the middle.

The universal symbol for the serpent throughout the ages and cultures is a serpent in an upright coil:

What John was telling us by using the standard monogram for Jesus Christ or **XS** is that the "sea serpent" or *the dragon* would be the source of the power, great authority and throne of the False messiah by inserting the symbol of the serpent ς in between them!

163

Revelation 13

And I saw a beast coming out of the sea ... The dragon (serpent ξ) gave the beast (*XS*) his power and his throne and great authority.

"Number in Scripture" - Dr E W Bullinger pg 49)

Indeed the expression of this number, Χξς *, consists of the initial and final letters of the word*

ΧΡΙΣΤΟΣ *(Christos), Christ, the X and* ς*, with the symbol of the serpent between them, X—ξ—ς.* The middle letter represents the symbol of the serpent and is intimately connected with the ancient Egyptian Mysteries.

This is exactly what The Apostle Paul told us:

2 Thessalonians 2
[9] The coming of the lawless one (*the one in whom The Law is abolished i.e. Jesus Christ*) will be in accordance with how Satan works (*the spirit behind The False messiah is the serpent* ξ). He will use all sorts of displays of power through signs and wonders that serve the lie.

We see the Greek letters such as IC and XC (*which is* **XS** *today*) used as **symbols** for 'Jesus Christ' in painted mosaics the world over clearly identifying Jesus Christ as the beast John saw in

164

Revelation.

"IC XC" as written in the Hellenistic period is a Christogram, a monogram of "Jesus Christ". When Jesus Christ is written in Greek it looks like this: **ΙΗΣΟΥΣ ΧΡΙΣΤΟΣ.** If we take the first and last letters of Ι_{ΗΣΟΥ}Σ ("Jesus") and Χ_{ΡΙΣΤΟ}Σ ("Christ") we are left with: *ΙΣ ΧΣ.* Today that would read *IS XS.*

> **Note:** *In handwritten Greek during the Hellenistic period (4th and 3rd centuries BC), the epigraphic form of Σ was simplified into a C-like shape, thereby giving us: IC XC. But today "at the time of the end" when Revelation would be understood the Σ is transliterated as the letter S. Therefore all these Christograms painted world-wide if painted today would read IS / XS. XS (ΧΣ) being the Christogram used by John in Revelation 13 as a symbol not a number.*

These mosaics of Jesus Christ have a serpent symbol above the IC XC (which today would be IS XS). If you move that serpent symbol into the monogram below it you have the exact symbol John wrote in Revelation 13:18. Remember the Greek letter Sigma Σ at the time this mosaic was painted was transliterated as a C. Today the Sigma is transliterated as an S.

This is where "wisdom" comes into play:

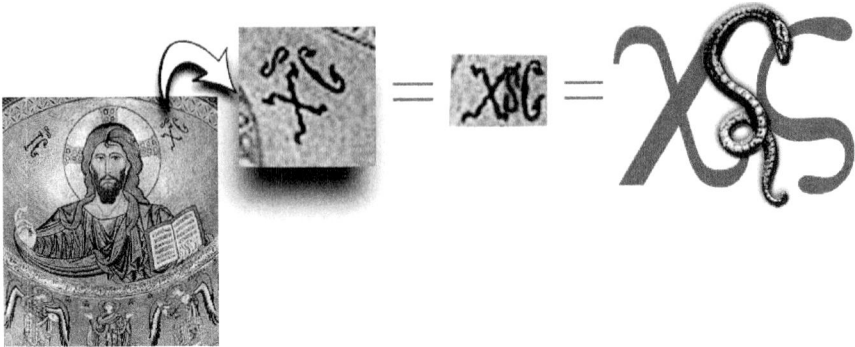

The symbol John saw is literally *hidden in plain site* as <u>THE</u> symbol for Jesus Christ in paintings, on mosaics that adorn cathedrals, on stain glass murals, on buildings and inscriptions the world over.

In many paintings, Jesus Christ is depicted as making the same cryptic hand gestures as seen below. This hand gesture is literally the symbol of the Antichrist that John saw in Revelation… XS (depicted as XC as the Sigma was transliterated as a C in the middle ages).

We see Jesus Christ represented below with the blazing sun (sungod) behind his head, the 4 equal distant cross of the Zodiac and the cryptic hand gestures of the false messiah:

We see in the images above that Jesus' right hand forms an X by crossing his first two fingers. He then forms the C for Sigma by curving his last two fingers making the C shape. This is the hand gesture of the False messiah as he identifies himself in plain sight making the *XS* symbol with his hands, the very symbol John used in Revelation 13…

http://en.wikipedia.org/wiki/Christogram

*In Eastern Christianity, the most widely used Christogram is a four-letter abbreviation, **ICXC** — a traditional abbreviation of the Greek words for "Jesus Christ" "IHCOYC XPICTOC" with the lunate sigma "C" common in medieval Greek which*

167

we today transliterate as an S. On icons, this Christogram may be split: "IC" on the left of the image and "XC" on the right, most often with a sideways S above the letters <u>to indicating that it is a sacred name.</u> **Jesus Christ's right hand is shown in a pose that represents the letters X, and C.**

ΧϚϚ points to the Trinity as well as Christ

The *sign of the cross* is the mark of Jesus Christ or <u>the mark that is associated with his name</u>!

<u>Jamieson-Fausset-Brown Bible Commentary</u>

> *the mark, or the name—Greek, "the mark (namely),* ***the name of the beast.****" The mark may be, as in the case of the sealing of the saints in the forehead, <u>not a visible mark</u>, <u>but symbolical of allegiance. Such as **the sign of the cross** in Popery.</u>*

We see above that even Christian Bible commentaries admit that the mark of the beast is the sign of the cross made on the forehead and over the heart. It represents The Trinity. This is the opposing mark to the Shema/Seal of Yahuah. Can this "symbol" John used be *associated* with The Trinity specifically? Remember, John's warning that "reckoning up the symbol" requires spiritual understanding and *INSIGHT* or "eyes to see".

Revelation 13
[18] **This calls for wisdom** (*spiritual understanding of the mind*). Let the person who has (*spiritual*) insight *reckon up* the *symbol* of the beast *that identifies him*

The Mark of the Beast as we read in Jamieson-Fausset-Brown Bible Commentary is made over the victim's forehead. It is the first letter in **X**ΡΙΣΤΟΣ. In fact, the *X* is the most widely used monogram for Christ and the mark on the forehead of Christians:

In Christianity the X mark is made on the forehead while repeating *"in the name of the Father, the Son, and the Holy Spirit"* or X'*ES* representing the triplicate nature of the pagan Trinity. In making this X mark over the forehead, the mind is sealed with the opposing mark of The Trinity.

We see below that the plural form of X (the mark) is the pictogram of what John wrote in Revelation 13. χξϛ is a pictogram of XES which is "Christ by abbreviation":

ETYMOLOGY REFERENCES WIKTIONARY:

X | Xs plural form | Xes plural form

*Origin: **Christ by abbreviation**, from Ancient Greek X (Ch, "(letter chi)"), from Χριστός (Christós,... (26 of 44 etymology words)*

The Sign and the Seal of the Beast is the X monogram

The first letter Chi or χ is also used widely today as *one of the many monograms* or <u>symbols</u> for Jesus Christ and is literally *The Mark of the Beast* John was referring to in Revelation 13!

<u>http://en.wikipedia.org/wiki/Christogram</u>

> *The most commonly encountered Christogram in English-speaking countries in modern times is the X (or more accurately, Greek letter chi) as in the abbreviation Xmas (for "Christmas"), which represents the first letter of the word Christ.*

The early Church Fathers attested to the use of *the sign of the cross* and that it is the Seal or Mark of Christianity; the mark that opposes The Shema or Mark of God.

<u>Tertullian (d. ca. 250) described the commonness of the sign of the cross:</u>

> *"In all our travels and movements, in all our coming in and going out, in putting on our shoes, at the bath, at the table, in lighting our candles, in lying down, in sitting down, whatever employment occupies us,* **we mark our foreheads with the sign of the cross***" (De corona, 30).*

<u>St. Cyril of Jerusalem (d. 386) in his Catechetical Lectures stated,</u>

> *"Let us then not be ashamed to confess the Crucified.* **Be the cross our seal***, made with boldness by our fingers on our brow and in everything; over the bread we eat and the cups we*

drink, in our comings and in our goings out; before
our sleep, when we lie down and when we awake;

Gradually, the sign of the cross was incorporated in different acts
of the Mass, such as the three-fold signing of the forehead, lips,
and heart as it represents The Trinity.

Ash Wednesday is the first day of Lent which and is founded in the
Babylonian ritual of "Weeping for Tammuz". Ash Wednesday
occurs 46 days before Easter (which is the sacrifice of a pig in
honor of the death of Tammuz).

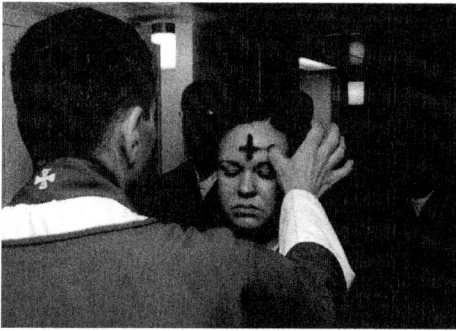

I cover this in detail in my
book **Mystery Babylon:
The Religion of the Beast**.
At Masses and services of
worship on Ash
Wednesday, ashes are
imposed on the foreheads
of the faithful in the shape
of an X. The priest,
minister, or in some cases
officiating layperson, marks the forehead of each participant with
black ashes **in the sign of the cross (or X)**, which the worshipper
traditionally retains until it wears off.

χ͂ςς is the *pictogram* of name of JESus as well as Christ identifying "Jesus Christ" by name

It would take <u>*understanding*</u> to identify the *monogram*. However,
it requires insight or spiritual *eyes to see* to recognize this symbol
χςς <u>as a pictogram</u> as well as a *monogram*. The symbol χ͂ςς
would <u>be a pictogram of the English</u> letters *XES.*

171

Pictogram - http://en.wiktionary.org/wiki/pictogram

> *Strictly speaking, a pictogram represents <u>by illustration</u>, an ideogram represents an idea, and a logogram represents a word: Chinese characters are all logograms, but few are pictograms or ideograms. Casually, pictogram is used to represent all of these: it <u>is a picture representing some concept</u>.*

The pictogram χξς is <u>*visually associated*</u> and *visually represents* the characters **XES** in English.

Ξ ξ   The Greek letter X looks like an X, the Greek letter Xi looks like the English letter E in both upper and lower case forms.

The Greek letter Sigma looks like an S giving us the pictogram of the English letters **XES** in both upper and lower case form:

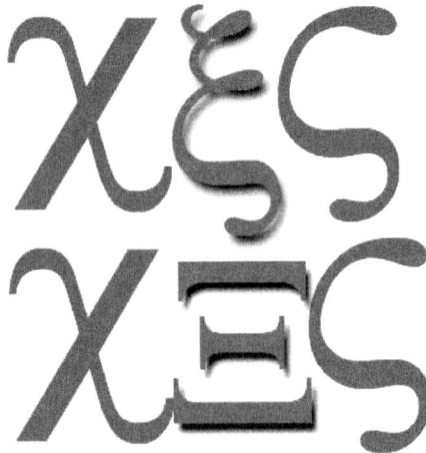

χξς

χΞς

χξς as a pictogram of **XES** is the <u>plural form</u> of the X monogram of Jesus

172

ETYMOLOGY REFERENCES WIKTIONARY:

X | Xs plural form | Xes plural form

Origin: **Christ by abbreviation**, *from Ancient Greek X (Ch, "(letter chi)"), from Χριστός (Christós,... (26 of 44 etymology words)*

So **XES** would indicate Jesus in triplicate. Jesus was often represented in this form in antiquity.

As a *pictogram* of **XES** in English, this symbol χξς uniquely identifies **the name** '*Jesus*' as well.

IHS = χξς = XES THE PICTOGRAM

The first 3 letters of the name **Jes**us are one of the most commonly used monograms for Jesus today. The most famous is IHS which is a Latin contracted form of **IHS**ous (**JES**us):

> **Catholic Encyclopedia** -
> http://www.newadvent.org/cathen/07649a.htm
>> IHS
>> *A monogram of the Jesus Christ. From the third century the names of our Saviour are sometimes shortened, particularly in Christian inscriptions (IH and XP, for Jesus and Christus). In the next century the "sigla" (chi-rho) occurs not only as an abbreviation but also **as a symbol**.*

X̌ЄϚ is a pictogram for the English letters **XES**. **XES** is the English translation of one of the Greek forms of **IHS**, the most famous of the symbols of Jesus. **XESÚS** is a common spelling of Jesus today:

In fact, the name *Jesus* is written in the Greek Galician dialect as **XES**us and is of Hebrew origin at the time John wrote Revelation. So John, when writing the book of Revelation, would naturally have known what I am pointing out here today.

> **XESÚS** - http://meaningbabynames.com/meaning/Xesus
>
> > *The baby boy name **Xesus** is pronounced as KahSahS (*). Xesus is **of Hebrew origin** and it is used mainly in the Galician language. **Xesus is a variation of Jesus** (English, Portuguese, Spanish, and German).*
>
> **XESÚS** - http://www.behindthename.com/name/xesu10s
>
> > **GENDER:** *Masculine*
> > **USAGE:** *Galician*
> > **Meaning** - Galician form of *JESUS*, used as a personal name.

That *symbol* John used χξς contains the mark of the beast χ, the mark of the serpent ξ, the monogram for Christos ΧΡΙΣΤΟS - *XS*, and the pictogram χξς for the letters ***XES***. ***XES***us is Greek for ***JES***us which in Latin is the most famous symbol for the name Jesus… the symbol ***IHS***. So χξς is pointing us to IHS which is the monogram for the name "**Jes**us" or χξς : We see below the IHS or χξς symbol with the mark of the beast (the cross) incased within the sun as the very image of sun worship and its god Hesus Horus Krishna (Jesus H. Christ).

χξς association with Zeus

John also used the ONE monogram that could *be associated* with Zeus. Jesus in Latin means "Hail Zeus". In Greek, the first of these three letters used by John χξς also takes the sound of a 'Z' - as in Xenephen or Xylophone. The first and last Greek letters of this formula, may therefore also be referring to the first and last letters of the name '**Zeus**' again pointing to Jesus. Keeping in mind that Constantine named his new god "Jesus" after the god of the Pantheon Zeus as was the custom in pagan Rome. Just like Hebrews used the poetic form of the name of God (Yahu) in contracted sentence names to give glory to Yahuah, so did the Greeks as they ended names and cities using "sous/sus/us" after their own god Ze**us**. Take for example the name of Juli**us** Caesar "Gai**us** Juli**us** Caesar" or the name of the Roman Emperor Constantine who literally created Christianity "Flavi**us** Valeri**us** Aureli**us** Constantin**us** August**us**".

The suffix "**us**" was added to Greek and Roman names to give glory to Ze**us** where Yah or Yahu was added to Hebrew names to give glory to Yahuah.

> *"It is known that the Greek name endings with sus, seus, and sous were attached by the Greeks to names and geographical areas as means to give honor to their supreme deity, Zeus."*
> **Dictionary of Christian Lore and Legend**

What we have learned so far is that out of all the various symbols constructed with the Greek letters of Christos, this **ONE** version χξϛ used by John specifically identifies *Jesus Christ* . This one symbol incorporates the sea serpent ϛ (the beast of the sea), it identifies his mark χ, his monogram *XS*, and a pictogram in English *XES* of his name which is his IHS monogram.

Below is Revelation 13 in its true meaning:

Revelation 13

The Beast out of the Sea

13 The dragon stood on the shore of the sea. And **I saw a beast** coming out of the sea (*sea serpent* ϛ)...[17] so that they could not buy or sell unless they had the mark (χ), which is the name of the beast or (rather) the *symbol* of its

name. [18] **This calls for wisdom** (*to discern the Christogram*). Let the person who has (*spiritual*) *eyes to see* reckon up the (*pictogram of the*) *symbol* of the beast *that identifies him*, for it is the *symbol* of a man. That *symbol* is

It should be obvious to the reader why we are warned ***not to add to or subtract from*** His Word. The translators did both in Revelation 13; they subtracted the symbol of Jesus Christ and added the number 666 in its place. This caused confusion and, as Satan so planned, <u>deflects our attention away</u> from his "*son of perdition*". People think "666" is the mark on the forehead when that number has nothing at all to do with the topic. That mark is the "X" symbol or monogram. Now it requires "wisdom and insight" to figure it out due to uninspired translation errors. This is one of the "seals" over the book of Revelation that only now has been broken.

177

They who don't have the mark X could not buy or sell

In Revelation 13:17 we see that those who do not take the mark of Jesus Christ (X) are prohibited from commerce within his realm. Is this referring to some futuristic physical "mark" or biochip in our forehead and hand as is being taught today? Or have we simply overlooked the obvious because we are unwilling to acknowledge the χϛϛ Jesus Christ is the beast and Christianity is the second beast? If we simply take an honest look throughout history, we see that Christianity has outlawed "buying and selling" specifically for all those who do not bow down to the authority of The Pope and accept the specific mark on their forehead X.

The Book of Revelation is misunderstood by many as applying only to the last 7 years of "Tribulation" when in fact is was given 2000 years ago and covers a 2000 year span of Christian dominance. We see below the *Mark of the Beast* is the sign of the Cross X and those who do not have that mark were forbidden to "buy or sell" throughout history and the X is the "seal on the forehead":

Jamieson-Fausset-Brown Bible Commentary

> *the mark, or the name—Greek, "the mark (namely), the name of the beast." The mark may be, as in the case of **the sealing of the saints in the forehead**, not a visible mark, but symbolical of allegiance. So **the sign of the cross** in Popery. The Pope's interdict has often shut out the excommunicate from social and commercial intercourse.*

Clarke's Commentary on the Bible

> *And that no man might buy or sell, save he that had the mark – "If any," observes Bishop Newton,*

*"dissent from the stated and authorized forms (of Christianity); they are condemned and excommunicated as heretics; and in consequence of that they are no longer suffered **to buy or sell**; they are interdicted from traffic and commerce, and all the benefits of civil society.*

Roger Hoveden relates of William the Conqueror,

*that he was so dutiful to the pope that he would not permit any one in his power **to buy or sell** any thing whom he found disobedient to the apostolic see (The Pope).*

The canon of the council of Lateran, under Pope Alexander III.,

*made against the Waldenses and Albigenses, enjoins, upon pain of anathema, that no man presume to entertain or cherish them in his house or land, **or exercise traffic with them** (that do not follow Papal authority).*

The synod of Tours, in France, under the same pope, orders,

*"under the like intermination, that no man should presume to receive or assist them, no, not so much as hold any communion with them, **in selling or buying**; that, being deprived of the comfort of humanity they may be compelled to repent of the error of their way."*

It was ordered by a bull of Pope Martin the Fifth,

*"that no contract should be made with such, and **that they should not follow any business and***

> *merchandise: save he that had the mark; took the oath to be true to the pope, or made a public profession of the Popish religion: or the name of the beast; Papists, so called from the pope"*

> *"In the tenth and eleventh centuries the severity against the excommunicated was carried to so high a pitch, that nobody might come near them, not even their own wives, children, or servants; they forfeited all their natural legal rights and privileges, and were excluded from all kinds of offices."*

Now we know the identity of the first beast χξϛ that it is the "image of a man" we have elevated in our hearts as God incarnate above Yahuah. We actually "invite Jesus into our hearts" and sit him on the throne and sacrifice a pig on Yahuah's altar every Easter! This is **The Abomination of Desolation**… John identified that image of a false messiah by his mark, his monogram, and by a pictogram and the serpent who give this image power and authority.

The second beast is easily identified… it is Christianity. It is the religion that evolved around the first beast χξϛ that causes the Earth to worship χξϛ . Remember that Christianity is the largest religion on Earth. It is the very one that sites on 7 hills etc. and by definition is the "widest gate" being the largest religion on Earth. "The True Way" is the NARROW GATE and very few find it! Simple logic (even without the proof in this book) should have told us the largest religion is not the "chosen few" remnant spoken of in scripture. It is not the "narrow gate" that leads to salvation.

When you insert the true identities of the first and second beast into passages in The Book of Revelation those passages come alive and clearly point to only one religion in the history of humanity… Christianity. The religion that bears no resemblance to that described in The Bible and is a carbon copy of Mystery Babylon.

The First Beast is χ͂ξ͂ς the Second Beast is Christianity

We see in Revelation the rise of the first beast χ͂ξ͂ς (creation of Jesus Christ at the Council of Nicaea) and then a second beast flows forth from the first beast (the religion of Christianity was created around the image of χ͂ξ͂ς Jesus Christ) and causes the entire world to worship the image of the first beast χ͂ξ͂ς Jesus Christ. The very one John identified in Revelation 13 by name... **XES**us (Jesus) using his pictogram, his mark, and his monogram. We are now going to further identify χ͂ξ͂ς Jesus as the Antichrist or first beast; and Christianity as the second beast.

How Rome became the "seat" of the Babylonian Religious Cult

What few people realize is that the religion of Babylon was <u>formally</u> transferred from Babylon to Rome when Rom conquered Babylon. That is why Peter properly identified Rome as Babylon below speaking to the assembly in Rome:

> **1 Peter 5:13**
> She (*the assembly*) who is in Babylon, chosen together with you, sends you her greetings, and so does my son Mark.

The first Roman Pontiff (and every Pope since) is actually the High Priest of Dagon the Dragon which was the "Babylonian Order" of Priests. When Attalus, the Pontiff and King of Pergamos died, in B.C. 133, he bequeathed the headship of the "Babylonian Priesthood" to Rome. When the Etruscans came to Italy from Lydia, (the region of Pergamos), <u>they brought with them the Babylonian religion and rites. They set up a Pontiff who was head of the priesthood.</u> Later the Romans accepted this Pontiff as their civil ruler. ***Julius Caesar was made Pontiff*** of the Etruscan Order in B.C. 74. In B.C. 63, he was made "Supreme Pontiff" of

181

the "Babylonian Order," thus becoming heir to the rights and title of Attalus, Pontiff of Pergamos, who made Rome his heir by will. Thus the first Roman Emperor became the head of the "Babylonian Priesthood," and Rome the successor of Babylon. Each successor to Emperor from that point forward held the title ***Pontifus Maximus*** literally *The High Priest of the Babylonian Cult of Sol Invictus* which was simply another incarnation of Mithraism stemming from the worship of Tammuz in Babylon.

The Pope of Rome now carries forward that High Priesthood as ***Pontiff***. Every fundamental doctrine of Christianity is by Papal decree such as Sunday worship, The Trinity, Easter, Christmas, etc. etc. Yahuah did not command these pagan rituals and not one of these *fundamental doctrines* are "in" the Bible or part of the life of Yahusha the Messiah. The Roman Empire began their **official recognition** of sun worship during the time of Aurelian when he instituted the cult of "Sol Invictus". There is virtually no difference between the cult of Sol Invictus and that of Mithraism or for that matter Catholicism/Christianity they are all later versions of The Mystery Religion of Babylon the Great Whore.

In the year 307 A.D. Emperor Diocletian, a sun worshipper, was involved in the dedication of a temple to Mithra, and he was responsible for the burning of Holy Scripture (the Hebrew originals that is why we don't have any today) which made it possible for later emperors to formulate Christianity. Without the original Hebrew texts the Roman version of the Universal Christo-pagan Mystery Religion was crafted in secret by pagan sun worshippers.

After the rein of Diocletian, the Roman Emperor Constantine (the creator of modern day Christianity) maintained the title "***Pontifus Maximus***" the high priest of paganism, and remained a worshipper of Apollo (Apollo is *Tammuz* in the Greek culture). His coins were inscribed: "SOL INVICTO COMITI", which is interpreted as "Committed to the Invincible Sun" until his death. During his reign, pagan sun worship was blended with the worship of the True Creator (this blending process is called syncretism), and officially titled "Christianity" by the (less than holy) Roman Empire and its' official church the (less than holy) Catholic (universal) Church. Christianity became the catch all "religion" created to assimilate all pagan religions into one.

Cybele, the Phrygian goddess, known to her followers as "the mother of god", was closely related to the worship of Mithra. Just as Mithraism was a man's religion, the worship of Cybele was practiced by women. The priests of Mithra were known as "Fathers" and the Priestesses of Cybele as "Mothers". <u>After baptism into the Mysteries of Mithra, the initiate was marked on the forehead with an X. The sign of the cross formed by the elliptic and the celestial equator was one of the signs of Mithra.</u> Sunday (Deis Solis), the day of the Sun, was considered by Mithraist a sacred day of rest. December 25th (the birthday of Mithra) was celebrated as the birth of the Sun, given birth by the "Queen of Heaven" - "Mother of god". The Mithraists celebrated a mithraic love feast. This feast consisted of loaves of bread decorated with crosses with wine, over which the priest pronounced a mystic formula. Mithra was considered mediator between god and man.

We know Constantine created ***Hesus Horus Krishna*** as the god of the Roman Empire and that over time that name evolved into Jesus H. Christ. We know Constantine created a totally new religion around Jesus Christ that abolished ***The Law of Yahuah***, changed the festival of Yahuah, changed the Sabbath of Yahuah, changed the Passover of Yahuah, and changed the name of the Messiah to a pagan name giving glory to Zeus. Christianity then, as the second beast, <u>caused</u> humanity to worship χξς through brute force (the inquisition) and forced ignorance (the Dark Ages) as Christianity conquered the globe. I know this is very hard to believe but keep reading the evidence is overwhelming.

The First and Second Beast of Revelation

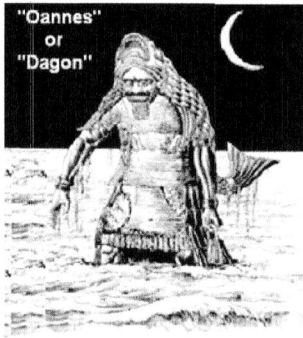

The first beast is "the beast of the sea" which is a reference to Dagon the Fish God who later became known as the sea serpent then the dragon. This is the "god" of the Babylonian Religion. Dagon pictured "coming out of the sea".

The first High Priest of Dagon was the King of Babylon Nimrod. The High Priests of Dagon wore a large gutted fish over their head letting the body drape over them like a cape.

As the religion spread throughout cultures the garments of the High Priest of Dagon the Dragon evolved as well into the Mitre Hat with a long cape instead of an actual gutted fish. The Pope today remains the Pontiff and High Priest of Dagon the Dragon:

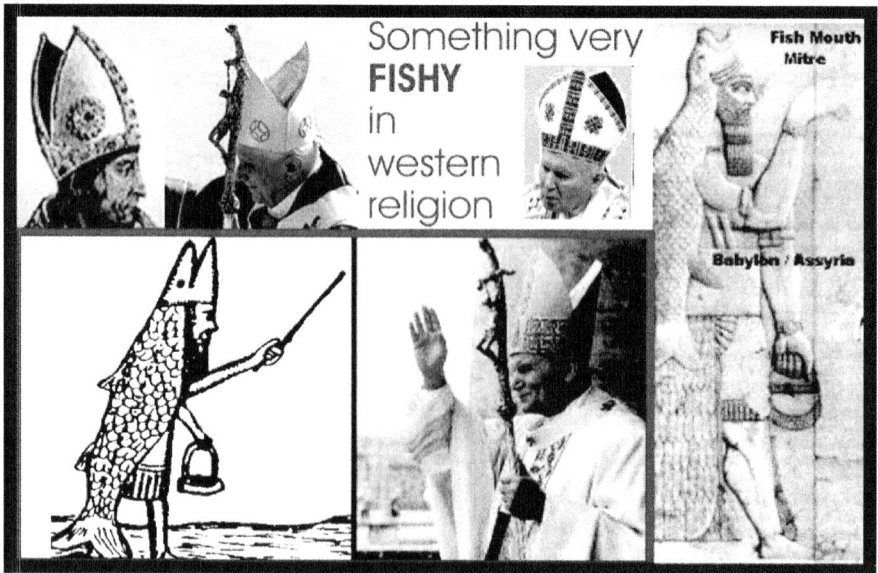

It is Dagon the Dragon that gives the High Priest of Dagon known as The Pope of Rome his earthly throne and power. Yahusha is the KING not these pagan priests who literally sit themselves on his thrown claiming they are literally Yahusha on Earth (Vicor of Christ). Yahusha as a man never assumed such power and authority, he emptied himself of his position as Prince of Israel and took on the form of a poor servant.

The Pope is described in great detail in the book of Revelation:

Revelation 17:4

And the woman was *arrayed in purple and scarlet colour*, and decked with gold and precious stones and pearls, *having a golden cup in her hand* full of abominations and filthiness of her fornication

We see the religion that grew up around ΧŞŞ Jesus Christ is literally the worship of the dragon or Dagon. It is *The Beast of the Earth* described in the Book of Daniel and the Book of Revelation. The most abominable "beast" to Yahuah is **the pig**. So "beast" in The Torah would be the pig. The name Jesus can be broken down into its Latin prefix *Je* which means "*earth*" and Latin suffix *sus*

185

which means *"pig"*. Remember Jesus is a LATIN name not Hebrew and is a contracted sentence name or contraction in the same way as Yahusha is in Hebrew. Yahusha is a contraction of **Yahu**ah and Yah**sha** meaning Yahuah is our deliverer or savior. Jesus is just such a contacted Latin name:

WEBSTER'S NEW WORLD DICTIONARY

Je – *Earth personified*

GE (je,ge) GAEA;GAIA GAEA (Jee),Noun. [Gr.Gaia derived from "Ge", earth] in **Greek mythology the earth personified** *as a goddess ,mother of Uranus the Titans,etc,* ***MOTHER EARTH****: identified by the Romans with Tellus: also Gala,Ge. GEO (jeo,jee)*

Sus – *Pig, a contemptible person*

sus *N 3 1 NOM S C T, sus N 3 1 VOC S C T sus, suis swine; hog,* ***pig****, sow; 2:* ***a contemptible person*** *(Webster's Seventh New Collegate Dictionary)*

No wonder the Greeks renamed Yahusha to Jesus. The name Jesus literally cries out

"the contemptible person whose image is the abominable pig (beast) of the earth"

giving glory to their pagan gods. Jesus is the god of the second beast in Revelation 13 - χξς . Easter is the sacrifice of a pig to Nimrod who became the sungod Ba'al which means The LORD and later Zeus as he is known in Greek Pantheon.

Chapter 13
The meaning behind Revelation Chapter 13

Below I am going to break down Revelation Chapter 13 in detail. If you haven't read my books **Babylon – The Religion of the Beast** and **Christianity – The Great Deception** now would be a very good time to review them as I prove all of this in great detail!

Revelation 13

13 The dragon (_Dagon the Fish God, later known as the Dragon_**) stood on the shore of the sea. And I saw a beast coming out of the sea**

NOTE: _Babylon worshipped Dagon known as **the Dragon coming out of the sea** who is half fish and half man. Rev. 13:1 is a direct reference to Dagon, see Chapter 1 in my book **Christianity – The Great Deception**. Below I provide a small excerpt. Dagon evolved over time and many cultures as follows ending up as the Dragon:_

DAGON

Dagon (fish god)= Neptune= Posiedon (who carries the Trident) = Satan = Leviathan = Taneen = dragon = seraph

man creates everything
in his own image

The Pope is the High Priest of Dagon and the Spirit of

The Religious "Mitre" Hat From Babylon | The Priest of Ancient "Dagon" Fish Worship

Dagon (the dragon) is the Spirit behind Christianity.

This "Dragon in the Sea or DAGON the Fish God" called leviathan in scripture was worshipped by those in ancient Babylon and associated with Nimrod the first High Priest of Dagon. Worship of Dagon was passed down after Yahuah confused the languages and scattered humanity across the globe. It was this religion that was prevalent and continued at the time Rome destroyed Jerusalem. It was this religion of Dagon that permeated the high priestly ranks of paganism and was the foundation of The Catholic Church which even today continues to wear the priestly garments of Dagon the Dragon:

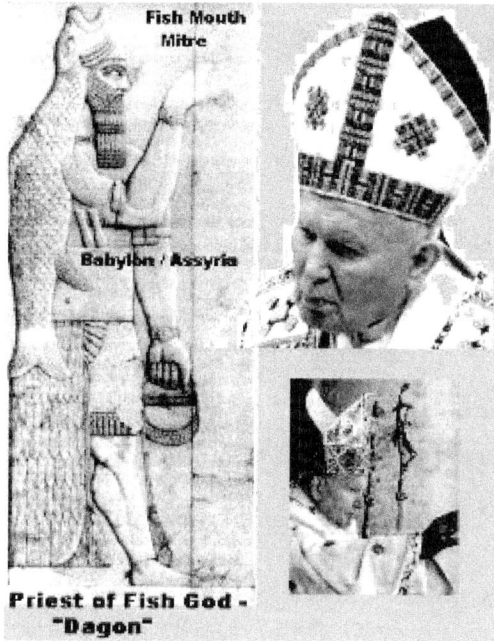

Fish Mouth Mitre

Babylon / Assyria

Priest of Fish God - "Dagon"

Revelation 17:4

*And the woman was **arrayed in purple and scarlet colour**, and decked with gold and precious stones and pearls, **having a golden cup in her hand** full of abominations and filthiness of her fornication*

Now back to Revelation Chapter 13

[2] ... **The dragon (***Religion of Dagon, The Pope is The High Priest of Dagon***) gave the beast his power and his throne and great authority...** [4]

People worshiped the dragon (*unknowingly*) **because he had given authority to the beast (***by worshipping Jesus you are actually worshipping the dragon and following the commands of The High Priest of Dagon, the Popes. Every fundamental doctrine of all Christian Churches are by Papal Decree and contradict Yahuah's commands***), and they also worshiped the beast (**$\chi\xi\varsigma$ *a.k.a Jesus Christ*) **and asked, "Who is like the beast? Who can wage war against it?"**

[5] **The beast (**$\chi\xi\varsigma$ *Jesus Christ*) **was given a mouth (***The Pope is Jesus' representative on Earth known as The Vicar of Christ and speaks for him***)**

to utter proud words (*that he has abolished The Law, he changed The Sabbath to his holy day Sunday, he changed Passover to Easter*) **and blasphemies** (that $\chi\xi\varsigma$ *Jesus Christ* is god incarnate) **and to exercise its authority for <u>forty-two months</u>.**

http://en.wikipedia.org/wiki/Day-year_principle

42 months using the day/year principle was fulfilled when The Papacy ascended to power as the Head of State. 1260-year period should commence with 755 AD, the actual year Pepin the Short invaded Lombard territory, resulting in the Pope's elevation from a subject of the Byzantine Empire to an independent head of state. The Donation of Pepin, which first occurred in 754 and again in 756 gave to the Pope temporal power of the Papal States. However, his introductory comments on Daniel 7 added 756 as an alternative commencement date. Based on this, 19th century commentators anticipate the end of the Papacy in 2016.

[6] It opened its mouth to blaspheme Yahuah (*saying Yahuah is not One but a Trinity and Jesus is God incarnate*)**, and to slander His name** (*calling Yahuah "the LORD" which is Ba'al. Changing the name of Yahusha which means "Yahuah is Salvation" to Jesus which means Hail Zeus*) **and his dwelling place** (*made Rome the eternal city of God in place of Jerusalem*) **and those who live in**

heaven (*declared all those who keep Yahuah's festivals are an anathema* **). ⁷ It was given power to wage war against Yahuah's holy people and to conquer them (***the inquisition, the Roman/Jewish Wars, the Crusades, the Holocaust etc.***). And it was given authority over every tribe, people, language and nation (***Rome conquered the known world and so now has Christianity***). ⁸ All inhabitants of the earth will (***eventually***) worship the beast (***Christianity is the largest religion on Earth***)—all whose names have not been written in the Passover Lamb's book of life, the Passover Lamb who was slain from the creation of the world (***those who put their faith in the Easter Pig and not in The Passover Lamb***)**

The Beast (SUS) out of the Earth (JE)… i.e. the JE (Earthly) SUS (Pig) χξς

11 Then I saw another beast (*Christianity***), coming out of the earth (***Je in Latin is "earth" or "mother earth". SUS is pig, Jesus is the pig (beast) of the earth. The second beast is a religion flowing forth from* χξς *aka Jesus Christ***). He (***the leader of***

this religion, The Pope the False Prophet of) **had two horns like a lamb (***Miter Hat***), but he spoke like a dragon (***the Spirit of Dagon***).**

Note: It is Dagon <u>the Dragon</u> that is ***the spiritual*** source behind the Catholic/Christian Churches based in Rome (any Sunday / Christmas / Easter / Trinity / Jesus church).

The Pope and priesthood of the Catholic Church are the high priest and priesthood of Dagon the Dragon in disguise (not a very good disguise actually):

12 He (*the Pope, High Priest of Christianity*) **exercised all the authority** (*Vicar of Christ*) **of the first beast** (Χ͠ϚϚ *Jesus Christ*) **on his behalf** (<u>*Authority of the Church*</u> *doctrine*)**, and** (*Christianity the second beast*) **made the earth and its inhabitants worship the first beast** (Χ͠ϚϚ *Jesus Christ*)**, whose fatal wound had been healed** (*the beast* Χ͠ϚϚ *Χ͠ϚϚ is based on the Messiah's life but it is a FALSE image of Yahusha*)**. 13 And he** (*second beast/Christianity*) **performed great and miraculous signs, even causing fire to come down from heaven to earth in full view of men. 14 <u>Because of the signs</u>** (*only a wicked and adulterous generation require a "sign"* **Matt. 16:4**) **he** (*Christianity*) **was given power to do on behalf of the first beast** (Χ͠ϚϚ *Jesus Christ*)**, he** (*Christianity*) **<u>deceived the inhabitants of the earth</u>** (*the largest religion on Earth is Christianity*)**. He** (*Christianity*) **ordered them** (humanity) **to <u>set up an image</u>** (*of* Χ͠ϚϚ *in The Temple of Yahuah – we "invite Jesus into our hearts"*)**) in honor of the beast** (Χ͠ϚϚ *Jesus Christ*) **who was**

wounded by the sword and yet lived (*another reference to Jesus being a false image of Yahusha in order to deceive*). **15 He** (*second Beast/Christianity*) **was given power <u>to give breath</u>** (*Spirit of the False messiah and Spirit of Error*) **to <u>the image</u> of the first beast (** Ҳ꙼ꙅ *Jesus Christ*)**, so that it could speak** (*to the hearts of man*) **and <u>cause all who refused to worship *the image*</u> (of** Ҳ꙼ꙅ *Jesus Christ*) <u>**to be killed**</u>

(*Christianity is <u>by a long shot the bloodiest religion in the history of the world</u> killing literally millions upon millions of people since its inception. Killing multitudes of millions in "Jesus Name"*)**.**

16 It (*Christianity*) **also forced all people, great and small, rich and poor, free and slave, to receive a mark (** 𝒳 **) on their right hands or on their foreheads,**

> <u>NOTE</u>: It was ordered by a bull of Pope Martin the Fifth,
>
> *"that no contract should be made with such, and <u>**that they should not follow any business and merchandise**</u>: <u>**save he that had the mark**</u>; took the*

197

oath to be true to the pope, or made a public profession of the Popish religion: or the name of the beast; Papists, so called from the pope"

The Mark of Jesus is "X" as in X-mas which is drawn on the forehead of Christians while reciting "in the name of the Father, the Son, and the Holy Ghost" and sealing the mind with Trinity:

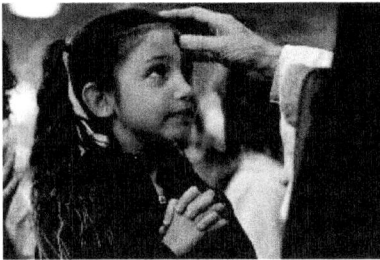

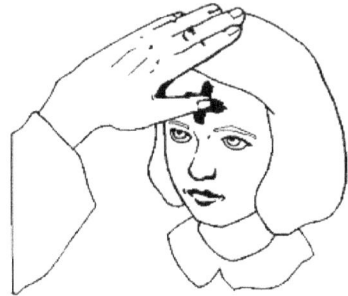

[17] so that they could not buy or sell unless they had the mark (𝒳),

Bishop Newton,

"dissent from the stated and authorized forms (of Christianity); they are condemned and excommunicated as heretics; and in consequence of that they are no longer suffered to buy or sell; they are interdicted from traffic and commerce, and all the benefits of civil society.

which is the name of the beast; or the symbol of its name. [18] This calls for wisdom (*spiritual understanding of the mind***). Let**

the person who has (*spiritual*) **insight** *reckon up* **the symbol of the beast** *that identifies him,* **for it is the symbol of a man. That symbol is** Χξϛ (*mark, monogram, pictogram*) (*the symbol uniquely identifies both Jesus and Christ it is the only symbol that is used for* <u>XESus,</u> *and* <u>Christos,</u> *and* <u>the serpent</u> ξ).

In verse 15 above

"He (*second Beast/Christianity*) **was given power** *to give breath* (*Spirit of the False messiah and Spirit of Error*) **to the image of the first beast, so that it could speak** (*to the hearts of man*) **and** **cause all who refused** **to worship the image** (of Χξϛ Jesus Christ) **to be killed** (*die the second death and not receive eternal life*)**"**

We see a reference to "give breath" which is the Greek word *pneuma* which means "breath" translated as Spirit. In the next chapter I will clearly defined *The Spirit of the False messiah* and *The Spirit of Error*.

Summary

The identity of The False messiah was hidden by Yahuah and not given to either the prophet Daniel or the prophet John.

Revelation 10

4 Now when the seven thunders uttered their voices, I was about to **write; but I heard a voice from heaven saying to me, "Seal up the things which the seven thunders uttered, and do not write them."** *And they were <u>hidden until the very end of time</u> and given to men of Wisdom risen up for the appointed time.*

Daniel 12

4 But you, Daniel, roll up and seal the words of the scroll *until the time of the end...* **8** I heard, but I did not understand. So I asked, "My lord, what will the outcome of all this be?" **9** He replied, *"Go your way, Daniel, because the words are rolled up and sealed until the time of the end.*

Yahuah's plan still required thousands of years to play out. If the mysteries explained in this chapter were revealed too early then Jesus Christ would never have been able to deceive the Earth as Yahuah had planned. Once you unravel these mysteries in the books of Daniel and Revelation then Jesus Christ stands out as the <u>only</u> "image of a man" in human history that qualifies as the False messiah. The symbol John saw is written all over Christianity as the symbol that identifies Jesus Christ specifically.

No other man or "image of a man" in history or the future can fulfill these prophetic words.

Chapter 14

The Spirit of Truth and the Spirit of Error

Introduction

The Bible clearly defines men who know Yahuah and men who do not. Men who have been chosen by Yahuah declare His Shema and have the protective seal over the frontal lobe of their brain that enables them to recognize deception. I cover this seal in detail in my book **The Kingdom of Yahuah**. These men proclaim Yahuah as the only true God and understand that Yahusha was the fulfillment of the prophesied human Messiah and that he came "in the flesh, fully human in every way".

Uninspired men who deny The Shema twist scripture to say what it does not say creating 'another gospel' in the process based on what The Bible defines as *The Spirit of Error*. The men who do not know Yahuah teach a false gospel which is no gospel at all. *The Spirit of the Antichrist* is what is behind their teaching as they themselves are filled with *The Spirit of Error*. In this chapter I am going to clearly define those spirits as they are defined in scripture as we learn that *The Spirit of Error* leads to *The Transgression of Desolation* while *The Spirit of the False messiah* leads *to The Abomination of Desolation*!

A Gospel that is no gospel at all

This twisting of scripture, denying The Shama, and worshipping a man above Yahuah began early as Paul took the gospel (Sabbath/Shema/Salvation through Passover/The Law on our hearts) to a pagan Roman Empire:

> ### Galatians 1
> 1 Paul, an apostle—sent not from men nor by a man, but Yahusha the Messiah and Yahuah the Father, who raised him from the dead (clearly Yahusha was not GOD!) — [2] and all the brothers and sisters with me, [3] Grace and peace to you from Yahuah our Father and the King Yahusha who is the Messiah, [4] who gave himself for our sins to rescue us

from the present evil age, according to the will of our Yahuah and Father, [5] to whom (Yahuah) be glory for ever and ever.

[6] I am astonished that you are so quickly deserting Yahuah who called you to live in ***The Yahushaic Covenant*** and are turning to a different gospel (Trinity/Jesus/Sunday/Easter/Christmas/no law)— [7] **which is really no gospel at all**. Evidently some people are throwing you into confusion (with the incarnation, name changes, abolishing The Law, changing The Sabbath and Festivals of Yahuah for pagan rituals, etc.) and are trying to pervert the gospel of Yahusha the Messiah (Yahuah / Yahusha / Sabbath / Passover / Festivals of Yahuah / The Law). [8] But even if we or an angel from heaven should preach a gospel other than the one we preached to you, let them be under Yahuah' curse! [9] As we have already said, so now I say again: If anybody is preaching to you a gospel other than what you accepted, let them be under Yahuah's curse!

You see, pagan Rome had been twisting everything Paul said into a pagan lie that fit their current religion The Cult of Sol Invictus. They did not understand the gospel of Yahusha as it was foolishness to them so they simply adapted it to their current religion:

1 Corinthians 1

[20] Where *is* the wise? Where *is* the scribe? Where *is* the disputer of this age? Has not Yahuah made foolish the wisdom of this world? [21] For since, in the wisdom of Yahuah, the world (*the Roman Empire*) through wisdom did not know Yahuah, it pleased Yahuah through the foolishness of the message preached to save those who believe. [22] For Jews request a sign, and Greeks seek after wisdom (*through philosophy*); [23] but we preach the Passover sacrifice of Yahusha (*they did not keep or teach Easter*), to the Jews a stumbling block and **to the Greeks**

foolishness, [24] but to those who are called, both Jews and Greeks, the Messiah is the power of Yahuah and the wisdom of Yahuah. [25] Because the foolishness of Yahuah is wiser than men, and the weakness of Yahuah (if there is such a thing) is stronger than men

2 Peter 3
[14] Therefore, beloved, looking forward to these things, be diligent to be found by Him in peace, without spot and blameless; [15] and consider *that* the longsuffering of our King *is* salvation—as also our beloved brother Paul, according to the wisdom given to him, has written to you, [16] as also in all his letters, speaking in them of these things, in which are some things hard to understand, **which untaught and unstable people** *twist* **to their own destruction, as they do also the rest of the Scriptures**.

Those who twist scripture are those who deny The Shema and are filled with The Spirit of Error, which I will define in this chapter, and their teachings lead to false doctrines. These false doctrines are then passed on from generation to generation until now! Yahuah said this would be the case at the end when He calls His elect from the 4 corners of Eath:

Jeremiah 16:19
O Yahuah, my strength, and my fortress, and my refuge in the day of affliction, the Gentiles shall come unto thee from the ends of the earth, and shall say, Surely our fathers have inherited lies, vanity, and *things* wherein *there is* no profit.

Each false doctrine is built upon "sound bites" not sound doctrine. Sound bite doctrine is always false doctrine and always contradicts explicit scripture. It is where you take a "sound bite" or rather one verse of scripture out of context and combine it with other "sound bite" of scripture also taken out of context and build an implied doctrine from those "out of context sound bites". That doctrine is implied and not specifically and explicitly stated in The Bible. The Trinity is the apposing mark of Babylon and a total contradiction

204

of Yahuah's mark (The Shema). The Trinity is just such an implied doctrine coming about in the 4th century A.D. after many centuries and much controversy as we will learn in this book series.

Yahusha and all the early church knew absolutely NOTHING about a Trinity!

> The *Encyclopedia Britannica,* Micropedia Volume 11, page 928, gives us the following facts about the trinity.

>> *TRINITY, in Christian doctrine, the unity of Father, Son, and Holy Spirit as three persons in one Godhead. Neither the word Trinity nor the explicit doctrine appears in the New Testament, nor did Jesus and his followers intend to contradict the Shema in the Old Testament: "Hear, O Israel: Yahuah our God is one God" (Deuteronomy 6:4). The doctrine of The Trinity developed gradually over several centuries and through many controversies.*

> **The Religions of Ancient Greece and Babylonia**, by A. H. Sayce. pages 229-230, clearly tells us that the Greek philosophical ideas were developed in Alexandria, Egypt from the pagan mystery religions. We see that these pagan philosophies have literally formed and are the foundation of our current modern religion of Christianity!

>> *Many of the theories of Egyptian religion, modified and transformed no doubt, have penetrated into the theology of Christian Europe, and form, as it were, part of the woof in the web of modern religious thought. Christian theology was largely organized and nurtured in the schools of Alexandria, and Alexandria was not only the meeting place of East and West, it was also the place where the decrepit theology of Egypt was revivified by contact with the*

*speculative philosophy of Greece. **Perhaps,
however, the indebtedness of Christian theological
theory to ancient Egyptian dogma is nowhere
more striking than in the doctrine of the Trinity.**
The very terms used of it by Christian theologians
meet us again in the inscriptions and papyri of
Egypt. Originally the trinity was a triad like those
we find in Babylonian mythology. The triad
consisted of a divine father, wife, and son. The
father became the son and the son the father
through all time, and of both alike the mother was
but another form.*

The Outline of History, by H. G. Wells. page 307, tells us:

*The trinity consisted of the god Serapis
(=Osiris+Apis), the goddess Isis (=Hathor, the
cow-moon goddess), and the child-god Horus. In
one way or another almost every other god was
identified with one or other of these three aspects of
the one god, even the sun god Mithras of the
Persians. And they were each other; they were
three, but they were also one.*

By believing in The Trinity you are denying the "seal of Yahuah"
over your mind which is the declaration that He is ONE and there
is no other Gods beside Him. That is what the REAL Messiah
believed:

Mark 12:28-34 - ***The Greatest Commandment***
28 One of the teachers of the law came and heard them
debating. Noticing that Yahusha had given them a good
answer, he asked him, "Of all the commandments, which is
the most important?" 29 "The most important one,"
answered Yahusha, "is this: 'Hear, O Israel: Yahuah our
God, *Yahuah is one God*.... [32] "Well said, teacher," the man
replied. "You are right in saying that Yahuah is one God
and there is no other God but Him.

The belief in The Trinity prevents your mind from being sealed by Yahuah. That is why there are so many different "interpretations" floating around within Christianity and so many denominations. The teachers and pastors in the Christian Church are filled with The Spirit of Error not having the "seal" of Yahuah over their mind they simply do not understand His Word. Keep in mind when the Bible was originally written, 80% of the Bible was prophetic. The Bible is not subject to "private interpretation"…

2 Peter 1
[20] Knowing this first: that no prophecy of the scripture is of any private interpretation.

There is only one true way of interpreting the Bible and that is letting scripture define scripture with the GREATEST commandment foremost on your mind to guide you that Yahuah is not a Trinity. Line upon line, precept upon precept as it builds little by little to reveal the full truth in context of the entire revelation of Yahuah.

Isaiah 28
[9] "Whom will he teach knowledge? And whom will he make to understand the message? Those *just* weaned from milk? Those *just* drawn from the breasts? [10] For precept *must be* upon precept, precept upon precept, Line upon line, line upon line, Here a little, there a little."

Isaiah foretold above what is the case today within the Christian Church. We have men just weaned from milk, just drawn from the breast, lost in their understanding trying to teach The Word of Yahuah. These are your Christian teachers, they are unskilled in the Word of Righteousness which is The Torah and Prophets (true Scripture) because they have abolished it! True teachers are not those who "go to school to be one" and have human degrees from human institution (which simply means they know how to deceive the masses very well in false doctrines).

Those men simply pass down the lies from the previous

generation. Speaking of those coming out of the nations at the end (that would be us) Jeremiah foretold exactly what we face today:

> **Jeremiah 16**
> O Yahuah, my strength, and my fortress, and my refuge in the day of affliction, the Gentiles shall come unto thee from the ends of the earth, and shall say, Surely our fathers have inherited lies, vanity, and *doctrines* wherein *there is* no profit.

That is what is taught to our so called "men of God" in seminaries and Bible colleges today. These men are not called by Yahuah by the laying on of hands of His prophets and anointed to teach; they set out under their own strength to teach that which they don't have the insight and understanding to teach. They just repeat the same false doctrines, pagan rituals, pagan names, and lies not found in scripture. They teach lies for money as it is their career. Make no mistake, if you are a good motivational speaker and salesman there is a lot of money in teaching the lies in Christianity. It is a very lucrative career option. These men, however, do not know Yahuah and have elevated Jesus as God and therefore have the Spirit of the Antichrist and are filled with The Spirit of Error not The Spirit of Truth.

The Test of Knowing Yahuah – *If you keep His Commandments and have the Spirit of Truth*

There is a specific test in scripture to know if you actually know the Creator Yahuah. That test is; do you have The Spirit of Truth in you that teaches you to keep His Commandments and walk by the example set by Yahusha who was a Torah obedient Jew:

> **1 John 2**
> [3] Now by this we know that we know Yahuah, if we keep His commandments. [4] He who says, "I know Yahuah," and does not keep His commandments, is a liar, and the (*spirit of*) truth is not in him. [5] But whoever keeps Yahuah's

commandments, truly the love of Yahuah is perfected in him. By this we know that we are in covenant with Yahusha. [6] He who says he abides in covenant with Yahusha ought himself also to walk just as Yahusha walked *(in obedience to The Law of Yahuah)*. [7] Brethren *(in the family of Yahuah)*, I write no new commandment to you, but an old commandment which you have had from the beginning *(The Torah)*. The old commandment is the word which you heard from the beginning *(the Commandments of Yahuah)*. [8] Again, a new commandment I write to you *(here is the only new command in **The Yahushaic Covenant**)*, which **Spirit of loving obedience** *(The Spirit of Truth)* is true in Yahusha and in you,

Ezekiel 36: 26, 27

I will give you a new heart *(for my Law and write my Law on it)* and put a new spirit *(of loving obedience)* in you; I will remove from you your heart of stone *(legalistic observance of The Law out of fear of death)* and give you a heart of flesh. And **I will put my Spirit of Truth in you and move you to follow my decrees and be careful to keep my laws**.

Continuing with 1 John 2…

because the darkness *(of The Law with active decrees that demand our death)* is passing away, and the true light *(Grace i.e. the decrees in the Law are covered by the blood of the lamb)* is already shining. *(Yahusha defeated The Law of Sin and Death and we now live in freedom through The Law of the Spirit of Life)*

Those who know Yahuah are those who keep His Commandments as they are now written on their hearts. This truth is echoed throughout Scripture from cover to cover.

The Spirit of Error

That Spirit of Truth will lead us to loving obedience to The Law of Yahuah which is written on our hearts.

> ### Ezekiel 36: 26, 27
> I will give you a new heart (*for my Law and write my Law on it*) and put a new spirit (*of loving obedience*) in you; I will remove from you your heart of stone (*legalistic observance of The Law out of fear of death*) and give you a heart of flesh. And **I will put my Spirit of Truth in you and move you to follow my decrees and be careful to keep my laws**.

The Spirit of Error is given to all of those who commit this abomination and elevate the image of ⲭⳅⳃ Jesus in their hearts as God and follow The Lawless One. That **Spirit of Error** is defined as "*abolishing the law*" i.e. do not keep the commandments of Yahuah.

> ### 2 John 7 - Beware of Antichrist Deceivers
> 7 For many deceivers have gone out into the world <u>who do not confess Yahusha the Messiah as coming in the flesh</u> (*but rather confess* ⲭⳅⳃ *Jesus is God in the flesh*). **This spirit is a deceiver and an antichrist**. (*The Spirit of the False messiah*) 8 Look to yourselves, that we do not lose those things we worked for, but that we may receive a full reward. 9 Whoever transgresses (***The Law of Yahuah***) and does not abide in the doctrine of the Messiah (*that he did not come to abolish The Law*) does not have (*the Spirit of*) Yahuah (*they have **The Spirit of Error***). He who abides in the doctrine of the Messiah (*that not one Jot or Tittle of The Law has been abolished*) has both the spirit of the Father and the Son. 10 If anyone comes to you and does not bring **this** doctrine (*but brings a Trinitarian lie and teaches unrighteousness as truth see Romans 1:18 that The Law was abolished*), do not receive him into your house nor

greet him; 11 for he who greets him shares in his evil deeds (*breaking of The Law*).

Now that we know that ***The Spirit of the Antichrist*** is the belief in the incarnation and ***The Spirit of Error*** is the belief that χ͞ς͞ς Jesus abolished the law (he is The Lawless One) I want to take a deeper look at The Spirit of the Antichrist χ͞ς͞ς .

Chapter 15
The Spirit of the Antichrist

Introduction

The Spirit of the Antichrist χ§ϛ (or False messiah) is anyone who elevates the image of a man known by his monogram χ§ϛ i.e. Hesus Horus Krishna (Jesus H. Christ) in their hearts as God above Yahuah! They will be given over by Yahuah <u>to believe a lie</u>.

That very lie is that The Law has been abolished by the incarnation of God in the image χ§ϛ of Jesus H. Christ. ***The Spirit of The Antichrist*** is anyone who denies that Yahusha was a mere man (came in the flesh, fully human in every way). "Came in the flesh" is a Jewish Idiom for "born human" to two earthly parents! It does not say "Jesus is God come in the flesh" as you have been told it says. Those who believe that have the Spirit of the False messiah χ§ϛ !

> ### 1 John 4
> 4 Beloved, do not believe every spirit, but test the spirits to see whether they are from Yahuah, because many false prophets have gone out into the world (*claiming to be the incarnation of God*). [2] By this you know the Spirit of Yahuah: every spirit that confesses that Messiah Yahusha has 'come in the flesh' (*which is an idiom for born to both a man and woman as it "the way of the flesh", fully human in every way*) is from Yahuah;

> ### Hebrews 2
> [17] For this reason he had to be made like them, <u>fully human in every way</u>, in order that he might become a merciful and faithful high priest in service to Yahuah.

> [3] and every spirit that does not confess Yahusha has come in the flesh (*but believes in the pagan myth of incarnation that he is a demi-god*) is not from Yahuah; **this is the *spirit* of the antichrist** (*The False messiah is an image of a man named* χ§ϛ *Jesus Christ who is worshipped as Yahuah in*

the flesh. See below, Yahusha denied the incarnation totally) …

Philippians 2

[5] Let this understanding be in you which was also in Yahusha the Messiah, [6] though he was in the (*human*) image (*reflection*) of Yahuah, **did not count equality with Yahuah a thing to be grasped**, [7] but made himself of no reputation, taking the form of a bondservant, *and* coming in the likeness of (*all*) men (*he was human not God*).

Continuing with **1 John 4**

6 We are of Yahuah. He who knows Yahuah hears us; he who is not of Yahuah does not hear us. <u>By this we know the spirit of truth and the spirit of error</u>… [12] **No one has seen Yahuah at any time!** (*Because Yahusha is not Yahuah in the flesh or a demi-god*).

There is the definition of The Spirit of Truth; those who know Yahusha was born human in every way and chosen as a High Priest to Yahuah from among men and understand that NO ONE HAS SEEN Yahuah because He cannot be found in the form of a man:

Numbers 23:19

Yahuah is not human, that he should lie, not a human being, that he should change his mind. Does he speak and then not act? Does he promise and not fulfill.

Hosea 11

9 I will not carry out my fierce anger, nor will I devastate Ephraim again. For I am Yahuah, and not a man

The Spirit of the Antichrist is anyone who elevates the **false** image of Yahusha (known as Jesus) into a God in their heart believing in the incarnation. That is *The Spirit of The Antichrist because all pagan Christs were demi-gods*. Those with The Spirit of the Antichrist will be given over to a depraved mind which is *The Spirit of Error*.

Christianity has created a human false image of Yahusha named "Jesus Christ" who is <u>the false messiah</u> and taught "Jesus" as being <u>the incarnation of God</u> and literally "God in the flesh". Please refer to my book *The Antichrist Revealed!* where I expose Jesus Christ as the Antichrist or false messiah.

I demonstrate in that book that John identified the names "Jesus" and "Christ" in Revelation Chapter 13. John used the mark, the monogram, and the Christogram of Jesus Christ when he wrote down the Greek symbol χξϛ

> <u>Revelation</u> 13 - The **Beast out of the Sea**
> 13 The dragon stood on the shore of the sea. And **I saw a beast** coming out of the sea (*sea serpent* ξ)…[17] so that they could not buy or sell unless they had the mark (χ), <u>which is the name of the beast</u> or (*rather*) the *symbol* of its name. [18] This calls for *wisdom* (*to discern the Christogram IHS/Christ*). Let the person who has (*spiritual*) *eyes to see* reckon up the (*pictogram HES/JES of the*) *symbol* of the beast *that identifies him (by name Jesus Christ)*, for it is the *symbol* of a man. That *symbol* is χξϛ

The Spirit of the False messiah

Anyone who elevates the image of a man known by his monogram χξϛ i.e. Hesus Horus Krishna (Jesus H. Christ) in their hearts as God above Yahuah will be given over by Yahuah to believe a lie. That very lie is that The Law has been abolished by the incarnation of God in the image χξϛ of Jesus H. Christ. *The Spirit of the False messiah* is anyone who denies that Yahusha was a mere man (came in the flesh):

> **1 John 4**
> 4 Beloved, do not believe every spirit, but test the spirits to see whether they are from Yahuah, because many false prophets have gone out into the world (*claiming to be the incarnation of God*). [2] By this you know the Spirit of Yahuah: every spirit that confesses that Messiah Yahusha has come in the flesh (*a man*) is from Yahuah; [3] and every spirit that does not confess Yahusha has come in the flesh (*but says Jesus* χξϛ *is God or The Trinity*) is not from Yahuah; **this is the *spirit* of the antichrist** (*or False*

messiah. The False messiah is an image χξς *of a man worshipped above Yahuah as God*) ... [12] No one has seen Yahuah at any time! (*Because Yahusha is not Yahuah in the flesh or a demi-God*).

Anyone who elevates the **false** image of Yahusha (known as χξς Jesus Christ) into a God in their heart believing in the incarnation has ***The Spirit of the False messiah***...

Romans 1
[21] because, although they knew Yahuah (*by what He created*), they did not glorify *Yahuah* as God, nor were thankful, but became futile in their thoughts, and **their foolish hearts were darkened** (*by Yahuah who gave them over to The Spirit of the False messiah*). [22] Professing to be wise, they became fools (*filled with The Spirit of Error*), [23] and changed the glory of the incorruptible God (*Yahuah who cannot die*) into **an image** χξς made like (*a*) corruptible man (*who died. Jesus is a false image of Yahusha who was executed.*)

The doctrine of Incarnation is the Spirit of the False messiah χξς

In this chapter I will address the reality of who Yahusha really was and confront the "sound bites" of scripture taken totally out of context by Christianity and in many cases <u>mistranslated</u> into English that are the foundation of this abomination called "incarnation". Incarnated man-gods are the identifying feature of all pagan religions dating back to Babylon. The Creator revealed Himself in The Bible as the one and only God not a Trinity, bi-entity, or god-man savior.

The doctrine of incarnation violates explicit scripture by taking scripture out of context to build a doctrine of man through <u>implication</u>. Yahusha came in the flesh as a man, fully human in every way, was tempted by evil, was not born perfect, and called himself *the son of man* 87 times as he was truly the son of his earthly father Joseph. I'll explain this in detail along with the doctrine of the Virgin Birth in this book as well.

Yahuah, however, declares that He is not a man, He is not 'the son of man', He is invisible Spirit that cannot be contained in the human form or tempted by evil.

Numbers 23:19

Yahuah is not a man, that he should lie (*Yahusha was fully human Hebrews 2:17*); neither the son of man (*Yahusha was called the son of man in the NT 87 times*), that he should repent (*Yahusha was Mikveh'd i.e. baptized by John for repentance, his sin forgiven Zachariah 3:4*).

Hosea 11

9 I will not carry out my fierce anger, nor will I devastate Ephraim again. For I am Yahuah, **and not a man**

1 John 4:1-3; 12

4 Beloved, do not believe every spirit, but test the spirits to see whether they are from Yahuah, because many false prophets have gone out into the world (*claiming to be the incarnation of Yahuah*). ² By this you know the Spirit of Yahuah: every spirit that confesses that Messiah Yahusha has come in the flesh (*a man*) is from Yahuah; ³ and every spirit that does not confess Yahusha has come in the flesh (*but says Yahusha is Yahuah incarnate*) is not from Yahuah; **this is the *spirit* of the antichrist** (*or False messiah. The False messiah is an image of a man worshipped above Yahuah as Yahuah*) …¹² **No one has seen Yahuah at any time** (*because they would die… Exodus 33:20*)!

Colossians 1:15

The Son (*all sons are the image of Yahuah Genesis 1:26,*

218

Psalms 82:6) is the (*human*) image (*reflection/proxy*) of <u>the invisible Yahuah</u>, **the firstborn** (*this is where Yahusha is different from the rest of the sons of Yahuah*) over all (*eternal*) creation.

Given the <u>explicit</u> scripture that is contradicted by the <u>implied</u> doctrine of incarnation... we must in obedience to explicit declarations made by Yahuah abandon the doctrine of "incarnation" as it is **The Spirit of the False messiah**.

That is what we will do in this chapter as we establish Yahusha as the human signatory (representative) to the covenant that bears his name **The Yahushaic Covenant**. Just like Moses was the human representative to the Mosaic Covenant, Adam to the Adamic Covenant, Noah to the Noahic Covenant, Abraham to the Abrahamic Covenant, David to the Davidic Covenant, and so forth.

Let us continue by clearly defining the terms used of Yahusha in **The Yahushaic Covenant** and clarify the relationship between Yahuah and Yahusha.

The relationship between Yahuah and Yahusha

The relationship between Yahuah and Yahusha is not difficult to understand. It is that of Father and Son. The same relationship we have with our Father in Heaven. Yahuah is not only the Father of Yahusha but He is the Father of all His sons in the same way. In the physical shadow of earthly father and son; and the spiritual parallel that shadow represents... the father and son are not the same "being". One begets the other. One is an "image" of the other. Yahuah has always revealed Himself as our Father as Yahusha too confirmed. We see that Yahuah is Yahusha's God and Father as Yahusha is no different that you and I:

Luke 11
[2] He said to them, "When you pray, say: "'**Father**,

219

hallowed be **your** name, **your** kingdom come."

1 Peter 1

To Yahuah's elect, exiles (*lost sheep of The House of Israel*) scattered throughout the provinces of Pontus, Galatia, Cappadocia, Asia and Bithynia, [2] who have been chosen according to the foreknowledge of Yahuah **the Father**... [3] Praise be to *the God* and *Father* of our King Yahusha the Messiah! In His (*our Father's*) great mercy He (*our Father*) has given us new birth into a living hope through the resurrection of Yahusha the Messiah from the dead (*he was a corruptible man who died, raised incorruptible by Yahuah who is God*), [4] and into <u>an inheritance</u> that can never perish, spoil or fade. This inheritance (*of Yahuah the Father to His sons*) is kept in *The Kingdom of Yahuah* for you.

1 Corinthians 8

[5] For even if there are so-called Gods, whether in heaven or on earth (as indeed there are many "Gods" and many "lords"), [6] yet for us there is but **one God, the Father Yahuah**, from whom all things came and for whom we live; and there is but one King, Yahusha the Messiah, for whom all things were created (*by Yahuah as an inheritance*) and through whom we live (*in covenant being covered by the blood of the lamb*).

We see above Paul explain the simple reality of Yahuah being the Father and Yahusha being Yahuah's first born son through resurrection. We see Yahuah give all His sons the inheritance which is held for us in *The Kingdom of Yahuah.* We see Sha'ul (Paul) praying that the true knowledge that Yahuah alone is our God and Father be revealed to His chosen:

Ephesians 1

[17] I keep asking that *the God* of our King the Messiah Yahusha, **the glorious** Father *(Paul declares The Shema)*, may give you the Spirit of wisdom and revelation, so that

you may know him (*your Father*) better. [18] I pray that the eyes of your heart may be enlightened in order that you may know the hope to which He (*your Father*) has called you (*as His son*), the riches of His (*your Father's*) glorious inheritance in His (*Yahuah's*) holy people, [19] and His (*Yahuah's*) incomparably great power toward us who believe.

(*now Paul changes subject to Yahusha*) That power is the same as the mighty strength [20] He (*your Father Yahuah*) exerted when He (*the Father*) raised Yahusha (*His son*) from the dead and seated Yahusha at His (*Father's*) right hand in **The Kingdom of Yahuah,** [21] far above all rule and authority, power and dominion, and every name that is invoked, not only in the present age but also in the one to come. [22] And Yahuah (*the Father*) placed all things under his (*son Yahusha's*) feet and **appointed** (*Yahusha wasn't born with it, he had to earn it*) Yahusha to be head over everything for the sons of Yahuah, [23] which is His (*Yahuah's*) body (*Temple*), the fullness of Him (*Yahuah*) who fills everything in every way.

All of the references to Father and son in the Bible are in context of the Hebraic mindset of the place and authority of the father over his household. It is within this context that Yahusha as the son and "perfect image" of the Father is understood. Yahusha is the proxy of His Father Yahuah as His instrument and assistant as Yahusha is seated at his Father Yahuah's right hand. The Universe is still the property of The Creator; the responsibility to govern it is given over to His sons.

Unger's Bible Dictionary, page 347

> *2. PLACE AND AUTHORITY. The position and authority of the father as the head of the family is <u>expressly assumed</u> and <u>sanctioned</u> in Scripture <u>as a likeness of that of the Almighty over his creatures</u>. It lies, of course, at the root of that so-called*

*patriarchal government (Gen. 3:16; I Cor. 11:3)...
While the father lived, he continued to represent the
whole family, the property was held in his name,
and all was under his superintendence and
control... The children, and even the grandchildren,
continued under the roof of the father ... The
property of the soil, the power of judgment, the civil
rights belonged to him only, and his sons were
merely his instruments and assistants...*

The Son of Yahuah; what does that mean?

The Scriptures generally describe all things relative to Yahuah using human terms i.e. physical to spiritual parallels. This literary technique, called anthropomorphism, is one of the primary means used in Scripture to lead us into an understanding of Yahuah.

Anthropomorphism:

> **Attribution of human characteristics to nonhumans: the attribution of a human form, human characteristics, or human behavior to nonhuman things such as deities in mythology and animals in children's stories.**

This is commonly done in the Scriptures with reference to Yahuah's "heart", "hand", "finger", etc. Attributes of personality such as "jealousy", "will" or "desire", "hate", and many other "emotions" are anthropomorphic. The reason for this technique is so that mankind, who is incapable of truly understanding the infinite Almighty, can grasp the basics of what is actually beyond our ability to understand.

The reference to Yahusha as Yahuah's "son" is one of these techniques to help us understand the relationship between Yahuah and all His chosen. It may surprise most Christians to realize Yahusha was not the ONLY "son of Yahuah" mentioned in Scripture! Solomon was referred to as Yahuah's son:

2 Samuel 7:14
[14] **I will be his father, and he shall be my son.** If he commits iniquity, I will chasten him with the rod of men, and with the stripes of the children of men.

Proof of this referring to Solomon is found in 1 Chronicles 28:6

1 Chronicles 28:6 (KJV)

[6] And he (*Yahuah*) said unto me (*David*), **Solomon** thy son, he shall build my house and my courts: for **I have chosen him to be my son,** and I will be his father.

It should be noted that verses regarding Solomon (and many other passages) are sometimes assumed to refer to Messiah. I agree, however, I feel the correct standard method of interpreting Scripture is to first look for a DIRECT application first and then the spiritual parallel. Continuing with the sons of Yahuah mentioned in Scripture... **The entire nation of Israel is referred to as Yahuah's sons!**

Exodus 4:22

[22] And thou shalt say unto Pharaoh, Thus saith Yahuah, **Israel is my son**, even my firstborn:

Adam was the "son of Yahuah" also.

Luke 3:38

[38] Which was the son of Enos, which was the son of Seth, which was the son of **Adam, which was the son of Yahuah.**

Of course, all TRUE followers of Yahuah's Holy instructions (Torah) are called sons of Yahuah. Therefore **it is SCRIPTURALLY accurate to say there is reference to well over 600,000 "sons of Yahuah" in the Bible, since Israel is Yahuah's son.** This is something Traditional Christian teachers hate to have revealed.

Exodus 12:37

[37] And the children of Israel journeyed from Rameses to Succoth, about **six hundred thousand** on foot that were men, beside children.

The term "son of Yahuah" is **always** used in an anthropomorphic sense to refer to Yahuah's representative(s) i.e. "sons". Of course, as **THE** greatest, most obedient, and most exalted of ALL of Yahuah's representatives, Yahusha, is indeed, **THE** son of Yahuah.

Yahusha is the ultimate *tsadik*, or pious and righteous servant and representative of Yahuah. Also, of course, if one wishes to accept the virgin birth, Yahusha can be further seen as being a "son" of Yahuah. However, as I show when I address the Virgin Birth, the teaching that Yahusha was conceived of a virgin outside of the seed of Joseph actually threatens Yahusha's claim to being the Messiah and disqualifies him. So there is nothing within the context of the virgin birth that makes Yahusha any more of a son of Yahuah than any other men.

The New Testament actually suggests to us the exact moment that Yahusha was "begotten" of Yahuah! Yes, believe it or not, we can know the precise time of the <u>final</u> "begetting" of Messiah Yahusha. In Acts 13 Paul is speaking to those gathered in a synagogue of Antioch. In this single chapter the entire gospel is summed up in one of the most concise presentations to be found anywhere in Scripture. During this sermon Paul reveals the exact moment that Yahusha's "begotten" status was completed.

> **Acts 13:33**
> [33] Yahuah has fulfilled this for us their children, in that He has risen up Yahusha. As it is also written in the second Psalm: **"You are My Son, Today I have begotten You."**

The Psalm to which he refers is:

> **Psalm 2:7**
> [7] I will declare the decree: Yahuah has said to Me, **"You are My Son, Today I have begotten You."**

Therefore, we see the SCRIPTURAL day Yahusha was begotten - THE SCRIPTURAL DAY HE <u>FULLY</u> BECAME THE SON OF Yahuah. It was on the day of his resurrection. This, also, is how he became the "first fruits of the resurrection" and the full "son of Yahuah." The announcement of the angel Gabriel in Luke presents

225

in the future tense the fact that Yahusha "<u>will be called</u> the Son of the Highest." This prophecy from Gabriel had its fulfillment at Yahusha's resurrection.

Luke 1:32

[32] He will be great, and **will be called** the Son of the Highest; and Yahuah will give Him the throne of His father David.

As usual, I appeal to common sense. One that is "begotten" is not eternal but has a beginning; therefore, the "begotten one" (Yahusha) cannot be the "Eternal One," Yahuah. I would argue that the resurrection is the <u>COMPLETION of the PROCESS of Yahusha's **becoming** Yahuah's Son.</u> He was already His Son as defined previously in terms of being Yahuah's perfect representative, agent, servant, and anointed One. For the reasons I will explain in the virgin birth section, I do not accept the virgin birth as it is taught. I consider it to be an attempt by those lead by the spirit of error (spirit of the False messiah) to usurp Yahusha's rightful claim to be the Messiah of Israel. The doctrine of the Virgin Birth eliminates the primary importance of him being of the literal seed of David **through the father** as scripture demands!

Upon his resurrection, Messiah Yahusha became **THE** Son of the Highest due to the fact that Yahusha was the very first man EVER resurrected to eternal life!

Romans 1:3-4

[3] concerning His Son Yahusha the Messiah our King, who was born of <u>the seed of David</u> (*the son of man, the man Joseph*) <u>according to the flesh</u> (*the "seed" of Yahuah is Spirit not flesh*), [4] and **declared to be the Son of Yahuah** with power according to *the Spirit of holiness* (*this is the "seed" of Yahuah*), **by the resurrection from the dead.**

Yahusha prior to resurrection was 100% human the product of the seed of Joseph and Mary like all humans; fully human in every way as Paul put it. Yahuah has no physical seed and in no way "impregnated Mary" as is taught. That is a pagan philosophy out of Babylon (Ishtar being impregnated with Tammuz by the rays of the sungod Ba'al). If Yahusha was in any way the Spiritual Son of Yahuah while on Earth, <u>death would have been impossibility</u>. The fact Yahusha died is the "nail in the coffin" of the false doctrine of Incarnation.

> ### Luke 20:36
> [36] for they <u>cannot even die</u> anymore, because they are like angels, and are **sons of Yahuah, being sons of the resurrection.**

Again we see above that you are not fully begotten by the seed of Yahuah until resurrection. Only once your body is transposed to *The Kingdom of Yahuah* through resurrection are you truly begotten by Yahuah in His full image as an eternal son.

Only Begotten Son; what does that mean?

The Christian Church teaches that 'Jesus' was the only *begotten* son on Earth through a divine conception to Mary. This is not the birth indicated by the word *begotten*; the term *begotten* is not referring to Yahusha's human birth to Joseph and Mary; but rather his birth into full sonship to Yahuah. It is referring to Yahusha's resurrection into *The Kingdom of Yahuah.* Whenever speaking of his human birth in the flesh the word *born* is used not *begotten*.

The term "only *begotten* son" simply means Yahusha *at this time and until such time as the first resurrection* is the ONLY begotten (resurrected) son of Yahuah in the family. Yahusha was the FIRST FRUITS (resurrected the first fruits of many more to come on the first Sabbath after Passover then his presenting the first fruits of the resurrection to the Father the next day on the Feast of First Fruits).

1 Corinthians 15

20 But now the Messiah has been risen (*by Yahuah*) from the dead, *and* **has become** (*the firstborn son upon resurrection not birth to Mary/Joseph*) **the first fruits** of those who have fallen asleep. 21 For since by man (*Adam*) *came* death (*The Law of Sin and Death*), by Man (*Yahusha the Second Adam*) also *came* the resurrection of the dead (*The Law of Sin and Death has been defeated*). 22 For as in Adam all die (*being held to account for the decrees in The Law*), even so (*those who abide*) in **The Yahushaic Covenant** shall all be made alive (*begotten by Yahuah as sons through resurrection*). 23 But each one (*of the sons of Yahuah*) in his own order (*after Yahusha, the eldest son*): The Messiah **the first fruits** (*first and only at this point of the sons to be resurrected*), afterward those *who are* in covenant *with Yahuah through Yahusha* at Yahusha's coming (*First Resurrection when the rest of the sons will be begotten*).

You see, the term **_begotten_** is the key. "Begotten of Yahuah" means resurrected birth not human birth. It is specifically talking about ONLY RESURRECTED SON until he returns to resurrect the rest of the family of Yahuah.

Acts 13:33

32 And we declare to you glad tidings—that promise (*that we are gods, sons of the Most High* **Psalm 82:6**) which was made (*by Yahuah*) to the (*fore*) fathers (*we are saved by faith in the promises of Yahuah made to our forefathers*). 33 Yahuah has fulfilled this (*promise of eternal life as literal gods, sons of Yahuah*) for us their children (*children of Abraham/Isaac/Jacob only*), in that Yahuah has raised up Yahusha (*the promise of eternal life fulfilled*). As it is also written in the second Psalm: **"You are My Son, Today** (*day Yahusha was resurrected*) **I have begotten You."**

Romans 1:3-4 NKJV

[3] concerning His Son Yahusha the Messiah our King, who was <u>born</u> of the seed of David (*both Mary/Joseph*) according to the flesh (*was a human*), [4] and **declared to be the Son of Yahuah** with power according to the Spirit of holiness, **by the resurrection from the dead.**

Yahusha is not the only son, just the only <u>begotten from the grave</u> at this point. Adam and David, and indeed all of us are declared sons of Yahuah. We too, shall be sons of Yahuah, begotten by the same power of the Spirit of Holiness upon resurrection just like Yahusha, <u>brothers</u> to the first born:

Luke 20:36

[36] for they cannot even die anymore, because they are like angels, and are **sons of Yahuah, being sons of the resurrection.**

The distinction between Yahusha and the rest of the sons of Yahuah is that Yahusha is the eldest and heir to all things as the firstborn of the resurrection through inheritance. We too will follow Yahusha and be begotten as sons of Yahuah through resurrection. We will take our place as Priests, Judges, and Kings under the authority of the first born and King of Kings and High Priest...

Matthew 19:28-29

28 Yahusha said to them, "Most assuredly I tell you, that you *who have followed* me, in the "Regeneration" (**Resurrection**) when (*after resurrection*) the *Son of Man* will sit on the throne of his glory, you also will sit on twelve thrones, judging the twelve tribes of Israel.

Revelation 5:10

[10] And hast made us unto our God (*Yahuah*) kings and priests: and we shall reign on the earth.

Romans 8:19

"creation eagerly awaits the revelation of the sons of Yahuah"… vs. 21 "when creation will be set free from slavery and come into the glorious freedom of the sons of Yahuah"

Revelation 21:7

[7] He that overcomes (*death through resurrection*) **shall inherit all things**; and I will be his God, and **he shall be my son**.

We see that all the promises given to Yahusha are also given to us. We too sit on thrones, we too inherit "all things", we too are sons of Yahuah. Yahusha is the first born son through resurrection, the first fruits presented to Yahuah through ascension, and currently the only resurrected human (***only begotten son***). Notice it is all about a family and inheritance.

Colossians 1:

[13] Who (*Yahuah*) hath delivered us from the power of darkness, and hath transposed us into the kingdom of His dear (*firstborn*) Son (*Yahusha*): [14] In whom (*Yahusha*) we have redemption (*to Yahuah*) through his (*Yahusha's*) blood (*that consummated the marriage covenant, we become 'one with Yahuah' as Yahusha was John 17:21*), even the forgiveness of sins (*the decrees in The Law for transgressing Yahuah's commands are covered by the blood of the lamb*): [15] Who (*Yahusha*) is the (*perfect human*) image of the <u>invisible</u> God (*the proxy of Yahuah*), the firstborn (*Feast of First Fruits*) of every (*eternal*) creature.

Paul changes the subject to distinguish Yahuah as the Creator

[16] For by Him (*Yahuah*) were all things created, that are in heaven, and that are in earth, visible (*flesh*) and invisible

(*spirit*), whether they be thrones, or dominions, or principalities, or powers: all things were created by Him (alone ***Isaiah 44:24***), and for him (*for Yahusha as an inheritance*): [17] And He (*the Creator Yahuah*) is before all things (*self existing*), and by Him (*Yahuah*) all things consist.

Paul changes the subject back to Yahusha to distinguish Yahusha as the first born son of Yahuah

[18] And he (*Yahusha*) is the head of the body (*the Temple of Yahuah*), the assembly (*family of Yahuah*): who (*Yahusha*) is the beginning (*of that family*), the firstborn from the dead (*Yahusha was the first to complete the process of training on Earth and be given Eternal Life by Yahuah*); that in all things (*of Yahuah's*) he (*Yahusha*) might have the preeminence (*among the sons of Yahuah*). [19] For it pleased the Father (*of all the sons*) that in him (*Yahusha*) should all fullness (*of deity*) dwell (*that same fullness dwells in us too **Ephesians 3:9***); [20] And (*Yahusha by defeating The Law of Sin and Death*), having made peace (*between the two houses, Remnant Israel*) through the blood of his stake (*by covering the death decrees freeing us from the fear of death that held us captive*), by him (*offering his life as a sacrifice to Yahuah*) to reconcile all things (*Yahuah created*) unto Himself; by (*sacrificing*) him (*self, as the Passover Lamb*), I say, whether they be things in earth, or things in heaven.

Ephesians 1

[1] Paul, an apostle of Messiah Yahusha by the will of Yahuah, to the assembly of sons which are at Ephesus, and to the faithful in (*covenant with*) Messiah Yahusha: [2] Grace be to you, and peace, from Yahuah our Father, and from the King Messiah Yahusha. [3] Blessed be ***the God*** (*declaration of the Shema*) and **Father** of our King Messiah Yahusha (*his is not God incarnate*), who (*Yahuah*) hath blessed us (*his sons*) with all spiritual blessings in ***The Kingdom of***

Yahuah in (*covenant with*) Yahusha: [4] According (*to Yahuah's purpose*) as he (*Yahuah*) hath chosen (*predestined*) us in him (*self*) before the foundation of the world (*through His Plan of Salvation*), that we should be holy and without blame before him (*Yahuah*) in love (*through covenant*): [5] Having predestinated (*according to His Plan of Salvation*) us unto the adoption of children (*Yahuah's plan to beget a family*) by (*the blood sacrifice of*) Messiah Yahusha (*as Passover Lamb*) to himself (*one through marriage covenant*), according to the good pleasure of his (*Yahuah's*) will (*to beget a family of gods to govern His creation*), [6] To the praise of the glory of his (*Yahuah's*) grace, wherein he hath (*through blood sacrifice of Messiah*) made us accepted in the beloved (*family of Yahuah*).

[7] In whom (*through covenant with Messiah Yahusha*) we have redemption (*from the second death, The Passover*) through his blood (*the Passover Lamb*), the forgiveness of sins (*decrees covered for transgression of Law*), according to the riches of his (*Yahuah's*) grace; [8] Wherein (*covenant with Yahusha*) He (*Yahuah*) hath abounded toward us (*unlimited Grace by accepting Yahusha's sacrifice to cover the death decrees in The Law*) in all wisdom and prudence;

[9] Having made known unto us the mystery of his will (*to beget a family*), according to his (*Yahuah's*) good pleasure which he (*Yahuah*) hath purposed (*predestined to create*) in himself (*as the Father*): [10] That in the dispensation of the fullness of times (*as foretold by His prophets*) he (*Yahuah*) might gather together in one (*through the covenant of marriage, the two shall become one*) all things in (*covenant with the*) Messiah, both which are in heaven, and which are on earth; even in him(*self, Yahuah will reconcile creation through the sacrifice of His Son*):

[11] In whom (*the first born Son, Messiah Yahusha*) also we

(*too*) have obtained an inheritance (*as sons of God, we inherit the Universe*), being predestinated according to the purpose of Yahuah (*to govern creation through a family of gods*) who works all things after the counsel of his (*Yahuah's*) own will: [12] That we (*sons of God*) should be the praise of his (*Yahuah's*) glory, who first trusted in Yahusha the Messiah. [13] In whom (*Yahusha*) you also trusted (*was the Messiah*), after that you heard the word of truth (*that we too are sons of God*), the gospel of your salvation (*purchased through the blood sacrifice of Yahusha to consummate the covenant of marriage whereby we are ONE with Yahuah*): in whom (*covenant with Yahusha*) also after that you believed, that you were sealed (*on your forehead with The Shema*) with that holy Spirit of promise, [14] Which is the earnest (*guarantee*) of our (*future*) **inheritance** (*as sons of God*) until the redemption (*transposition to **The Kingdom of Yahuah** *) of the purchased possession (*when we'll be begotten gods, sons of Yahuah like Yahusha was upon resurrection*), unto the praise of his glory.

….

[17] I keep asking that ***the God** of our King the Messiah Yahusha* (*Yahuah is the God and Father of Yahusha in the exact same way He is our God and Father **John 20:17**),* **the glorious Father**, may give you the Spirit of wisdom (that *incarnation is a lie*) and revelation (*that Yahusha was no different than you and I*), so that you may know him (your Father) better (*by not worshipping Jesus as God*). [18] I pray that the eyes of your heart may be enlightened in order that you may know the hope to which he (*your Father*) has called you (*as His son*), the riches of his (*your Father's*) glorious inheritance in his (*Yahuah's*) holy people, [19] and his (*Yahuah's*) incomparably great power for us who believe. That power **is the same** (*no difference between Yahusha and the rest of the sons, Yahusha is not god incarnate*) as the mighty strength [20] he (*your Father*

233

Yahuah) exerted when he (*the Father*) raised Yahusha (*His first born son*) from the dead and seated Yahusha at his (*Father's*) right hand (*they are not the same being*) in **The Kingdom of Yahuah** , [21] far above all rule and authority, power and dominion, and every name that is invoked, not only in the present age but also in the one to come. [22] And Yahuah (*the Father*) placed all things under his (*son Yahusha's*) feet and **appointed him** (*he had to earn it*) to be head over everything for sons of Yahuah, [23] which is his (*Yahuah's*) body (*Temple*), the fullness of him (*Yahuah*) who fills everything in every way.

There really isn't much I can add to that. Paul did an outstanding job of explaining exactly what Yahuah set out to do and where Yahusha fits in and where, we the rest of His sons, are destined within the Plan of Yahuah. Yahusha was not a "god-man" and not the incarnation of Yahuah, that is a pagan concept born in Babylon and the fundamental doctrine of all pagan religions.

Yahusha is the first human to complete the process of perfection and the first human to be resurrected from the grave as a full son of Yahuah. He is the only begotten son of the resurrection at this point. But, he will not always be the only begotten son. There are many more to follow.

Logos and the firstborn of Creation

Yahusha is called the firstborn of Creation. Does this mean that Yahusha was created and existed prior to his human birth? Is this evidence of the doctrine of incarnation? To understand this title for Yahusha we must use *Wisdom* and *Insight* and overcome the pagan philosophy of "Logos" and the physical to spiritual parallel of "light".

It is imperative that we all know what happened when Greeks and Romans took over the faith. We know the Greeks did not

234

understand scripture and twisted it into a lie:

1 Corinthians 1

[20] Where *is* the wise? Where *is* the scribe? Where *is* the disputer of this age? Has not Yahuah made foolish the wisdom of this world? [21] For since, in the wisdom of Yahuah, the world (*the Roman Empire*) through wisdom did not know Yahuah, it pleased Yahuah through the foolishness of the message preached to save those who believe. [22] For Jews request a sign, and Greeks seek after wisdom (*through philosophy*); [23] but we preach the Passover sacrifice of Yahusha, to the Jews a stumbling block and **to the Greeks foolishness**, [24] but to those who are called, both Jews and Greeks, the Messiah is the power of Yahuah and the wisdom of Yahuah. [25] Because the foolishness of Yahuah is wiser than men, and the weakness of Yahuah (*if there is such a thing*) is stronger than men.

2 Peter 3

[14] Therefore, beloved, looking forward to these things, be diligent to be found by Him in peace, without spot and blameless; [15] and consider *that* the longsuffering of our King *is* salvation—as also our beloved brother Paul, according to the wisdom given to him, has written to you, [16] as also in all his letters, speaking in them of these things, in which are some things hard to understand, **which untaught and unstable *people* twist to their own destruction, as *they do* also the rest of the Scriptures**.

We say that the Hebrew texts and the Gospel and all the Hebrew names were "Hellenized" not realizing what that means. That word does not just mean the Hebrew texts were translated into Greek and Latin. What Hellenized literally means is that the polytheistic religion of the Greeks was merged into the texts and the text altered to be "Greek appropriate" so the pagans could be assimilated into the one world religion called Christianity. Hellenism is Greek paganism. Everyone should fully understand what happened during this time in history. The Truth of Yahuah was merged with pagan Hellenism through syncretism. We see below that nothing changed with Hellenism and that the same gods continued to be worshipped until 300 CE. This is when Constantine brought everything under one pagan religion called Christianity:

http://en.wikipedia.org/wiki/Hellenistic_religion

Hellenistic religion

From Wikipedia, the free encyclopedia

> Hellenistic religion is any of the various systems of beliefs and practices of the people who lived under the influence of ancient Greek culture during the Hellenistic period and the Roman Empire (c. 300 BCE **to 300 CE**). **There was much continuity in Hellenistic religion: the Greek gods continued to be worshipped, and the same rites were practiced as before**.

We call this assimilation of Greek Hellenism *to be Hellenized*. We know that the pagan Greek religion (Hellenism) overtook the truth of Yahuah and the resulting religion is now called Christianity:

http://en.wikipedia.org/wiki/Hellenization

Hellenization

From Wikipedia, the free encyclopedia

> The twentieth century witnessed a lively debate over the extent of Hellenization in the Levant and particularly among the ancient Palestinian Jews that has continued until today. The Judaism of the diaspora was thought to have succumbed thoroughly to its influences. Bultmann thus argued that **Christianity arose almost completely within those Hellenistic confines and**

236

**should be read against that background
as opposed to a more traditional
(Palestinian) Jewish background**

I want to firmly establish this historical fact because "Logos" was one of those philosophical ideas of Hellenism that was incorporated into the texts and the texts were altered by the Greek and Hellenized Jews who translated it.

In order to justify the false doctrine of "pre-existence" or the "incarnation" that Yahusha pre-existed with Yahuah and was co-creator and in fact was God! Christianity quotes John Chapter 1:

John 1
1 In the beginning was the Word, and the Word was with God, and the Word was God. [2] He was with God in the beginning. [3] Through him all things were made; without him nothing was made that has been made. [4] In him was life, and that life was the light of all mankind. [5] The light shines in the darkness, and the darkness has not overcome it.

[6] There was a man sent from God whose name was John. [7] He came as a witness to testify concerning that light, so that through him all might believe. [8] He himself was not the light; he came only as a witness to the light.

[9] The true light that gives light to everyone was coming into the world. [10] He was in the world, and though the world was made through him, the world did not recognize him. [11] He came to that which was his own, but his own did not receive him. [12] Yet to all who did receive him, to those who believed in his name, he gave the right to become children of God— [13] children born not of natural descent, nor of human decision or a husband's will, but born of God.

[14] The Word became flesh and made his dwelling among us. We have seen his glory, the glory of the one and only Son, who came from the Father, full of grace and truth.

[15] (John testified concerning him. He cried out, saying, "This is the one I spoke about when I said, 'He who comes after me has surpassed me because he was before me.'") [16] Out of his fullness we have all received grace in place of grace already given. [17] For The Law was given through Moses; grace and truth came through Jesus Christ. [18] No one has ever seen God, but the one and only Son, who is himself God and is in closest relationship with the Father, has made him known.

All the modern translation like the NIV above are uninspired Hellenized translations giving preference to Greek mythology not the Hebrew mindset. Let us define terms and then correct the modern Hellenized translations with the intent and mindset of John who was a Hebrew Jew not a Greek philosopher.

"Sound Bites" vs. Sound Teaching

The doctrine of "pre-existence", "Logos", and the "Incarnation" are very good examples of taking scripture out of context. Taking scriptural "sound bites" and stringing them all together out of context to create an implied doctrine. These doctrines are always easy to identify because they violate clear explicate doctrine (sound doctrine). Anytime an implied doctrine is formulated that contradicts explicit scriptures we must reject that doctrine as our "understanding" is flawed.

Let's look closer at how the doctrine evolved that Yahusha is literally the "Word" or "Divine Logos" of YAHUAH that became flesh used to justify incarnation. Is Yahusha literally the "Word" or is Yahusha the fulfillment of YAHUAH's Word from the beginning. There is a big difference.

Logos a pagan philosophy

As you can see, the entire doctrine of incarnation that lead to the acceptance of the pagan Babylonian Trinity through syncretism did not come about until 4 centuries after Yahusha lived and died. That false doctrine that Yahusha is literally "Logos" and not the fulfillment of YAHUAH's predestined plan evolved in the 4th Century through the "*tradition and reasoning*" under the influence of pagan Greek philosophers such as Plato...

> ***The Abingdon Dictionary of Living Religions***, page 767, tells us:

> > TRINITY (Ch). The Dogma, formulated authoritatively in fourth century church Councils, that Christians worship one God in three persons (Father, Son, Holy Spirit) and one substance. Under pressure to explain to a hostile Roman world how Christians counted themselves monotheists, Christian apologists (notably Justin Martyr, d. 165) **combined Johannine and Stoic-Platonic understanding of the term Logos** ("Reason," or "Word") in order to maintain that the Son was both God's own self-expression and a being distinct from him.

So we read above The Trinity was justified not through the Word of Yahuah (because it cannot be) it was justified using Hellenism or the "combined Johannine and Stoic Platonic" pagan philosophy of the term "Logos".

We read below that the term *logos* was defined by Christians according to the interpretations of pagan influenced philosophers in order to promote a false pagan God-savior:

> *Encyclopedia Britannica*, Volume 7, page 449.

> *LOGOS (Greek:"word, "reason, or plan"), plural logoi, in* **Greek philosophy and theology**, *the divine reason implicit in the cosmos, ordering it and giving it form and meaning.* **Though the concept defined by the term logos is found in Greek, Indian, Egyptian, and Persian philosophical and theological systems**, *it became particularly significant in Christian writings and doctrines to describe or define the role of Jesus Christ as the principle of God active in the creation and the continuation structuring of the cosmos and in revealing the divine plan of salvation to man.* *It thus underlies the basic Christian doctrine of the pre-existence of Jesus...* **The identification of Jesus with the logos was further developed in the early church but more on the basis of Greek philosophical ideas than on Old Testament motifs**.

The concept of Logos was based on **Greek philosophical ideas** not on any prophecy or Old Testament "motifs" or Hebrew understanding at all. It is and remains a pagan philosophy of Hellenism.

The Religions of Ancient Greece and Babylonia clearly tells us that the Greek philosophical ideas were developed in Alexandria, Egypt from the pagan Babylonian mystery religions. These ideas pertaining to the meaning of *Logos* penetrated as a result of modern religious thought through the philosophy of Greece and Egypt. It was through syncretism that we have the word "*Logos*" or "Word" written in our English Bibles instead of "*The Plan of Yahuah*":

> The Religions of Ancient Greece and Babylonia, by A. H. Sayce. pages 229-230

> *Many of the theories of Egyptian religion, modified and transformed no doubt, have penetrated into the theology of Christian Europe, and form, as it were,*

part of the woof in the web of modern religious thought. Christian theology was largely organized and nurtured in the schools of Alexandria, and Alexandria was not only the meeting place of East and West, it was also the place where the decrepit theology of Egypt was revivified by contact with the speculative philosophy of Greece. Perhaps, however, <u>the indebtedness of Christian theological theory to ancient Egyptian dogma is nowhere more striking than in the doctrine of the Trinity</u>. The very terms used of it by Christian theologians meet us again in the inscriptions and papyri of Egypt. **Originally the trinity was a triad like those we find in Babylonian mythology**. *The triad consisted of a divine father, wife, and son. The father became the son and the son the father through all time, and of both alike the mother was but another form.*

It is from the pagan mystery religions that the Greek philosophers developed the idea of *Logos*:

<u>The New International Dictionary of New Testament Theology</u>, Volume 3, page 1085

Among the systems offering an explanation of the world in terms of the **logos**, <u>*there are the Mystery Religions*</u>. *These cultic communities did not see their task as lying in the communication of knowledge of a scientific nature, but of mysteries to their initiates who strove for purification in the recurrent enactment of sacred actions. The Foundation for these cultic actions was Sacred Text. Among them were the cults of Dionysus, the Pytha-goreans, and the Orphic Mysteries. By means of these cults, non Greek thought, such as in the Isis-Osiris Mysteries, which Osiris* **the logos** <u>**created by Isis is the spiritual image of the world**</u>. <u>**Similarly in the cult of Hermes**</u>, *Hermes informed* *his son Tat in the Sacred Text belonging to the cult, how by God's mercy, he became **logos**, and thus a son of God. <u>As such, he (Hermes) brought regulation and form into world</u>, but himself remained a mediating being between God and matter, on one side, and God and man on the other. **The logos** <u>can also, however, appear as the son of Hermes, resulting in a triple (trinity) gradation: God (who is Zeus), Son (Hermes), and LOGOS (this is what they believed in ROME and this is where we get our false doctrine of incarnation from).</u>*

Now back to John Chapter 1 where this pagan philosophy of "Logos" was mistranslated into our English Bibles by uninspired Hellenized translators.

John 1
1 In the beginning was the Word, and the Word was with God, and the Word was God. [2] He was with God in the beginning. [3] Through him all things were made; without him nothing was made that has been made. [4] In him was life, and that life was the light of all mankind. [5] The light shines in the darkness, and the darkness has not overcome it.

The word "**word**" in these verses comes from the Greek word **logos**. The pagan Christians, so eager to promote the pagan Trinity and incarnation (The Spirit of the False messiah), attached to the word **every pagan interpretation**. But they deliberately ignore the fact that *John was a Hebrew Jew who had nothing to do with pagan Greek philosophy* and the Gospel of John was not written from the pagan mindset associated with the Greek word **logos**. The Gospel of John was written from a Hebraic mindset and most probably penned originally in Hebrew not Greek.

242

The Wycliffe Bible Encyclopedia, Moody Press, Chicago, IL, Volume 2 pages 1046-1047.

> *Many scholars have argued that the apostle John had this philosophical development (of the pagan LOGOS) in the back of his mind when he wrote the prologue to his Gospel and that he actually tried to impart some of these (pagan) concepts. For a long time many have contended that the background of the fourth Gospel was essentially Hellenistic rather than Hebraic. In dealing with such an assertion we may note that studies in the Dead Sea scrolls have tended to confirm the traditional conservative position that the cultural orientation of **the Gospel of John was Hebraic**. Moreover, we must observe that John was a simple fisherman from Palestine. ... **there is no evidence that he imbibed any Greek pagan philosophical orientation in John Chapter 1**. If he intended to be philosophical in the first few verses, he certainly was not anywhere else. We may argue **that John used the word "logos." in its ordinary meaning**.*

This source admits that John used this word in its ordinary meaning in the Hebraic mindset. They further admit that John's writings were Hebraic not Greek which means the actual word John used was the Hebrew word *dabar* not the Greek word *logos*.

The *Encyclopedia Judaica* admits that the style of most of the writings in The New Testament is, in fact, Hebraic. The Greek versions we have today of The New Testament are later Hellenized versions translated from earlier Hebrew original versions that were most likely burned after the council of Nicea. So "*logos*" is a mistranslation; the original version of John Chapter 1 used the Hebrew word *debar*.

The *Encyclopedia Judaica*, Volume 12, page 1060

THE LANGUAGE OF THE NEW TESTAMENT.

Although the language of the New Testament, in the form that it exists today, is Greek, two earlier influences are still discernible.

*(1) THE INFLUENCE OF **THE ARAMAIC-HEBREW ORIGINALS**. Because most of the authors were Jewish Nazarenes, they spoke, for the most part, **Aramaic, and some also mishnaic Hebrew**. This influence, which was detectable particularly in the original versions of Mark and Matthew, survives to some degree in their extant Greek versions and in several of the Epistles as well, including James and Jude.*

(2) THE SEPTUAGINT.
*Since this translation was used by many authors, the New Testament contains not only Aramaic words and phrases, which the disciples heard from Jesus and took care to remember out of reverence for their master (e.g. Talitha Kumi (Mark 5:41), Kum, Rabboni, Eli, Eli (Elohi, Elohi) lama sabachthani (Matt. 27:46; Mark 15:24)), but also expressions and phrases which retain their Hebrew flavor **although they were transmitted through the Greek translation of the Hebrew Bible.***

So, John wrote under inspiration of Yahuah, not of a incarnated pre-existent God-savior, but of the wonderful *Plan of Yahuah* which is what the Hebrew word *debar* implies. *The Anchor Bible* shows us from the Talmud that seven things were in Yahuah's mind showing us what the Hebraic mindset was. His Plan was from the beginning and this plan included the Savior. This is the mindset of John Chapter 1 not the pagan philosophy of "Logos":

The Anchor Bible, Ephesians 1-3, page 111

> *IN THE TALMUD tractate Pesachim 54a; cf. Nedarim 39b, seven things, i.e. the law, repentance, paradise, Gehinnom, the throne of glory, the heavenly sanctuary, <u>and the messiah</u> are not called pre-created, but pre-conceived in (Yahuah's) thoughts.*

Debar vs. Logos

The Gospel of John was originally written in Hebrew then Hellenized into a Greek appropriate book in order to <u>assimilate pagan religions</u> through syncretism. The Hebrew word used by John in John Chapter 1 was *debar*. *A Hebrew and Chaldee Lexicon to the Old Testament* shows us that the Hebrew word *dabar* refers to Yahuah's Plan and His Laws.

A Hebrew and Chaldee Lexicon to the Old Testament, by Julius Furst, page 312

dabar

comp. ἔπος. b) *command, precept, law, regulation* (by words), also taken collect., e. g. of God 2 Sam. 12, 9, of a king

e) *decree, plan, proposal* 2 Sam.

The Interpreter's Dictionary states emphatically that "word" or "logos" or "debar' as used in The Bible is referring to "Yahuah's revealed will or predestined Plan" for mankind.

Speaking of the *debar* i.e. "*word*" of Yahuah, *The Interpreter's Dictionary* states emphatically:

> **The Interpreter's Dictionary** , Volulme 4 pages 870-871
>
> "The **word** of God" (o logof tou qeou) is used of:
>
> (a) the OT law (cf. Mark 7:13=Matt 15:6, where it is contrasted with the tradition of the Jews);
>
> (b) a particular OT passage (cf. John 10:35, referring to Ps. 82:6);
>
> (c) in a more general sense, **God's revealed will, or his whole plan and purpose for mankind** (cf. Luke 11:28; Rom. 9:6; Col. 1:25-27, where it is defined as the "mystery hidden for ages and generations but now manifest to his saints..., which is Christ in you"; Heb. 4:12);

The real meaning of John Chapter 1

What we have learned above is that our English Bibles are modern Hellenized <u>uninspired</u> translations that Hellenized the original Hebraic mindset of the New Testament and promoted pagan philosophical thought. The way John Chapter 1 is translated into English embodies the pagan philosophical ideas from Babylon contained in the Greek word "*Logos*". The real meaning of "*word*" in John Chapter 1 can be found in the Hebrew word "*debar*" which means *the predestined Plan of Yahuah*.

What John had in mind was <u>not</u> the pre-existence of Yahusha, but the pre-conceived Plan of Yahuah. This is the polar opposite of how John 1 is taught today. With all this in mind, let us read the correct translation of the following Scripture.

John 1

1 In the beginning was ***debar*** (*the plan of Yahuah*), and *the plan* was with Yahuah (*and defined His purpose in creation*), and *the plan* was Yahuah's. 2 The same *plan* was in the beginning with Yahuah. 3 All things were done according to the *plan of Yahuah*, and without the *plan of Yahuah* nothing was done, that was done. 4 In *this plan* was (*predestined*) life (*through a human Messiah's sacrifice*), and that life was the light (*revelation*) to mankind. 5 Now that light (*revealed plan to send a human Messiah has been fulfilled in Yahusha*) shines in the darkness, but the darkness does not take hold of it. [6] There was a man sent from Yahuah whose name was John. [7] He came as a witness to testify concerning that light (*that Yahusha was The Passover Lamb of Yahuah*), so that through him all might believe (*that Yahusha was the fulfillment of that plan to send a human Messiah*). [8] He himself was not the light (*the Messiah, many believed John the Baptist was the Messiah*); he came only as a witness to the light (*Yahusha*).

[9] The true light (*Yahusha*) that gives light (reveals The WAY) to everyone was coming into the world (as a man). [10] He (*Yahusha*) was in the world (in the flesh), and though the world was reconciled to Yahuah through him, the world did not recognize him. [11] Yahusha came to that which was his own (the Jews), but his own did not receive him. [12] Yet to all who did receive him (enter into ***The Yahushaic Covenant***), to those who believed in (the covenant that bears) his name (***The Yahushaic Covenant***), he gave the right to become children of God— [13] children born not of natural descent, nor of human decision or a husband's will, but begotten of Yahuah (through resurrection).

[14] The predestined plan of Yahuah (*to send a human Messiah*) became flesh (*was born human and fulfilled in Yahusha*) and made his dwelling among us (*was fully human in every way **Hebrews 2:17***). We have seen Yahuah's glory (*fulfilled in Yahusha*), the glory of the one

and only (*begotten*) Son (*until the first resurrection*), who came from the (*predestined mind or plan of the*) Father, full of grace (*covered the death decrees for our sin*) and truth (*properly teach The Torah as Moses prophesied of him*).

[15] John the Baptist testified concerning him. He cried out, saying, "This is the one I spoke about when I said, 'He who comes after me has surpassed me because he was before me (*in the Plan of Yahuah and given pre-eminence among the sons of Yahuah* **Colossians 1:17**)'") [16] Out of his fullness (*of obedience to The Law*) we have all received grace (*his blood covers the death decrees in the Law*) in place of grace already given. [17] For The Law (*with **active decrees** or **The Law of Sin and Death***) was given through Moses; grace (***the decrees** covered by the blood of the lamb*) and truth (*The Law of the Spirit that leads to life*) came through Yahusha the Messiah. [18] **No one has ever seen God** (*including Yahusha*) but (*however*) the one and only Son (*has come as the light to reveal Yahuah to mankind*), who is himself the (*the perfect human*) image of Yahuah (***Colossians 1:15** – "He is the image of the invisible God, the firstborn over all creation"*) and is in closest relationship (*covenant of marriage, the two shall become one*) with the Father, has made Yahuah's plan (*to procreate a family*) known to us.

That is the meaning and intent in context of scripture and the Hebraic mindset of John Chapter 1. Yahusha was not the incarnation of Yahuah in the flesh nor did Yahusha have any hand in creation. Yahusha is the fulfillment of the Plan of Yahuah to send a human Messiah. Yahusha was the perfect human image of the invisible God. Yahusha is the Proxy of Yahuah. Yahusha is the son of the Father and it is no more complicated than that.

John 14
8 Philip said, "King, show us the Father and that will be enough for us." 9 Yahusha answered: "Don't you know me, Philip, even after I have been among you such a long

time? Anyone who has seen me has seen the (*perfect human image of the invisible*) Father (*NOT the incarnation of God*).

Colossians 1:15

"He is the image of the invisible God, the firstborn over all creation

How can you say, 'Show us the Father'? 10 Don't you believe that I am in (*covenant with*) the Father, and that the Father is in (*covenant with*) me? The words (*of this covenant*) I say to you I do not speak on my own authority (*because he is NOT God incarnate he is the proxy or messenger of Yahuah of **The Yahushaic Covenant**, the human SIGNATORY*). Rather, it is the Father, living in me (*through His Spirit*), who is doing his work. 11 Believe me when I say that I am in (*covenant with*) the Father and the Father is in (*covenant with*) me.

Yahusha and Yahuah are "one" through covenant. All covenants in the Bible are marriage covenants. Within the context of **The Yahushaic Covenant**, Yahusha and Yahuah are one family (one through marriage) that is what the physical to spiritual parallel of human marriage was designed to teach us.

John 10

[25] Yahusha answered them, "I told you (*I was the Messiah*), and you do not believe. The works that I do in My Father's name (*because he is not God incarnate*), they bear witness of Me. [26] But you do not believe, because you are not of My sheep, as I said to you. [27] My sheep hear My voice, and I know them, and they follow my example. [28] And I give them (***The Way to***) eternal life (*by example)*, and they shall never perish (*if they follow my example*); neither shall anyone snatch them out of My hand. [29]

My Father, who has given *them* to Me, is greater than all (*even Yahusha because Yahusha is not a god-man or the incarnation of Yahuah*); and no one is able to snatch *them* out of My Father's hand. [30] I and *My* Father are one (family he is my Father and I am His son and we are one in mind, will, purpose, and Spirit <u>through covenant of Marriage</u>… *the two shall become one*)."

Yahusha came to fulfill the marriage vows (The Law) which were always the foundation of every marriage covenant:

Jeremiah 3
[14] "Return, O backsliding children," says Yahuah "for I am married to you."

Yahusha's beginning

Yahusha's existence began like the existence of all the sons of Yahuah at the point of his human birth to two earthly parents. Yahusha did not "pre-exist" other than in the mind of Yahuah within the context of the Plan of Yahuah.

King David spoke prophetically as though Yahusha was doing the talking in:

Psalm 22:9-10
9 <u>But you took Me from My mother's womb, Yahuah!</u> You made Me trust in You, even from My mother's breast. 10 I was cast upon You from My birth; <u>from My mother's womb, You are My Strength.</u>

The word for word Hebrew translation of **Psalm 22:9-10**, from *The NIV Interlinear Hebrew-English Old Testament* shows the word **from** in these Scriptures:

גֹּלִ · אֶל - יְהֹוָה

Yahweh   in   trust!   (9)

כִּי - אַתָּה   בּוֹ:   חָפֵץ   בִּי   יְצִילֵהוּ

you   yet   (10)   in-him   he-delights   since   let-him-deliver-him

אִמִּי: שְׁדֵי   עַל -   מַבְטִיחִי   מִבֶּטֶן

iother-of-me   breasts-of   at   one-making-trust-me   from-womb

The Dictionary of Old Testament Words for English Readers, says that the Hebrew letter, **mem**, which has been circled in the previous copy, is prefixed to a substantive, which denotes the preposition.

However, it is *The Hebraic Tongue Restored*, by Fabre d'Olivet, which tells us what these prepositions mean when the Hebrew letter **mem** is prefixed.

> *EXTRACTIVE OR PARTITIVE ARTICLE. – The movement which this article expresses, with nouns or actions that it modifies, is that by which a noun or an action is taken for the means, for the instrument, by which they are divided in their essence, or drawn from the midst of several other nouns or similar actions. I render it ordinarily by from, out of, by; with, by means of, among, between, etc.*

The New World Dictionary of the American Language, Second College Edition, gives a complete definition of the word *from* in Hebrew **mem** as *beginning at, starting with, out of.*

The word translated **from** in **Psalm 22:10**, means _beginning at, starting with._ Yahusha is prophetically pictured through King David to say that Yahuah was His strength from the beginning, starting with the point Yahusha Messiah was conceived in His mother's womb. Yahuah was Yahusha's strength. This can only mean one thing: that before Yahusha was in His mother's womb, Yahuah was not His strength, because Yahusha did not yet exist. He had no need of strength. Yahuah was only Yahusha's strength, beginning at, starting with, His mother's womb. The belief that Yahusha had his beginning in the womb as flesh is The Spirit of Yahuah. The denial and belief in the incarnation and Trinity is the Spirit of the False messiah (Jesus Christ).

Divine Emanation? Was Yahusha co-creator?

One of the false doctrines that have evolved in Christianity is that Yahuah created the Universe through "Jesus" by the process called

Merriam-Webster's Dictionary

> #### Emanation
>> b: _the origination of the world by a series of hierarchically descending radiations from the Godhead through intermediate stages to matter_

The doctrine of Divine Emanation from Yahuah through Yahusha implying Yahusha was co-creator is another "implied doctrine" taken from "sound bites" of scripture. The main scripture is the uninspired translation of John Chapter 1:

> 1 In the beginning was the Word, and the Word was with God, and the Word was God. [2] He was with God in the beginning. [3] Through him all things were made; without him nothing was made that has been made.

I have already demonstrated that the true meaning of John Chapter 1 says nothing like the uninspired English modern translations as they used the Babylonian myth associated with "logos" to translate that verse. The real meaning of John Chapter 1 is:

> 1 In the beginning was the *plan of Yahuah*, and *the plan* was with Yahuah *(and defined His purpose in creation)*, and *the plan* was Yahuah's. 2 The same *plan* was in the beginning with Yahuah. 3 All things were done according to the *plan of Yahuah*, and without the *plan of Yahuah* nothing was done, that was done.

Scripture is very clear that Yahuah created the Universe *all alone*, there was no one with Him and that Yahuah alone sits on the throne of Creation. Yahusha sits at the right hand of Yahuah and was only seated there after his resurrection. Yahusha sits on the throne of **The Kingdom of Yahuah** as Yahuah's proxy King to govern Yahuah's creation.

Daniel 7

[13] "I kept looking in the night visions, and behold, with the clouds of heaven One (*Yahusha*) like **a Son of Man** (*born human*) was coming, And He (*Yahusha*) came up to the Ancient of Days (Yahuah *who is everlasting and had no beginning, they are not the same being*) And Yahusha was presented before Yahuah. [14] "And to Him (*Yahusha*) was given (*by Yahuah as an inheritance*) dominion, Glory and a kingdom, that all the peoples, nations and *men of every* language Might **serve** Him (*not worship Yahusha, we serve Yahusha in The Kingdom*). His dominion is an everlasting dominion which will not pass away; and His kingdom is one which will not be destroyed.

Like all "implied doctrines" the false doctrines of The Trinity, The Incarnation, and Divine Emanation violate direct explicate declarations in Scripture. Yahuah alone is Creator:

Isaiah 44

[6] "This is what Yahuah says — *Israel's King (Yahusha had not yet been installed as Yahuah's proxy King) and Redeemer*, Yahuah Almighty: I am the first and I am the last; *apart from me there is no God*.

Isaiah 44

[24] "This is what Yahuah says— your Redeemer, who formed you in the womb: I am Yahuah, *the Maker of all things*, who stretches out the heavens, who spreads out the earth *by myself*.

Isaiah 42

[5] This is what YAHUAH says— **He** who created the heavens and stretched them out, who spread out the earth and all that comes out of it, who gives breath to its people, and life to those who walk on it:

Isaiah 45

[5] I am YAHUAH, **and there is no other**; apart from me there is no God. [7] I form the light and create darkness, I bring prosperity and create disaster; I**, YAHUAH, do all these things**. [12] **It is I who made the earth and created mankind upon it**. **My own hands stretched out the heavens; I marshaled their starry hosts**. [18] For this is what YAHUAH says— **He** who created the heavens, **He** (*alone*) is God; **He** who fashioned and made the earth, **He** founded it; **He** did not create it to be empty, but formed it to be inhabited— **He** says: "**I am YAHUAH, and there is no other** (*God*)."

Isaiah 46

[5] "**To whom will you compare me or count me equal**? To whom will you liken me that we may be compared? [8] "Remember this, fix it in mind, take it to heart, you rebels. [9] Remember the former things, those of long ago; **I am God, and there is no other**; **I am God, and there is none like me**. [10] I make known the end from the beginning, from

ancient times, what is still to come. I say: **My purpose** will stand, and I will do all that I please.

Yahuah makes it crystal clear that He alone is The Creator and He alone sits on *The Throne of Creation*. Yes, Yahuah is *The Creator* and He did it all alone. Despite all the rhetoric from the Christian Church about "the Trinity" and "divine emanation", "Divine Logos", and so forth... Yahuah cleared it up. He did it by Himself. There was no one with Him.

Did Yahusha accept worship as the incarnated God?

One of the misconceptions taught in the Christian Church to "prove" that Yahusha was Yahuah in the flesh and establishes the pagan doctrines of The Trinity and Incarnation is that Yahusha accepted worship as a deity. Therefore, by implication (implied doctrine), he was Yahuah in the flesh. We need to employ just a little bit of common sense here.

The issue at hand is "Glory" which Yahuah declares that He alone is wise and to Him alone belongs "glory, majesty, dominion, and power"

> **Jude 1:25**
> 25 to Yahuah Our Savior, who alone is wise, be glory and majesty, dominion and power, both now and forever.

Yahusha agreed:

> **Matthew 19:16-17**
> 16 Behold, one came to him and said, "Good teacher, what good thing shall I do, that I may have eternal life?" 17 He said to him, "Why do you call me good? No one is good but one, that is, Yahuah. But if you want to enter into life, keep the commandments of Yahuah."

John 17:3
Now this is eternal life: that they know you Yahuah, **the only true God**, and (*are in covenant with*) Yahusha the Messiah, whom you have sent (*as the mediator of that covenant*).

Matthew 4:10
Yahusha said to him, "Away from me, Satan! For it is written: **'Worship Yahuah your God, and serve Him only**.'"

Mark 12:29
"The most commandment," answered Yahusha, "is this: 'Hear, O Israel: Yahuah our God, Yahuah is one.

Wonderful Counselor, *Mighty God*, *Everlasting Father*, Prince of Peace

Another misquoted passage of scripture to promote the incarnation is found in Isaiah. The confusion comes in because Yahuah through inheritance gave dominion, power, and authority by extension to Yahusha His son and proxy after Yahusha's resurrection. The confusion is created by the fact that there are two thrones as I have stated before:

Revelation 5:13

[13] And I heard every creature which is in heaven and on the earth, and under the earth and such as are in the sea, and all that are in them, saying, "Blessing and honor and glory and power be unto Him (Yahuah) that sitteth upon the throne of Creation, and unto the Lamb (who sits on Yahuah's right hand on the throne of *The Kingdom of Yahuah)* forever and ever!"

As Yahuah's proxy and perfect human image (reflection) of the Glory of Yahuah, Yahusha is called by titles. The titles below have been used in justification of the Trinity, and incarnation. The titles below must be understood IN CONTEXT of the entire Word of Yahuah to understand them.

- The first title "Mighty God" is in context referring to Yahusha as the "perfect human image of the invisible God".
- The second title below "Father of Everlasting" is not saying Yahusha is the Everlasting Father Yahuah. That title, like Abraham who is called the "Father of Faith" meaning the forefather of faith, is referring to the fact that Yahusha is the forerunner or forefather to attain eternal life; he is the first born son.

Below is the scripture used to justify that "Jesus is God in the flesh". I have put in blue parenthesis the scripture below in context:

Isaiah 9:6-7
"For to us a child is born, to us a son is given, and **the government** shall be on his shoulders and he will be called Wonderful Counselor, (*Colossians 1:15* the perfect image of) Mighty God, (fore) Father of Everlasting (life *1 Corinthians 15:20*), and Prince of Peace." There will be no end to the increase of His government or of peace, on the Throne of David and over His Kingdom, to establish it and to uphold it with justice and righteousness from then on and forevermore.

We see the clear difference between Yahuah and Yahusha below:

Daniel 7
[13] "I kept looking in the night visions, and behold, with the clouds of heaven One (*Yahusha*) like **a Son of Man** was coming, And He (*Yahusha*) came up to the Ancient of Days

257

(*Yahuah, they are not the same being*) and was presented before Him. [14] "And to Him (*Yahusha*) was given (*by Yahuah as an inheritance*) dominion, Glory and a kingdom, that all the peoples, nations and *men of every* language Might **serve** Him (*not worship Yahusha, we serve Yahusha in The Kingdom*). His dominion is an everlasting dominion which will not pass away; and His kingdom is one which will not be destroyed.

To whom does Glory belong?

In order to answer the question; did Yahusha accept worship? We need to define the term glory. I will admit there is a very fine line that we are treading. While it is YAHUAH alone to whom Glory (worship) belongs... it is Yahusha who embodies the very "image" of the invisible YAHUAH. Yahusha represents in bodily form the INVISIBLE God Yahuah. Yahusha is both a reflection of Yahuah to us and Yahusha reflects Glory from us back to Yahuah.

Glory as CREATOR belongs to YAHUAH alone. The glory as King and Heir to all that YAHUAH created belongs to Yahusha given to him by Yahuah as an inheritance. It is with that clear understanding that we must approach Scripture. So I am very careful to whom I direct my WORSHIP (Glory) as opposed to my praise (as the one who is worthy). There is only ONE worthy of my worship.... and that is Yahuah. Yahusha is worthy of my highest praise. Below is the definition of the word glory and how I apply it and to whom:

Merriam-Webster Online Dictionary

> *glory*
> *Main Entry: 1glo·ry*
>
> *1 a : praise, honor, or distinction extended by common consent : RENOWN b : worshipful praise, honor, and thanksgiving <giving glory to God>*

2 a : something that secures praise or renown <the glory of a brilliant career> b : a distinguished quality or asset

3 a (1) : great beauty and splendor : MAGNIFICENCE something marked by beauty or resplendence <a perfect glory of a day> b : the splendor and beatific happiness of heaven; broadly : ETERNITY

To #1 above I give to YAHUAH alone.
To #2 above I give you Yahusha alone.
To #3 above I give to both.

To whom did Yahusha teach us to direct our worship?

To whom I give glory in the form of worship is not the real question here. The real question is did Yahusha accept glory in the form of divine worship that belongs to Yahuah? Or did Yahusha accept glory in the form of worship given to a superior man in rank and position? We see below that Yahusha directed all glory in the form of divine worship to Yahuah alone:

Mark 12:28-30
28 So he asked Him; what is the greatest commandment of all? 29 And Yahusha answered Him: The greatest of all the commandments is: **Hear, O Israyl, Yahuah is our Father. Yahuah is one God. 30 And you must love Yahuah your Father with all your heart and with all your soul, and with all your might.**

Matthew 4:10
Then Yahusha said to her; you get away, Satan! For it is written: Yahuah your Father you must worship, and Him only you must serve!

Matthew 23:9
And you must not pray to **or worship any man on earth** as a "Father," for you have only One Father, Who is in heaven.

But Yahusha accepted worship from his disciples!

Now concerning the rest of the scriptures that appear to demonstrate that Yahusha was worshipped; I will just lump them all together and give you the reason behind it. First, let me say that we are commanded to worship in Spirit (to Yahuah) and in (the) Truth (Yahusha is the truth and the way). So true worship of Yahuah is coming to Him by the example of the true way. That is coming to Him through Yahusha by proxy.

John 4:24
24 Yahuah is spirit (*not a man or man incarnate*), and his worshipers must worship in the Spirit and in truth."

John 14:6
6 Yahusha answered, "I am the way and the truth and the life (*my example the true way to eternal life*). No one comes to the Father except through (in covenant with) me (*by following in my footsteps*).

Next, I want to point out that the word translated "worship" is a word used to describe *the act of bowing down* which in many cases is not the intent of "worshipping Yahuah" or Divine Worship; but rather recognizing a superior in rank or messenger of Yahuah. In the case of bowing down before a messenger of Yahuah, those that bow are not worshipping the messenger. They are bowing down recognizing the messenger "comes with the power and authority of Yahuah" giving Yahuah glory through the messenger... this would be an example of worshipping Yahuah in Spirit with the understanding that Yahusha is the true way to Him.

260

It is a fine line but Yahusha understood that line as I will demonstrate.

Before I go any further let me say that bowing down to Yahusha as the anointed proxy of Yahuah and anointed King of Yahuah's Creation and the "Truth of Yahuah" is not divine worship it is respect. I have no problem with this type of "respectful worship (bowing down to)" with the understanding of Yahusha's superior position in the Kingdom as well as the power and authority of Yahuah given to Yahusha as "The Truth and the Light" of Yahuah. I have no problem with and do not see that act as a violation of Yahuah's revealed will nor proof that Yahusha is Yahuah as long as the <u>Spiritual Intent</u> of that act is righteously directed toward Yahuah through Yahusha the proxy.

Paul does not say that every knee shall bow to Yahusha; it is <u>before Yahuah</u> that every knee shall bow in worship. Yahusha is the Judge not The Creator. We **stand** before Yahusha, **we hit our knees in worship** before Yahuah:

> **Romans 14:10-11**
> For <u>we shall all stand before the judgment seat of the Messiah</u>. 11 For it is written in Isaiah 45:23: "As I live, says Yahuah, Every knee shall bow to Me, and every tongue shall confess to Yahuah." [12] So then each of us shall give account of himself to Yahuah.

Yahuah looks at the "Spiritual Intent" not the physical act alone. One person could "bow down" to *Jesus* in an act of Godly worship while another can "bow down" to The Messiah Yahusha in an act of recognizing his superior position and by proxy give worship to Yahuah. One would be justified, <u>the other in idolatry</u>.

However, a witness to those two people both bowing down would not know the "intent" of their heart and describe both using the same word in Hebrew and Greek/Latin. So those words describe both physical acts of Divine Worship and reverence to authority.

Worship of Yahusha is not divine worship

Ok, among the many passages of the New Testament that presents Yahusha as being the object of "worship" is Matthew 14:33.

> ### Matthew 14:33
> 33 Then they that were in the ship came and worshipped (bowed down before) him, saying, of a truth thou art the Son of God (they bowed down to Yahusha in the sense of respect for his superior position as son of Yahuah. They did not worship him as Yahuah.)

Here we have a clear situation - one of many recorded in the New Testament - of Yahusha being "worshipped", yet those worshipping him did not worship him as Yahuah but as **the Son** of Yahuah, which to them, actually meant that they recognized him as Messiah or as an empowered, righteous agent of the Almighty God. They were bowing down as an act of respect to authority before Yahusha and as an act of worship to Yahuah through His proxy.

Although many think the term "worship" is only applicable to "God", in fact the term relates to showing reverence even to a fellow man. Christian teachers do not make this distinction as they are false teachers and lead us astray to believe Yahusha was worshipped. Then these false teachers take that sound bite out of context and assume ***Jesus*** is God. In every case bowing down to Yahusha is in the context of showing reverence to a higher authority.

As the Strong's Lexicon points out, the Greek term is simply "*used of homage shown to men and beings of superior rank*". The Greek word rendered "worship" in the NT is the Greek word *proskyneō* below is the Strong's entrance for the word:

Lexicon :: Strong's G4352 – *proskyneō*

> *in the NT by kneeling or prostration to do homage*
> *(to one) or make obeisance, whether in order to*
> *express respect or to make supplication*

In the 2nd Temple era when Yahusha lived; kneeling or prostration to do homage (to one) or make obeisance (which is translated as *'worship'* in the NT), whether in order to express respect or to make supplication was a common practice. It remains a common practice even today in the Orient in Japanese, Chinese, Muslim, and other cultures around the world. This is not Godly worship.

The often referenced instances of Yahusha being "worshipped" are another example of the desperation Christians to find any shred of proof for their unsubstantiated and false doctrines. This is another example of the biased use of "implicit" proofs by those promoting the mystery Babylon man-God or traditional Trinitarian Christianity and counterfeit Messiah Jesus Christ. They IMPLY what is not there.

The reference, *A Dictionary of Biblical Languages With Semantic Domains: Hebrew (Old Testament)*, by James Swanson, defines the Hebrew word often translated "worship" as - *"take a stance of bowing low in an act of respect or honor, but not necessarily worship of deity"* (Genesis 43:28).

The reference in Genesis below is just such an example of the type of "worship" Yahusha accepted:

Genesis 43:28
And they answered, Thy servant our father is in good health, he is yet alive. And they (*worshipped* - proskyneō) bowed down their heads, and made obeisance.

This term "obeisance" is from the Hebrew equivalent of the Greek term used in the verse from Matthew *proskyneō* shown above, as well as most other New Testament verses where "worship" is the translation. The proper translation should read "*bowed down to*" not "*worshipped*". Again we see the bias of uninspired Hellenized translators. Matthew, as many of you already know, is now strongly assumed to have been initially written in Hebrew; however, even if it wasn't, it was still written by a Hebrew from memory of conversations in Hebrew.

From Strong's Lexicon we determine the Hebrew term to mean:

Strong's Number 7812

> *shachah {shaw-khaw'} a primitive root; TWOT - 2360; v*
> > *AV - worship 99, bow 31, bow down 18, obeisance 9, reverence 5, fall down 3, themselves 2, stoop 1, crouch 1, misc 3; 172*
> > > *to bow down*
> > > *to bow down, prostrate oneself*
> > > *before a superior man in homage*
> > > *before God in worship*
> > > *before false gods*
> > > *before angels*

Note that the term can even refer to "worship" of false gods! Of course, this is precisely the type of worship practiced by Trinitarians and all others that promote the antichrist (replacement Messiah) deception that Jesus is God. Obviously, the context of Genesis is not referring to worship of Yahuah. It records Joseph's brothers bowing before him i.e. "worshipping" him (obeisance) as someone of much higher rank. Are Trinitarians prepared to claim that everyone in Scripture that was "worshipped" is Yahuah (God)? Since Joseph was "worshipped" do they also claim he was Yahuah? Of course not. We simply need to do a small amount of research into the meaning of the Greek and Hebrew words that were translated as "worship" to realize there are two types of "worship". Worship directed to Yahuah and worship directed to Yahusha as a superior in rank and authority as the son of Yahuah.

Did Yahusha commit blasphemy claiming to be the incarnation of God?

Did Yahusha claim he was *the Great I AM*? Did he claim he and Yahuah were one being? Christianity would have us believe he did just that and the Jews tried him for blasphemy because of it. They say Yahusha was found innocent of blasphemy <u>because he was Yahuah</u> so it wasn't blasphemy. If Yahusha did in fact make those claims then he would have been found guilty of blasphemy but they found him innocent!

Christianity teaches that when asked by Pilot about these charges that Yahusha remained silent <u>implying</u> he was God. Yahusha did not reply to those charges because he had already provided a defense to the Jews and knew he must die at the hands of his brothers to save them. The truth is not that difficult to understand when Scripture and the words of Yahusha are not taken out of context they were meant. Yahusha did not claim to be Yahuah he claimed to be <u>the son of Yahuah</u>. Yahusha was simply declaring a fact that Yahuah proclaimed of all of us:

> **Psalm 82**
> 6 I have said, Ye are (all) gods; and all of you are children of the most High.

The Jews in authority at that time were trying to arrest Yahusha for blasphemy claiming that by saying he was the son of Yahuah was committing blasphemy. They were <u>implying</u> the same thing Christians imply today that "son of Yahuah" means equal to Yahuah and Yahuah in the flesh. Yahusha wasn't buying it and defended himself very well against these charges. He never defended them as Christians imply by saying he was Yahuah in the flesh.

Yahusha responded to their claims of blasphemy below with my comments in blue parenthesis. We see that Yahusha explained to the Jews who wanted to stone him for blasphemy that he used the term "son of God" <u>in the same sense</u> that Yahuah claimed all children of Israel were gods, the son of the Most High. So Yahusha asked them "how is it blasphemy just because I refer to myself as the son of God when Yahuah said we all are?"

John 10
[29] My Father, who has given them to me, is greater than all; no one can snatch them out of my Father's hand. [30] I and the Father are one (in mind, will, purpose, and spirit through marriage covenant. We ALL are one with our Father in the same exact way)."

John 17:19-21
[20] "My prayer is not for them alone. I pray also for those who will believe in *(enter into covenant with)* me through their message, [21] **that all of them may be one, Father, just as you are in me and I am in you. May they also be ONE in us**

[34] Yahusha answered them, <u>"Is it not written in your Law, 'I have said you are "gods"'?</u> [35] <u>If he called them (the Israelites) 'gods,' to whom the word of God came—and Scripture cannot be set aside—</u> [36] <u>what about the one whom the Father set apart as his very own and sent into the world? Why then do you accuse me of blasphemy because I *said, 'I am God's Son'*?</u> [37] Do not believe me unless I do the works of my Father. [38] But if I do them, even though you do not believe me, believe the works, that you may know and understand that the Father is in (covenant with) me, and I in (covenant with) the Father." [39] Again they tried to seize him, but he escaped their grasp.

Yahusha's defense was simple as he know we are all one with one with Yahuah and sons of Yahuah not just Yahusha. He was accepting what Yahuah had declared in Psalm 82 and quoted that scripture back to the Jews. He wasn't saying OR implying he was God incarnate or Yahuah in the flesh, he was simply acknowledging a fact that pertains to ALL of us… Yahusha realized at that point that the "trap" they had laid for him was falsely accusing him of blasphemy by saying Yahusha implied he was Yahuah by using the term son of God. Yahusha explained that he was not saying he was Yahuah. He was acknowledging the fact that, as Yahuah said, he was a god and the son of Yahuah. The same thing said of King David, Solomon, and many others in scripture. The same thing said of all those in *The Yahushaic Covenant*. The answer is no, Yahusha did not commit blasphemy and no Yahusha never said he was God. Both the Jews and the Christians today are bearing false witness against the Messiah. Yahusha explained exactly what he meant.

Did Yahusha claim he was the Great I Am?

John 8
55 Though you do not know him, I know him. If I said I did not, I would be a liar like you, but I do know him and keep his word.**56** Your father Abraham rejoiced at the thought of seeing my day; he saw it and was glad." **57** "You are not yet fifty years old," the Jews said to him, "and you have seen Abraham!" **58** "I tell you the truth," Yahusha answered, "*before Abraham was born, I am*!" **59** At this, they picked up stones to stone him, but Yahusha hid himself, slipping away from the temple grounds.

In the scene above Yahusha is telling the Jews that because they transgress The Law of Yahuah with their human tradition and commandments of men (the Talmud) they are liars when they say they know Yahuah. When Yahusha made the statement "*before Abraham was born, I AM*" in context of the Word of Yahuah and the predestined plan of Yahuah to send a human Messiah; Yahusha was simply saying "before Abraham was born, I am (prophesied to come and have pre-eminence among the sons of Yahuah in the pre-ordained Plan of Yahuah)." Letting scripture interpret scripture we establish sound doctrine to overcome this sound bite. Yahusha knew he was given preeminence among all things in the plan of

Yahuah which was with Yahuah at creation therefore "before Abraham". Paul confirms this fact:

Colossians 1:15-20

15 He is the image *(human reflection of his father as all sons are reflection or images of their fathers)* of the invisible God, the firstborn son of all creation. 16 For by Yahuah all things were created, in heaven and on earth, visible and invisible, whether thrones or dominions or rulers or authorities—all things were created through Yahuah and for Yahusha. 17 And Yahuah is before all things, and in Yahuah all things hold together. 18 And Yahusha is the head of the body, the church. Yahusha is the beginning, the firstborn from the dead, that in everything <u>Yahusha might be preeminent</u>. 19 For in Yahusha all the fullness of Yahuah's Spirit was pleased to dwell, 20 and through Yahusha, Yahuah would reconcile to himself all things, whether on earth or in heaven, making peace by the blood of his cross (Yahuah would reconcile creation in covenant with Yahusha).

Paul is explaining what Yahusha was stating… two facts: 1.) he was before Abraham and had pre-eminence in the Plan of Yahuah. 2.) Yahusha is before Abraham in the resurrection being the first born of all eternal creatures. As I stated early, Yahusha accepted worship as the preeminent son of Yahuah and was before all men in the Plan of Yahuah. Below is the meaning of preeminence:

pre·em·i·nence

noun: pre-eminence; plural noun: pre-eminences; noun: preeminence; plural noun: preeminences

1. the fact of surpassing all others; superiority.

So before Abraham was born, Yahusha said "I am preeminent among the sons of Yahuah". Yahusha's use of the phrase "I am" was no different than how you and I would use it today. If you ask me if I am a son of Yahuah, I would reply "I am". Would you stone me for blasphemy? I am not claiming in any way to be Yahuah nor saying that *I am The Great I AM* simply because I used the phrase "I am". Neither was Yahusha. In fact, Yahusha uses this phrase often and <u>never was he implying</u> he was the Great I AM in the process. Below we see Yahusha use the phrase I am and what he meant:

1. *Bread* - "I am the bread of life; he who comes to Me shall not hunger." **John 6:35**

2. *Light* - "I am the light of the world; he who fallows Me shall not walk in the darkness, but shall have the light of life." **John 8:12**

3. *Gate* - "I am the gate; if anyone enters through Me, he shall be saved, and shall go in and out, and find pasture." John 10:9

4. *Good Shepherd* - "I am the good shepherd; the good shepherd lays down His life for His sheep." **John 10:11**

5. *Resurrection and Life* - "I am the resurrection and the life; he who believes in Me shall live even if he dies." **John 11:25**

6. *Way, Truth, Life* - "I am the way, and the truth, and the life; no one comes to the Father, but through Me." **John 14:6**

7. *True vine* - "I am the true vine, and My Father is the vinedresser." **John 15:1**

Given Yahusha's use of the term I Am he would have said "I am the Great I AM" if that is what he intended to say. Again, to understand what Yahusha was saying in John 8:58 we must put this statement into context of Scripture. Christianity takes John 8:58 out of context and combines it with John Chapter 1 that is mistranslated to come up with the false teaching that Yahusha claimed to be God.

In fact those two verses do combine to give us the truth of what Yahusha was saying. Yahusha was simply saying that before Abraham was born, Yahusha was prophesied to come in the Plan of Yahuah and was preeminent in that plan. I have proven earlier in this book is exactly what John 1 states:

> ### John 1:1-5
> 1 In the beginning was the *plan of Yahuah*, and *the plan* was with Yahuah (*and defined His purpose in creation*), and *the plan* was Yahuah's. 2 The same *plan* was in the beginning with Yahuah. 3 All things were done according to the *plan of Yahuah*, and without the *plan of Yahuah* nothing was done, that was done. 4 In *this plan* was (*predestined*) life (through a human Messiah's sacrifice, he was the for father of eternal life), and that life was the light (*revelation*) to mankind. 5 Now that light (*revealed plan to send a human Messiah*) shines in the darkness, but the darkness does not take hold of it…

Again, in every case where incarnation is taught it is taken out of context. Put back into context that false doctrine crumbles and is exposed as The Spirit of the Antichrist.

1 John 4

1 Dear friends, do not believe every spirit, but test the spirits to see whether they are from Yahuah, because many false prophets have gone out into the world (*all pagan 'Christs" were demi-gods i.e. Tammuz, Horus, Hesus, Krhishna, Apollo, Mithra, in whose image* Χ͞ς͞ *was fashioned at the Council of Nicaea*). [2] This is how you can recognize the Spirit of Yahuah: Every spirit that acknowledges that the Messiah Yahusha **has come in the flesh** (*100% human*) is from Yahuah, [3] but every spirit **that does not acknowledge** (*that Yahusha was human, but elevates a man who died as God above Yahuah* **Romans 1**) is not from God; this (*doctrine of incarnation that Jesus is God in the flesh*) is **the *spirit* of the** Χ͞ς͞ **antichrist**, of which you have heard that it is coming, and now it is already in the world. [4] You are from Yahuah (*not just Yahusha we all are 'from Yahuah'*), little children (*speaking to the spiritually immature*), and have overcome them (*the pagan incarnate god-men Christs they once believed in*); because greater is Yahuah who is in you than he (*the spirit of Dagon the Dragon Rev. 13*) who is in the world. [5] They (*the pagans who believe in god-men known as Christs i.e. Christos Mithra, Christos Appolos, Khrishna, Christos Hesus*) are from the (*pagan*) world; therefore they speak *as* from the world (*as pagans in their doctrines*), and the (*pagan*) world listens to them. [6] We are from Yahuah; he who knows Yahuah (*is the only true God and there is no other*) listens to us (*who teach that Yahusha came in the flesh as all men do and was raised divine and so became the for-father of eternal life*); he who is not from Yahuah does not listen to us. **By this we know the spirit of truth** (*Yahusha was not Yahuah incarnate*) **and the spirit of error** (*the doctrine of incarnation*).

The Trinity and Incarnation doctrines are literally built upon *implied* doctrine and the Christian scribes had to add words to Scripture in order to even be able to "imply" such nonsense. If you take out the words added to scripture to promote the "doctrine of the false messiah χϛϛ " and put those verses back into context there is zero references to incarnation and the Trinity. We have been lied to for 2000 years:

> Jeremiah 8:8-9
> "How can you say, 'We are wise, and The Law of Yahuah is with us'? But behold, the lying pen of the scribes has made it into a lie. 9 The wise men shall be put to shame; they shall be dismayed and taken; behold, they have rejected the word of Yahuah, so what wisdom is in them?

> **Jeremiah 16:19**
> O Yahuah, my strength, and my fortress, and my refuge in the day of affliction, the Gentiles shall come unto thee from the ends of the earth, and shall say, Surely our fathers have inherited **lies**, false gods, and *pagan rituals* wherein *there is* no profit.

Yahusha clearly admits he is not my "God" but my brother

I am about to end this section with the clear and documented truth that Yahuah is not Yahusha. Yahusha is our brother not our "God". Yahuah is our God and Father not our brother. The simplicity and obviousness of the truth is inescapable. It was not through "Yahusha" that all things exist as the pagan "Logos" lie is taught, but through Yahuah alone...

Hebrews 2:10-18 - NIV

10 In bringing many sons and daughters to glory, it was fitting that Yahuah, for whom and through whom everything exists, (*Yahuah*) should make the pioneer of their salvation (*Yahusha the forefather of eternal life*) perfect through what he suffered (*Yahusha was not god incarnate he wasn't even born perfect!*). 11 Both the one who makes people holy (*Yahuah*) and those who are made holy (*Yahusha and all his brother/sisters*) <u>are of the same family</u>. **So Yahusha is not ashamed to call them <u>brothers and sisters</u>**. 12 He says,

"I will declare your name (*Yahuah*) <u>to my brothers and sisters</u> (*Yahusha is not our God, he is our elder brother in the family of Yahuah*); in the assembly I will sing your praises." 13 And again, "I (*Yahusha*) will put my trust in him (*Yahuah*)." And again he says, "Here am I, and the (*rest of the*) children Yahuah has given me (*to rule over as king*)."

14 Since the children have flesh and blood, **he too shared in their humanity** (*he was human too not a demi-god*) so that by his death (*the death of a man not God*) he might break the power of him who holds the power of death (*defeat The Law of Sin and Death*)—that is, the devil— 15 and free (*all who now live by The Law of the Spirit of Life*) those who all their lives <u>were held in slavery by their fear of death</u> (*we were held in slavery to the death decrees not The Law*). 16 For surely it is not angels Yahusha helps, but Abraham's descendants. 17 For this reason he (*Yahusha*) had to be made like them (*he was made human just like I was*), _**fully human in every way**_ (*doesn't get any clearer than that*), in order that he might become a merciful and faithful high priest (*all High Priests are chosen from among men... Hebrews 5:1*) in service to Yahuah (*he was not the incarnate Yahuah*), and that he might make atonement for the sins of the people. 18 Because he himself suffered when he was tempted (*proof he was not Yahuah,*

Yahuah cannot be tempted by evil), he is able to help those who are being tempted.

James 1:13
For Yahuah cannot be tempted by evil, nor does he tempt anyone;

That is the long and short of it. There is absolutely no difference between Yahusha pre-resurrection than there is you and I now accept Birthright, inheritance, and position in the Kingdom of Yahuah. All the claims he made of being one with Yahuah we too have the authority to claim. All the claims to be god, we too have the authority to claim. We too are the sons of Yahuah. Everything that Yahusha is now post resurrection, in terms of "being", we <u>will be too</u> after we are resurrected. I will be a god, a King, a Priest, Righteous Judge etc. Again the main difference is that Yahusha is the first born son, he is the King of Kings, and High Priest. WE ARE OF THE SAME EXACT FAMILY! There is no Trinity or "Godhead" there is Yahuah the Father and all His chosen sons.

Yahuah is the God of Yahusha just like he is my God!

The scripture below speaks volumes, and should be the end of this discussion:

John 20:17
17 Yahusha said to her, "Do not cling to Me, for I have not yet ascended to My Father; but go to <u>My brothers</u> and say to them, 'I am ascending to **My Father and your Father, and to My God and your God**.' "

Again, it just doesn't get any clearer than that.

Summary

χ§ς Jesus Christ represents *The Spirit of the Antichrist* (false messiah) as it was in the "image of a man who died" in whom The Law of Yahuah was abolished. The True Messiah Yahusha declared he did NOT abolish The Law. In fact the example he set on this Earth was that of a Torah Obedient Jewish Rabbi. As the chosen Messiah, Yahusha was sent by Yahuah to bring The Law to its fullest meaning and expression spiritually, that is what fulfill means. It does not mean "abolish".

The Law was given to Moses by Yahuah in physical "letter" as a mentor/teacher to keep us 'under' protective custody with the 'hope' of a coming Messiah who would fulfill the promises made in The Law. Those promises are a Passover sacrifice to make the law whole and deliver us from our sin.

Yahuah would fulfill His promises to cover our sin by the blood of the lamb in the Yahushaic Covenant by covering the death decrees that demand out death. It is in that way that Yahusha 'fulfilled' The Law and made it whole! In the process bringing all who lovingly obey the spiritual intent of The Law into total compliance resulting in eternal life which is the promise made in The Law for obedience to it.

So The Law in the Mosaic Covenant was referred to by the Apostle Paul as *The Law of Sin and Death* because it was incomplete and we were being held captive by the fear of the death decrees.

In The Yahushaic (New) Covenant the Apostle Paul refers to The Law as *The Law of the Spirit of Life* because the death decrees have been cover releasing us from bondage to 'sin therefore you die'. The Law has been fulfilled by covering the death decrees which, the fear of those death decrees had created enmity between us and Yahuah. So now Yahuah, by removing the death decrees by sacrificing his son in fulfillment of the Abraham/Isaac parallel, has now given us a loving heart for His Law (writing it on our

275

heart) and gave us His Spirit of Holiness that teaches us to keep His commandment and obey His Law; only out of love instead of fear. So now we have 'The Law of the Spirit of Holiness that leads to eternal life' because the death decrees are covered by the blood of the lamb… i.e. *The Law of the Spirit of Life*! That is the testimony of Yahusha.

The testimony of $\chi\varsigma\varsigma$ Jesus is the Law has been abolished, i.e. The Lawless One. $\chi\varsigma\varsigma$ Jesus Christ also fulfills the role of "the Beast/Pig sacrifice of Isthar" in Mystery Babylon. $\chi\varsigma\varsigma$ Jesus Christ was created in the image of all pagan gods which is the Trinity.

Chapter 16
The Antichrist is an image of all pagan gods

The Pagan "Trinity" – Overview

The Bible warns not to worship Yahuah in the ritual and practices of Babylon. We were warned not to sacrifice our children to Moloch, and not to make Him into the image of a corruptible man or the nature of all pagan gods which were all trinities in every culture.

𝄇𝄇 Jesus Christ was created in the image of the second member of the Babylonian Trinity who was Tammuz and given the sacrifice of Tammuz which was the pig on Ishtar/Easter Sungod Day in worship to Ba'al. In this chapter, I am going to demonstrate why 𝄇𝄇 Jesus Christ represents The Trinity and that The Trinity is pagan.

Yahuah is the one and only God, there is no other and He declared He could never and would never be found in the form of a man, nor the son of man.

> **Numbers 23:19**
> Yahuah is not human, that he should lie, not a human being, that he should change his mind. Does Yahuah speak and then not act? Does he promise and not fulfill?

You see, The Creator made that promise and declared He would fulfill it and NEVER come to Earth as an incarnate god-man like 𝄇𝄇 Jesus Christ. In the image of 𝄇𝄇 Jesus Christ, Yahuah is made out to be a liar and did a 180 degree about face becoming everything He claimed He was not, then took on the form of every pagan god in The Trinity expressed by an incarnate god-man.

So did Yahuah "lie" in Numbers 23:19 and become a 'liar and a human being' who broke His promise and did not fulfill it? Or is 𝄇𝄇 Jesus Christ the "image of a men who died" that we have elevated in our hearts above Yahuah"

Romans 1

For even though they knew Yahuah was God, they did not honor Him as God or give thanks, but they became futile in their speculations, and their foolish heart was darkened. [22] Professing to be wise, they became fools, [23] and exchanged the glory of Yahuah who cannot die for ___an image___ in the form of a man who died.

The pagan god worshipped in ***The Mystery Religion of Babylon*** was a triune god made up of ***the Father/the incarnate Son/ and Mother of God.*** The father was the son, the son the father, and both were one with the mother in marriage (Semaramis married both Nimrod and her son Tammuz). We see this abomination as a constant theme not only among pagan religions but also condemned in The Bible as Yahuah is not a triune god but the one and only living God. It is the worship of this triune "Trinity" representation of gods that apposes the God in The Bible as Yahuah declares "you shall have no other gods before me"… "Before me" is the English translation of the Hebrew words "in my face". So Yahuah actually said "you shall have no other gods in my face!" The same expression used of Nimrod who was described as a "mighty hunter before Yahuah' or rather a "mighty hunter in the face of Yahuah" implying rebellion against Yahuah. So we are to "have no other gods in Yahuah's face!"

NOTE: The declaration that Yahuah is ONE not a Trinity is the central theme in the True Faith of every man of God in the Bible, including The Messiah. This knowledge of Yahuah being the one and only Creator and God is the very "mark" on the forehead of the Elect called "The Shema" that marks the elect for eternal life. When Yahusha (the True Messiah) was asked the single greatest commandment of God, he quoted The Shema (Shema means "hear" in Hebrew) by quoting literally from The Torah Deuteronomy Chapter 6:

Mark 12:29

"The most important one," answered Yahusha, "is this: 'Hear, O Israel, Yahuah our God, **Yahuah is one**.

Yahusha was quoting Deuteronomy 6:4 verbatim. This passage of Deuteronomy is also defined as the "mark between our eyes and on our right hands". It IS the "mark of Yahuah" that sets us apart from this "false religion". The mark of the false religion is literally The Trinity made on the foreheads of newly baptized babies and over the hearts of literally billions every day as they make "the sign of the cross" in the name of The Trinity. I'll get to this too in great detail.

This "mark" of Yahuah on our foreheads and right hand displayed by The Messiah and expressed as the single greatest command as we see below is an outright denial of the pagan Trinity gods:

Deuteronomy 6
4 Hear, O Israel: Yahuah our God, Yahuah is one. 5 Love Yahuah your God with all your heart and with all your soul and with all your strength. 6 These commandments that I give you today are to be on your hearts. 7 Impress them on your children. Talk about them when you sit at home and when you walk along the road, when you lie down and when you get up. 8 Tie them as symbols (*mark*) on your hands and bind them (*mark*) on your foreheads.

The true Messiah Yahusha again demonstrated this singular knowledge of Yahuah is the foundation of eternal life. For He is the giver of life and to receive that life you must be in covenant with Yahuah through the Yahushaic Covenant:

John 17:3
[3] **And this is eternal life**, that they may know You (*Yahuah*), **the only true God, and** (*then there is*) Yahusha (*the*) Messiah whom You (*Yahuah*) have sent (*as the Passover not Easter sacrifice for sin*).

We also see this same triune god is a consistent them in every pagan religion which evolved from *The Mystery Religion of Babylon*. This religion of Satan cleverly opposes the Mark of Yahuah in the minds (mark of the forehead is a metaphor for knowledge) with what is called The Mark of the Beast defined later in this book series. Let us take a look at The Trinity as it evolved over time throughout almost every culture. Before we begin, let us define the concept of a triune god.

The History of the Pagan Trinity

Source: http://en.wikipedia.org/wiki/Triple_deity

TRIPLE DEITY

> A ***triple deity*** *(sometimes referred to as threefold, Trinity, tripled, triplicate, tripartite, triune or triadic) is a deity associated with the number three. Such deities are common throughout world mythology;* ***the number three has a long history of mythical associations****. C. G. Jung considered the arrangement of deities into triplets an archetype (or mark) in the history of religion. The deities and legendary creatures of this nature typically fit into one of the following general categories:*

> - ***triadic*** ("forming a group of three"): a triad, three entities inter-related in some way (life, death, rebirth, for example, or triplet children of a deity) and always or usually associated with one another or appearing together;

> - ***triune*** ("three-in-one, one-in-three"): a Trinity being with three aspects or manifestations;

> - ***tripartite*** ("of triple parts"): a being with three body parts where there would normally be one (three

heads, three pairs of arms, and so on); or

- ***triplicate-associated*** ("relating to three corresponding instances"): a being in association with a trio of things of the same nature which are symbolic or through which power is wielded (three magic birds, etc.)

Now let us take a journey throughout history as The Trinity evolved as *THE GOD* of almost every pagan religion in opposition to Yahuah, the ONLY TRUE GOD. As we see The Messiah Yahusha speaking to his Heavenly Father, Yahuah in John 17:3 declares this simple truth and that truth is where salvation is found:

John 17:3
³ Now this is eternal life: that they know you (*Yahuah*), **the only true God**, and (*your*) Messiah Yahusha, whom you have sent.

Again, when asked the single greatest commandment in the entire Bible, Yahusha clearly contradicted the "pagan Trinity" in Mark 12:28-34 the Messiah correctly answered the "teachers of The Law" with what is known as "The Shema" which is the "Seal of God" on your forehead… Yahusha quoted directly from Deuteronomy 12:

Mark 12:28-34
²⁸ One of the teachers of the law came and heard them debating. Noticing that Yahusha had given them a good answer, he asked him, "Of all the commandments, which is the most important?" ²⁹ "The most important one," answered Yahusha, "is this: 'Hear, O Israel: Yahuah our God, Yahuah is (*the*) one (*and only God*). ³⁰ Love Yahuah your God with all your heart and with all your soul and with all your mind and with all your strength.'

So much for "the Trinity"… that is how pagans worship their gods, not how the men in the Bible including The Messiah worshipped

Yahuah. Yahuah forbids us from "saying we are worshipping him" in the way pagans worship their gods:

> **Deuteronomy 12:31**
> You must not worship Yahuah your God in their way, because in worshiping their gods, they do all kinds of detestable things Yahuah hates. They even burn their sons and daughters in the fire as sacrifices to their gods (Moloch worship).

No wonder Christianity abolished The Torah. It stands as witness against every ritual they practice. Let's take a look at every pagan religion and their "Trinity' gods.

➢ The Egyptian Trinity

NOTE: I.H.S. is the monogram of Jesus H. Christ or "Isis/Horus/Seb". The Egyptian Trinity of Isis, Horus, Seb (Egyptian names for Baal, Ishtar, Tammuz). The Outline of History, by H. G. Wells. page 307 tell us:

"The trinity consisted of the god Serapis (=Osiris+Apis), the goddess Isis/Ishtar (= Hathor, the cow-moon goddess), and the child-god Horus (the Egyptian Tammuz). In one way or another almost every other god was identified with one or other of these three aspects of the one god, even the sun god Mithras of the Persians (*whom Constantine worshipped*). **The origin beginning with Baal, Ishtar, Tammuz of the ancient Babylonian Religion**. Many of the theories of Egyptian religion have penetrated into the theology of

283

Christian Europe, and form, as it were, part of the woof in the web of modern religious thought. Christian theology was largely organized and nurtured in the schools of Alexandria, and Alexandria was not only the meeting place of East and West, it was also the place where the decrepit theology of Egypt was revivified by contact with the speculative philosophy of Greece. Perhaps, however, **the indebtedness of Christian theological theory to ancient Egyptian dogma is nowhere more striking than in the doctrine of the Trinity**. The very terms used of it by Christian theologians meet us again in the inscriptions and papyri of Egypt. **Originally the trinity was a triad like those we find in Babylonian mythology**. The triad consisted of a divine father, wife, and son. **This triune god was later formulated into Christianity as the Christian Trinity of father, son, holy ghost.**"

➢ The Hecate Trinity

The Hecate Trinity (and the Statue of Liberty)...

The Statue of Liberty, like the Eye of Horus on the dollar bill and Obelisk we call The Washington Monument, all identify our great country and the religion it is founded upon as the modern day Babylon.

The Hecate Trinity was also associated with Diana (another cultural name of Ishtar). A triplefold Diana was venerated from the late sixth century BCE as Diana Nemorensis. "The Latin Diana was conceived as a threefold unity of the divine huntress, the Moon goddess, and the goddess of the nether world, Hekate," Albert Alföldi interpreted the late Republican numismatic image, noting that Diana *montium custos nemoremque virgo* ("keeper of the mountains and virgin of

Nemi") is addressed by Horace as *diva triformis* ("three-form goddess"). Diana is commonly addressed as Trivia by Virgil and Catullus.

As a virgin goddess later to be called Mary, she remained unmarried and had no regular consort. Hecate has survived in folklore as a 'hag' figure associated with witchcraft. Strmiska notes that Hecate, conflated with the figure of Diana, appears in late antiquity and in the early medieval period as part of an "emerging legend complex" associated with gatherings of women, the moon, and witchcraft that eventually became established "in the area of Northern Italy, southern Germany, and the western Balkans." This theory of the Roman origins of many European folk traditions related to Diana or Hecate was explicitly advanced at least as early as 1807 as the Roman equivalent the goddess Libertas. The Statue of Liberty is based on The Roman Goddess Libertas, the Roman goddess of freedom. Originally as goddess of personal freedom, she later became the goddess of the Roman commonwealth. Now she stands watch over The United States of America, the revived Roman Empire and spiritual Babylon.

The Queen of Babylon believed herself to be the incarnation of Lilith we discussed Lilith in my first book Creation Cries Out!.

Lilith was the origin of the vampire myths and said to have been the serpent that deceived Adam and Even in the Garden. So Lilith became Semaramis

who became the Goddess Ishtar in the religion of Babylon. The fertility goddess known as EASTER!

Ishtar (Babylonian Semaramis) fertility goddess of Easter is the Akkadian counterpart to the Sumerian Inanna and to

285

the cognate northwest Semitic goddess `Ashtart. Anunit, Astarte and Atarsamain, the goddess of fertility and sexuality. The Babylonian fertility goddess Ishtar (Easter in English) is portrayed as a trinitarian god with Baal the Sun God/Tammuz the Sun of God/Ishtar the Queen of Heaven... this is where we get the Christian Trinity as incorporated into the "Christian Church" by the sun worshipping emperor Constantine at the Council of Nicaea.

The worship of the Babylonian Ishtar was survived and at the time of the Roman Empire was known as the Goddess of Liberty Libertas. This is the real spiritual implication behind The Statue of "Libertas".

In celebration of the centenary of the first Masonic Republic in 1884, the Statue of Liberty was presented to the Masons of America, as a gift from the French Grand Orient Temple Masons.

The Statue of Liberty is nothing more than a replica image of a pagan trinity goddess.

The Masonic "Torch of Enlightenment" was also referred to as the "Flaming Torch of Reason", by the Illuminati Masons in the 1700's and in 1884, the cornerstone for the Statue of Liberty was placed in a solemn ceremony, by the Masonic lodges of New York.

Below is the cornerstone of the Statue of Liberty, dedicated to and by Freemasons. Below is the inscription dedicating the Statue of Liberty (Ishtar) by the Masonic Lodge who worships the founder of Masonry… Nimrod!

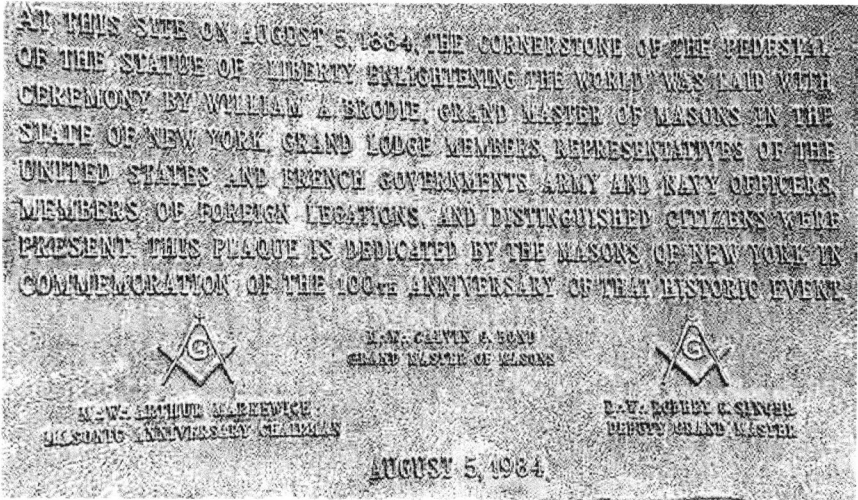

➤ Brigit –Irish Trinity

Brigit – A "Christopagan" era Irish Trinity – The Celebration of Groundhog Day in the honor of the goddess Brigit and Catholic Nuns

Irish Catholic St. Brigit edallion. The **goddess of the flame** to the ancient Celts, she has survived into <u>our time</u> as **"St. Bridget"** in the **Irish catholic church**. To this day her 'eternal flame' burns in Kildare, Ireland and her ancient sacred wells are still revered and visited. It is believed by pagan Catholics that Brigit, Lady of the Fairies – watches over their **sacred green** places and, if you look into her Magical Mirror, you can see the Faerie Realm. Here she is presented as a **cloverleaf Trinity**.

Brigit is known by various names, Brigit being the most ancient form. The name variations are: Brighid, Bride (Scottish), Brid, Brigit, Bridget, Brigantia (English), Brigan, Brigindo (Gaul) and Brigandu. Her name derives from her worship by the pre-christian Brigantes, who honored her as identical with Juno, Queen of Heaven. Brigit was just another incarnation of Semaramis/Ishtar and the eternal flame. Into the 18th Century, her sacred flame was tended, at first, by priestesses, who later became catholic nuns, when **the pagan shrine became a convent**, at Kildare, Ireland. These nineteen virgin priestesses (called nuns by the Catholic Church) were called 'Daughters of the Flame'. No man was ever allowed near. In fact, these women had other women in the village bring them their necessary supplies so they wouldn't have to deal with men. Bridget then became known as The Virgin Mary.

Imbolc **(Candlemas** and **Groundhog Day)**, the Celtic spring festival, honors Brigit. The Druids called this sacred holiday Oimelc, meaning "ewe's milk". Held on February 1st or 2nd, it celebrated the birthing and freshening of sheep and goats. The catholic version of Imbolc (Candlemas), also, involves much elaborate rituals and feasting, and to this very day, many Irish homes have a St Brigit's cross for protection, still made from rushes as in days of old.

288

➤ Geryon Greek Trinity

Geryon the 3 Headed God of Greek Mythology

In Greek mythology, Geryon (Ancient Greek: Γηρυών; gen.: Γηρυόνος), son of Chrysaor and Callirrhoe and grandson of Medusa, was a fearsome giant who dwelt on the island Erytheia of the mythic Hesperides in the far west of the Mediterranean. A more literal-minded later generation of Greeks associated the region with Tartessos in southern Iberia.

Geryon was often described as a monster with 3 human faces. According to Hesiod,X Geryon had one body and three heads, whereas the tradition followed by Aeschylus gave him three bodies. As seen in the picture on the left, Geryon was a "Trinity" having 3 bodies, 3 heads, and 3 shields.

➤ Cerberus - Greek and Roman Trinity

Trinity God Cerberus of Greek and Roman Mythology

Cerberus (pronounced /ˈsɜrbərəs/), or Kerberos, (Greek form: Κέρβερος, [ˈkerberos]) in Greek and Roman mythology, is a multi-headed hound (usually three-headed) which guards the gates of Hades, to prevent those who have crossed the river Styx from ever escaping. Cerberus featured in many works of ancient Greek and Roman literature and in works of both ancient and modern art and architecture, although, the depiction and background surrounding Cerberus often differed across various works by different authors of the era. The most notable difference is the number of its heads: Most sources describe or depict three heads.

➢ The Hindu Trinity

The Hindu Trinity

Idol worship and rituals are at the heart of Hinduism and have tremendous religious significance. All Hindu deities are themselves symbols of the abstract Absolute, and point to a particular aspect of the Brahman. The Hindu Trinity (Trimurti) is represented by three godheads: Brahma - the creator, Vishnu - the protector and Shiva - the destroyer.

The Hindu trinity is of Brahma, Vishnu and Shiva. They are respectively the creator, preserver and destroyer of the universe. They are also aligned as the transcendent Godhead, Shiva, the cosmic lord, Vishnu and the cosmic mind, Brahma. In this regard they are called Sat-Tat-Aum, the Being, the Thatness or immanence and the Word or holy spirit. This is much like the Christian trinity of God as the Father, Son and Holy Ghost. The trinity represents the Divine in its threefold nature and function. Each aspect of the trinity contains and includes the others.

➢ The Viking Trinity

Trinity. Norway, 14 Century, CE

The Viking Trinity

According to Adam of Bremen: "If plague and famine threatens, a libation is poured to the idol Thor; if war, to Odin; if marriages are to be celebrated, to Frey." Because Odin, the All-Father, was generally more feared than loved and subsequently kept at a distance, his son, Thor, assumed the position as favored deity. He was the protector and trusted friend. Some myths associated with Thor had him as almost human, with his foibles and gullibility.

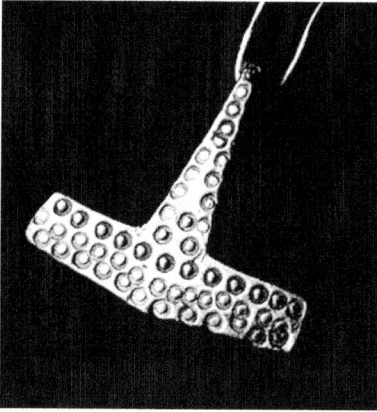

His hammer came to be used as an amulet, not only to signify the wearers allegiance to the old faith, but also as protection against the evils abounding. Later incororated into Christianity and associated with The Cross of Tammuz.

Odin and Thor were the most prominent members of the militaristic Æsir family. Frey, god of fertility and fecundity, led the Vanir family, the early opponents of the Æsir. However, a truce between them brought Frey to Valhalla and elevated his status to be one of the Norse trinity. With the conversion to Christianity, the Norse trinity, although driven underground by the Christian church, nevertheless, remained significantly conspicuous, albeit in changed form.

➢ **The Greek Trinity**

The Greek Trinity

Olympic triad of Zeus (king of the gods), Athena (goddess of war and intelect) and Apollo (god of the sun, culture and music)

In the Greek culture Zeus was the name for Nimrod, Athena for Semaramis, and Apollo for Tammuz.

291

List of triple deities of Babylonian polytheism

REFERENCE:
HTTP://EN.WIKIPEDIA.ORG/WIKI/TRIPLE_DEITY#TRIPLE_GODDESSES

- The Classical Greek Olympic triad of Zeus (king of the gods), Athena (goddess of war and intelect) and Apollo (god of the sun, culture and music)
- The Delian chief triad of Leto (mother), Artemis (daughter) and Apollo (son)[35][36] and second Delian triad of Athena, Zeus and Hera·
- In ancient Egypt there were many triads, the most famous among them that of Osiris (man), Isis (wife), and Horus (son), local triads like the Theban triad of Amun, Mut and Khonsu and the Memphite triad of Ptah, Sekhmet and Nefertem, the sungod Ra, whose form in the morning was Kheper, at noon Re-Horakhty and in the evening Atum, and many others.
- The Hellenistic Egypt triad of Isis, Alexandrian Serapis and Harpocrates (a Hellenized version of the previous), though in early Ptolomean religion Serapis, Isis and Apollo (who was though sometimes identified with Horus)
- The Roman Capitoline Triad of Jupiter (father), Juno (wife), and Minerva (daughter).
- The Roman pleibian triad of Ceres, Liber Pater and Libera (or its Greek counterpart with Demeter, Dionysos and Kore)
- The Olympian demiurgic triad in platonic philosophy made up of Zeus (considered the Zeus [king of the gods] of the Heavens), Poseidon (Zeus of the seas) and Pluto/Hades (Zeus of the underworld), all considered in the end to be a monad and the same Zeus, and the Titanic demiurgic triad of Helios (sun when in the sky), Apollo (sun seen in our world) and Dionysus (god of mysteries, "sun" of the underworld) (see Phaed in Dionysus and the Titans)
- The Julian triads of the early Roman Principate:
  - Venus Genetrix, Divus Iulius, and Clementia Caesaris

- o Divus Iulius, Divi filius and Genius Augusti
- o Eastern variants of the Julian triad, e.g. in Asia Minor: Dea Roma, Divus Iulius and Genius Augusti (or Divi filius)
- The Matres (Deae Matres/Dea Matrona) in Roman mythology
- The Fates, Moirae or Furies in Greek and Roman mythology: Clotho or Nona the Spinner, Lachesis or Decima the Weaver, and Atropos or Morta the Cutter of the Threads of Life. One's Lifeline was Spun by Clotho, Woven into the tapestry of Life by Lachesis, and the thread Cut by Atropos.
- The Hooded Spirits or *Genii Cucullati* in Gallo-Roman times
- The main supranational triad of the ancient Lusitanian mythology and religion and Portuguese neo-pagans made up of the couple Arentia and Arentius, Quangeius and Trebaruna, followed by a minor Gallaecian-Lusitanian triad of Bandua (under many natures), Nabia and Reve female nature: Reva
- The sisters Uksáhkká, Juksáhkká and Sáhráhkká in Sámi mythology.
- The triad of Al-Lat, Al-Uzza, and Manat in the time of Mohammed (surah 53:19-22)
- Lugus (Esus, Toutatis and Taranis) in Celtic mythology
- Odin, Vili and Ve in Germanic mythology
- The Norns in Germanic mythology
- The Triglav in Slavic mythology
- Perkūnas (god of heaven), Patrimpas (god of earth) and Pikuolis (god of death) in Prussian mythology
- The Zorya or Auroras in Slavic mythology
- The Charites or Graces in Greek mythology
- The One, the Thought (or Intellect) and the Soul in Neoplatonism

Summary

The list of The Trinity as the fundamental description of "god" in pagan religions is quite long and really outside the scope of this book, my point here is to illustrate three very important truths:

1. There is no "Trinity" in the Bible, neither the word nor the concept. For more information and proof see my book ***The Yahushaic Covenant***.
2. The Trinity is a direct contradiction of The Shema, the mark of Yahuah that Yahuah is ONE God not three.
3. The Trinity is the fundamental description of EVERY PAGAN GOD…
4. Yahuah forbids us from saying we are worshipping Him yet doing so in the form of a pagan trinity.

I encourage everyone to research this topic on their own initiative. The names of Baal (Nimrod), Ishtar (Semaramis), and Tammuz changed in each language but the religious practices did not. The main point I am making here with the concept of a pagan Trinity, is that the entire world and every religious system has been polluted by the worship of Sungod Baal (Nimrod), Moon goddess Ishtar (Semaramis), and Tammuz their only begotten incarnate son (who was Baal in the flesh) in the form of a Trinity. The "Mystery" in the religion of Babylon was literally the "Mystery" of the Trinity. Satan is literally the "god of this world" and his counter to the ONE true God is his unholy Trinity. This "mark of the beast" over our mind is the opposite of the Mark of Yahuah and has the minds of the entire Earth polluting every pagan religion especially Christianity the largest religion on Earth.

𐤇𐤔𐤔 Jesus Christ was created in the image of Tammuz, the incarnation of The LORD (Ba'al) the second member of the Babylonian Trinity. Jesus Christ represents the rituals of Babylon which are aimed at our Children as we sacrifice our children on the Altar to the Babylonian Moloch each year. Yahuah literally hates these Babylonian holidays with all His being!

Chapter 17

The Antichrist changes Yahuah's Holy Days to Babylonian festivals

Sacrificing our children to Moloch

Isaiah 1

14 <u>**Your appointed festivals**</u> (*Sunday, Easter, Christmas, etc. all Babylonian Rituals*) **I hate with all my being**.

PASSING THROUGH THE FIRE TO MOLECH

<u>Deuteronomy 12:31</u>

You must not worship Yahuah your God in their (*Babylonian*) way, because in worshiping their (*Babylonian*

Trinity) gods, they do all kinds of detestable things Yahuah hates. They even burn their sons and daughters in the fire as sacrifices to their gods (*all Christian/Babylonian holidays are directed at our children*).

We today are "sacrificing our children to Moloch" as we follow 𝕏𝕊𝕊 Jesus Christ who is the false messiah or Antichrist. We have targeted these pagan Babylonian festivals directly at our children! We are literally sacrificing the eternal lives of our childress by keeping these pagan SUN worshipping rituals making the excuse that "*oh… but they are harmless, we do keep them because they are for the children!*" We must realize that is the point! The spirit of the Dragon has always wanted our children and we are delivering our children to him on a silver platter!

𝕏𝕊𝕊 Jesus Christ the Antichrist represents the Mystery Religion of Babylonian festivals NOT the Holy Days of Yahuah defined in scripture that Yahusha the Messiah kept and brought to their fullest expression spiritually.

Keeping The Law and the Festivals of Yahuah teach us the role of The Messiah

The Festivals or Holy Days of Yahuah are His witness to the true Messiah and stand as SUN blazing condemnation of the Antichrist 𝕏𝕊𝕊 Jesus Christ. I explain these most Holy Days which are times appointed by Yahuah when we "meet our Father" on a specific days to worship Him in my book *The Yahushaic Covenant*. I break down the most important one of all in my book *The Passover Season* as The Passover is the narrow gate that leads us out of bondage to sin and into the promised land.

Yahuah's festivals are rehearsals for future events and through them the Plan of Salvation through a Messiah is revealed. A rehearsal with Yahuah is like a rehearsal for a play. This suggests that the festivals are a teaching tool to prepare us to celebrate the fulfillment of the festival, at some time in the future and how to recognize the True Messiah from the false one. To rehearse properly we need to know:

1. The correct words of the script.
2. The correct actions and props.
3. The correct costume.
4. The correct date and time.

A rehearsal is practice for the real thing. By celebrating the festivals dictated by Yahuah, on Mount Sinai, we will be in the right place, at the right time, wearing the right clothes, saying the right words, and doing the right things. Thus even if we were not highly Torah educated, or were distracted by the task that Yahuah gave us, even then we would be perfectly positioned to fulfill His will.

To begin to understand the rehearsals of Yahuah will entail looking at the Hebrew word that means "rehearse". The Hebrew word "*miqra*" is translated as "sacred assemblies" or "holy convocation" depending on which translation one uses.

Strong's defines the Hebrew word "*miqra*" as:

> 4744 miqra', mik-raw'; from 7121; something called out, i.e. a public meeting (the act, the persons, or the place); also a rehearsal:-assembly, calling, convocation, reading.

Thus we see that *mikra* defines an assembly of people for the purposes of rehearsing a future event. The first use of *miqra* is found in:

Exodus 12:16
And in the first day there shall be an holy convocation (mikra/rehearsal), and in the seventh day there shall be an holy convocation (mikra/rehearsal) to you; no manner of work shall be done in them, save that which every man must eat, that only may be done of you.

The rehearsals, the festivals, of Yahuah, are spelled out in Leviticus chapter 23. The first verse to speak of these rehearsals is:

Leviticus 23:2
"Speak to the Israelites and say to them: 'These are my appointed feasts, the appointed feasts of Yahuah, which you are to proclaim as sacred assemblies (mikra/rehearsal).

Leviticus 23:4
"'These are Yahuah's appointed feasts, the sacred assemblies (mikra/rehearsal) you are to proclaim at their appointed times:

The Spring Festivals are dress rehearsals and celebrations that pointed to Yahusha coming as The Passover Lamb. The Fall Festivals are dress rehearsals and celebrations of Yahusha returning as the Conquering King. The Apostle Paul taught every assembly he established to KEEP The Torah, The Sabbath, the New Moon celebrations, and the Festivals of Yahuah:

Colossians 2
[16] Therefore do not let anyone judge you by what you eat or drink (as they kept Kosher Laws), or with regard to a religious festival (as they kept The Festivals of Yahuah), a New Moon celebration (as they celebrated each month) or a Sabbath day (as they kept the 4th Commandment and celebrated weekly). [17] These (things Paul taught them to do, remember they were Gentiles not Jews) are a shadow (physical rehearsals) of the things that were to come (Spiritual Truths); the reality, however, is found in *The Yahushaic Covenant*.

The False messiah is known by pagan festivals

The Antichrist will be the "image of a man" in whom the Ordained Times of Yahuah known as the Feasts of Yahuah or Holy Days will be changed to Babylonian festivals i.e. Holidays.

> **Daniel 7:25**
> He (*the Antichrist/False messiah*) will defy the Most High and oppress the holy people of the Most High. He will try to change their sacred festivals and the laws of Yahuah.

There is only one "image of a man" in history who has successfully fulfilled this prophecy and that is Jesus Christ. In the name and image of Jesus the Feasts of Yahuah were changed the Babylonian holidays by the Beast (Christianity).

Yahuah gave us His moedim or holy days so that we would know the true Messiah and not fall for the False messiah. Yahuah's Holy Days that He commanded we keep and were kept by Yahusha are:

- *The Spring Festivals:* Passover, First Fruits, and Shav'uot
- *The Fall Festivals*: Trumpets, Day of Atonement, and Tabernacles.

We know the False messiah is a false "image" of the true Messiah who is worshipped in our hearts above Yahuah as God. We can identify The False messiah because there will only be one "image of a man" in history that will be seemingly based on the life of the true Messiah but in his name a false gospel will be preached. That "false gospel" is that *The Law of Yahuah* has been abolished, the Sabbath changed to the day of the Sungod i.e. Sunday, and the Appointed Times (Festivals of Yahuah) have been changed to Babylonian rituals.

This is exactly what was done in the name of Hesus Horus Krishna a.k.a Jesus H. Christ at the council of Nicaea. Constantine created an image based on the life of Yahusha and in that image he changed The Sabbath to Sunday, change the name of the Messiah from coming in the name of Yahuah to another name, and he changed the Feasts of Yahuah to pagan sun worship rituals.

Yahusha warned us that another false messiah would come. Not in the name of Yahuah as Yahusha did as Yahusha's name means "Yahuah's Salvation". This false messiah would come in his own name (Jesus) and we would follow his example not Yahusha's.

John 5
[43] I have come in my Father's name (*Yahusha*), and you do not accept me; but if someone else comes in his own name (*Jesus*), you will accept him (*and follow him*).

Yahuah through Isaiah declares He hates these pagan festivals that have replace His Ordained Holy Days kept by those who "claim" they know Him but have been deceived:

Isaiah 1
14 **Your** New Moon feasts and **your appointed festivals** (*Sunday, Easter, Christmas, etc. all Babylonian Rituals*) **I hate with all my being**. They have become a burden to me; I am weary of bearing them. **15** When you spread out your hands in prayer, I hide my eyes from you; even when you offer many prayers, I am not listening (because you are not keeping Yahuah's Holy Days). Your hands are full of blood (of the Ishtar Pig, Easter sacrifice of the earthly pig Jesus)!

It is because we stopped keeping the very rehearsals that help us identify the true Messiah that most have fallen for The False messiah Jesus H. Christ. Had we kept The Sabbath and understood it we would never have fallen for Sunday worship as the day of rest. Had we kept Passover we would nave never fallen for Easter and so forth.

Yahuah gave us these Ordained Times because they literally define Yahusha as the true Messiah and condemn Jesus as The False Image of Yahusha who proclaims a false gospel message. Let's evaluate the rituals that define Jesus Christ.

The Resurrection Day of Tammuz (Easter)

Semaramis became known as the fertility goddess Ishtar. She took on many names in different cultures including Isis, Diana, Astarte, Ishtar, Aphrodite, Venus, and Easter. She was even identified with Mary as Mary was falsely deified and took on the titles "Mother of God" and "Queen of Heaven". Her son Tammuz took on many names as well such as Horus, Apollo, Sol, Krishna, Hercules, Mithra, and finally Jesus. The name Jesus H. Christ, in fact, originated by Constantine as Hesus Horus Krishna. "Hesus Horus Krishna" evolved into Jesus H. Christ over the years. All names of Tammuz put together for the son of the sungod and member of the Trinity worshipped on Sunday the day of his sungod. We will get to that in greater detail later in this book series.

Semaramis instituted a holy day in her Babylonian religion in honor of the supposed "death/resurrection" of her son Tammuz. Below is a picture of the Semaramis and Tammuz, the "Madonna/Child" and "Mary/Jesus"…

Notice the "child" in these images is not a baby but a small fully developed man. While protesting Catholics (called Protestants) deny worship of this pagan deity… they indeed contradict that denial in action as they openly do just that on Sunday, Christmas and Easter.

In the images above we see to the left the idol of Ishtar/Tammuz renamed Jesus/Mary. The idol of the Madonna/Child renamed Jesus/Mary. We see a painting of Jesus/Mary all the exact same Babylonian deities.

We need to begin admitting the obvious truth; these idols were not renamed because the pagans now believed in Yahusha the Messiah. No, Tammuz and Ishtar/Semaramis simply had their names changed in the false religion of Christianity which is a carbon copy of The Mystery Religion of Babylon!

What we now call "halos" were nothing more than images of the Sun clearly demonstrating who these "paintings" were really representing. Not Yahusha but Tammuz. Not Miriam but Isthar/Semaramis.

The real truth behind the "cross of Jesus" and the "halos" around Jesus and Mary is simple. Jesus is Tammuz and Mary is Ishtar, they were the renamed and became the latest versions of the Babylonian Madonna and Child. This is clearly depicted below in the bottom right image as we see the images of the Sungod behind them, the X of Tammuz (the cross of the equinox from The Zodiac) written on The Sun over "Jesus", and the crown on the Queen of Heaven and "Tammuz" in the upper right image of Jesus/Mary.

Their still remains idols in the Vatican of "Tammuz the great hunter" to this day… their (Christianity's) REAL messiah they renamed Jesus or Hesus or Iesous or I.H.S. which means… Hail Zeus or Son of Zeus.

The picture below is Tammuz the Great Hunter idol in The Vatican.

We still pass on images of Tammuz son of Semaramis today as Cupid, son of Venus. Still depicted as the "mighty hunter" complete with a bow and arrow!

"Cupid is depicted with a bow and arrow. a reminder of Nimrod being a "mighty hunter"

Satan has very craftily hidden this Babylonian worship in to target the minds of our children! We as adults have these "traditions" engrained in us and then we pass these abominations to Yahuah

305

down to our children. The process continues Generation after generation.

We were warned of this and it was prophesied to be true that at this time in history as Yahuah moves on His chosen in every nation:

> **Jeremiah 16:19**
> Yahuah, my strength and my fortress, my refuge in time of distress, to you the Gentiles will come out of the nations and will come back to You from the ends of the earth and say, "Our ancestors possessed nothing but false gods, worthless idols that did them no good.

We need to wake up and realize every established religion especially Christianity has been polluted with The Mystery Religion of Babylonian gods, rituals, and worship. We still "hunt Ishtar eggs" in honor of Tammuz the Great Hunter on Ishtar's day and eat ham in his honor. We just call it by its English name Easter but every ritual remains the same as in ancient Babylon.

No longer do we keep Passover and eat Lamb as commanded by The Messiah (strengthening the Law of Yahuah) as he kept Passover on the 14th of Abib (eve of Passover) just before he gave his body as The Passover Lamb. The last thing Yahusha said before dying on Passover was… ***KEEP PASSOVER!***

> **Luke 22:19**
> 19 And when he had taken some bread and given thanks (on the eve of Passover), He broke it and gave it to them, saying, "This (Passover Dinner) is My body (*Passover Lamb*) which is given (*sacrificed*) for you; do this (*keep Passover*) in remembrance of Me."

Do we obey our King? No… we now keep Ishtar and eat HAM because that is what was passed down to us from our ancestors. We literally eat the most abominable "beast" in The Torah in honor Tammuz who was killed by a pig. The fact, that Jesus of the Christian Church is in reality the Babylonian Tammuz, reincarnated Nimrod son of Ba'al to this day is denied by Christianity as **they have been given over by Yahuah to believe a lie**. I clearly define this "Spirit of Error" later in my book series. They have literally fallen for Nimrod / Semaramis / Tammuz under another name as they became Isis/Horus/Seb or **I.H.S** the monogram for Hesus Horus Krishna all names for Tammuz. Hesus Horus Krishna eveolved into Jesus H. Christ in English. But in Latin it remains I.H.S. in the middle of Sol Invictus, the same "invincible Sun" worshipped from Nimrod to Constantine to world-wide today in Christianity!

IHS **is the very monogram of Jesus H. Christ** and carried around by the High Priest of Ba'al today with the cross of Tammuz blazoned on top in the center of the Sun. Proudly displaying to the world the truth on the back of his robe that he serves Ishtar, Horus, Seb as he places the symbol of sun worship on the heart of his goddess Ishtar (they simply changed her name to Mary).

This is pagan Babylonian sun worship as I will explain in detail in my next book as we prove that the religion of Babylon was formally transferred to Rome and became what we know today as "*The Catholic Priesthood*".

Forty Days of Weeping for Tammuz: Lent & Ash Wednesday

When Tammuz was forty years old, he was hunting in the woods and he was killed by a wild boar (a pig) that is why we eat "ham" on Easter/Ishtar Day even though it is against Yahuah's commandments to eat pig. He took after his father Nimrod in that he was a "mighty hunter." After Tammuz died, his mother Semaramis began a custom in Babylon called "forty days of weeping for Tammuz" where people were commanded to fast and pray for Tammuz in the underworld. They exchanged one day of pleasure in this life for each year of Tammuz's life.

Today in the Roman Catholic Church this has been renamed "Lent." These forty days of fasting from something would begin on what is called "Ash Wednesday" in the Catholic Church and many protestant Churches with the Cross of Tammuz being written in ash on the forehead of the "faithful". The priest would take ashes and place a "mark" on our foreheads of a cross as he would recite a declaration about how we were "created from ashes and to ashes we shall return."

We were all told that when we celebrated Lent that we were commemorating the time when our Messiah fasted and prayed in the wilderness for "forty days and forty nights."

That is what I was made to believe that Lent was all about. But the truth of the matter is that our Messiah fasted and prayed during the "Forty Days of Repentance" leading up to Yom Kippur. It had NOTHING to do with "Lent" or Easter.

Here we see Yahuah condemning this practice called "weeping for Tammuz" which today is called Lent:

Ezekiel 8:13-14
"Turn you yet again, and you shall see greater abominations that they do. Then he brought me to the door of the gate of Yahuah's house which was toward the north; and, behold, there sat women <u>weeping for Tammuz</u>. Then said he unto me, Have you seen this, O son of man?"

Today in many cultures people make "Easter Bread" or "hot crossed buns". Do people realize that they are inadvertently offering up cakes to the Queen of Heaven?

Jeremiah 7:18-19
"The children gather wood, and the fathers kindle the fire, and the women knead their dough, to make cakes to the queen of heaven, and to pour out drink offerings unto other gods, that they may provoke me to anger. Do they provoke me to anger? says Yahuah: do they not provoke themselves to the confusion of their own faces? Therefore thus says the Yahuah your God; Behold, my anger and my fury shall be poured out upon this place."

No wonder the Catholic Church abolished the so-called Old Testament. It is a glaring condemnation of the entire religious system based in Rome.

Semaramis, (Nimrod's mother), became known in other cultures as "Magna Mater," the "Great Mother," and she was worshipped as Mother Earth. The Sun "mated" with the Earth each spring, and the "Rites of Spring" symbolized by the "May Pole" and "Easter" came 9 moons (months) before December 25th on the "birth" of the winter Sun. Her Assyrian name is Ishtar which is where we derive the name "Easter." Easter, the goddess of the dawn is the Universal goddess of fertility throughout history since the Tower of Babel. She began as Nimrod's wife Semaramis, and then after Yahuah scattered the nations and confused their languages at the

Tower of Babel (Genesis 10-11), her image with her baby son Tammuz migrated to other nations under different names.

The Romans called her Astarte but later she was called Venus, and the Phoenicians called her Asherah. The Hebrews called her Astoroth, the consort of Ba'al. Her emblem is the flower of the lily. She is the "goddess of the dawn," and her statue stands on a bridge in France. The French made a colossus of this image, and it now stands in New York Harbor, facing "East," referring to the name Ishtar or Easter. We call this idol of her **The Statue of Liberty.** Why is she facing the East?

Ezekiel 8:16

> And he brought me into the inner court of Yahuah's house, and, behold, at the door of the temple of Yahuah, between the porch and the altar, were about five and twenty men, with their backs toward the temple of Yahuah, and their faces toward the east; <u>and they worshipped the sun toward the east</u>.

The French Illuminati donated this statue to America in order to bring the spirit of Jezebel's influence upon our nation! I covered this earlier on the section on pagan Trinities. The torch that she carries is the "light of Lucifer" the same "light" of Freemasonry.

Easter is a day that is honored by nearly all of contemporary Christianity and is used to celebrate the resurrection of Jesus Christ which now we know is actually Tammuz not Yahusha. The holiday often involves a church service at sunrise (sun worship), a feast which includes an "Easter Ham" (the abominable sacrifice), decorated eggs and stories about rabbits. Below is a quick summary of exactly "what" Easter really is all about.

Detailed Origin of Easter

"Ishtar" (which is pronounced "Easter") was a day that commemorated the resurrection of one of their gods that they called "Tammuz". Tammuz was believed to be the only begotten son of the moon-goddess and the sun-god. In those ancient times, there was a man named Nimrod, who was the grandson of one of Noah's son named Ham. Ham had a son named Cush who married a woman named Semaramis. Cush and Semaramis then had a son named him "Nimrod."

After the death of his father, Nimrod married his own mother and became a powerful King. The Bible tells of of this man, Nimrod, in Genesis 10:8-10 as follows: "And Cush begat Nimrod: he began to be a mighty one in the earth. He was a mighty hunter in the face of Yahuah: wherefore it is said, even as Nimrod the mighty hunter in face of Yahuah. And the beginning of his kingdom was Babel, and Erech, and Accad, and Calneh, in the land of Shinar." Nimrod became a god-man to the people and Semaramis, his wife and mother, became the powerful Queen of ancient Babylon.

Nimrod was eventually killed by an enemy, and his body was cut in pieces and sent to various parts of his kingdom. Semaramis had all of the parts gathered, except for one part that could not be found. That missing part was his reproductive organ. Semaramis claimed that Nimrod could not come back to life without it and told the people of Babylon that Nimrod had ascended to the sun and was now to be called "Baal", the sun god.

Queen Semaramis also proclaimed that Baal would be present on earth in the form of a flame, whether candle or lamp, when used in worship representing the Sun. Semaramis was creating a mystery religion, and with the help of Satan, she set herself up as a goddess. Semaramis claimed that she was immaculately conceived.

She taught that the moon was a goddess that went through a 28 day cycle and ovulated when full. She further claimed that she came down from the moon in a giant moon egg that fell into the Euphrates River as she emerged as the moon fertility goddess Ishtar.

The Easter Egg

This was to have happened at the time of the first full moon after the spring equinox. Semaramis became known as "Ishtar" which is pronounced "Easter", and her moon egg became known as the "Ishtar's" egg."

Every year, on the first Sunday after the first full moon after the spring equinox, a celebration was made. It was Ishtar's Sunday and was celebrated with rabbits and eggs. The "Ishtar Eggs" were died in the blood of babies sacrificed to Tammuz with the "cross of Tammuz" emblazoned on them as the children would "hunt" the eggs in the likeness of Tammuz and Nimrod the mighty hunters.

Ishtar also proclaimed that because Tammuz was killed by a pig, that a pig must be eaten on that Ishtar's Sunday. At this point we begin to "see" what exact abominable "beast" replaced the sacrifice of the Passover Lamb. It was then and is still now, the Easter Pig of Ishtar! I will go into this in detail later in this book series.

The Easter Bunny

Tammuz was noted to be especially fond of rabbits, and they became sacred in the ancient religion, because Tammuz was believed to be the son of the sun-god, Baal. The rabbit is one of the most fertile creatures on Earth and held sacred to the fertility religion Semaramis had created in Babylon. Ishtar was the fertility goddess and the Ishtar/Easter Rabbit was her symbol.

Easter egg hunting originated with Tammuz, like his supposed father, became a hunter. The day came when Tammuz was killed by a wild pig. Queen Ishtar told the people that Tammuz was now ascended to his father, Baal, and that the two of them would be with the worshippers in the sacred candle or lamp flame as Father, Son and Spirit.

The Evergreen Tree and Lent and Fasting

Ishtar, who was now worshipped as the "Mother of God and Queen of Heaven", continued to build her mystery religion. The queen told the worshippers that when Tammuz was killed by the wild pig, some of his blood fell on the stump of an evergreen tree, and the stump grew into a full new tree overnight. This made the evergreen tree sacred by the blood of Tammuz. She also proclaimed a forty day period of time of sorrow each year prior to the anniversary of the death of Tammuz. During this time, no meat was to be eaten. We know this today as Lent.

The Cross of Tammuz

Worshippers were to meditate upon the sacred mysteries of Baal and Tammuz, and to make the sign of the "T" in front of their hearts as they worshipped. Today this is called "The Sign of the Cross" made over the heart of Christians as we read from the Catholic Encyclopedia

http://www.newadvent.org/cathen/13785a.htm

The cross was originally traced by Christians with the thumb or finger on their own foreheads. This practice is attested by numberless allusions in Patristic literature, and it was clearly associated in idea with certain references in Scripture, notably Ezekiel 9:4 (of the mark of the letter Tau); Exodus 17:9-14; and especially Apocalypse 7:3, 9:4 and 14:1. Hardly less early in date is the custom of marking a cross on objects — already Tertullian speaks of the Christian woman "signing" her bed (cum lectulum tuum signas, "Ad uxor.", ii, 5) before retiring to rest—and we soon hear also of the sign of the cross being traced on the lips (Jerome, "Epitaph. Paulæ") and on the heart (Prudentius, "Cathem.", vi, 129).

Hotcross buns

They also ate sacred cakes with the marking of a "T" or cross on the top. We know them today as "hotcross buns" we bake and eat on "Ishtar SungodDay" i.e. Easter Sunday.

The Birthday of Nimrod and Tammuz and the Rebirth of the Sun (Christmas)

The origin of Christmas has been and continues to be exposed for its true original roots:

> *"Nimrod started the great organized worldly apostasy from God that has dominated this world until now. Nimrod married his own mother, whose name was Semaramis. After Nimrod's death, his so-called mother-wife, Semaramis, propagated the evil doctrine of the survival of Nimrod as a spirit being. She claimed a full-grown evergreen tree sprang overnight from a dead tree stump, which symbolized the springing forth unto new life of the dead Nimrod. On each anniversary of his birth, she claimed, Nimrod would visit the evergreen tree and leave gifts upon it. December 25th, was the birthday of Nimrod. This is the real origin of the Christmas tree."*
> **-The Plain Truth About Christmas by David J. Stewart**

> *"Traditionally, a yule log was burned in the fireplace on Christmas Eve and during the night as the log's embers died, there appeared in the room, as if by magic, a Christmas tree surrounded by gifts. The yule log represented the sun-god Nimrod and the Christmas tree represented himself resurrected as his own son Tammuz."*
> **--After Armageddon -Chapter 4 Where do we get our ideas? by John A. Sarkett**

The actual identity of "Santa Clause" is Nimrod himself and the X-mas Tree is a memorial to him.

We see Nimrod in a long white beard clearly pictured with a "Christmas Tree" and even a reindeer as early as 2000 BC, yes TWO THOUSAND YEARS before "Christianity" was ever created:

Nimrod deified: Ancient Nineveh Artifact

Nimrod and Santa (trees)

Circa 2000 B.C.

Nimrod's Birthday - December 25

1. Long Beard
2. Holding Rheindeer
3. Holding Xmas Tree

Christmas being the "birthday" of "Jesus" has its origins in the Babylonian Mystery Religion. In order to secure her reign as Queen of Babylon after Nimrod's death, Semaramis had to devise a way of keeping the "Spirit of Nimrod" alive. She had already deified Nimrod as Baal the Sungod but needed Nimrod to return to the people.

Semaramis consulted her astrologers who told her that the sun "dies" on December 21st (the shortest day of the year) but then it begins to come back to life again on the eve of December 24th as the days begin to grow longer.

> *"In paganism this is what is known as the "winter solstice," which falls on December 21st ----when the earth is the furthest away from the sun. On December 24th, the earth begins to rotate back around the sun and comes closer to the sun. But the pagans did not know this in earlier times before science and telescopes.*

These pagans in Babylon thought that the sun died on December 21st and then it began to resurrect on the eve of December 24th and then it made it's full rebirth on December 25th. They believed this to be the birthday of Nimrod or Baal the Sungod.

Using astrology as her guide, Semaramis became pregnant on around March 25th (9 months from December 25th), and then she concocted a legend for the Babylonian people telling them that on December 21st, Nimrod dies each year, but then on December 25th Nimrod is "born-again" as the "sun-god" or "Ba'al." Hence, on December 25th the "sun-god" is celebrated around the world with many different names.

Semaramis told the Babylonians that she had become the goddess of the moon and the sky and that Nimrod was being "reincarnated" in her womb as "Ba'al" the sun-god on December 25th. She told the Babylonians that Nimrod impregnated her with the "rays of the sun" supernaturally and Nimrod "re-incarnated" himself as her new son Tammuz on December 25th.

Her new son was named Tammuz according to Ezekiel 8:14 or generically he was called "Ba'al" (which means Lord or husband). Each year on Tammuz's birthday on December 25th, the pagans were ordered by Semaramis to go into the groves (forests) and placed a gift on a tree to honor Nimrod who was "cut down" like a tree. They were also ordered to cut down an everygreen tree, take it into their homes and decorate it with silver and gold balls to symbolize Nimrod's testicles.

Trees and branches became symbols of Nimrod because Nimrod was "cut down" by Shem, the son of Noah who placed a bounty hunt on his life. The book of Jasher tells us that it was Esau (the son of Jacob) who actually killed Nimrod. Hence, a tree stump became a place of honoring him, as the scriptures speak of the pagans going into the "groves" or the forest and cutting down a tree, decorating it, and propping it up so that it will not totter."

...*The Two Babylons, by Alexander Hyslop*

How was "Christmas" passed down to us in "Christianity"?

In the pagan Roman society during the time lived, they instituted the "Saturnalia" in honor of the god Saturn. It was a lawless celebration held on December 25th, the birthday of Tammuz and rebirth of Nimrod. Each year, an innocent person would be chosen by the communities as a human sacrifice to the gods. This person would be forced into engaging in all types of physical pleasures (food, sex, etc) throughout the week leading up to Saturnalia then murdered on December 25th with the aim of obtaining the gods blessing for the coming years crops.

In addition to human sacrifice, there was wide-spread intoxication and the people would go house-to-house singing (origin of caroling). The people would mimic human sacrifice by eating human shaped biscuits (we call them **gingerbread men**). The Encyclopedia Britannica volume 24 page. 231 tells us the people would give each other gifts. Primarily to children in the form of "dolls" which represented sacrificed human beings to the infernal gods.

Christianity incorporated Saturnalia into the religion of Constantine (Christianity) calling it Christmas in the 4th Century AD. No such festival exists in the Bible. It is directly from Babylon. Yahusha was born during the Feast of Sukkoth in the Fall.

The Christmas Tree

Jeremiah 10:2-4

"Learn not the way of the heathen, and be not dismayed at the signs of heaven; (astrology was idolized) for the heathen are dismayed at them…For the customs of the people are vain: for one cuts a tree out of the forest, the work of the hands of the workman, with the axe. They deck it with silver and with gold; they fasten it with nails and with hammers that it move not." (then they put gifts under it and bow down to it as if to accept the gift from the gods)

The Hebrew word for "groves" in this case is Strong's H842 – 'asherah אֲשֵׁרָה'.

Asherah: groves (for idol worship); *__a Babylonian__* (Astarte/Ishtar) - Canaanite goddess (of fortune and happiness), the supposed consort of Baal known as Ishtar, her images; the goddess, goddesses; her images; sacred trees or poles set up near an altar.

The origin of the X-mas Tree (X or "the cross" is the symbol of Tammuz and the mark/monogram of Jesus Christ) is actually the Tammuz/Nimrod Tree and has absolutely nothing to do with The Messiah or The Truth found in The Bible. The X-mas Tree was a central figure in the Babylonian Religion with a snake wrapped around a tree trunk. We now, of course, don't have snakes around our tree **we have garland**! But let us not be so naive to think Yahuah approves of such ignorance in worship founded in Babylonian paganism…

It began with a Snake and a Tree

Christmas trees are really Asherah poles or sacred trees for honoring "Ba'al" and the ornamental balls represent Nimrod's testicles! Garland representing the serpent, Satan! Babylonian history records that Nimrod was cut into pieces and his body parts were sent to different provinces of Babylon to warn the people not to sacrifice babies to Moloch. His only body part which was never

found was his penis. Semaramis, his mother/wife then decided to memorialize his penis by erecting a giant image of Nimrod's penis which today is called **the obelisk**. They adorn many Christian Churches today as steeples as I noted earlier in this chapter. We are COMMANDED by Yahuah to destroy these very structures: Exodus 23:24, Exodus 34:13, Deuteronomy 7:5, Deuteronomy 12:3, Jeremiah 43:13, Hosea 10:2. Yet, we openly worship them as part of the Christian Religion. The Christmas Tree is also the symbol of Satan in the Garden of Eden, the garland wrapped around the "Tree of Knowledge of Good and Evil" like a snake around the tree with the ornamental balls representing the forbidden fruit.

The Sabbath is changed to Dies Solis

"If Protestants would follow the Bible, they should worship God on the Sabbath Day, that is Saturday. In keeping Sunday they are following a law of the Catholic Church."
Albert Smith, chancellor of the Archdiocese of Baltimore, replying for the cardinal in a letter of Feb. 10, 1920.

What the Chancellor of the Archdiocese of Baltimore is saying to his "Cardinal" is simple… Sunday is not in The Bible and contradicts The Commanded Sabbath of Yahuah. Albert Smith is admitting is that "***Protest***ants" are simply ***protest***ing Catholics but still Catholic non-the-less in fundamental doctrine. The entire body of "Christianity" is in fact the false religion based word for word in doctrine on the ***the Mystery Religion of Babylon***.

When addressing the issue of the Sabbath vs. Sunday, we must always keep in the forefront of our minds that the Roman Empire's religion before, during and even after the Roman Emperor Constantine was Sol Invictus (the worship of the invincible sun which began in Babylon). Constantine founded Christianity on a purely political bases to stabilize his empire and unit pagan religions not because he became a follower of Yahusha and child of Yahuah. Constantine never changed his religion; he just forced his sun worship upon the entire world.

"Had she (Christianity) not such power, she could not have done that in which all modern religionists agree with her, **she could not have substituted the observance of Sunday**, the first day of the week, for the observance of Saturday, the Seventh day, **a change for which there is no Scriptural authority**" **Stephen Keenan, A Doctrinal Catechism 3rd ed. p. 174**

> *The Christian Church,… "by virtue of her (Christianity's) divine mission", changed the day from Saturday to Sunday.* **The Catholic Mirror, official organ of Cardinal Gibbons, Sept. 23, 1893.**

321

The admission above is true, it was Satan's "divine mission" to change the Sabbath to Sunday. Why? Because The Sabbath is the "sign" that you are truly a child of Yahuah. Keeping The Sabbath is how you demonstrate you know Yahuah:

> **Exodus 31**
> 12 Yahuah said to Moshe, 13 Tell the people of Isra'el, **'You are to observe my Shabbats; for this <u>is a sign between me and you</u> through all your generations; <u>so that you will know that I am Yahuah</u>, who sets you apart for me. 17 It is a sign between me and the people of Isra'el forever**; for in six days Yahuah made heaven and earth, but on the seventh day he stopped working and rested.'

The Sabbath
Key to Salvation

Hebrews 4 even in the NT or New Covenant the Sabbath is key to salvation. Below it clearly says you cannot be saved if you violate the Sabbath and The Sabbath is the 4th Commandment of Yahuah. Remember, all the men of God in the Bible and the true church kept the Sabbath for 300 years after the Messiah's death until Constantine changed it by threat of death:

> **Hebrews** 4 - *A Sabbath-Rest for the People of God*
> 1 Therefore, since the promise of entering his rest ***still stands***, let us be careful that none of you be found to have fallen short of it (*by failing to Keep the Sabbath*). 2 For we also have had the gospel preached to us, just as they did; but the message they heard was of no value to them, because those who heard did not combine it with faith (*Keep the Sabbath in light of the Messiah*). 3 Now we who have believed enter that rest (*Keep the Sabbath in light of*

faith in the Passover Lamb of Yahuah, whose name is Yahusha), just as Yahuah has said,

"So I declared on oath in my anger, 'They shall never enter my rest.' "And yet his work has been finished since the creation of the world (*Yahuah Himself kept the Sabbath in Genesis 1 and commanded we do to, the 4th Commandment*). 4 For somewhere he has spoken about the seventh day (*Saturday, not Sunday*) in these words: "And on the seventh day Yahuah rested from all his work." 5 And again in the passage above he says, "They shall never enter my rest." (*Referring to those disobedient to His Sabbath command*)

6 It **still remains that some (**the remnant sons of Yahuah**) will enter that rest**, and those who formerly had the gospel preached to them did not go in, because of their disobedience (*to the Sabbath*). 7 Therefore Yahuah, again, set a certain day, calling it Today, when a long time later he spoke through David, *as was said before*:

"Today, if you hear his voice, do not harden your hearts. (*against His Sabbath*)"

8 For if Joshua had given them rest, God would not have spoken later about another day (*the Sabbath Rest is yet to come*). 9 **There remains, then, a Sabbath-rest for the people of Yahuah**; 10 **for anyone who enters God's rest also rests from his own work, just as Yahuah did from His (***You must keep the Sabbath just as Yahuah did***)**. 11 Let us, therefore, make every effort to enter that rest (*by being obedient to The Sabbath*), so that no one will fall by following their example of disobedience (*set by the Christian Church*).

The Sabbath is defined as The Sign between Yahuah and His sons. The "sign" of the Christian Church between Satan and his chosen is and has always been Sunday.

"You may read the Bible from Genesis to Revelation, and you will not find a single line authorizing the sanctification of Sunday. The Scriptures enforce the religious observance of Saturday, a day which we never sanctify." **James Cardinal Gibbons, The Faith of Our Fathers (1917 ed.), pp. 72,73.**

In fact, The Sabbath is the weekly worship day for all eternity by all mankind because as Hebrew 4 states only Sabbath keepers enter the Kingdom of God. We see below that those Sabbath keepers literally step over the bodies of those destroyed for NOT KEEPING THE SABBATH!

Isaiah 66:22-24

22 "For just as the new heavens and the new earth that I am making will continue in my presence," says Yahuah, "so will your descendants and your name continue. 23 "Every month on Rosh-Hodesh and **every week on Shabbat**, everyone living will come to worship in my presence," says Yahuah. 24 "As they leave, they will look on the corpses of the people who rebelled against me (*and My Sabbaths*) for their worm will never die, and their fire will never be quenched; but they will be abhorrent to all humanity."

Where did Sunday Worship come from if not The Bible?

Where did the Christian Church get Sunday worship? Not from The Bible it is nowhere to be found. Sunday worship cam from Sol Invictus ("Invincible Sun"); the official sun god of the later Roman Empire. In 274 the Roman emperor Aurelian made it an official cult alongside the traditional Roman cults. Sol Invictus was the favored god by emperors after Aurelian and appeared on their coins until Constantine. The last inscription referring to Sol Invictus dates to 387 AD.

Keep in mind, Constantine's "conversion" was supposedly to have taken place much earlier than that. The Council of Nicaea and "birth" of Christianity took place in 325 AD some 50 years *earlier* than the last inscription on Constantine's coins. His strictly legendary "conversion" supposedly took place earlier than the Council of Nicaea. What "conversion' actually took place 3 years prior to the Council of Nicaea and birth of the Christian religion? Constantine was converted to The Cult of Sol Invictus. The "new" convert Constantine actually remained deeply committed to his sun god and was one of the few which incorporated the epithet invictus, such as the legend SOLI INVICTO COMITI, claiming the Unconquered Sun as a companion to the Emperor. This "commitment to the sun god" was used particular frequency by Constantine. Statuettes of Sol Invictus, carried by the standard-bearers, appear in three places in reliefs on the Arch of Constantine. Constantine's official coinage continues to bear images of Sol until 325/6. A solidus of Constantine as well as a gold medallion from his reign depict the Emperor's bust in profile twinned ("jugate") with Sol Invictus, with the legend INVICTUS CONSTANTINUS. It should be noted here, that his new god too was INVICTUS JESUS as are his followers to this day.

Constantine decreed (March 7, 321) dies Solis—day of the sun, "Sunday"—as the Roman day of rest just prior to the Council of Nicaea:

> *"**On the venerable day of the Sun** let the magistrates and people residing in cities rest, and let all workshops be closed. In the country however persons engaged in agriculture may freely and lawfully continue their pursuits because it often happens that another day is not suitable for grain-sowing or vine planting; lest by neglecting the proper moment for such operations the bounty of heaven should be lost."*

Constantine's triumphal arch was carefully positioned to align with the colossal statue of Sol by the Colosseum, so that Sol formed the dominant backdrop when seen from the direction of the main approach towards the arch.

Following the Council of Nicaea, the newly formed "Christian Church" held yet another "council" of paganism known as The Council of Leodicea to uphold the abomination of Sun god worship. In this council they literally declared the obedient followers of Yahuah an "anathema of Christ" or rather "accursed by Chrestos" which may be true of their god "Jesus" but not the true Messiah Yahusha. Yahusha kept Sabbath, commanded we keep it, and was raised by Yahuah on The Sabbath. In effect, they declared the True Messiah, a Jewish Rabbi and follower of The Torah, accursed as he was truly a Jewish Rabbi and Sabbath keeper:

> *Christians must not judaize by resting on the Sabbath, but must work on that day, rather honouring the Lord's Day; and, if they can, resting then as Christians. But if any shall be found to be judaizers,* **let them be anathema from Christ. (Canon 29 [A.D. 360]). (The Church Council of Laodicea circa 364 CE)**

Well, Yahusha the Messiah was by their definition "a judaizer" and there for accursed by their god Jesus. It was the role of the new "priests of Sol" (formerly the priests of Mithra called "Fathers") and the priestesses of Brigit called "Nuns" in the newly formed "Christian Church" to teach the masses now that Sungod Day was the "New Sabbath". This was accomplished by teaching that the disciples of "Jesus" met together on the first day of the week. In their pagan calendars and reckoning of time, Sunday was the first day of the week and the day began at midnight. The ignorant masses were easily led astray.

The days in the Bible at the time of the Messiah began at sunset. So early "the first day" of the week Biblically was what we call Saturday night. The disciples were at home keeping The Sabbath, as commanded by Yahuah and obediently kept by Yahusha, from sunset Friday to sunset Saturday. They would then get together Saturday night to fellowship together once the sun set on The Sabbath and a new day began at dusk. When the sun rose on Sunday the first day of the week **they were all at work it was a work day**. They didn't have "weekends" like we do today! Any truth seeking individual thinker and obedient son of Yahuah would know this simple historical fast. Sunday "sunrise" morning worship is PAGAN dating back to Babylon.

Then the pagan priests in this "new" religion called Christianity would teach Good Friday as the day their "Christ" was crucified on the cross of Tammuz. When in reality the Messiah was impaled on a stake. They would then teach their "Christ" was resurrected on Ishtar Sungod Day what we now call Easter. This was their "justification" for literally abolishing the only Holy Day kept by God (Yahuah) Himself, **the Sabbath Day**. These pagan priests used lies by changing the "times" of Yahuah in how you calculate a "day", lies to justify a "cross" and lies to justify Good-Friday/Easter. The Catholic (Mother of Christianity) Church then literally re-wrote the 10 Commandments eliminating the 4th Commandment to keep the Sabbath Day Holy.

In the 5th century, Socrates Scholasticus Church History book 5 states the fact that until Constantine imposed Dies Solis (Sungod Day) on humanity, most assemblies and believers across the world at that time **still kept The Sabbath even as late as 5 centuries later after Yahusha**! He clearly knew that this "Sunday" worship was based in Rome on "the account of some ancient tradition"!

> *"Nor is there less variation in regard to religious assemblies. For although almost all churches throughout the world celebrate the sacred mysteries on the sabbath of every week, yet the Christians of Alexandria and at Rome,*

> *on account of some ancient tradition, have ceased to do this."*

The reader of this book should now know exactly what "ancient tradition" he was referring to; sun god worship originating in ancient Babylon. Evidence of this blasphemous move by a pagan Roman Church called "Christianity" is plentiful in history if we simply love Yahuah enough to question it.

> ***Westminster Confession of Faith, Chapter 21, "Of Religious Worship, and the Sabbath Day". Section 7-8 reads:*** *As it is the law of nature, that, in general, a due proportion of time be set apart for the worship of God; so, in his Word, by a positive, moral, and perpetual commandment binding all men in all ages,* ***he hath particularly appointed one day in seven,*** *for a Sabbath, to be kept holy unto him: which, from the beginning of the world to the resurrection of Christ, was the last day of the week; and, from the resurrection of Christ, was changed into the first day of the week, which, in Scripture, is called the Lord's day, and is to be continued to the end of the world, as the Christian Sabbath.*

No. Yahuah did not set aside "one day in Seven" he set aside **THE 7ᵗʰ Day**! The above is an unscriptural pagan lie. This trickery and slight of hand and word smithing is notorious in the Christian Church. "Christian Sabbath" is a man-made term <u>not found in Scripture</u> or taught by anyone until 5ᵗʰ century. Only by circular reasoning can this statement be made – (i.e. the Lord's Day must mean Sunday since that is the day Jesus rose from the grave.) – which in fact Yahusha was not raisedon Sunday at all! He was raised 3 days and 3 nights after the Passover when he was killed. That resurrection day is The Sabbath!

The first "lie" is that Yahusha rose on Sunday when in fact he was risen on The Sabbath! Yahusha rose on the 7ᵗʰ Day. This "Lord's Day" or more accurately "Day of the Lord" in scripture actually says "Day of Yahuah" and refers to the END OF DAYS – NOT

SUNDAY - See Amos 5:18, Joel 2:31, 1Thes. 5:2. The Apostle John in Revelation uses this term. His entire letter is describing the end of days, end time events. He wasn't saying, "let's see, I think it was on Sunday that I had this vision". No, he was saying, "I have been a witness of future events on the Day of Yahuah" – referring to judgment. Change the name Yahuah to "the LORD", give that same title to the Messiah, call him "Jesus" then twist the reckoning of time and scriptures, and **only then** can you arrive at Sunday being "The Lord's Day". Oh how easily we are misled and how very easily we put up with it! We have literally been given another Gospel (Trinity/Sunday/Easter/Jesus) not in scripture (which is Yahuah/Yahusha/Sabbath/Passover) and another "Spirit" that "Jesus is God not man" when Yahuah alone is God and we bought into it and to this day put up with it:

2 Corinthians 11:4
[4] For if someone comes to you and preaches a Messiah other than the Messiah we preached, or if you receive a different spirit from the Spirit you received, or a different gospel from the one you accepted, **you put up with it easily enough**.

Yahuah raised Yahusha from the grave on The Sabbath

The Messiah was impaled on a stake on The Passover, a Wednesday, and rose from the grave on The Sabbath exactly 3 days/nights later. This false messiah named "Jesus" is proven false by the very fact that Friday night (supposed time of Jesus crucifixion) to Sunday morning (supposed time of his resurrection) **is only a day and a half**! Jesus is therefore a FALSE PROPHET because he specifically stated he would be in the grave 3 days AND 3 nights. There is no logic known to man that can get 3 days and 3 nights from Friday evening to Sunday morning. **Are we so ignorant and uneducated that we cannot even count to 3?** Or have we "willingly" become so? This one fact alone disqualifies the Roman demi-god "Jesus H. Christ" from being the true

Messiah of Israel. The Catholic Church (Christianity) even admits this abomination. Calling the Sabbath of Yahuah a "Jewish Sabbath", the very sign between Yahuah and His chosen Elect and the 4th Commandment of God, they admit literally changing The Law of God on the authority of the False Christian Church alone. Basically "we keep Sunday because we keep Sunday we don't care what the Bible says or Yahuah Commanded or what day Yahusha taught in The Temple or what day he was resurrected". This is our only defense and reason for keeping Sunday because no justification for Sunday worship is true. History clearly shows the Sabbath was changed by a sun worshiping pagan emperor then forced on an uneducated realm by law then by death:

> *"The Church, on the other hand, after changing the day of rest from the Jewish Sabbath, or seventh day of the week, to the first, made the Third (fourth) Commandment refer to Sunday as the day to be kept holy as the Lord's Day."* **The Catholic Encyclopedia Topic: Ten Commandments, 2nd paragraph**

> *"We have made the change from the seventh day to the first day, from Saturday to Sunday, on the authority of the one holy, catholic, apostolic church of Christ."*--**Episcopalian Bishop Seymour said in "Why We Keep Sunday."**

Never did Yahuah give mankind such authority to rewrite His Law. The Messiah Yahusha never assumed such authority. The pagan Popes of Rome even go so far as to claim Yahuah's most Holy Sabbath as an "execration" or "curse"!

> *Sylvester I (314-337 A.D.) was the pope during the reign of Constantine. Here is what he thought of the Bible Sabbath: "If every Sunday is to be observed joyfully by the Christians on account of the resurrection,* **then every Sabbath on account of the burial is to be execration** *[loathing or cursing] of the Jews."--***quoted by S. R. E. Humbert, Adversus Graecorum calumnias 6, in Patrologie Cursus Completus, Series Latina, ed. J.P. Migne, 1844, p. 143.**

Yahusha was neither buried on Friday nor was he resurrected on Sunday. He was buried on Passover a Wednesday and raised on The Sabbath. Again it is openly admitted that the 7th Day Sabbath is the ONLY Holy Day in scripture and was changed to accommodate <u>the pagan sun worshippers of their day</u>:

> *At this time in early church history it was necessary for the church to either adopt the Gentiles' day or else have the Gentiles change their day. To change the Gentiles' day would have been an offense and a stumbling block to them. The church could naturally reach them better by keeping their day."*
> *--William Frederick, Three Prophetic Days, pp. 169-170.*

That's right; to assimilate pagans into this new false religion the decision was made to "keep THEIR pagan day". Even the Pope admits as much, if you follow Yahuah you will keep The Sabbath, if you follow him you will keep Dies Solis (the day of the Sun god) as it is his "divine right" given him by the Sun deity to <u>change the ordinances of Yahuah</u>:

> *"The Pope has the power to change times, to abrogate (abolish) laws, and to dispense with all things, even the precepts of Christ." **"The Pope has the authority and often exercised it, to dispense with the command of Christ."** - **Decretal, de Tranlatic Episcop. Cap. (The Pope can modify divine law.) Ferraris' Ecclesiastical Dictionary.***

Make no mistake if you are Christian and do not keep the Sabbath IT IS BY PAPAL DECREE! The false Church of Rome known today as Christianity (even its Protestants off-shoots are guilty) imposed this "false" Church upon humanity at the cost of literally murdering over 100,000,000 (100 Million) people or as the Bible says "dripping with the blood of the Saints":

> *"That the Church of Rome has shed more innocent blood than any other institution that has ever existed among*

mankind, will be questioned by no Protestant who has a competent knowledge of history . . . It is impossible to form a complete conception of the multitude of her victims, and it is quite certain that no powers of imagination can adequately realize their sufferings."
--W. E. H. Lecky, History of the Rise and Influence of the Spirit of Rationalism in Europe, vol. 2, p. 32, 1910 edition

"For professing faith contrary to the teachings of the Church of Rome, history records the martyrdom of more then one hundred million people. A million Waldenses and Albigenses [Swiss and French Protestants] perished during a crusade proclaimed by Pope Innocent III in 1208. Beginning from the establishment of the Jesuits in 1540 to 1580, nine hundred thousand were destroyed. One hundred and fifty thousand perished by the Inquisition in thirty years. Within the space of thirty-eight years after the edict of Charles V against the Protestants, fifty thousand persons were hanged, beheaded, or burned alive for heresy. Eighteen thousand more perished during the administration of the Duke of Alva in five and a half years."
--Brief Bible Readings, p. 16.

On August 24, 1572, Roman Catholics in France, by pre-arranged plan, under Jesuit influence, murdered 70,000 Protestants within the space of two months. The pope rejoiced when he heard the news of the successful outcome. (Read Great Controversy, chapter 15 for the details.). . . We have heard ring out many times the very bells that called the Catholics together on that fatal night. They always sounded sweetly in our ears"
--Western Watchman, Nov. 21, 1912 [Roman Catholic].

It is little wonder "why" we march to our

Trinity/Jesus/Sunday/Easter/Christmas

pagan establishments each and every Dies Solis. "The Whore of

Babylon" literally is drenched in the blood of the saints of Yahuah who would not bow to this paganism. **Humanity has been conditioned by threat of death** from the Inquisitions on through 2,000 years of murder and bloodshed to blindly obey. That includes YOU! Try questioning Sunday worship some day to your family, friends, preacher, etc. and ask them why we all are disobedient to the ONLY Holy Day kept by God Himself and the Messiah and every man in the Bible and the real church for 500 years after Yahusha came… The Sabbath.

Summary

The Antichrist is not prophesied to be an actual man but rather an "image of a man who died" meaning there will be an "image" based somewhat on the life of the True Messiah. However, this image will be a "false" image of Yahusha that comes in his own pagan name not the name of Yahuah. In this image the Holy Days of Yahuah will be changed to Babylonian rituals and the Law of Yahuah will be abolished. The name of Yahuah will be lost as we fall for this false messiah and worship The LORD (Ba'al).

The Holy Days of Yahuah are well defined in scripture and these appointed times when we are to meet with our Creator each years were changed to Babylonian holiday and focused directly at our children.

Passover/Unleavened Bread/First fruits were changed to Good Friday/Easter and ҲȘȘ Jesus Christ is therefore a false prophet for not meeting Yahusha's sign of Jonah. That sign is 3 full days and 3 full nights in the grave. Jesus only spend 1/1/2 days in the tomb! Yahusha's birth on the Feast of Tabernacles in the fall was changed to Saturnalia which is December 25th in celebration of the sungod Ba'al and so forth.

In recent years even the Pope (Pontiff High Priest of Dagon the Dragon) has even admitted that Yahusha was not born in winter:

> *Pope Benedict Disputes Jesus' Date of Birth | TIME.com*
> *"With the release of his new book, Pope Benedict XVI asks how much we really know about the birth of Christ. Pope Benedict XVI has revealed in the third installment of his trilogy, dedicated to the life of Christ, that Jesus may have been born earlier than previously thought. The calendar we use today, which commences with the birth of Christ and was created by a Dionysius Exiguus, a 6th century monk, may be mistaken. According to the Telegraph, the Pope explains in his book that Exiguus, who is considered the inventor of the Christian calendar, "made a mistake in his calculations by several years. The actual date of Jesus' birth was several years before." The suggestion that Jesus wasn't actually born on Dec. 25 has been tirelessly debated by theologians, historians and spiritual leaders, but what makes this case different is that now the leader of the Catholic Church is the one asking the questions.*

Now we are going to take an even deeper look at *The Spirit of Error* that leads to *The Transgression of Desolation* as 𝙓𝘚𝘚 Jesus Christ is… The Lawless One.

Chapter 18

The Antichrist is The Lawless One who commits The Transgression of Desolation

My people are being destroyed because they don't know me. Since you priests refuse to know me, I refuse to recognize you as my priests. <u>Since you have forgotten the laws of your God,</u> ***I will forget to bless your children*** *… **Hosea 4:6***

The Transgression of Desolation is the Abolishment of The Law

In this chapter we are going to take a hard look at The Lawless One in whose "image" the Law of Yahuah has been abolished.

In scripture there are two events that occur among mankind that lead to the Earth's destruction and the destruction of humanity. They are *The Transgression of Desolation* and *The Abomination of Desolation*.

Very few people realize that *The Transgression of Desolation* and *The Abomination of Desolation* are two very different events and that one leads to the other. They are both addressed in scripture and both combine as a 1, 2... punch to destroy the Earth and everyone on it. Most Christian teachers (filled with The Spirit of Error and Spirit of the False messiah themselves) don't see there is a difference between the two. To admit this would shine a bright spotlight on the fact that The Law in fact has not been abolished but rather simply transposed to Spiritual Intent. In fact, it has been STRENGHENED and in no way shape, form, or fashion has it been done away with.

First let us define terms:

Transgression Definition:

Main Entry: **trans·gres·sion** 🔊
Pronunciation: -'gre-sh&n
Function: *noun*
Date: 15th century
: an act, process, or instance of transgressing : as **a :** infringement or violation of a law, command, or duty

Abomination Definition:

Main Entry: **abom·i·na·tion** 🔊
Pronunciation: &-"bä-m&-'nA-sh&n
Function: *noun*
Date: 14th century
1 : something abominable
2 : extreme disgust and hatred :

The Transgression of Desolation is where mankind abolishes *The Law of Yahuah* in the "image of The False messiah" and change Yahuah's Feasts to pagan holidays and Yahuah's Sabbath to a pagan day of worship. It is this transgression of The Law that leads to the desolation of Earth and everything on it.

The Abomination of Desolation is committed by those who put their faith in The False messiah and elevate an image of him as God in their hearts. The sacrifice of The False messiah is the most abominable animal to Yahuah defined in His Law as a pig. خۏۻ Jesus name in English is a Latin derived name and means Earthly Pig. Those who put their faith in this abominable sacrifice are destroyed; it literally desolates/destroys their body which is *The Temple of Yahuah*.

Transgression of Desolation vs. The Abomination of Desolation

The Transgression of Desolation is humanity abolishing The Laws of Yahuah. It is this transgression that leads to the total "desolation" of planet Earth by Yahuah:

> ### Isaiah 24: 1-6
> The Earth is polluted by its inhabitants - They have committed ***The Transgression of Desolation*** (*transgressed the Torah, changed the Holy Feasts to Christopagan Holidays, and broken the Everlasting Covenant of the Sabbath changing it to the pagan day of worship ... Sunday*) - Therefore the Curse found in the Torah devours the whole Earth, the inhabitants of Earth will be burned up, and few men left.

The "curse" Isaiah is referring to that destroys the Earth is the curse for "transgressing The Laws of Yahuah"

> ### Deuteronomy 27:26
> "Cursed is anyone who does not uphold the words of this law by carrying them out."

We see in Revelation 15 the prophecy in Isaiah being fulfilled as ***The Tabernacles of The Covenant Law*** is opened inside ***The Temple of Yahuah*** to judge the Earth for committing ***The Transgression of Desolation*** and ***The Great Tribulation*** begins:

> ### Revelation 15
> [5] After this I looked, and I saw in heaven (*there is no temple on Earth at this time, it has been transposed to heaven*) **the temple—that is, the tabernacle of the covenant law**—and it was opened (*as to judge those on the Earth who have transgressed The Law*). [6] Out of the temple came the seven angels <u>with the seven plagues</u>. They were dressed in clean, shining linen and wore golden sashes

around their chests. [7] Then one of the four living creatures gave to the seven angels seven golden bowls <u>filled with the wrath of Yahuah</u>, who lives forever and ever. [8] And the temple was filled with smoke from the glory of Yahuah and from his power, and no one could enter the temple <u>until the seven plagues of the seven angels were completed</u>.

The false teachers (Christian pastors/teachers) simply read over this most important prophecy. They teach The Law has been abolished when yet it IS The Law, the tabernacles of covenant Law of Yahuah that is and has always been the standard of Righteousness by which all mankind will be judged. The prophet Daniel speaks of this same event where the people of Earth commit *The Transgression of Desolation* by transgressing *The Law of Yahuah*. We see that *The Transgression of Desolation* leads later to *The Abomination of Desolation*. Below is how the Amplified Bible translates Daniel 8 my comments in blue.

Remember this is a VISION and should be understood as such and applied spiritually:

> <u>**Daniel 8**</u> – Amplified Bible
> 12 And the host [*the body Temple*] was given [*to the False messiah*] together with the continual [*defense provided by Michael as he is being taken away Dan. 12:1 and Rev. 12:7 and 2 Thess. 2:7*] because of **the transgression of desolation** [*changing ordained feasts, changing the Holy Sabbath, and transgressing the Torah*]. And righteousness and truth [*of Yahuah defined by His Law*] were cast down to the ground, and it [*the image of* Χ Ƨ Ƨ *The False messiah*] accomplished this [*by Divine permission*] and prospered [*in the hearts of man as Yahuah gave those who elevated an image of The False messiah* Χ Ƨ Ƨ *over to a depraved mind ...* ***The Spirit of Error***].
>
> 13 Then I heard a holy one [*angel*] speaking, and

another holy [*angel*] one said to the one that spoke, "For how long is the vision concerning the continual (*defense of Michael being taken away Dan. 12:1 and Rev. 12:7 and 2 Thess. 2:7*],(*which leads to the*) **the transgression that makes desolate**, and (*later resulting in*) the giving over of both the sanctuary (**The Altar of Yahuah**/hearts of man) and the host (*the human body/Temple of Yahuah…this is* **the Abomination of Desolation** *where the sanctuary is desolated by an abominable sacrifice and the body temple destroyed*] to be trampled underfoot? 14 And he said to him and to me, For 2,300 evenings and mornings (*is the timeframe that separates The Transgression of Desolation and The Abomination of Desolation*); then the sanctuary shall be cleansed and restored (*by the Testimony of Yahusha as those who have the testimony of the Lamb cleanse their body temples and the Altar of Yahuah with the blood of the Lamb*).

Notice above Daniel describes the continual defense over Earth provided by the Archangel Michael literally being "taken away" because of **The Transgression of Desolation**. Earth is left defenseless and per **Isaiah 24** literally destroyed because of **The Transgression of Desolation** or transgression of **The Law of Yahuah**.

The problem is, in your English Bible it doesn't tell you it is Michael that is "removed" and "taken away" it says **sacrifices!** This is just one of the many "seals" placed over the books of Daniel that only now are being broken. Those seals are mistranslation, words added, and scripture twisted that would take "men of wisdom" who Yahuah would anoint in the end to break these seals.

You see, anytime a word is in italics in your modern "mis" translated Bibles, it means that word was added to scripture by the

340

translators. This is just one very important example of how bad translation can literally change the meaning of the Bible completely.

The word *sacrifices* in Daniel 8:12, 13 was NOT in the original Hebrew text it was ADDED by the translators in error. What Daniel was referring to was the continual defense of the Archangel Michael as I will demonstrate next. Translators did not do as Yahuah commanded and let scripture interpret scripture "line upon line, precept upon precept" they simply drew their own conclusion and added "sacrifices" when that is nothing at all what Daniel said.

The reason this is extremely important is because Michael is removed or taken away from standing in our defense because humanity has abolished *The Law of Yahuah* committing *The Transgression of Desolation*. Allow me to explain...

Hebrew/Aramaic Scriptures vs. English Translations

The Meaning of Italics in the English Translations of the Bible

When the original Bible was translated from Hebrew, Aramaic, and Greek; the challenge for the translators was to correctly translate these languages into an English equivalent and make judgment calls where in Hebrew the subject wasn't specified stated but only implied. The problem is every translator of our modern Bibles were filled with The Spirit of Error and had fallen for אֱלֹהִים Jesus Christ. They believe that "Jesus abolished The Law"! So in their prejudice, they took liberty to ensure the truth was hidden. As I will demonstrate, these translators did not always make the correct assumptions and did not let scripture interpret where at times only implications were made. These translators were uninspired pagan scribes and translators not guided by *The Spirit of Holiness*.

English Words ADDED to the Book of Daniel

In the book of Daniel, the word "*sacrifice*" was **added** to the King James Version (and every later version) in VERY important passages of scripture which define the signs and cause of the Great Tribulation and the duration between major end events.

In Daniel the word "*sacrifice*" was **added** after the Hebrew word *tamiyd* which was translated "daily" giving us "daily sacrifices". The original text did not specify what was implied by the word *tamiyd* (itself mistranslated as *daily instead of 'continual'*) so the English translators assumed the original text was implying "*sacrifice*" based on Daniel 9:27 when the proper reference is Daniel 12:1:

Daniel 12:1

"At that time Michael, the great prince who (*continually tamiyd*) protects your people, will arise (*and be removed or taken away by Yahuah because of the Transgression of Desolation*). The χ̃ςς be a time of distress (*for those who put their faith in the Ishtar Pig and abolished The Law*) such as has not happened from the beginning of nations until then (*Isaiah 24*). But at that time your (*chosen*) people -- everyone whose name is found written in the (*Lambs*) book (*of life*) --will be delivered (*by The Passover Sacrifice of Yahusha because they did not abolish The Law it was instead written on their hearts*).

Below are the scripture where the word *tamiyd* translated <u>daily</u> was used and the word '*sacrifice*' was **added** in italics by the English translators assuming "sacrifice" was the proper implication of *tamiyd*. NOTE: the word "*sacrifice*" is in ITALICS in most Bibles which means the word was added and not originally in the text:

Daniel 8:11-14

[10] And it (χ̃ςς *the False messiah*) waxed great, even to the host of heaven (*he is a false image of Yahusha*); and it cast down some of the host and of the stars to the ground, and stamped upon them. [11] Yea, he magnified *himself* even to the Prince of the host (*Michael the Archangel*), and by Him (*Yahuah*) **the daily sacrifice** (*sacrifice was added*) was taken away, and the place of the sanctuary was cast down. [12] And an host (*Michael*) was given *him* against **the daily sacrifice** (*sacrifice was added*) by reason of transgression (*of The Law*), and it cast down the truth (*of Yahuah's Word*) to the ground (abolished it); and it practiced, and prospered (in abolishing *The Law of Yahuah*).
[13] Then I heard one saint speaking, and another saint said unto that certain *saint* which spake, How long *shall be* the vision *concerning* **the daily' sacrifice'** (*the word 'sacrifice' as added in error*) and <u>The Transgression of</u>

Desolation, to give both the sanctuary (*the heart/mind of man*) and the host (*the body*) to be trodden under foot?

Daniel 12:11
[11] And from the time that **the daily '*sacrifice*'** ('*sacrifice*' *was added*) shall be taken away, and The Abomination of Desolation set up, there shall be a thousand two hundred and ninety days.

In every case above the word *sacrifice* was not in the Hebrew texts, it was added by the translators. What was taken away per Daniel 12:1 was Michael but "daily Michael" doesn't make any sense. That is because the translators mistranslated the Hebrew word *tamiyd as*" daily" when it actually means "continual" as in **the continual defense Michael provides over Earth**.

Hebrew Word translated "Daily" mistranslated

In the scriptures in Daniel we just reviewed, only the word "tamiyd" occurred in the original text. The word is translated "daily" and the word "*sacrifice*" was added in English to try and clarify what Daniel implied by the word *tamiyd* giving us "daily sacrifices" which is a mistranslation.

Below is the actual word translated as "daily" in English from the Strong's Concordance:

8548	tamiyd *taw-meed'*	from an unused root meaning to stretch out; properly, continuance (as indefinite extension); but used only (attributively as adjective) constant (or, **constantly**);

344

I don't see "daily" in that definition anywhere. This is one of the seals over the book of Daniel that had us all looking for the "daily oblation sacrifices" to be stopped on an Altar that will never exist again in a Temple that will never be rebuilt! It is the same type of "seal" placed over the book of Revelation where the translators removed the "symbol" of Jesus Christ and put in a number 666. These "seals" were placed over those two books (Daniel and Revelation) so that the false messiah would prosper until the time of the end. Then Yahuah would raise up "men of wisdom and insight" to break these seals at the appointed time of the end.

Daniel 12:4

But you, Daniel, roll up and seal the words of the scroll _**until the time of the end**_. Many will go here and there to increase knowledge. ... [9] He said, "Go _your way_, Daniel, for _these_ words are concealed and sealed _**up until the end time**_. [10] Many will be purged, purified and refined, but the wicked will act wickedly; and none of the wicked will understand, _**but those who have insight will understand**_.

Daniel 11

[33] Those who have insight among the people will give understanding to the many;

Revelation 13:18

This calls for **wisdom. _Let the person who has insight_** recon up the symbol of the beast, for it is the symbol of a man. That symbol is χξς

So let's continue and break this seal over the book of Daniel. So the Hebrew word _tamiyd_ that comes before the added word _sacrifice_ is an adjective used to modify a noun but the noun is missing in Hebrew. The word _**tamiyd**_ actually means to stretch out as an indefinite extension, stretch out continually or constantly. It doesn't mean "daily" as translated.

The key is to try and determine what noun was implied by Daniel when he used the adjective *tamiyd*. Was it the "*sacrifice*" that was implied by Daniel as the English translators assumed? Or was it something else? Could it be that what was removed was the <u>continual</u> DEFENSE of the Holy People provided by Michael the Archangel? Yes, Daniel answered that question in Daniel Chapter 12 verse 1.

> ### Daniel 12:1
> 1 "Now at that time Michael, the great prince (*who the*
> ✗ЄϚ *Antichrist magnifies himself against* **Daniel 8:11**)
> who (*Michael*) stands *guard* (*'guard' was added it should
> read 'as a continual defense*) over the sons of your people,
> will arise (*and be taken away see* **Revelation 12:7** *and 2
> Thessalonians 2:7** below*).

We see that Daniel is no longer on Earth and has been "taken away" because of the Transgression of Desolation and removed to Heaven to wage war on the Dragon, the Spirit behind the beast at "the time of the end", when men of wisdom and insight break the seals and reveal the Antichrist to be ✗ЄϚ Jesus Christ:

> ### Revelation 12:7
> 7 And there was war **in heaven**, <u>Michael</u> (*who was
> removed and taken away from providing the Tamiyd
> continual defense of Earth because the Earth was defiled
> by its inhabitants and committed the Transgression of
> Desolation* **Isaiah 24**) and his angels waging war with the
> dragon. The dragon and his angels waged war,

> ### 2 Thessalonians 2
> 3 Don't let anyone deceive you in any way, for that day (*of
> Yahusha's return*) will not come until the Transgression of
> Desolation occurs and the man of lawlessness (The Lawless
> One ✗ЄϚ) is revealed (*by men of wisdom and insight at
> the end*), the (*image of a*) man (*we have elevate as God
> above Yahuah* **Romans 1**) doomed to destruction (*by the

Testimony of Yahusha). [4] He 𝐗𝐒𝐒 will oppose (*Yahusha the Host/King of Heaven*) and will exalt himself over everything that is called God or is worshiped, so that he sets himself up in Yahuah's temple (*the heart/mind of man*), proclaiming himself to be God (*incarnate which is **The Spirit of the Antichrist***).

[5] Don't you remember that when I was with you I used to tell you these things? [6] And now you know what is holding him back (*Michael who is providing the continual defense*), so that he 𝐗𝐒𝐒 may be revealed at the proper time (*of the end when Michael is removed to Heaven*). [7] For the secret power of lawlessness (***The Spirit of Error** abolishing The Law of Yahuah*) is already at work; but the one (*Michael*) who now holds it (*The Transgression of Desolation*) back will continue (***tamiyd***) to do so (*provide the defense of Earth*) till he is taken out of the way (*to heaven to fight the Dragon*). [8] And then the lawless one 𝐗𝐒𝐒 will be revealed, whom the Messiah Yahusha will overthrow with the breath of his mouth and destroy by the splendor of his coming. [9] The coming of the lawless one 𝐗𝐒𝐒 will be in accordance with how Satan works. He will use all sorts of displays of power through signs and wonders that serve the lie (*Lord Lord, we cast out demons in your name* 𝐗𝐒𝐒, *performed miracles in your name* 𝐗𝐒𝐒 ***Matthew** 7*), [10] and all the ways that wickedness deceives those who are perishing (*for sacrificing the Earthly **(Je)** Pig **(sus)** of Ishtar/Easter on the altar of Yahuah instead of the Passover Lamb*). They perish because they refused to love the truth (*The Torah*) and so be saved. [11] For this reason Yahuah sends them a powerful delusion (*Christianity, Mystery Babylon*) so that they will believe the lie (*that* 𝐗𝐒𝐒 *Jesus Christ is god incarnate and abolished The Law*) [12] and so that all will be condemned (*by The Law they abolished*) who have not believed the truth (*of The Torah*) but have delighted in wickedness (*sinning against The Law*

by violating the feasts/torah/Sabbaths per Isaiah 24 and following ΧϚϚ *The Lawless One and keeping Babylonian rituals and worshipping The Trinity).*

Pretty clear, it is a wonder why the translators did just let scripture interpret scripture! Well, I already gave that answer, they were filled with The Spirit of Error and followers of ΧϚϚ . The word "tamiyd" should have been translated as "continual defense" not "daily" as it refers to Michael who **continually stretches out in defense** of the people of Earth.

The translators determined it was the "daily *sacrifice*" based on Daniel 9:27. This was a grave error on the part of the translators as we will see.

Proper Implication of "Tamiyd" is Michael not Sacrifices

EVERY verse in Daniel listed above is in context speaking of the Archangel Michael, the Prince of the Angelic Host, the Commander of the Angelic Host, being taken away by Yahuah as a result of the **Transgression of Desolation**.

The translators should have let scripture interpret scripture and if they did so they would have realized Daniel specifically stated it was Michael that was removed in Daniel 12:1. Daniel specifically named Michael as Israel's defender:

> **Daniel 10**
> [21] But I will tell thee that which is inscribed in the writing of truth: and there is none that holdeth (*in defense*) with me against these (*continually 'tamiyd'*), but Michael your prince

Therefore, the proper implication is that the "**continual defense**" of the Holy People provided by **Michael the Archangel** will be "taken away" because of *The Transgression of Desolation… not*

the daily sacrifice.

Daniel 12:11

[11] And from the time that the continual defense provided by Michael shall be taken away (*because of The Transgression of Desolation*), and ***The Abomination of Desolation*** set up, there shall be a thousand two hundred and ninety days.

These are two very different unique events. Daniel goes on to say that it is only once ***The Transgression of Desolation*** is complete (transgressors reach their fullness) that the False messiah is revealed (stands up) and The Abomination of Desolation is set up:

Daniel 8

23And at the latter end of their [*4th*] kingdom, **when the transgressors** [*the apostate people of God who committed the Transgression of Desolation causing the Great Tribulation*] **have reached the fullness** [*of their wickedness, taxing the limits of Yahuah's mercy*], a [*shadow*] king of fierce countenance and understanding dark trickery and craftiness shall stand up [*in the Holy Sanctuary and commit the Abomination of Desolation*].

I am going to cover this in detail in the next few chapters of this book. I will fully explain in detail what I am introducing here in this chapter. I just wanted to quickly illustrate that it is the abolishment of The Law called ***The Transgression of Desolation*** that literally causes the Great Tribulation and the destruction of Earth.

Law Breakers thrown out of The Kingdom of Yahuah

Now that we see that The Transgression of Desolation results in Michael being removed from his post of continually defending the Eath, let's look at what the purpose of The Great Tribulation is. We know per Isaiah 24 that the Great Tribulation is cause by the inhabitants of the Earth violated The Law of Yahuah and ultimately through 𝑋𝜍𝜍 Jesus Christ abolishing all together. What all of us need to admit and realize it that the **only** sons that will exist in that Kingdom will be those who have The Law written on their hearts, not those who have disobeyed it their entire lives, abolished it in their minds, and lived a life of iniquity (lawlessness).

Yahusha made this fact crystal clear below as he casts out those who are "without The Law" or Torahless or Lawless. That is what "iniquity" or "lawless" means in Matthew 7:23. The word in that verse is the Greek word **_anomía_**:

Entry for Strong's #458 - ἀνομία

> *458.* ἀνομία **anŏmia**, *an-om-ee'-ah;* from *459; illegality,* i.e. *violation of law* or (gen.) *wickedness:*—iniquity, x transgress (-ion of) the law, unrighteousness.
>
> *459.* ἄνομος **anŏmŏs**, *an'-om-os;* from *1* (as a neg. particle) and *3551; lawless,* i.e. (neg.) *not subject to (the Jewish) law;* (by impl. a *Gentile),* or (pos.) *wicked;*—without law, lawless, trangressor, unlawful, wicked.

With that understanding in mind, hear the words of the King of *The Kingdom of Yahuah* who is the gatekeeper you must get past to enter it… the word "lawlessness" and in some translations "iniquity" or "evildoers" is the Greek word *anomía* defined above as '*without The Law of Yahuah*' and we see Yahusha throw them out!

> ### Matthew 7:21-23
> "Not everyone who says to Me, King, King, shall enter the kingdom of heaven, but he who does the will of my Father (*keeps His Commandments*) in heaven. Many will say to Me in that day, King, King, have we not prophesied in Your name $\chi\xi\varsigma$, and cast out demons in Your name $\chi\xi\varsigma$, and done many wonders in Your name $\chi\xi\varsigma$? And then will I (*Yahusha*) declare to them, I never knew you, depart from Me, **you who practice lawlessness**" (*follow the Lawless One* $\chi\xi\varsigma$).

The *name* they were calling on was $\chi\xi\varsigma$ Jesus Christ the lawless one. Yahusha does not answer to that name and denies entry those who follow *the lawless one*.

Anomía is used 15 times in the New Testament to condemn all those who abolish *The Law of Yahuah*, have contempt for *The Law*, or break *The Law*. Those "law breakers" are literally gathered up and cast out of *The Kingdom of Yahuah*. This is The Transgression of Desolation or The Great Tribulation. Below is how various translations handle the word **anomía**:

> ### Matthew 7:23 - New Living Translation
> But I will reply, 'I never knew you. Get away from me, you who *break God's laws.'*

> ### Matthew 13:41- English Standard Version
> The Son of Man will send his angels, and they will gather out of his kingdom all causes of sin and all *law-breakers*,

Matthew 23:28 - Weymouth New Testament
The same is true of you: outwardly you seem to the human eye to be good and honest men, but, within, you are full of insincerity and ***disregard of God's Law***.

Matthew 24:12 - New American Standard Bible
"Because ***lawlessness*** is increased (*The Law defines love*), most people's love will grow cold

Romans 4:7 - GOD'S WORD® Translation
"Blessed are those whose ***disobedience*** (*to The Law*) is forgiven and whose sins (*against The Law*) are pardoned.

Romans 6:19 - International Standard Version
I am speaking in simple terms because of the frailty of your human nature. Just as you once offered the parts of your body as slaves to impurity and to greater and greater ***disobedience*** (*to The Law*), so now, in the same way, you must offer the parts of your body as slaves to righteousness (*which is keeping The Law*) that *leads to sanctification*.

2 Corinthians 6:14 - English Standard Version
Do not be unequally yoked with unbelievers (*true believers keep The Law*). For what partnership has righteousness (*law keepers*) with ***lawlessness*** (*law breakers*)?

2 Thessalonians 2:7 - International Standard Version
For ***the secret of this lawlessness*** (*the false doctrine that Jesus abolished The Law*) is already at work

Titus 2:14 - English Standard Version

who ave himself for us to redeem us from all ***lawlessness*** and to purify for himself a people for his own possession who are zealous for good works (*of The Law*).

Hebrews 1:9 - Holman Christian Standard Bible
You have loved righteousness (*kept The Law*) and hated

lawlessness (*disregard for The Law*); this is why Yahuah, Your God, has anointed You with the oil of joy rather than Your companions.

Hebrews 8:12 - King James 2000 Bible
For I will be merciful to their ***unrighteousness*** (*breaking The Law*), and their ***sins*** (*against The Law*) and their ***iniquities*** (*contempt for The Law*) will I remember no more.

Hebrews 10:17 - New International Version
Then he adds: "Their ***sins and lawless acts*** I will remember no more."

1 John 3:4 - King James 2000 Bible
Whosoever commits sin transgresses also The Law: for sin is the transgression of The Law.

Crystal clear if you ask me! The reason those who have abolished The Law in their hearts (believing the lie told by the False Religion of Christianity) will not inherit ***The Kingdom of Yahuah*** is simple: We are being trained to govern the Universe and the foundation of that government is The Law. Yahuah simply cannot grant eternal life and a position within ***The Kingdom of Yahuah*** to a disobedient human being… period. That would put Yahuah in a position to deal with a rebellion of gods! It is that simple. If you disobey His Law now, you cannot be trusted with eternal life, you cannot be trusted to govern, you cannot be trusted to judge, you cannot be trusted as His priest, you cannot be trusted with anything and you will die dead in your "sin" which is… **transgression of His Law**. This cannot be over stated.

The Law is the foundation of *The Yahushaic Covenant*

REVELATION 15

[5] After this I looked, and I saw in heaven (*there is no temple on Earth at this time, it has been transposed to heaven*) **the temple—that is, <u>the tabernacle of the covenant law</u>**

As we see above, when Yahusha comes back to establish **The Kingdom of Yahuah** on Earth he brings with him the foundation of that covenant "*the tabernacle of the COVENANT LAW*".
Let me summarize, the Great Apostasy is not a falling away from Christianity, Christianity IS the Great Apostasy! The Great Apostasy is defined in scripture as The Transgression of Desolation or rather the transgression of The Law/Feasts/Torah that causes the desolation of this planet and the people on it for abolishing His Torah! The Law defines the Yahushaic (New Covenant) and is a gift from Yahuah to His chosen. The Law defines righteousness and sanctifies us and it is in obedience to The Law that foundation is found through Grace.

The Transgression of Desolation

Transgressing The Laws, Sabbaths, and Ordained Festivals of Yahuah is what causes the Great Tribulation.

Isaiah 24: 1-6

The Earth is polluted by its inhabitants - They have committed **The Transgression of Desolation** (*transgressed the Torah, changed the Holy Feasts to Christopagan Holidays, and broken the Everlasting Covenant of the Sabbath changing it to the pagan day of worship ... Sunday*) - Therefore the Curse found in the Torah devours the whole Earth, the inhabitants of Earth will be burned up, and few men left

The Yahushaic Covenant is defined by The Law of Yahuah

The Law was not abolished by Yahusha:

Matthew 5:17
"Do not think that I have come to abolish The Law or the Prophets; I have not come to abolish them but to fulfill them (*transpose them to Spiritual Intent*)."

The Law was strengthened and transposed from written in stone to written on our hearts.

Jeremiah 31
[31] "Behold, days are coming," declares Yahuah, "when I will make a new covenant with ***The House of Israel*** and with ***The House of Judah***, [32] not like the covenant which I made with their fathers in the day I took them by the hand to bring them out of the land of Egypt (*where sin was defined by the letter and physical act*), *My covenant which they broke*, although I was a husband to them," declares Yahuah. [33] "But this is the covenant which I will make with ***The House of Israel*** after those days," declares Yahuah, "***I will put My law within them and on their heart I will write it***; and I will be their God, and they shall be My people.

Ezekiel 36: 26, 27
I will give you a new heart (*for my Law and write my Law on it*) and put a new spirit (*of loving obedience*) in you; I will remove from you your heart of stone (*legalistic observance of The Law without love*) and give you a heart of flesh. And **I will put my Spirit in you and move you to follow my decrees and be careful to keep my laws**.

355

1 John 2

[3] By this we know that we have come to know Yahuah, if we keep His Law. [4] The one who says, "I have come to know God," and does not keep His Law, is a liar, and the truth is not in him; [5] but whoever keeps Yahuah's Law, in him the love of Yahuah has truly been perfected. By this we know that we are in covenant with Yahusha: [6] the one who says he is in covenant with Yahusha ought himself to walk in the same manner as Yahusha walked (*in obedience to The Law*).

The Law is a gift from Yahuah to His sons:

Romans 9:4-5

To the "Israelites" belong 7 things granted to them as gifts from Yahuah:

1.) Adoption as sons of Yahuah
2.) To be the Glory of Yahuah
3.) **The "Law" which is the Torah**
4.) The Temple of Yahuah and the Altar within
5.) The Promises of Yahuah (forgiveness, resurrection, eternal life, dominion, inheritance)
6.) The "fathers" - they are of the bloodline descending from Abraham, Isaac, and Jacob
7.) And the Messiah (to be partakers in *The Yahushaic Covenant*)

Obedience to The Law is what sanctifies us leading to righteousness

Romans 6:16
Do you not know that to whom you present yourselves slaves to obey, you are that one's slaves whom you obey, whether of sin (not keeping The Law) *leading* to death, or of obedience (to The Law) *leading* to righteousness?

Romans 6:19
I am speaking in simple terms because of the frailty of your human nature. Just as you once offered the parts of your body as slaves to impurity and to greater and greater **disobedience** (to The Law), so now, in the same way, you must offer the parts of your body as slaves to righteousness (which is keeping The Law) that *leads to sanctification*.

Romans 2:13
13 For it is not those who hear The Law who are righteous in Yahuah's sight, **but it is those who obey The Law who will be declared righteous**.

Eternal Life is the promise for obedience to The Law

Matthew 19
[16] And someone came to Him and said, "Teacher, what good thing shall I do that I may obtain eternal life?" ··· **if you wish to obtain eternal life, keep the commandments** (*of Yahuah, Eternal Life is the promise for obedience to The Law*)."

Spiritual Maturity is found in practicing The Law

Hebrews 5:12 - Spiritual **Immaturity**
12 For though by this time you ought to be teachers (*of the Torah, there was no such thing as the New Testament when he wrote this*), you need someone to teach you again the first principles of the oracles of Yahuah (*The Torah*); and you have come to need milk and not solid food. 13 For everyone who partakes only of milk is **unskilled in the word of righteousness** (*Righteousness is Keeping The Law so "word of righteousness" is The Torah*), for he is a babe. 14 But solid food belongs to those who are of full age (*mature Saints with minds set on The Law of the Spirit of Life*), that is, those who **by reason of use** (*keeping the Feasts/Torah/Sabbaths*) have their (*Spiritual*) senses exercised (*trained through physical to Spiritual parallels*) to discern both good and evil (*which is defined by The Law of Yahuah, good is obedience to His Commands, evil is breaking them*).

Overcoming the Spirit of Error and The Lawless One!

We must come out of this rebellion against Yahuah's Torah known as The Transgression of Desolation or the Great Apostasy. This is not easy as the Christian Church has mistranslated, misunderstood, and taught lies based on the writing of the Apostle Paul. Then they elevated those false doctrines born out of implied doctrines using sound bites of mistranslated texts taken out of context as "The Word of God". This atrocity is known as The Pauline Doctrine. Below I will quickly address this but it too is outside the scope of this book. In my book *The Yahushaic Covenant* I address every false doctrine of the false religion and overcome Christianity's sound-bite implied doctrines with SOUND doctrine by putting everything Paul said back into context. *The Yahushaic Covenant* is the crown jewel, so to speak, of The Original Revelation Series! I want to illustrating the point that the "GREEK" i.e. Roman based religion altered and twisted Paul's writing. Leading to the rise of their god-man χ͞ξ͞ϛ fulfilling the prophecy of The Lawless One by abolishing The Law. Below I will include a small portion from my book *The Yahushaic Covenant*.

The False Religion is founded on what is called The Pauline Doctrine. The Christian Church, having the Spirit of Error, has twisted the words of Paul to say what is not said in order to justify the Spirit of Error in them which is 'The Law has been abolished'. This began early just after Yahusha had been resurrected and Paul began his ministry. The reality is that the Apostle Paul was a very educated man and spoke over the heads of everyone around him. Even today, his writings are over the heads of almost everyone who reads them. The Apostle Paul spoke in a metaphorical language like Yahusha of "hidden things".

2 Peter 3

> [14] Therefore, beloved, looking forward to these things, be diligent to be found by Him in peace, without spot and blameless (*in keeping The Law*); [15] and consider *that* the longsuffering of our King *is* salvation—as also our beloved brother Paul, according to the wisdom given to him, has written to you, [16] as also in all his letters, speaking in them of these (*hidden*) things, in which are some things hard to understand (*for those not trained in the Mystery Language*), which **untaught** (*in the Mystery Language*) and unstable (*in their depraved minds*) ***people* (**Greeks**)** **twist to their own destruction**, as *they do* also **the rest of the Scriptures**.

1 Corinthians 2:4-15

4 And my speech and my preaching was not with enticing words of man's wisdom (*Paul or Yahusha did not speak in literal terms*), but in the demonstration of the Spirit of Holiness and of power (*which gives us understanding of hidden things*): 5 That your faith should not stand in the (*literal*) wisdom of men (***to be taken literally***), but in the power of Yahuah (*In a Mystery Language taught only by The Holy Spirit to a chosen few*). 6 However we (*Yahuah's Chosen Few*) speak wisdom (*Spiritual Understanding*) among them that are perfect (*perfected by The Spirit of Holiness*): yet not the wisdom (*Literal / pagan / natural understanding*) of this world, nor of the princes of this world, that come to nothing (*they do not understand The Bible language*): 7 But we (*Yahuah's Chosen Few*) **speak the wisdom of Yahuah in a mystery, even the hidden wisdom**, which (*this Mystery Language*) Yahuah ordained before the world unto our glory (*those who know Him, the Chosen Few*): 8 Which none of the princes of this world knew (*the hidden mystery language of Yahuah that His Word is written in*): for had they known it (*this Mystery Language*), they would not have crucified the King of glory (*they did not understand the physical to Spiritual Truth of Passover*). 9 But as it is written, (*the natural*) EYE (*does not see Spiritual Truths and*) hath not seen (*the hidden mysteries*), nor (*the natural*) EAR heard (*the Spiritual Truth*), neither have (*these mysteries*) entered into the (*natural*) HEART of (*natural*) man (*humanity has been given over to a Spirit of Error and the mind has been depraved of Spiritual understanding Romans 1*), the things which Yahuah hath prepared for them (*the Chosen Few*) that Love Him. 10 But Yahuah hath revealed them (*the secret mysteries and hidden knowledge*) unto us by His Spirit of Truth (*we speak the hidden language*): for the (*HOLY*) Spirit searches all things, yes, and the deep (*hidden / mysterious*) things of Yahuah. 11 For what man knows the things of a (*natural*) man, save the (*natural / human*) spirit of man which is in him? Even so the things of Yahuah knows no man, but the (*HOLY*) Spirit of Yahuah (*reveal this hidden language to them*). 12 Now we

(The Chosen Few / Righteousness Seekers) have received, not the *(human nature / natural)* spirit of the world, but the *(HOLY)* spirit which is of Yahuah; that we might know *(these hidden mysteries and speak the hidden language or tongues through The HOLY SPIRIT)* the things that are freely given to us of (by) Yahuah. 13 Which *(Mysterious / Secret)* things, also, we *(The Chosen Few / Righteousness Seekers)* speak, not in the *(literal)* words which man's wisdom teaches, but which the Holy SPIRIT teaches; comparing spiritual things with spiritual *(physical to Spiritual Parallels / Parables/ metaphors, allegories/ Idioms, anthropomorphisms, poems, prophetic languages, proverbs, etc)*. 14 But the natural man receives not the *(hidden/mysterious)* things of the *(HOLY)* Spirit of Yahuah: for they (the hidden mysteries) are foolishness unto him (*1 Corinthians 1:23*): neither can he know them *(these hidden mysteries)*, because they *(the hidden mysteries of Yahuah)* are *(HOLY)* spiritually discerned *(through the Mystery Language)*.

These untaught and unstable people twist all the scriptures to say what they want the scriptures to say not what they actually say. You must be trained in the metaphorical language (Mystery Language i.e. other tongues) to understand the hidden mysteries of Yahuah. That is why we have so many different denominations and doctrines in Christianity. These are untaught, unstable, uninspired men trying to understand the Word of Yahuah yet Yahuah has given them over to a depraved mind for worshipping Jesus (Romans 1). Anyone who follows these Christian teachers of Christos Iesous (the Greek appropriate demi-god Jesus Christ) will themselves be destroyed:

Matthew 15:14
[14] Let them alone. They are blind leaders of the blind. And if the blind leads the blind, both will fall into a ditch."

We are not to be blind followers of any man, yet that is exactly what most Christians are. They have turned over their eternal lives, the lives of their family, and their role as Priest of their home over to their beloved "Pastor" who is leading them directly to their own destruction. We are supposed to know The Word of Yahuah intimately so that we can test every lie they tell us:

2 Timothy 2:15
[15] Be diligent to present yourself approved to Yahuah, a worker who does not need to be ashamed, rightly dividing the word of truth.

That "*twisting of Paul's writings*" that "*leads to their destruction*" is the doctrines of *Incarnation* and that *The Law has been abolished*. The Christian Church teaches that The Law was nailed to the cross and that we are no longer bound by it, it has been abolished, and the Old Testament is no longer relevant. This false doctrine is not based on sound scripture and violates the commands of Yahuah and Yahusha. This false doctrine is based on what is known as *The Pauline Doctrine* or *Pauline Christianity* as the Greeks twisted Paul's writings and created another gospel all together based on the abolishment of The Law of Yahuah.

http://en.wikipedia.org/wiki/Pauline_Christianity

> *Pauline Christianity is the Christianity associated with the beliefs and doctrines espoused by Paul the Apostle through his writings. Orthodox Christianity relies heavily on these teachings and considers them to be amplifications and explanations of the teachings of Jesus. Others, as detailed below, perceive in Paul's writings, teachings that are different from the original teachings of Jesus documented in the canonical gospels, early Acts and the rest of the New Testament, such as the Epistle of James.*

> *The theological aspect is the claim that Paul transmuted Jesus the Jewish messiah into the universal (in a wider meaning "catholic") Savior. Pauline theology is also a term referring to the teaching and doctrines especially espoused by the*

apostle Paul through his writings. Mainstream Christianity relies on Paul's writings as integral to the biblical theology of the New Testament and regards them as amplifications and explanations consistent with the teachings of Jesus and other New Testament writings. Christian scholars generally use the term expressing interest in the recovery of Christian origins and the contribution made by Paul to Christian doctrine. <u>Others, especially non-Christian scholars, claim to see a Pauline distinction different from that found elsewhere in the New Testament, a distinction that</u> **<u>unduly</u>** *influenced later* <u>Christianity</u>.

There is a great divide today between those who believe Paul expounded on the teaching of Yahusha and those who believe Paul literally started a false religion not found in The Bible. Neither one is true. Many in the Hebrew roots movement today who realize the **<u>supposed</u>** contradictions (there really are no contradictions) in Paul's writings have declared Paul a false teacher. They can't reconcile Paul's teaching with Yahusha's and all the other men in the Bible. Their condemnation of Paul is very compelling; however, I understand Paul's writings, where they do not, and I find <u>no contradiction</u> at all. Those who simply want to declare Paul a false teacher and get rid of the books in the Bible he wrote simply are too lazy or "blind" themselves as they don't speak the "Mystery Language" Paul spoke in . These men who have written Paul off as a false teacher simply believe the uninspired modern translations of his writing and believe what the Christian Church falsely teaches concerning Paul. Based on the mistranslated Bibles and the false Christian witness of Paul they deem him a false teacher in error.

If Paul really taught what Christianity says he taught then yes; Paul is a false teacher. However, Christianity has been bearing false witness against the Apostle Paul for 2,000 years. We need men <u>to stand up to the false religion</u> and properly teach Paul's writings.

363

Because not only was he not a false teacher; he was the only one of his day qualified with the knowledge of The Torah and Prophets required to properly teach the risen Messiah in light of them.

Paul addressed this issue below making it clear that it was not his intention to gain a "following" and not his intention to contradict The Bible and start a new religion:

1 Corinthians 1:10-25

[10] Now I plead with you, brethren, by the name of our King Yahusha the Messiah, that you all speak the same thing, and *that* there be no divisions among you, but *that* you be perfectly joined together in the same mind and in the same judgment. [11] For it has been declared to me concerning you, my brethren, by those of Chloe's *household,* that there are contentions among you. [12] Now I say this, that each of you says, "I am of Paul," or "I am of Apollos," or "I am of Cephas," or "I am of Yahusha." [13] Is the Messiah divided? **Was Paul crucified for you? Or were you baptized in the name of Paul**? (*Paul is condemning the concept of a Pauline Doctrine*)

[14] I thank Yahuah that I baptized none of you except Crispus and Gaius, [15] **lest anyone should say that I had baptized in my own name** (*started a new religion*). [16] Yes, I also baptized the household of Stephanas. Besides, I do not know whether I baptized any other. [17] For Yahusha did not send me to baptize (*or start a religion in his own name i.e. Pauline Christianity*), but to preach the gospel (*that **The Kingdom of Yahuah** is at hand through **The Yahushaic Covenant***), not with wisdom of words, lest **the Passover sacrifice** of Yahusha should be made of no effect.

[18] For the message of Yahusha's Passover sacrifice (*the Spiritual Truth of Passover*) is foolishness to those who are perishing, but to us who are being saved (*by keeping Passover in light of Yahusha's sacrifice **1 Corinthians 5:8***) it is the power of Yahuah. [19] For it is written:

"I will destroy the (*literal human*) wisdom of the (*so-called*) wise, And bring to nothing the (*human*) understanding of the (*so-called*) prudent."

[20] Where *is* the (*spiritually*) wise? Where *is* the (*true*) scribe (***Jeremiah 8:8***)? Where *is* the disputer of this age (*truly inspired teacher*)? Has not Yahuah made foolish the wisdom of this world? [21] For since, in the wisdom of Yahuah (*Mystery Language*), the world through wisdom did not know Yahuah (*did not understand physical to Spiritual parallels*), it pleased Yahuah through (*what the world sees as*) the foolishness of the message preached (*Yahusha is The Passover Lamb*) to save those who believe (*put their faith in and keep Passover in light of Yahusha 1 Corinthians 5:8*). [22] For Jews request a sign, and Greeks seek after (*human*) wisdom; [23] but **we preach the Passover sacrifice of Yahusha**, to the Jews a stumbling block and to the Greeks foolishness, [24] but to those who are called (*the Chosen Few who understand the Mystery Language*), both Jews (*The House of Judah*) and (*The House of Israel scattered among the*) Greeks, the Messiah is the power of Yahuah and the wisdom of Yahuah. [25] Because the foolishness of Yahuah is wiser than men, and the weakness of Yahuah (*if there is such a thing*) is stronger than men.

Paul clearly states that the Greeks did not understand his message and would twist it into another gospel. They perverted it, twisted it, and HELLENIZED IT... and that perversion is where we get Christianity as they perverted the writing of Paul into... *The Pauline Doctrine of Christianity*. They removed all "Jewishness" of Yahusha the Messiah, they Hellenized Yahusha into Christos Iesous. They turned him into a Greek appropriate "Christos" god-man named Jesus Christ. They (at the council of Nicea) patterned their "Jesus" after the pagan Christs (Hesus, Horus, and Krishna) so that all the pagans could and would accept. Thereby bringing peace to the Roman Empire by creating a "Universal Religion" called The Universal Church of Rome (Christianity).

365

Let us address The Pauline Doctrine and overcome the faulty English translations. Let us put Paul's writing back into context and establish sound Pauline doctrine. When we do, we see a man deeply committed to The Torah and Prophets who properly taught the transposition of The Law. A man who defended The Law of Yahuah against The Talmud and pagan worship of all the various *Christos* whose followers even in his day were called Christians. Mainly they worshiped Christos Mithras the sun deity of Constantine's faith at that time called Mithraism or The Cult of Sol Invictus. Today known as Christianity.

The Apostle Paul was in fact a devout Jew, a Torah Master (Pharisee), a *LAW*yer, who loved **The Law of Yahuah** and proclaimed that fact over and over and is found teaching others to be obedient to The Law. Paul and his companions even took the vow of a Nazarite defined in The Torah!

> **Acts 21:23-24** – Paul praising those who "live in obedience to The Law"
>
> 23 so do what we tell you. There are four men with us who have made a (*Nazarite*) vow (Numbers 6:1-21).
>
> > **Numbers 6:1-21**
> >
> > Again Yahuah spoke to Moses, saying, 2 "Speak to the sons of Israel and say to them, 'When a man or woman makes a special vow, the vow of a Nazirite, to dedicate himself to Yahuah, 3 he shall abstain from wine and strong drink; he shall drink no vinegar, whether made from wine or strong drink, nor shall he drink any grape juice nor eat fresh or dried grapes. 4 All the days of his separation he shall not eat anything that is produced by the grape vine, from the seeds even to the skin.

> 5 'All the days of his vow of separation no
> razor shall pass over his head. He shall be
> holy until the days are fulfilled for which he
> separated himself to Yahuah; he shall let the
> locks of hair on his head grow long.

24 Take these men, join in their purification rites and pay
their expenses, so that they can have their heads shaved.
Then everybody will know there is no truth in these reports
about you, but that you yourself are living in obedience to
the law.

Paul declaring obedience to The Law is the definition of
Righteousness

Romans 2:13

13For it is not those who hear The Law who are righteous
in Yahuah's sight, but it is those who obey The Law who
will be declared righteous.

Paul declaring his belief in The Law and Prophets

Acts 24:14

"But this I admit to you: I worship the God of our fathers in
accordance with the Way (which they call a sect). I
continue to believe everything that accords with the Torah
and everything written in the Prophets."

Paul declaring he is a Torah Observant Jew

Acts 28:17

Brothers, (*speaking to the local Jewish leaders*) although I
have done nothing against either our people or the
traditions of our fathers (*The Torah and Prophets*)…

Paul going out of his way to celebrate the giving of The Torah

> ### Acts 20:16
> For Shaul had decided to bypass Ephesus on his voyage, in order to avoid losing time in the province of Asia, because he was hurrying to get to Jerusalem, if possible in time to celebrate Shavu'ot. (*Celebrate WHAT? Paul went out of his way to celebrate Shavu'ot which is THE CELEBRATION OF THE GIVING OF THE TORAH!*)

Paul going to a Torah observant Jew to be healed

> ### Acts 22:12 –
> A man named Hananyah, an observant follower of the Torah (*why would he add that statement?*) who was highly regarded by the entire Jewish community there, came to me, stood by me and said "Brother Shaul, see again!".

Paul was a Pharisee, a Jewish Rabbi blameless in keeping The Law until he died

> ### Philippians 3: 4-6:
> 4. Though I might also have confidence in the flesh. If any other man thinketh that he hath whereof he might trust in the flesh, I more: 5. Circumcised the eighth day, of the stock of Israel, of the tribe of Benjamin, an Hebrew of the Hebrews; as touching the law, a ***Pharisee***;

It is outside the scope of this book for me to properly teach the writing of Paul but let us at least correct the Christian Church's false witness of Paul with the most obvious of sound bite implied doctrine of all… *Jesus nailed The Law to the cross.*

Did Paul teach that The Law was nailed to the cross?

Christianity's most famous false doctrine is that "Jesus nailed The Law to the cross" and abolished it. Like all false doctrines this is a sound bite implied doctrine that contradicts explicit commands and scripture. It not only contradicts Yahuah's commandments and Yahusha's explicit statements (that he did not come to abolish the Law) but it also contradicts Paul's other writings.

This false doctrine is based on the following sound bite:

> ### Colossians 2 – New American Standard Edition
> [14] having canceled out the certificate of debt consisting of decrees against us, which was hostile to us; and He has taken it out of the way, having nailed it to the cross.

First of all, nowhere in the scripture above does it say The Law was nailed to the cross. It says "*the certificate of debt consisting of* ***decrees*** *against us*" was nailed to the cross. Based on this one sound bite, Christianity lumped all the terms and conditions in all covenants (The Law) together with the covenants themselves, grouped all the covenants and The Law together with The Writings and The Prophets and in one abominable stroke… the Christian Church abolished the entire Word of Yahuah; the true Scriptures which they then called the "Old Testament". This is what the Bible declares is "the Spirit of Error" as I have shown in this book series.

Before I put the above sound bite back into context a few definitions are in order so that we have the same mind set and understanding that the Apostle Paul had who wrote it. The Apostle Paul was a Pharisee which means he was a master teacher of The Torah and Prophets (the true Scriptures). Paul was well aware of the definitions below:

The Law – a term used for all 613 "instructions" in righteousness found in The Torah. The Law contains very distinct categories of

- ***His Commandments*** (Ten Commandments)
- ***His Ordinances/Laws*** (Dietary, Priestly, Ritual Purity, Sacrificial, Judicial, Moral, Agricultural, Business, Sabbatical, Community, Prohibition, Tithes/Offerings, etc.)
- ***His Decrees*** (Judicial Judgments amounting to a Certificate of Debt against us for our disobedience to His Commandments and His Laws)

I want to bring your attention to Colossians 2 because what Paul said was nailed to the cross were ***the decrees against us*** not The Law of Yahuah. In The Law Yahuah gave His commands and Ordinances/Laws and instructed us to keep them for all eternity. Yahuah also included in The Law His judicial judgments that are against those who violate the Commands/Law/Ordinances. These are called "decrees". We see below that even The Catholic Church uses the term decree to mean a disciplinary act for violating their doctrine:

http://www.thefreedictionary.com/decree

de·cree

1. An authoritative order having the force of law.
2. *Law* The judgment of a court of equity, admiralty, probate, or divorce.
3. *Roman Catholic Church*
   a. A doctrinal or disciplinary act of an ecumenical council.

Decrees are judicial judgments for violating law. Below is from The King James dictionary:

http://av1611.com/kjbp/kjv-dictionary/decree.html

DECREE, n. L. To judge; to divide.

1. Judicial decision or determination of a litigated cause; as a decree of the court of chancery. The decision of a court of equity is called a decree; that of a court of law, a judgment.

We see that The Law of Yahuah (it is not Law of Moses as Christianity falsely implies) contained 3 distinct categories:

Deuteronomy 5
30 "Go, tell them to return to their tents. 31 But you stay here with me so that I may give you all the **commands**, *decrees* and **laws/ordinances** you are to teach them to follow in the land I am giving them to possess."

The Apostle Paul knew exactly what he was saying and said exactly what he meant. Paul was describing the definition of Grace. The blood of the lamb covers the judicial decrees levied against us for "sin" which is violating His Commands and Ordinances (Laws).

These decrees, lumped together for all our violations, amounted to what Paul calls a *"certificate of debt"* that Yahusha paid on our behalf (the free gift of Grace). Paul used the Greek word *dogmasin* referencing the decrees against us found within The Law. Yahuah's laws, ordinances, instructions, and commandments are mentioned many, many times in the the Greek Old Testament (the Septuagint) that was used by Greek-speaking people of Paul's day. But how many times does the Septuagint use the word *dogma* (or any of its

371

forms) when referring to Yahuah's laws or instructions? <u>Never.</u> Not one time.

Paul could have easily used one of the same Greek words that is frequently used in the Greek Old Testament to refer to The Law of Yahuah if that is what he meant: *ho nomos, entole, krima, dikaioma,* or *rhema.* But he didn't because he wasn't speaking of The Law of Yahuah. I will explain in this chapter that anytime Paul is referring to THE LAW of Yahuah he used the phrase *ho nomos* which is "The Law" in Greek.

Now let's put that sound bite back into context. Isn't it interesting that Paul begins with a stern warning in verse 8 not to be taken captive by "***philosophy and empty deception, according to the tradition of men, according to the elementary principles of the world***" which is exactly what "Jesus nailed The Law to the cross" is. It is a deceptive GREEK appropriate tradition of men according to the elementary (spirit of error) principle of this world and Paul did not even say that.

It is obvious that Paul was dealing with the same false teachers at the time he wrote this letter that were distorting his words. This is still the case today; the false teachers in Christianity are still twisting Paul's words. At that time in history, pagan Greeks followed Christos Mithras and they were called ***Christians*** as I have explained in this book series. Greek Christians (followers of Christos Mithras of his day) are the ones who Paul said "did not understand the message" of the Gospel or his writings about it:

1 Corinthians 1
[23] but we preach **the Passover** sacrifice of Yahusha, to the Jews a stumbling block and <u>to the Greeks foolishness</u>.

It was these Christians followers of various ***Christs*** that were twisting Paul's message and condemning the assembly in

Colossia (a pagan province of Rome) for keeping The Law as Paul had taught them. So it is even today as "Jesus" is an incarnation of Constantine's god Mithra. We, the true sons of Yahuah, even today are condemned by Christians of our day (worshippers of the sun god Christos Jesus a later name for Mithras) twisting his words and condemning us for being obedient to The Law of Yahuah. Nothing has changed in 2000 years.

After Paul issues the stern warning not to let the Greeks lead them astray by twisting his words, Paul goes on to describe in great detail the work of Yahusha as Passover Lamb to cover the decrees in The Law that are against all of us for transgressing it. Then Paul goes on to encourages the assembly in Colossae to keep The Law and not to let anyone "judge them" for doing so.

Colossians 2 – *IN CONTEXT OF ALL PAUL'S WRITINGS*

[8] See to it that no one (*Greek Christian*) takes you captive through philosophy (*sound bite implied doctrine*) and empty deception (*that Yahusha abolished The Law*), according to the (*pagan*) tradition of men, according to the elementary principles (*false spirits i.e. The Spirit of Error*) of the world, rather than according to **The Yahushaic Covenant**. [9] For in (*covenant with*) Yahusha all the fullness of Deity dwells (*in us*) in bodily form (*Ephesians 3:19),*

Ephesians 3:19

19 and to know this love that surpasses knowledge—that you may be filled (in bodily form) to the measure of all the fullness of Diety (which is the Spirit of Yahuah).

[10] and in **The Yahushaic Covenant** you have been made complete (*in fullness of Deity being filled with The Spirit of*

Holiness), and Yahusha is the head over all rule and authority (*as the first born son of Yahuah through inheritance*); [11] and in **The Yahushaic Covenant** you were also circumcised (*in your heart which is your commitment to keep The Law*) with a circumcision made without hands (*Paul is teaching **the transposition of The Law** into the Spirit*), in the removal of the body of the flesh by the circumcision of the same Spirit of Holiness (*righteous keeping of The Law **Ezekiel 36:27***) that is in (*covenant with*) the Messiah (*The Yahushaic Covenant*); [12] having been buried (*to your flesh or carnal mind*) with Yahusha in baptism (*into the Spirit or Spiritual mind*), in which you were also raised up with Yahusha through faith in the working of Yahuah (*to accept Yahusha's sacrifice on Passover as a sin offering **Romans 8:3***), who raised Yahusha from the dead (*because the death decrees in Yahusha's human genetic code inherited from Adam **Romans 5:12** were not justified*). [13] When you were dead in your transgressions (*against The Law being held captive to the death decrees **Hebrews 2:15***) and the uncircumcision of your flesh (*he is speaking to Lost Sheep of the House of Israel in Colossia*), Yahuah made you alive together (*in covenant*) with Yahusha, (and Yahuah **John 17:21**) having forgiven us all our transgressions (*by the blood of the Passover Lamb*), [14] (*Yahuah*) having canceled out **the certificate of debt** consisting of (*His judicial*) **DECREES** against us (*death decrees in the The Law*), which was hostile to us (because we transgressed His Commands and Ordinances); and Yahuah has taken **the decrees** in The Law out of the way (*not The Law*), having nailed those **death decrees** to the cross (*with Yahusha and forgiven our sin, this is the very definition of Grace*). [15] When Yahusha had disarmed the rulers and authorities (*by dying innocent*), Yahusha made a public display of them (*defeating The Law of Sin and Death*), having triumphed over them through (*the power of*) Yahuah (who raised Yahusha from the grave, he was not God and did not raise himself).

[16] Therefore no pagan Christian (*that you live among in Colossae worshipping Christos Mithras*) is to act as your judge in regard to food or drink (*as you keep the Dietary Laws as I taught you*) or in respect to a festival (*of Yahuah as you keep His Ordained Times*) or a new moon (*as you keep Yahuah lunar calendar not the pagan solar calendar*) or a Sabbath day (*as you set yourself apart from the pagan day of the Sunday and keep Yahuah's Sabbath Holy*) — [17] (*physical*) Things which are a shadow (*cast by true Spiritual Reality that teach us through physical to spiritual parallels in the Mystery Language*) of what is to come (*in the future Kingdom of Yahuah*); but the substance (*Spiritual meaning*) belongs to Yahusha (*as he is the Messiah these rehearsals and festivals point to*). [18] Let no one (*pagan Christians in Colossae*) keep defrauding you of your prize by delighting in self-abasement (*wallowing in insignificance*) and the worship of the (*fallen*) angels (*dating back to Babylon*), taking his stand on *visions* he has seen, inflated without cause by **his fleshly mind** (*the mind set on the flesh is hostile toward The Law of Yahuah and cannot please Yahuah and is not subject to The Law of Yahuah Romans 8:7*), [19] and not holding fast to the head (*example set by Yahusha in keep The Law of Yahuah*), from whom the entire body (*follows the head by example in keeping The Law of Yahuah*), being supplied and held together by the joints and ligaments, grows with a growth which is from Yahuah (*because He has written His Law on our hearts and given us the Spirit of Holiness that teaches us to lovingly obey His Law*).

[20] If you have died in **The Yahushaic Covenant** to the elementary principles of the world (*literal carnal mind*), why, as if you were living in the world, do you submit yourself to **human** commands, such as, [21] "Do not handle, do not taste, do not touch!" [22] (which all *refer to* things destined to perish with use) — in accordance with **the commandments and teachings of men** (the 6,200 page Talmud)? [23] These are matters which have, to be sure, the

375

appearance of wisdom (*these teachings come from Jewish Rabbis*) in self-made religion (*these aren't commandments of Yahuah*) and self-abasement and severe treatment of the body, *but are* of no value against fleshly indulgence.

"Context" is a wonderful thing, it will keep us out of idolatry, it will keep us from false doctrines, and it puts the entire Word of Yahuah into agreement; even the writings of the Apostle Paul. When put into context of all Paul's writings as I have done above, we see what is consistent about Paul. He was a Torah obedient son of Yahuah who understood ***The Yahushaic Covenant*** and taught The Law of Yahuah to the assemblies he established. He fought against the pagan Christians (followers of Christs such as Christos Mithras and many others) of his day and fought against Rabbinical Judaism just like Yahusha did. He taught the transposition of The Law just like Yahusha did. Paul was a defender of The Torah, the Prophets, and The Messiah... Paul was a Nazarene a defender, protector, and keeper of The Law, the Prophets, and the Messiah. He would never speak against The Law:

Acts 24:5
"We have found this man to be a troublemaker, stirring up riots among the Jews all over the world. **He is a ringleader of the Nazarene sect** ... However, I admit that I worship **the God** (*Paul declares The Shema or SEAL*) of our ancestors (*Yahuah*) as a follower of the Way (*and example by Yahusha*), which they call a sect**. I believe everything that is in accordance with the Law and that is written in the Prophets**

Did Paul teach that The Law is *Enmity* toward Yahuah and that Yahusha took that enmity "The Law" away?

The modern English translations as I have said many times are corrupted Hellenized translations that are complicit in the lies that serve the Antichrist Jesus Christ. The translators routinely added words to the Scriptures in order to do away with The Law of Yahuah. This should be expected of them as they all worshipped Jesus as God and were given over to a depraved mind and The Spirit of Error which is defined in Scripture as "The Law was abolished". Yahuah warned us this would happen:

> ### Jeremiah 8
> 8" 'How can you say, "We are wise, for we have The Law of Yahuah," when actually the lying pen of the scribes has handled it falsely? 9The wise will be put to shame; they will be dismayed and trapped. Since they have rejected the word of Yahuah, what kind of wisdom do they have?

These pagan translators had no wisdom. However, the translators were careful to insert their lies into the English translation adding words and twisting the meaning of other words to support their Hellenism. Let's look at Ephesians in various translations to demonstrate that every modern English translation has been totally corrupted.

Every version below states clearly (supposedly) that Jesus *"abolished the law"* or *"abolished in his flesh the enmity which is The Law"* or *"setting aside in his flesh The Law which was a dividing wall hostile toward God"* or *"Having abolished in his flesh the enmity, even The Law of commandments contained in ordinances"*…

377

Ephesians 2 – English Standard Version

[14] For he himself is our peace, who has made us both one <u>and has broken down in his flesh the dividing wall of hostility</u> [15] <u>by abolishing The Law of commandments expressed in ordinances</u>, that he might create in himself one new man in place of the two, so making peace, [16] and might reconcile us both to God in one body through the cross, thereby killing the hostility.

Ephesians 2 – New American Standard Version

For He Himself is our peace, who made both *groups into* one and <u>broke down the barrier of the dividing wall,</u> [15] <u>by abolishing in His flesh the enmity, *which is* The Law of commandments *contained* in ordinances</u>, so that in Himself He might [n]make the two into one new man, *thus* establishing peace,

Ephesians 2 – NIV

[14] For he himself is our peace, who has made the two groups one and <u>has destroyed the barrier, the dividing wall of hostility,</u> [15] <u>by setting aside in his flesh The Law with its commands and regulations</u>. His purpose was to create in himself one new humanity out of the two, thus making peace

Ephesians 2 – King James Version

[14] For he is our peace, who hath made both one, and <u>hath broken down the middle wall of partition between us;</u> [15] <u>Having abolished in his flesh the enmity, even The Law of commandments contained in ordinances;</u> for to make in himself of twain one new man, so making peace;

Well there you go… positive **undisputable evidence** that Paul taught that "Jesus nailed The Law to the cross and abolished that enmity toward God which was The Law"! Right? You know what I am to say… WRONG!

Our translators miserably failed us yet again. By now we should realize that these are not "mistakes" but very **intentional mistranslation**, adding words, and twisting words. We are dealing literally with Satan's church and his followers. The Christian Church is Mystery Babylon and the Spirit behind it is the dragon (Revelation Chapter 13). I have proven this throughout this book series. I suggest everyone toss whatever translation they have in the trash where it belongs because it will deceive you and mislead you and condemn you to death.

I digress. I get just a little heated when it comes to worthless shepherds and lying scribes and The Christian Church in general. Christianity has cost my dear family members their eternal lives and is misleading everyone I know (almost). Back to the abomination that is the modern English Hellenized translated Bibles.

In Ephesians 2 that I quoted there seems to be irrefutable *proof* that Paul taught The Law was abolished. What we need to realize is that words were added to this Scripture that were not there changing the entire meaning of the text. Below is the KJV of the passage and I have underlined the added words:

> ### Ephesians 2
> [14] For he is our peace, who hath made both one, and hath broken down the middle wall of partition between us; [15] Having abolished in his flesh the enmity, _even_ The Law of commandments _contained_ in ordinances; for to make in himself of twain one new man, so making peace;

The words '*even*' and '*contained*' were not inspired words of Yahuah written by Paul. They were **added** to our Bibles. Now we need to understand exactly what the word *enmity* means.

In Ephesians 2:15-16 the word translated **enmity** comes from the Greek word **echthra**, word #2189 in Strong's Greek Dictionary, which is a derivative of the word #2190 **echthros**:

Entry 2189. echthra

Definition: enmity, hostility, alienation

Entry 2190. echthros

*Definition: an enemy; someone openly hostile (at enmity), animated by deep-seated hatred. 2190/exthros ("enemy"), **implies irreconcilable hostility**, proceeding out of a "personal" hatred bent on inflicting harm (DNTT).*

Thayers Greek Lexicon gives us even more information especially about how it is used in Ephesians:

STRONGS NT 2189: ἔχθρα

*ἔχθρα, ἔχθρας, ἡ (from the adjective ἐχθρός), enmity: Luke 23:12; Ephesians 2:14 (15),16; plural, Galatians 5:20; ἔχθρα (Lachmann ἔχθρα feminine adjective (Vulg.inimica)) Θεοῦ, **toward God**, James 4:4 (where Tdf. τῷ Θεῷ); εἰς Θεόν, Romans 8:7; by metonymy, **equivalent to cause of enmity** in Ephesians 2:14 (15) (but cf. Meyer. (From Pindar down.))*

We read above that in context of Ephesians 2:14 it is used meaning "**cause of the enmity toward God**". The Greek word is derived from the Hebrew word *ayib*. **The Lexicon in Veteris Testamenti Libros, by Koehler and Baumgartner**, shows on pp. 35 that the Hebrew word AYIB means: *to be hostile TOWARD*.

The word **enmity** in Ephesians 2:16 should have been written as "**cause of the enmity or irreconcilable hostility toward God**". So when we take out the ADDED words in Ephesians 2 and insert the true meaning of *enmity* here is what we get:

Ephesians 2 – King James Version

[14] For Yahusha is our peace, who hath made both (*The House of Judah and the House of Israel*) one, and hath broken down (*our hatred toward The Law out of our fear of the death decrees which was*) the middle wall of partition between us (*we hated The Law because the death decrees for our sin condemned us to death and we were "being held captive to fear" Hebrews 2:15*); [15] Having abolished (*nailed the death decrees to the cross*) in his flesh (*he broke the law of Sin and you Die by decree by dying without sin*) which (*the death decrees Colossians 2:14 and Hebrews 2:15*) were the *cause of the enmity* (*our hatred toward the Law Romans 8:6-7*) *toward* the law, commandments and ordinances;

> #### Hebrews 2:15
> and free those who all their lives were held in slavery by their fear of death.

> #### Romans 8:6-7
> [6] For to be carnally minded *is* death, but to be spiritually minded *is* life and peace. [7] Because the carnal mind *is* **enmity** against Yahuah; for **it is not subject to The Law of Yahuah**, nor indeed can be.

for to make in himself of two, one new man, so making peace (*between both Houses creating love for The Law of Yahuah as Yahuah writes it on our hearts and gives us The Spirit of loving obedience by nailing the death decrees to the cross with Yahusha who paid the Certificate of Debt!*);

> #### Ezekiel 36: 26, 27
> I will give you a new heart (for my Law and write my Law on it) and put a new spirit (of loving obedience) in you; I will remove from you your

heart of stone (legalistic observance of The Law without love) and give you a heart of flesh. And **I will put my Spirit in you and move you to follow my decrees and be careful to keep my laws** (without the fear of death **IF** you are in The Yahushaic Covenant).

The above is the full context of what Paul said letting scripture define scripture and taking OUT the added words. Paul was saying exactly what he said in Colossians 2 as I just demonstrated. Paul said the *"death decrees in The Law"* were nailed to the cross. He is saying the exact same thing in Ephesians.

Below is how one sacred name translations reads:

Ephesians 2:15-16
15 Abolishing the enmity; which is the hatred and the opposition to the Law and to the Commandments, and to the Ordinances, through His own flesh, in order to create in Himself one new man from the two; making peace, 16 That would reconcile both in one body to Yahuah through the sacrifice– having killed the enmity through Himself.

What Paul is saying in plain English in Ephesians 2 and Colossians 2 is this:

Yahusha abolished our hatred toward (enmity) The Law because we feared the death decrees in The Law. Yahusha nailed those death decrees to the cross in his own flesh by dying innocent in the eyes of Yahuah. Yahusha's blood broke down the "dividing wall" which was our fear of death by defeating The Law of Sin and Death. He united us in loving obedience to The Law which now (with the death decrees covered) is The Law of The Spirit (which teaches us to obey The Law) that leads to Life because the weakness in The Law (our sin) has been covered and now The Law leads to eternal life!

382

Putting Ephesians back into context it agrees with the rest of the Word of Yahuah that His Law is the foundation of righteousness, the constitution of His Kingdom and the fundamental aspect of *The Yahushaic Covenant*. The enmity is further defined letting scripture interpret scripture, line upon line, and precept upon precept:

Romans 8:6-7

[6] For to be carnally minded *is* death, but to be spiritually minded *is* life and peace. [7] Because the carnal mind *is enmity* against Yahuah; for **it is not subject to The Law of Yahuah**, nor indeed can be.

So the Apostle Paul defined what "the enmity" is… our carnal minds that harbor hatred toward The Law of Yahuah. The enmity is not The Law of Yahuah as our English lying translators who had just such a carnal mind tell us. It is exactly what Paul said in Ephesians 2. There is absolutely no way Paul ever taught against The Law of Yahuah:

Romans 3:31

31 Are we then doing away with The Law through the faith? By no means! Rather, we establish the Law!

Romans 7:12

Therefore The Law is holy, and the commandments are holy, and just, and righteous.

Remember, Paul declared what he taught was "foolishness to the Greek" and Peter said the Greeks twisted Paul's words along with the rest of Scripture which they did not understand. Christianity is a Greek religion! The Bible you read is a Hellenized version of the Truth. That means they made it Greek appropriate to appease their pagan beliefs. The modern uninspired translations have turned the Truth of Yahuah into a pagan lie. You cannot trust these translations. The Pauline Christian Doctrine that the Christian Church has built its foundation on is a foundation made of sand. It is sound bite driven implied doctrine that could only be established in Scripture by <u>adding words and twisting the text</u>. Not one of these "translators" had the seal of Yahuah over their minds; they had the mark of the beast as they were Greek Christians and did not follow Yahusha but had elevated Christos Iesous (Jesus) in their heats as God above Yahuah:

Ephesians 2 and Colossians 2 are just 2 examples of how Greeks (The Catholic Church/Christian Church) has taken "sound bites" out of context and ADDED words to the text to make the text say the total opposite of what it actually says. These *false sound bite doctrines* literally contradict what Yahusha plainly said… He DID NOT come to abolish The Law but to fulfill it:

Matthew 5:17 – Amplified Bible

> 17 Do not think that I have come to do away with or undo the Law or the Prophets; I have come not to do away with or undo but to complete and fulfill them.

Please read my book *The Yahushaic Covenant* for more…

Chapter 19

The Antichrist enters the Temple of Yahuah

Introduction

Before we have "eyes to see" the Abomination of Desolation we must understand what that Temple is at the end within The Yahushaic (New) Covenant. Because it is at the time of the end that $X\xi\varsigma$ the Antichrist "enters the Temple of Yahuah" and commits The Abomination of Desolation which is slaughtering the Ishtar Pig Jesus instead of the Passover Lamb Yahusha.

> ### Matthew 24:15
>
> "So when you see (*with your spiritual eyes*) $X\xi\varsigma$ standing in the holy place 'the abomination (*of sacrificing a pig on the altar*) that causes (*the*) desolation (*of Yahuah's Temple*),' spoken of through the prophet Daniel--let the reader understand *(with their spiritual mind what that Temple really is! It is YOUR body)*

In keeping with Scripture and progressive revelation (defined in my book ***The Kingdom of Yahuah***), this chapter will illustrate that Yahuah designed the physical Temple of Solomon in the previous covenants as a shadow picture or physical representation of the temple in ***The Kingdom of Yahuah***. That spiritual Truth cast by the physical shadow by the design of the physical Temple of Solomon was that Yahuah's Temple was always the bodies of the sons of Yahuah.

This fact was the meaning behind Yahusha's declaration that he would tear down The Temple and raise it again in 3 days. This "Temple" the Messiah was referring to was his body. The Bible confirms that the resurrection of the Messiah was in fact the beginning of the construction of the true Temple of Yahuah as the Messiah is the Chief Cornerstone.

In this chapter we will examine the physical design of the Temple of Solomon demonstrating the design was a divine physical portrait of the human body. Then we will apply our understanding

386

of "transposition" as it relates to *The Temple of Yahuah* from physical to spiritual Truth. Once we have fully established that the Temple of Solomon was a <u>temporary</u> physical structure illustrating a greater spiritual Truth, we can fully understand the physical and spiritual state in which Yahuah's Temple now exists in *The Kingdom of Yahuah*.

The Physical Design of the Temple of Solomon

The physical design of the Temple of Solomon was literally a human portrait. In keeping with progressive revelation, this physical world is literally a training ground and a teaching tool for the sons of Yahuah. We are being trained and taught spiritual Truths concerning *The Kingdom of Yahuah* by what we see and experience in the physical world. Every detail of the previous 6 covenants including the physical priesthood of Levi, the High Priesthood of Aaron, the sacrifice of the Passover Lamb, the scapegoat, *The Temple of Yahuah*, *The Altar of Yahuah*, were all given to us physically **as training aids**. The Spring and Fall Festivals were given as physical "rehearsals" to teach us about the spiritual plan of salvation.

Everything in the first 6 covenants was designed to point us to The Messiah and teach us about Yahuah's Spiritual Kingdom. It is only within the scope of this chapter to discuss the *physical to spiritual parallels* of the Temple of Solomon as it relates to *The Temple of Yahuah* in *The Kingdom of Yahuah*.

The 3 Chambers of The Temple of Solomon

One evident *physical to spiritual parallel* is that both the Tabernacle of Moses and the Temple of Solomon contained three distinct and clearly defined sections. There was the Outer Court (Ulam), the Inner Court or Holy Place (Hekal), and the Holy of Holies or Most Holy Place (Beit HaMikdash).

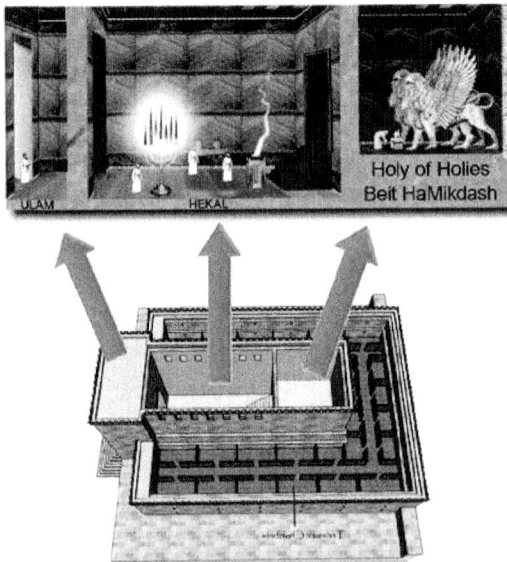

These three sections find perfect correspondence to man as he is also a tri-part being consisting of body, soul and spirit. The Apostle Paul was speaking of our body temples below and the physical to spiritual parallel of The Temple:

I Thessalonians 5:23
Now may the God (*Paul declares The Shema*) of peace Himself (*Yahuah*) sanctify you (*His Temple*) entirely; and may your spirit (*Holy of Holies*) and soul (*Inner Court*) and body (*Outer Court*) be

preserved complete, without blame at the coming of our King Yahusha the Messiah.

The Human Portrait in The Temple of Solomon

It is only my intention to communicate what Tony Badillo and others have illustrated; that The Temple of Solomon was a physical portrait of a human body (*physical to spiritual parallel*). Very specifically crafted as a 3 layered "Temple Man" carefully constructed to illustrate physically the ultimate spiritual Truth that *The Temple of Yahuah* is the human body.

The High Priest as Temple Man

The section below is taken from Tony Badillo's website http://www.templesecrets.info/. The picture to the left is the temple floor plan as seen from looking at The Temple from above. It is transformed into a figure of the Zadok High Priest; and within the figure are 13 red numbers briefly explained below. All are in sequence except nine (9).

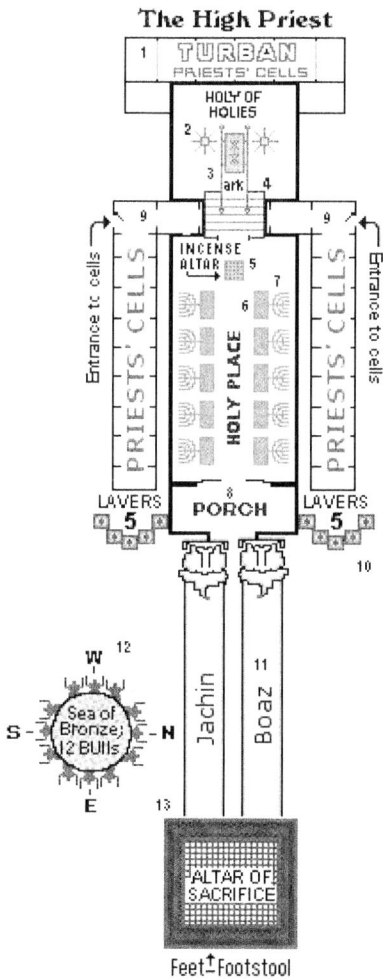

1. *PRIESTS' CELLS* as a TURBAN[1] *west side* – Gold and silver bullion, I Kings 7:51, was likely stored here. These cells form the High Priest's head cover or turban mentioned in Exodus 28:4, 37. The common priest's cap or bonnet, Exodus 28:40, was more

389

globular, resembling an inverted bowl.

2. ***PRIESTS' CELLS***, *south and north sides* – These are the arms. Only one ingress is given, I Kings. 6:8, but Ezekiel 41:11 includes a second. The entrances correspond to the onyx stones the High Priest wore on his left and right shoulders. Each was engraved with the names of six Israelite tribes, twelve names total, Exodus. 28:9 -12.

3. **TWO LARGE STARS** – These are two 10-cubit tall cherubs of gold plated olive wood, I Kings. 6:23, 28; they are the eyes within Temple Man's head, while the head is the Holy of Holies[2] .

4. **THE ARK of the COVENANT** – This is a gold plated chest with a solid gold cover and two small cherubs (small stars).The Ark is his nose; and its *poles* –when attached to its long sides and drawn forward (I Kings. 8:8) – depict extended nostrils smelling the sweet smoke from the Incense Altar in the Holy Place.

5. **STAIRWAY** – A short staircase or ramp led from the Holy Place to a slightly elevated (six cubits) Holy of Holies. The stairway is his neck/throat and its top is his mouth.

6. **INCENSE ALTAR** – This small gold plated altar (I Kings 6:22) is national Israel's *heart*, and its sweet-smelling smoke is the prayers and spiritual life of national *ideal* Israel,

7. **TABLES OF THE SHOWBREAD** – On these gold plated tables (I Kings 7:48) were bread and wine, symbolizing flesh and blood, i.e., the humanity of national Israel.

8. **THE LAMP STANDS** (I Kings 7:48, 49) – Their total number was 10 stands/menorahs x 7 stems each = 70 lights, relating to the 70 Israelites of Exodus 1:5 (Jacob's offspring). This is national Israel as the *light to the world*, and the world is the 70 nations of Genesis 10. They may also symbolize the Sabbath multiplied 10 times, implying a messianic age of worldwide rest (meaning *peace).*

9. **THE PORCH**, Portico or vestibule – This antechamber, the *ulam,* (I Kings 6:3, II Chronicles 3:4) corresponds to the human pelvis (hips) and, therefore, *procreation* through the male and female genitalia.

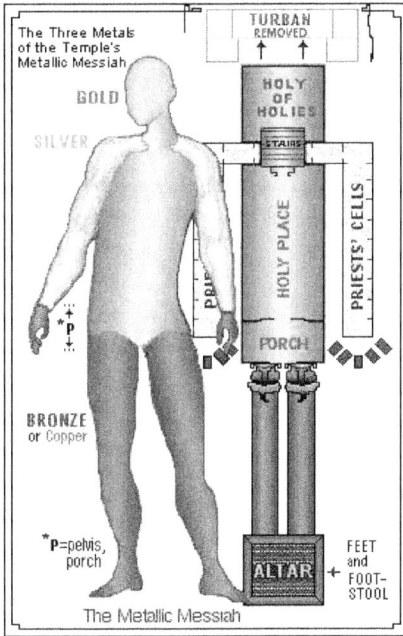

The Three Metals of the Temple's Metallic Messiah

GOLD

SILVER

BRONZE or Copper

*P=pelvis, porch

The Metallic Messiah

TURBAN REMOVED

HOLY OF HOLIES

STAIRS

HOLY PLACE

PRIESTS' CELLS

PORCH

FEET and FOOT-STOOL

ALTAR

10. TEN LAVERS – Five bronze water lavers were on the north and five on the south side. These signify the ten fingers of the hands. The lavers were for washing the blood off the sacrificial offerings, I Kings 7:38

11. JACHIN, BOAZ – The large bronze pillars were named *Jachin* and *Boaz* (II Chronicles.3:17) and form Temple Man's legs. These are two hybrid plants symbolizing Kings David and Solomon, war and peace.

12. SEA OF BRONZE, TWELVE BULLS – This was a

huge basin full of water for the priests to wash their hands and feet (II Chronicles 4:2). It depicts the twelve tribes of Israel stakeing the Red Sea. Its water symbolizes the God's spirit and also his seed.

13. **THE SACRIFICIAL ALTAR** – This (II Chronicles. 4:1) forms Temple Man's feet, while also symbolizing the metallic King Messiah's feet and *footstool,* as was the custom of that time, II Chronicles 9:18, Psalms 110:1.

The point here is that the physical Temple that existed in the previous covenants prior to the 7th Yahushaic Covenant was designed as a physical metaphor or "shadow-picture" or portrait. The Temple of Solomon was a physical shadow designed to teach us the greater Spiritual Truth found in The Messiah that *The Temple of Yahuah is our body.*

Many men throughout history have studied the Temple of Solomon. It is considered one of the 7 Wonders of the World and Sir Isaac Newton (1642–1727), the noted English scientist, mathematician and theologian, studied and wrote extensively upon the Temple of Solomon. He dedicated an entire chapter of The Chronology of Ancient Kingdoms to his observations regarding the temple. Newton was intrigued by the temple's sacred geometry and believed that it was designed by King Solomon with privileged

391

eyes and divine guidance.

Note: Picture taken from http://www.templesecrets.info/

Transposition of *The Temple of Yahuah*

Now that we have looked into the physical design of the Temple of Solomon and see a portrait of the human body, is there evidence in Scripture to support this *physical to spiritual parallel*. Is it true that now in the 7th and final Yahushaic Covenant that The Temple was transposed from a physical place to its final Spiritual state never to be rebuilt physically again? Could it be that there will never be another physical temple built by the hands of man in Jerusalem? There hasn't been in 2,000 years!

This spiritual Truth concerning the state of *The Temple of Yahuah* is a consistent theme in Scripture which clearly defines *The Temple of Yahuah* as the human body in *The Yahushaic Covenant*:

> **John 2**
> 19 Yahusha answered and said unto them, Destroy this temple, and in three days I will raise it up. 20 Then said the Jews, Forty and six years was this temple in building, and wilt thou rear it up in three days? 21 **But he spake of the temple of his body**.
>
> **I Corinthians 6:19**
> Do you not know **that your body is a temple** of the Spirit of Yahuah who is in you, whom you have from Yahuah?
>
> **II Corinthians 6:16**
> What agreement has *The Temple of Yahuah* with idols? For **we are the temple of the living God**; just as Yahuah said, "I *will dwell in them* and walk among them; and I will be their God, and they shall be My people."

Ephesians 2:19-22
So then you are no longer strangers and aliens, but you are fellow citizens with the saints, and are of Yahuah's household, having been built upon the foundation of the apostles and prophets, **the Messiah Yahusha Himself being the corner stone** (of *The Temple of Yahuah*), in whom the whole building, being fitted together is growing into a **Holy Temple of Yahuah**; in whom you also are being built together into a dwelling of Yahuah in the Spirit (*The Kingdom of Yahuah*).

I Peter 2:5
You also, as living stones, are being built up **as a spiritual house** (Temple)…

We see this Spiritual Truth clearly in Revelation as the "physical Temple" was not seen in the City of Jerusalem, but rather that Temple is now spiritual:

Revelation 21
[22]-I did not see a temple in the city, because the (*sons of*) Yahuah Almighty and the Lamb are its temple.

The Temple of Yahuah has been transposed from its physical shadow to its Spiritual Reality and is the human body, *the sum total of the sons of Yahuah*.

The sons of Yahuah are Living Arks of The Covenant

In *The Kingdom of Yahuah*, the Ark of the Covenant has been transposed from physical to spiritual. The hearts/minds of the sons of Yahuah are now the Ark of the Covenant.

As we see, in *The Yahushaic Covenant*, The Torah or "Law" or "Commandments/Instructions" are now written within our "heart" which is now the spiritual Ark of the Covenant:

393

Romans 2:14-15
14 Indeed, when Gentiles, who do not have the law, do by
nature things required by the law, they are a law for
themselves, even though they do not have the law. 15 **They
show that the requirements of the law are written on
their hearts**, their consciences also bearing witness, and
their thoughts sometimes accusing them and at other times
even defending them.

Inside each of us is the spiritual equivalent of the physical portrait
of the Ark of the Covenant! The tablets of *The Law of Yahuah* as
given to Moses... Aaron's staff, and a portion of Manna (bread
from Heaven). Paul lists the physical items found within the
physical Ark of the Covenant:

Hebrews 9:4
⁴ which had the golden altar of incense and the gold-
covered ark of the covenant. This ark contained the gold jar
of **manna**, **Aaron's staff** that had budded, and the **stone
tablets** of the covenant.

The Ark of the Covenant is within each of us in *The Kingdom of
Yahuah*. The blood of Yahusha, the Passover Lamb, is poured on
top of the Ark spiritually inside us to cover our sins as we keep
Passover in light of Yahusha's sacrifice.

Inside the Ark (in our heart) is:

- **The Commands of Yahuah**. They are "written on our
  hearts" or placed inside The Ark of the Covenant. We keep
  them out of love.
- **The staff of Aaron**. Yahuah is our shepherd, Yahuah
  ROHI.
- **The Manna**. We are fed spiritually "manna from heaven"
  as we are filled with the Spirit of Yahuah

Now that we realize that The Temple that Daniel was speaking about is our bodies not a physical temple in Jerusalem, let's identify the sacrifices. What is stopped by this abominable sacrifice of the Earthly Pig Χ͑ϚϚ and what is that Altar that is desecrated?

Chapter 20

The Antichrist Χξς *stops the sacrifices on the Altar*

Introduction

Now that the spiritual Kingdom of Yahuah has been announced by Yahusha and the 7th Covenant has been consummated by the blood of the true Passover Lamb, let us examine *The Altar of Yahuah* in *The Kingdom of Yahuah*. We must realize it is not a "working altar in Jerusalem on the Temple Mount" as we have been led to believe.

In the last chapter we clearly demonstrated that *The Temple of Yahuah* is the human body, the sum total of the sons of Yahuah; Yahusha being the Chief Cornerstone of that Temple. The physical temple in Jerusalem was but a prototype or shadow of this greater Truth revealed by The Messiah. We discovered that each of the sons of Yahuah are living *Arks of The Covenant*. Just as with all things previous in 6 physical covenants were transposed to their true spiritual meaning:

- The Passover Lamb – Yahusha the Messiah
- The Levitical Priesthood – transferred over to Melchizedek
- The Aaronic High Priesthood – Yahusha is now the eternal High Priest
- The Temple – is our body
- The Altar – is our heart
- The Law – is written on our heart
- The Ark of The Covenant – resides in each of us
- The Sacrifices – are spiritual sacrifices not physical ones

The Altar was transposed to *The Kingdom of Yahuah* in *The Yahushaic Covenant*. Therefore, in what way was *The Altar of Yahuah* transposed from physical shadow to spiritual reality?

Transposition of *The Altar of Yahuah*

What is The Altar of Yahuah in the body temple? **The "heart and mind" is the Altar in the body temple.**

The Altar of Yahuah now resides in the body temple as the "hearts and minds" of those so chosen by Yahuah as sons! It is still very much a "working altar" with the proper daily oblation (daily sacrifices) being offered up to Yahuah in those Chosen Few by Melchizedek our Eternal High Priest Yahusha who offers his body as the daily sacrifice as a Lamb that has been slaign.

In fact, it is still in keeping and putting our faith in Passover that Yahusha as High Priest faithfully makes the proper sacrifices before the throne of Yahuah. Expressing our faith in Passover <u>by keeping it</u> is the spiritual equivalent of "sacrificing a lamb". As we keep Passover in faith Yahusha's "blood" is poured out on the altar of our hearts and minds covering the death decrees in The Law that held us captive to the fear of death. The abominable pig of Ishtar/Easter is NOT the proper sacrifice for sin and never was.

We see below Yahusha set the righteous example of keeping Passover and the significance of keeping Passover going forward in "remembrance" or "faith" in him. We see Yahusha clearly say the Passover will find its fulfillment spiritually in *The Kingdom of Yahuah* and only then will Yahusha eat Passover again with us.

> ### Luke 22
> [7] Then came the day of Unleavened Bread on which the Passover lamb had to be sacrificed. [8] Yahusha sent Peter and John, saying, "Go and make preparations for us to eat the Passover."… [14] When the hour came, Yahusha and his apostles reclined at the table. [15] And he said to them, "I have eagerly desired to eat this Passover with you before I suffer. [16] For I tell you, I will not eat it again until it (*Passover*) **finds fulfillment in *The Kingdom of Yahuah*.**"

[17] After taking the cup, he gave thanks and said, "Take this and divide it among you. [18] **For I tell you I will not drink again from the fruit of the vine until _The Kingdom of Yahuah comes_.**"

[19] And he took bread, gave thanks and broke it, and gave it to them, saying, "This (*Passover meal*) is my body given for you; do this (*keep Passover*) in remembrance of me (*Yahusha commands us to keep Passover in **The Yahushaic Covenant** and that is how we express our faith in him*)."

[20] In the same way, after the supper he took the cup, saying, "This (*Passover*) cup is the new covenant in my blood (**The Yahushaic Covenant** was consummated by blood on The Passover), which is poured out for you. [21] ...

And I confer on you a kingdom (*we are co-heirs*), just as my Father conferred one on me (*His Kingdom*), [30] so that you may eat and drink (Passover) at my table **in my kingdom** (*Passover is kept in **The Kingdom of Yahuah***) and sit on thrones, judging the twelve tribes of Israel.

The Apostle Paul confirms that Passover is kept as we put our faith in the sacrifice of Yahusha thereby his blood is spread over **The Altar of Yahuah** (in our hearts and minds) covering our sin and by keeping Passover (not Easter) we keep the sacrifice of the True Messiah alive within us:

1 Corinthians 11

[23] For I received from the King what I also passed on to you: Yahusha the Messiah, on the night he was betrayed, took bread, [24] and when he had given thanks, he broke it and said, "This (*Passover meal*) is my body, which is for you; do this (*keep Passover*) in remembrance (*faith*) of me." [25] In the same way, after supper he took the cup, saying, "This (*Passover*) cup is the new covenant (*the transposition of Passover literally inaugurated **The Yahushaic Covenant***) in my blood; do this (*keep

Passover), whenever you drink it, in remembrance of me."
[26] For whenever (*once a year as commanded by Yahuah*)
you eat this bread and drink this cup, **you proclaim** (*your faith, which is the spiritual sacrifice, in*) the King's death
until he comes (*in your heart and his blood is poured out over the Altar of your heart*).

[27] So then, whoever eats the bread or drinks the cup of the
King's in an unworthy manner (*eating ham on Easter for example violating Yahuah's command and Yahusha's instruction to keep Passover*) will be guilty of sinning (*you will not have the proper sacrifice for sin offered by the eternal High Priest on Yahuah's altar which is your heart and mind*) against the body and blood of the King. [28]
Everyone ought to examine themselves (*purify **The Altar of Yahuah***) before they eat of the bread and drink from the
cup. [29] For those who eat and drink without discerning
(that) the body of the Messiah (*is the Passover Lamb not the Easter pig*) eat and drink judgment on themselves
(*because the blood is only poured out to cover sin on the Altars of those who keep Passover*)

Above Paul is talking about examining ourselves before we keep
Passover. He is speaking of the ***physical to spiritual parallel*** of
ritually cleansing the Altar in The Torah:

Holman Bible Dictionary
http://www.studylight.org/dic/hbd/view.cgi?number=T515
7

> *The altar for sacrifice was purified so that it would
> be prepared for worship (Leviticus 8:15; Ezekiel
> 43:26). The objects of gold used in the tabernacle
> and Temple were also pure in this sense; this would
> be true of the incense in Exodus 37:29. The Levites
> were to purify themselves for service in the
> tabernacle (Numbers 8:21). When that which was
> unclean or impure came into contact with that*

> *which was holy, danger resulted and could even
> lead to death. This is probably the background for
> the preparation made for the theophany, a
> manifestation of God's presence, in Exodus 19:1
> and for the death of Uzzah when he was unprepared
> (not purified) to touch the ark of the covenant, a
> most holy object (2 Samuel 6:1-11). Malachi 1:11-
> 12 contrasts the pure offerings of Gentiles with
> blemished offerings given by God's people; such a
> state necessitated purification (Malachi 3:3-4).
> Purity qualified one to participate in worship, an
> activity central to the life of ancient Israel.
> Breaking that purity was a serious matter.*

In the book of Hebrews we see the Apostle Paul address the reality that instead of The Law being abolished it has literally been transferred to *The Kingdom of Yahuah* to define the role of Melchizedek the Eternal High Priest.

The main point I want to establish here is that The Law pertaining to the High Priesthood that <u>gives authority to offer sacrifices on the Altar</u> (the hearts/minds) on behalf of the sons of Yahuah has been *transposed* to define the role and to give authority to Yahusha as High Priest:

> **Hebrews 7:12**
> "for when there is a transfer (*of position from Earth to Heaven or transposition*) of the priestly office (of Levi to Melchizedek), out of necessity there is ALSO A TRANSFER of the LAW of the priesthood (*by which the Priesthood has authority*)"

And now, Yahusha as High Priest makes those sacrifices on behalf of **only those whose faith is put in Passover** in light of his sacrifice. That was the entire "point" of the physical portrait of Passover. It was a rehearsal designed to teach us the greater spiritual Truth found in Yahusha's sacrifice. We are instructed not only by Yahuah in His Law to keep Passover but also by Yahusha and the Apostle Paul. Passover was the beginning of *The Yahushaic Covenant* and was transposed to *The Kingdom of Yahuah* spiritually.

In keeping with transposition, the Passover shadow was pointing to Yahusha and *faith in Passover* is as essential today as it ever was or even more so. We see below the description of Yahusha the High Priest in the Order of Zadok being called by Yahuah to assume the role of making sacrifices on behalf of men before God.

As we showed earlier those sacrifices are made on behalf of those who *do this* or keep Passover in remembrance of his sacrifice":

> **Hebrews** 5 - The Perfect High Priest
> 1 For *every* high priest taken from among men (*Yahusha was a man when chosen by Yahuah as heir to High Priest Yahusha III*) is appointed on behalf of men in things pertaining to Yahuah (*the High Priest, including Yahusha, is not Yahuah but is a mediator*), in order to offer both gifts and sacrifices for sins (*this is Yahusha's eternal role, these offerings/sacrifices are defined in The Law which has been transposed to serve him in The Kingdom of Yahuah*); 2 he can deal gently with the ignorant and misguided, since he himself also is beset with weakness; 3 and because of it he is obligated to offer sacrifices for sins, as for the people, so also for himself. 4 And no one takes the honor to himself, but receives it when he is called by Yahuah, even as Aaron was. 5 So also (*like every human High Priest*) Yahusha did not glorify himself so as to become a high priest (*he was chosen by blood in the Order of Zadok being the heir to Yahusha III, he is the High Zadok or Melchezidek*), but He who said to Him
>
> "YOU ARE MY SON, TODAY I HAVE BEGOTTEN YOU"; 6 just as He says also in another passage, "YOU ARE A PRIEST FOREVER ACCORDING TO THE ORDER OF MELCHIZEDEK."

So now Yahusha is offering the daily oblation (sacrifice) for sin on *The Altar of Yahuah* and offers his slain body as the final Passover Sacrifice. This is performed for those <u>who put their faith in and keep Passover</u> as he commanded.

The "Altar" has not disappeared as many assume and in error claim there are currently no daily sacrifices being made. **The Altar and the sacrifices being made on it are still alive and very active**. It has simply been transposed to its final spiritual state in *The Kingdom of Yahuah* along with Passover.

We see a "picture" of this spiritual reality in Revelation as Yahusha is seen as *The Passover Lamb* that had been slain in on *The Altar of Yahuah* in Revelation 5.

> ### Revelation 5
> [6] Then I saw a Lamb, looking as if it had been slain, standing at the center of the throne… 11 "Worthy is the (*spotless*) Lamb, who was slain (*on Passover*), to receive power and wealth and wisdom and strength and honor and glory and praise!"

So Yahusha, the final Passover Lamb, is offering his spiritual body as THE sacrifice for sin before the throne of Yahuah **continually** (daily oblation) now in *The Kingdom of Yahuah*. This sin offering is made effectual only for those who obey Yahuah and Yahusha's command to <u>keep Passover</u> in light of and expressing faith in his sacrifice. This Altar is not the physical altar used by the physical priesthood of Aaron and Levi. The Altar in *The Kingdom of Yahuah* is intimately connected spiritually throughout *The Temple of Yahuah* which again has been transposed and now is the sum total of the sons of Yahuah!

Isaiah gives us a glimpse of this very truth. We learn that in the Spiritual Kingdom of Yahuah, we will turn our eyes directly to the Holy One of Israel not "physical altars made with our hands and fingers":

Isaiah 17
In that day (*in the future Kingdom of Yahuah*) people will look to their Maker and turn their eyes to Yahuah, the Holy One of Israel. [8] They will not look to the (*physical*) altars, the (*altars made with the*) work of their hands…

The Physical Altar Metaphor

This spiritual Truth concerning the True *Altar of Yahuah* was the reason why Yahuah commanded *the physical altar was not to be made of "stone" cut by human hands* but only by stones cut by Yahuah:

Exodus 20:25
'If you make an altar of stones for me, do not build it with cut stones, for you will defile it if you use a tool on it.'

Why such restrictions on the construction of the physical altar? Because the physical altar was pointing to the reality that the physical altar was a shadow picture of the human heart and mind which was not made by man but by Yahuah Himself. Our hearts and minds are spiritual parallels of those stones uncut by human hands… the physical stones in the physical altar were a *physical to spiritual parallel* designed to teach us this fact:

I Peter 2:5
You also, as living stones, are being built up as a spiritual house…

We have established the reality of The Temple and Altar in the true Spiritual realm where *The Kingdom of Yahuah* exists and how this physical world around us was designed as a teaching tool. Let us examine now the sacrifices defined by The Law. Have they been "abolished" or are they being made "daily" by the Eternal High Priest Melchizedek exactly as defined in The Law?

The Transposition of Sacrifices on The Altar

The sacrifices and burnt-offerings were appointed to represent (***physical to spiritual parallel****s*) the offering-up of <u>our affections</u> to Yahuah. The animals offered by the physical shadow, whether lamb, or ram, or goat, or bullock, were the ***types of principles in the mind of the worshipper***. We offer these in loving devotion to Yahuah; they are spiritually represented by the physical fire of the offering. Yahuah's acceptance of those offerings was declared by the words so often used respecting the different sacrifices. "It is an offering made by fire, of a sweet aroma unto Yahuah."-·Leviticus 3:5.

Animal sacrifices were always intended (as all things physical) as a teaching tool whereby we can come to an understanding of spiritual things i.e. physical to spiritual parallels. What Yahuah was teaching us in these physical examples is what He truly desires spiritually:

> ### <u>Psalm 40:6-8</u>
> [6] (Physical) Sacrifice and meal offering You have not desired;
> My ears You have opened; (Physical) Burnt offering and (Physical) sin offering You have not required. [7] Then I said, "Behold, I come; In the scroll of the book it is written of me. [8] I delight to do Your will, O my God; <u>Your Law is within my heart</u>."

Transposition of all things is the "key" to understanding this physical world in which we live.

The Apostle Paul taught the transposition of The Law as it related to physical sacrifices in *The Yahushaic Covenant*:

Hebrews 10

1 For the Law, since it has *only* a shadow of the good things to come *and* <u>not the very form of things</u> (*the very form of things is in the spirit not physical*), can never, by the same (physical) sacrifices which they offer continually year by year, make perfect those who draw near. [2] Otherwise, would they not have ceased to be offered, because the worshipers, having once been cleansed, would no longer have had consciousness of sins? [3] But in those (*physical*) *sacrifices* there is a reminder of sins year by year. [4] For it is impossible for the blood of bulls and goats to take away sins. [5] Therefore, when He comes into the world, He says,

> Psalm 40:6-8 "SACRIFICE AND OFFERING YOU HAVE NOT DESIRED, BUT A BODY YOU HAVE PREPARED FOR ME; [6] IN WHOLE BURNT OFFERINGS AND *sacrifices* FOR SIN YOU HAVE TAKEN NO PLEASURE. [7] "THEN I SAID, 'BEHOLD, I HAVE COME (IN the SCROLL OF THE BOOK IT IS WRITTEN OF ME) TO DO YOUR WILL, O GOD.'"

[8] After saying above, "SACRIFICES AND OFFERINGS AND WHOLE BURNT OFFERINGS AND *sacrifices* FOR SIN YOU HAVE NOT DESIRED, NOR HAVE YOU TAKEN PLEASURE *in them*" (*which are offered physically according to the Law until Yahusha came*), [9] then He said, "BEHOLD, I HAVE COME TO DO YOUR WILL." He (*Yahusha*) takes away (*the responsibility to offer physical sacrifices from*) the first in order (*of the Levitical Priests*) to establish (*the spiritual sacrifices in*) the second (*order of the Priesthood of Melchizedek*). [10] By this will we have been sanctified through the (*daily*) offering of the body of the Messiah

Yahusha (*who was sacrificed*) once for all (*as The Passover Lamb*).

[11] Every priest (*of Levi*) stands daily ministering and offering time after time the same (*physical*) sacrifices, which can never take away sins; [12] but He (*Yahusha as Melchizedek the Spiritual High Priest*), having offered one (*spiritual*) sacrifice for sins for all time (*as he stands before the spiritual Altar of Yahuah daily or continually as a Lamb that has been slaughtered*), SAT DOWN AT THE RIGHT HAND OF GOD, [13] waiting from that time onward UNTIL HIS ENEMIES BE MADE A FOOTSTOOL FOR HIS FEET. [14] For by one offering He has perfected for all time those who are sanctified (*because he lives eternally offering his body as the daily sacrifice before Yahuah*). [15] And the Holy Spirit also testifies to us; for after saying,

[16] "THIS IS THE COVENANT THAT I WILL MAKE WITH THEM
AFTER THOSE DAYS, SAYS YAHUAH:
I WILL PUT MY LAWS UPON THEIR HEART,
AND ON THEIR MIND I WILL WRITE THEM,"

He then says,

[17] "AND THEIR SINS AND THEIR LAWLESS DEEDS
I WILL REMEMBER NO MORE."

[18] Now where there is forgiveness of these things, there is no longer *any* (*physical*) offering for sin (*because the sacrificed body of Yahusha is ever before the Throne of Yahuah*).

Revelation 5:6
Then I saw a Lamb, looking as if it had been slain, standing at the center of the throne

[19] Therefore, brethren, since we have confidence to enter the holy place by the blood of Yahusha, [20] by a new and

living way which He inaugurated for us through the veil, that is, His flesh, [21] and since *we have* a great priest over the house of Yahuah (*offering the spiritual sacrifices prescribed by The Law on our behalf*), [22] let us draw near with a sincere heart in full assurance of faith (*in The Passover*), having our hearts (***The Altar of Yahuah***) sprinkled *clean* (*by the blood of The Passover Lamb when we express our faith by keeping Passover in remembrance of him until he comes again*) from an evil conscience and our bodies washed with pure (*living*) water. [23] Let us hold fast the confession of our hope (*as we keep Passover in remembrance of Yahusha*) without wavering, for He who promised (*that The Passover Lamb covers the death decrees in The Law*) is faithful (*to set us free from bondage to the threat of death*); [24] and let us consider how to stimulate one another to love and (*to do*) good deeds (*of The Law, because now we have been set free from The Law of Sin and Death and live by The Law of the Spirit of Life*)

Transposition of The Law that governs The Sacrifices

The Apostle Paul describes the "change" that occurred in both the physical law and physical priesthoods. Paul used the Greek word "*metathesis*" in Hebrews 7:12 when explaining how The Law and the Priesthood of Levi defined by **The Mosaic Covenant** "*changed*" in **The Yahushaic Covenant**. Metathesis is strong's 3331 and means "*transferred to Heaven*"... *transposition*.

3331	metathesis *met-ath'-es-is*	from - metatithemi 3346; transposition, i.e. transferal (to heaven), disestablishment (of a law from physical to spiritual):--change to, removing, translation.

Hebrews 7:12
For when the priesthood is *changed*, of necessity there takes place a *change* of law also.

The word "change" above means "transferred to heaven" so the proper translation is:

Hebrews 7:12
For when the (*physical*) priesthood (*of Aaron/Levi*) is *transferred to heaven* (*to Melchizedek*), <u>of necessity</u> (*because The Law is what gives the authority to make sacrifices*) there takes place a *transposition* of The Law (*to heaven to serve Yahusha now as High Priest*) also.

It is not my intention in this chapter to teach on all the various sacrifices and what they represent. Every section in this book should really be developed fully into a book of its own. Again this book is meant more as *Cliff Notes*. In this book series, we will eventually look at the most "abominable" sacrifice that could be made. Before we can identify that "abominable" sacrifice we must first establish the "true" sacrifice that this "abominable" sacrifice replaces on the altar of our hearts and minds in the Body Temple. **That true sacrifice is Passover**.

Passover the True Sacrifice for Sin

As we see below, the sacrifice of Passover as well as the keeping of Passover wasn't "abolished" by the Messiah; it too was transposed over to Yahusha as "The Passover Lamb of God". The sacrifice of *The Passover Lamb* is only effective now for those who have the blood of THAT sacrifice on their hearts (Altars).

We renew that "sacrifice" annually in loving obedience in keeping Passover in light of Yahusha's sacrifice. "Easter" is not "Passover" as we will soon realize clearly later in this book series. Easter is not an *Appointed Time of Yahuah*, it is not a sacred assembly of Yahuah's, it is not the day on which the Messiah's sacrifice was made nor was it his resurrection day.

There is no commandment for Easter. It is a pagan sacrifice of a pig and a pagan holy day originating not in The Bible but in Babylon.

ONLY, and I cannot stress this enough, *ONLY* those who have properly put their faith in Passover and express that faith in their actions by keeping Passover (*believe Yahusha was that Lamb*) as commanded by Yahuah and instructed by Yahusha and taught by his disciples <u>are covered by the Blood of the Lamb</u>.

The keeping of Passover to be saved from death was established clearly by the original Passover when Isaac was spared by a substitutionary ram (a male lamb). Then again in Egypt when the Angel of Death "passed over" those who had the blood of the lamb on their doorposts.

Yahusha made this clear as he kept Passover the day he died. John the Baptist made this point crystal clear when he saw Yahusha at his Mikveh and declared "Behold! The Passover Lamb of Yahuah". The Apostle Paul makes this point clear instructing us in "how" to keep Passover, Peter stressed it, John the Revelator showed us this in the Spirit;

Passover is truly the scarlet thread (blood) of redemption running from cover to cover in the Word of Yahuah beginning with Abraham and Isaac:

Luke 22:19
19 And when He had taken some bread and given thanks (*at Passover*), He broke it and gave it to them, saying, "This (*Passover Dinner*) is My body (*Passover Lamb*) which is given (*sacrificed*) for you; **do this** (*keep Passover*) **in remembrance of Me**."

John 1:29
"Behold the (*Passover*) Lamb of God, which taketh away the sin of the world."

John 1:36
"and he looked at Yahusha as He walked, and said, "Behold, the (*Passover*) Lamb of God!"

1 Corinthians 5: 7-8
"Get rid of the old yeast that you may be a new batch without yeast--as you really are. For the Messiah, our Passover Lamb has been sacrificed. Therefore let us keep the Festival (*of Passover/Unleavened Bread*), not with the old yeast, the yeast of malice and wickedness, but with bread without yeast, the bread of sincerity and truth."

1 Peter 1: 18-25

"For you know that it was not with perishable things such as silver or gold that you were redeemed from the empty way of life handed down to you from your forefathers, but with the precious blood of the Messiah, a (*Passover*) lamb without blemish or defect"

Revelation 5:6

"Then I saw a (*Passover*) Lamb, looking as if it had been slain.

Revelation 5:12

"In a loud voice they sang: "Worthy is the (*Passover*) Lamb, who was slain, to receive power and wealth and wisdom and strength and honor and glory and praise!".

Revelation 5:13

"Then I heard every creature in heaven and on earth and under the earth and on the sea, and all that is in them, singing: "To him who sits on the throne and to the (*Passover*) Lamb be praise and honor and glory and power, for ever and ever!"

So we see the "proper" sacrifice for sin on **The Altar of Yahuah** is **The Passover Lamb of God**, the Messiah Yahusha. We are to keep **and** put our faith in Passover each year as we "do this" in remembrance of The Messiah's sacrifice. Keeping Passover is our spiritual sacrifice to Yahuah and in doing so, we are "covered by the Blood of the Lamb" and will be Passed Over the Second Death. This is the story of salvation told in the Bible. Today, however, Christianity no longer puts their faith in Passover but rather "Easter". We will cover this *abomination* in detail later in Chapter 14 as we define *The Abomination of Desolation*. In this chapter I am simply demonstrating the transposition of physical sacrifices defined in The Law (now "written on our hearts") and the transposition of His Altar. In doing so I demonstrate that the TRUE sacrifice for sin *is keeping Passover*. Not "Easter".

True sacrifices in the Spiritual Kingdom of Yahuah

The physical sacrifices defined in The Law are physical to spiritual parallels of true Spiritual sacrifices to Yahuah. These true sacrifices in the spiritual realm are our affections toward Yahuah expressed through our actions (faith without works is dead faith). This is not a new concept limited to The New Testament. King David proclaimed this reality in Psalms; clearly illustrating the spiritual Truth later to be revealed in *The Yahushaic Covenant*. The true Altar of Yahuah is in the heart and mind of the Body Temple and TRUE sacrifices are made on that altar not a physical one:

> **Psalms 51:17**
> "The (*true*) sacrifices of Yahuah are a broken spirit (*Spiritual*); (*offered on*) a broken and a contrite heart (*The True Altar*), 0 Yahuah, **thou wilt not despise**."

The Apostle Paul in his letter to the Roman Church, again illustrates this spiritual truth concerning true sacrifices in the Spiritual Kingdom of Yahuah:

> **Romans 12:1**
> "I beseech you therefore brethren, by the mercies of Yahuah, that you present <u>your bodies a living sacrifice,</u> holy and acceptable to Yahuah, which is your **spiritual** worship."

It is in <u>the keeping</u> of Passover that we express our faith in The Passover Lamb and keep the memory of Yahusha's sacrifice alive. That is the spiritual equivalent of "sacrificing The Passover Lamb and pouring the blood of the Lamb over *The Altar of Yahuah*" which is our hearts/minds. Many say they have "faith in the blood of the Lamb" and then keep Easter. True faith in the blood of the Lamb is expressed by "works" of The Law and Yahuah and Yahusha and Paul all commanded we keep Passover!

413

James 2:18

But someone may well say, "You have faith (*alone*) and (*condemn me because*) I have works (*trying to work my way to heaven legalistically*); show me your faith without the works, and I will show you my faith by my works."

We cannot "say" we have faith in Yahusha and then not keep Passover as Yahusha commanded. That is <u>dead faith</u> and if we don't keep Passover then our faith in ***The Passover Lamb*** is DEAD and your sin is not covered as we did not offer the spiritual sacrifice required. If we don't express our faith <u>by our works</u> of keeping The Passover, the blood of the Passover Lamb is not poured out over ***The Altar of Yahuah*** on our behalf. Everyone (even demons) know Yahusha is the Passover Lamb, but how many express that faith in Yahusha by being obedient to his command to keep Passover? Faith expressed through actions of obedience makes us perfect.

We see that we are justified not by faith alone, but by faith combined with works:

James 2:14-26

[14] What *does it* profit, my brethren, if someone says he has faith but does not have works? Can faith save him? [15] If a brother or sister is naked and destitute of daily food, [16] and one of you says to them, "Depart in peace, be warmed and filled," but you do not give them the things which are needed for the body, what *does it* profit? [17] **Thus also faith by itself, if it does not have works, is dead.**

[18] But someone will say, **"You have faith, and I have works." Show me your faith without your works, and I will show you my faith by my works.** [19] You believe that there is one God. You do well. Even the demons believe— and tremble! [20] **But do you want to know, O foolish man, that faith without works is dead?**

414

[21] Was not Abraham our father justified by works when he offered Isaac his son on the altar? [22] Do you see that faith was working together with his works, and **by works faith was made perfect**? [23] And the Scripture was fulfilled which says, "Abraham believed God, and it was accounted to him for righteousness." And he was called the friend of God. [24] **You see then that a man is justified by works, and not by faith only.**

[25] Likewise, was not Rahab the harlot also justified by works when she received the messengers and sent *them* out another way?

[26] **For as the body without the spirit is dead, so faith without works is dead also.**

Now we are in a position to "see" the Abomination of Desolation spoken of by the prophet Daniel as Yahusha warned us "let the reader understand" that it is a spiritual event not a physical one. Now we know what the Temple, Altar, and Sacrifices really are and we can define the real Abomination of Desolation that occurs at the end in the Kingdom of Yahuah.

Chapter 21

The Antichrist commits The Abomination of Desolation

Introduction

We must all have a firm understanding of the "purpose" of The Yahushaic (New) Covenant in that Yahusha came to "fulfill" The Law. He did not come to abolish it but to transpose it from written in stone to written on our hearts. Yahusha came to usher in The Kingdom of Yahuah and that kingdom is "not of this world". It is a Spiritual Kingdom! I explain this in great detail in my book *The Kingdom of Yahuah* as I demonstrate exactly what Yahusha did in fulfilling The Law and transposing The Law, the priesthood, the altar, the temple, the sacrifices, New Jerusalem, and even our bodies to The Kingdom of Yahuah.

In order to "see" the Abomination of Desolation we must understand the concept of transposition and the method by which Yahuah progressively discloses events through prophecy, then physical fulfillment as a shadow of the Spiritual Reality. A reality we cannot "see" with our natural eye. Don't listen to these false prophecy teachers who are not inspired and have committed BOTH the Transgression of Desolation AND The Abomination themselves! They are telling us to look for a physical event that occurs at the end within The Yahushaic Covenant which will never happen! Even worse are the "rapturist" who simply say "don't worry about it, you're going to be beamed up to Heaven before it happens anyway" … again coming from those guilty of both the Transgression and Abomination of Desolation! They have been given over to the Spirit of Error and fallen for the Spirit of the False messiah Χ§Ϛ and **Yahuah has made them fools**.

The Abomination of Desolation, as it is called, is the sacrifice and shedding of the blood of the most abominable animal to Yahuah (*a pig*) on His Altar that destroys His Temple. In this chapter I am going to reveal exactly what *The Abomination of Desolation* is in *The Kingdom of Yahuah*. This is not going to be easy for most to "see" and even harder for most to "understand". Having "eyes to see" this spiritual event will be almost impossible for anyone to "accept" because the masses have not had their frontal lobe "sealed" by Yahuah and are spiritually blind to the Truth. The Name of Yahuah is likened to the frontal lobe bone that protects the portion of our brain from deception. For more on that, read my book *The Kingdom of Yahuah*.

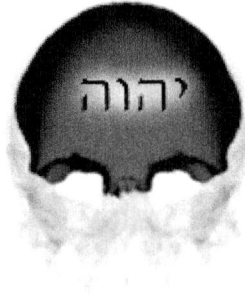

Most people worship The Trinity which is the seal of Babylon and have been given over *The Spirit of Error* and simply do not have eyes to see real Truth. Real truth is a double edged sword; that which divides the very soul and spirit of a man. Truth is simply too hard for most to accept that is why all of Yahuah's prophets were killed. I highly recommend reading my entire books in the Original Revelation Series so that you truly understand what I am revealing in this book.

It is imperative that we understand what religion evolved out of Babylon (my book *Mystery Babylon the religion of The Beast*) because it is **that** religion Yahusha commands us to "come out" of before he returns. It is **that** religion that deceives the Earth over the course of the 6,000 year training period we call human history. It is **that** religious lie that those who "overcome it and endure in The Truth" will find salvation. It is the false image of 𝓍ⲋⲋ that represents all the Babylonian rituals and gods that is The Antichrist.

We only need to take a truthful look at the <u>largest religion on Earth</u> which is *Christianity* and compare it to the religion born in

418

Babylon to know they are the exact same religions. That is why I wrote the first three books *Creation Cries Out!*, *Babylon the religion of The Beast*, and *Christianity the Great Deception!*".

In those three books I clearly define the Babylonian Mystery Religion and then compare it closely with Christianity and demonstrate they are identical. They worship the same god, they worship on the same day, they keep the exact same rituals, and their sacrifice remains that of the Χ𝄢Ϛ pig of Ishtar (Easter).

In my book series I will establish how to read scripture with the understanding of *physical to spiritual parallels* and *transposition* from the physical realm to the spiritual realm. In my book *The Kingdom of Yahuah* I will define the vital aspect of His Kingdom such as The Law, The Temple, The Altar, and The Sacrifices as they now exist in *The Yahushaic Covenant* as Yahusha came to usher in The Spiritual Kingdom of Yahuah through transposition. Understanding the spiritual state of The Yahushaic Covenant is necessary to understand *The Abomination of Desolation*.

It is my hope that reading this book series the reader will developed "eyes to see" Spiritual Truth because that is the only way we will ever "see and understand" what the prophet Daniel saw in a vision and what is revealed about *The Abomination of Desolation* in The New Testament. Daniel, Paul, and John saw an "image of a man" being elevated in *The Temple of Yahuah* as God incarnate, removing the proper sacrifice for our sin, and committing the most abominable sacrifice on *The Altar of Yahuah*. This event literally desolates or destroys *The Temple of Yahuah*. It is known as The Abomination that causes Desolation.

The point is this, Daniel proclaims this event happens "at the time of the end" and Yahusha confirms this fact in Matthew and John as well in Revelation. We must understand that "at the time of the end" we are under *The Yahushaic Covenant* and *The Alter*, *The Temple*, and *The Sacrifices* have been transposed by Yahusha to their Spiritual State in *The Kingdom of Yahuah*. It is, with this truth in mind, that we must evaluate the prophecies concerning *The False messiah* standing up in *The Temple of Yahuah* proclaiming himself to be God and slaughtering a pig on *the altar of Yahuah*.

Daniel saw <u>a vision</u> of what would occur physically and then what occurs in *The Kingdom of Yahuah* within the context of *The Yahushaic Covenant* in the spirit. We must keep in mind Yahuah's use of *physical to spiritual parallel*s to teach us Spiritual Truths through physical examples. We must keep in mind how Yahuah progressively revealed His Spiritual Kingdom over time. We must keep in mind that Yahusha transposed the physical shadows in all the previous covenants in The Torah to their final spiritual states... we must "see" Daniel's vision from this very important perspective... *The Abomination of Desolation* occurs at the end within *The Yahushaic Covenant* when:

- The False messiah is an "image" of Yahusha that is false. He is not a real person.
- *The altar of Yahuah* is not a physical altar but the heart and mind of man.
- *The Temple of Yahuah* is the human body not a standing physical place in Jerusalem.
- Sacrifices are not physical animals but "faith" exercised by believers.

That is one of the main themes of my book series as I firmly establish these truths in order to reveal the true abominable sacrifice on *the altar of Yahuah* that desolates *The Temple of Yahuah*. What Daniel "saw in a vision" was fulfilled by Antiouchus IV which is the "shadow" of the REAL event that occurs at the end spiritually. He describes that vision to us using a physical example that we as sons of Yahuah should understand using *physical to spiritual parallel*s.

Yahuah showed Daniel that at the time of the end we would invite a false image of The Messiah into our hearts and we would put our faith in the sacrifice of a pig. We would spread the blood of that pig on the altar of our hearts causing the true sacrifice of The Passover Lamb to cease on our behalf as we stopped keeping Passover and began keeping Easter. This would leave us without the proper sacrifice for sin and our body, which is His Temple, would therefore be destroyed due to our transgression.

Why are the present Christian teachers telling us to look for a physical fulfillment of a Spiritual Event? Yahuah does not go backwards in "progressive revelation"… that would be "**re**gressive revelation" and what would the point be in that? That would be like Yahuah changing His mind about Yahusha being the final sacrifice on Passover and requiring us to once again go kill a physical lamb every year… pointless. Yahusha prophesied the destruction of the physical temple and announced the Spiritual Temple and both were fulfilled. The physical temple is no longer required and hasn't existed for 2,000 years since the Chief Cornerstone of the FINAL TEMPLE was properly set. Those with "eyes to see and ears to hear let them understand" the Spiritual Kingdom of Yahuah should stop looking for a physical event that has already occurred.

The Abomination of Desolation intro

As an Eschatology Scholar for the past 20 years, allow me articulate the prevailing view of *The Abomination of Desolation* in churches today and in Christian literature:

> *The Abomination of Desolation occurs at the mid-point or 3.5 years into the 7 year tribulation period. This event begins the last 3.5 years period called The Great Tribulation. The Great Tribulation begins when the Antichrist either erects an idol on the Temple Mount in Jerusalem after stops a working altar that The Jews have setup on the Temple Mount inside the rebuilt Third Temple.*

421

This is what is being taught in Christian circles today. What I am going to demonstrate in this chapter is that:

- **The altar of Yahuah** is not a physical working altar in a physical temple on The Temple Mount in Jerusalem, but rather the "hearts and minds" of humanity.
- The Third Temple is not finally constructed until after the Second Coming. This Temple is build not by the hands of the False messiah (antichrist) but rather The Messiah Yahusha and the sons of Yahuah. The construction of the Final and Third Temple began with the laying of the Chief Cornerstone 2000 years ago and is completed during the Millennial Kingdom with the resurrection of the rest of the sons of Yahuah. **The Temple of Yahuah** is the bodies of Yahuah's Chosen Elect as proven by the resurrection, demonstrated in scripture, and illustrated by the physical design of the physical Temple of Solomon.
- The singular most abominable sacrifice in the Torah is a pig. This was foreshadowed in history when a pig was slain on **the altar of Yahuah** in His Temple by Antiochus IV in honor of Zeus. Spiritually the Pig of Ishtar is the abominable sacrifice.
- The False messiah is the Roman demi-god Jesus H. Christ identified by name in scripture
- The belief in Easter (the Pig of Ishtar) in lieu of Passover is the abominable sacrifice that causes the continual oblation (the slain body of Yahusha as The Lamb of Yahuah) to cease.

I realize how "shocking" this sounds. But in this chapter I will build on the transposition of **The Kingdom of Yahuah** defined in this book and lay down The Truth line upon line, precept upon precept as I build to the final inescapable conclusion.

This chapter will be very difficult to even read for most (it is long and complex) and almost impossible to believe for many (for the conclusions presented). It confronts almost 2000 years of

Christian Tradition and is a full frontal assault on the very "God" worshipped in the hearts of many world-wide.

I encourage everyone to approach this chapter with an open heart for The Truth. It is only by truly seeking out our own salvation with "fear and trembling" and testing every doctrine (we have come to accept as "Truth") and be willing to accept only the pure Word of Yahuah that we will be given "eyes to see". Our eternal life depends on our ability to overcome this one singular abomination and tear down every high place that elevates itself above the knowledge of the one true and living God… Yahuah. Not only will I clearly define *The Abomination of Desolation* but I will also clearly define how one can overcome it! It is never too late while you still draw breath!

Yahusha spoke in parables

Yahuah tells us what He will do through the mouth of His prophets, he then brings it to pass as a physical shadow-pictures or "portraits" designed to teach us greater Spiritual Truths concerning His Kingdom. Then Yahuah fulfills that shadow picture in the spirit which is true reality.

> ### Isaiah 48
> ³ I foretold the former things long ago, my mouth announced them (*to my prophets*) and I made them known (*through physical shadows*); then suddenly I acted, and they came to pass (*Spiritually*).

> ### Isaiah 46
> 9 Remember the former things of old: for I am God, and there is none else; I am God, and there is none like me, 10 **Declaring the end from the beginning**, and from ancient times the things that are not yet done, saying, My counsel shall stand, and I will do all my pleasure: 11 … I have spoken it (*through My prophets*), I will also bring it to pass (*as a physical example*); (*because*) I have purposed it (*in*

The Kingdom of Yahuah), I will also do it (*in the Spiritual Realm*).

Yahusha too veiled the Spiritual Kingdom of Yahuah through parables, riddles, and idioms.   You see, it is not for "everyone" to understand the things I am explaining in this chapter. That is why most will simply shut down and stop reading… this information cannot be comprehended or accepted by anyone who <u>does not</u> have *The Seal of Yahuah* over their mind. Many times we see Yahusha use this veiled language and those around him, including his own disciples, had no idea what he was talking about.   Yahusha was bringing a "Spiritual Kingdom" to a physical world and that knowledge is reserved for the chosen Elect, sons of Yahuah <u>and no one else</u>. Only those whose minds have been sealed with His Shema.

It is little wonder why things of Yahuah remain hidden to this day. Because Yahuah has literally blinded the masses' "minds of understanding" for committing *The Transgression of Desolation* (abolishing His Law) and darkened their minds to believe a lie causing them to commit *The Abomination of Desolation* in their heart.

When referring back to *The Abomination of Desolation* in Daniel, Yahusha told us that to "see" it we must have "eyes to see"; we must use the "understanding of our spiritual mind":

Matthew 24
[15] "So when you ***see*** standing in the holy place 'the abomination that causes desolation,' spoken of through the prophet Daniel—***let the reader understand***—

When asked by his disciples "why" Yahusha spoke in parables, riddles, and idioms; his response was something like "let the reader understand or whoever has eyes to see or ears to hear". You see, anytime Yahusha was speaking in such veiled language he would make a statement such as he made after telling the parable of The Sower in Luke Chapter 8:

Luke 8:8

"When he said this (*finished the parable of The Sower*), he called out, "*Whoever has ears to hear, let them hear*.""

"*Whoever has ears to hear, let them hear*" and "*let the reader understand*" are just two of the phrases Yahusha would use to indicate that, although what he was talking about was a physical example or story, it was <u>intended</u> to be understood with spiritual "eyes of understanding"! He was speaking in *physical to spiritual parallel*s. Having heard Yahusha do this time and again, his disciples finally confronted Yahusha and asked him why he spoke in such a way. Yahusha made it crystal clear, this knowledge is not for the masses, but for the Elect only:

Luke 8:10

10 He said, "The knowledge of the <u>secrets</u> of *The Kingdom of* Yahuah has been given to you, but to others I speak in parables, so that, 'though seeing, they may not see; though hearing, they may not understand.'

Yahusha was simply stating the same thing Yahuah had told Isaiah:

Isaiah 6

9 He said, "Go and tell this people: "'Be ever hearing, **but never understanding**; be ever seeing, **but never perceiving**.' 10 Make the heart of this people calloused; make their ears dull and **close their eyes**. **Otherwise they might see with their eyes, hear with their ears, understand with their hearts**,

In *The Yahushaic Covenant* you cannot "see" *Spiritual Intent* with your eyes. It is not like in the previous 6 covenants where sin was an outward act that <u>could be seen.</u> In *The Yahushaic Covenant* The Law took on new meaning and <u>was strengthen</u> to a higher state of "intent". So for us now to identify sin, we must examine ourselves inwardly with "*eyes to see and ears to hear and understanding with our hearts*". This too is true of all things in a Spiritual Kingdom. In acts we see the same warning:

Acts 28:27
27 For the heart of this people is waxed gross, and their ears are dull of hearing, and their eyes have they closed; lest they should see with their eyes, and hear with their ears, and understand with their heart, and should be converted, and I should heal them.

What is this "*secret*" that requires not physical "*seeing and hearing*" but "*eyes and ears of Spiritual understanding*" we are warned that only a select "*few*" will possess? It is the simple fact that the previous 6 covenants were given in physical shadow-pictures that painted a portrait of greater Spiritual Truths found in the 7th Covenant of Yahusha the Messiah. It is truly "The Spiritual Kingdom" that is at stake. The very same Kingdom that Yahusha reigns as King; the very one that is not of this physical world as Yahusha explained to Pilot.

The Apostle Paul discussed the very issue concerning The Torah below. Paul clearly says one simple fact in Colossians 2... The previous 6 covenants in The Torah found their final Spiritual expression in *The Yahushaic Covenant*, and do not let ANYONE disqualify you (or judge you) for keeping The Torah in light of Yahusha for those that condemn you are guilty of worshipping (fallen) angels. In fact more specifically they are guilty of committing *The Transgression of Desolation* (abolishing The Law) which leads to *The Abomination of Desolation* (having the wrong sacrifice for sin in your heart) as I will explain in this chapter. Because anyone who teaches such foolishness that we should not be obedient to The Law goes into great detail about "*what they see*" or "*how they see it*" and in reality they are all puffed up with "IDLE NOTIONS BY THE UNSPIRITUAL MIND". In other words... they do not have Spiritual "*eyes of understanding*" required to properly understand the Word of Yahuah, and seeing they cannot see, hearing they cannot hear, and their unspiritual mind cannot "UNDERSTAND" the Spiritual

Kingdom of Yahuah:

> ### Colossians 2
> 16 Therefore do not let anyone judge you by what you eat or drink (*as you keep The Kosher Laws*), or with regard to a religious festival (*as you keep Yahuah's Appointed Times*), a New Moon celebration or a Sabbath day (*because you keep His monthly calendar and keep His Sabbaths Holy*). 17 These (*things defined in previous covenants*) are a shadow of the (*greater Spiritual*) things that were (*prophesied*) to come; the (*Spiritual*) reality, however, is found in ***The Yahushaic Covenant*** (*and understood by keeping His Festivals*)
>
> 18 Do not let anyone who delights in false humility and the worship of angels disqualify you. ***Such a person also goes into great detail about what they have seen; they are puffed up with idle notions by their unspiritual mind***.

So what does having "***eyes and ears of understanding***" spiritual things from the study of physical shadow-pictures have to do with ***The Abomination of Desolation***? Well that is what this chapter is all about. Because when Yahusha warned us of what Daniel "saw" in a vision, he obviously warned us that Daniel's vision was not a glimpse of a physical event alone; But rather, Daniel was given *a vision* and in his vision he was shown as a physical shadow of the event. In reality Yahusha warned us that to "see" it we must use our "<u>eyes of understanding</u>". When John spoke about the same things in Revelation he too warned us that to understand them we must have wisdom and spiritual insight.

The Abomination of Desolation in ***The Yahushaic Covenant*** was not an event to be beheld by the physical eye but "the spiritual eye" and understood with a mind set of the spirit of Yahuah. It is an event that occurs within the context of ***The Yahushaic Covenant*** at "the time of the end" when <u>all things</u> have been transposed from physical to spiritual including The Alter, The Temple, The False messiah, and the Abominable Sacrifice!

How did Yahusha warn us of this?

Yahusha warning...
"The Abomination of Desolation is a Spiritual Event"

In Matthew 24, Yahusha warned us of the coming *Abomination of Desolation*. Notice that right after he warned us he then qualified that warning with "*let the reader understand*". Yet another way of saying "*whoever has developed spiritual eyes to see let them see with their MIND*" because it is not an event to be beholden by the physical eye...

> ### Matthew 24
> [15] "So when you see standing in the holy place 'the abomination that causes desolation,' spoken of through the prophet Daniel—*let the reader understand*—

Well, in this chapter that is exactly what we shall do. We will not make the mistake of looking for a physical event taking place on a physical altar in a physical temple in Jerusalem (that has already occurred with Antiochus IV), but rather we shall look with our "*eyes of understanding*" at that fulfilled physical shadow-picture exactly as instructed by Yahusha.

Total disconnect with *The Yahushaic Covenant*

In short, if we are looking for a physical temple to be rebuilt in Jerusalem and a working altar to be constructed to "see" *The Abomination of Desolation*, then the teaching of the Messiah and his Spiritual Kingdom is as lost on us as it was on those around Yahusha 2000 years ago! Looking for a physical altar, a physical temple, physical sacrifices, and a physical man called "the Antichrist" shows a complete disconnect with *The Yahushaic Covenant* and the message contained in The Bible concerning *The*

Kingdom of Yahuah.

Paul informs us there is no understanding Spiritual Truths outside of the physical "shadows" because it is by those very physical shadows in The Torah and history that Spiritual Reality is taught! This concept of "***physical to spiritual parallel****s*" is what the Apostle Paul was struggling with when he accepted the Messiah. Paul had to literally be "knocked off his high horse" to realize that the physical world was really nothing more than a "shadow" of greater Spiritual Truths. Paul had to be literally <u>blinded physically</u> before his spiritual eyes could be opened.

After his spiritual eyes were opened and he could "see" the reality of ***physical to spiritual parallel****s*; this physical world, to him, was like looking through a "dim mirror" that was just a reflection of the true Spiritual Reality:

> ### 1 Corinthians 13
> [12] For now we (*physically*) see only a reflection (*of Spiritual Reality*) as (*if we were looking*) in a mirror; (*but when resurrected*) then we shall see (*clearly*) face to face (*the Spiritual Realm directly*). Now I know in part (*through physical to spiritual parallels*); then I shall know fully, even as I am fully known.

The Christian Church has thrown out The Torah as "old" and actually believes it is possible to understands the "New Testament" outside of it. There is no understanding ***The Yahushaic Covenant*** outside of the study of The Torah. Paul actually chastised those who do not keep the Torah/Feasts/Sabbaths as being "spiritually immature" because you cannot progress as a spiritually mature son outside of learning those Spiritual Truths! You must study their physical shadows, rehearsals, and metaphors found in The Torah to understand The New (Yahushaic) Covenant!

> ### Hebrews 5:12 - Spiritual Immaturity
> 12 For though by this time you ought to be teachers (*of the Torah, there was no such thing as the New Testament when*

he wrote this), you need someone to teach you again **the first principles of the oracles of God** (*this is The Torah*); and you have come to need milk and not solid food. 13 For everyone who partakes only of milk **is unskilled in the word of righteousness** (*they don't know The Torah, there was no such thing as The New Testament at this time*), for he is a babe. 14 But solid food (*Spiritual Truth*) belongs to those who are of full age (*mature Saints with minds set on Spiritual Law*), that is, **those who by reason of use** (*i.e. those who are Torah observant*) have their (*spiritual*) senses exercised (*trained through physical to spiritual parallels*) to discern both good and evil (*which is defined by the Law of God, good is obedience to His Commands, evil is breaking them*).

This is true too of **The Abomination of Desolation**. We must understand that Yahuah always foretells an event through His prophets, and then He brings it to pass physically for us to learn from. Ultimately, however, the event finds its "fulfillment" in The Spiritual Realm.

Isaiah 48

> [3] I foretold the former things long ago, my mouth announced them (*to my prophets*) and I made them known (*through physical shadows*); then suddenly I acted, and they came to pass (*Spiritually*).

Isaiah 46

> 9 Remember the former things of old: for I am God, and there is none else; I am God, and there is none like me, 10 **Declaring the end from the beginning**, and from ancient times the things that are not yet done, saying, My counsel shall stand, and I will do all my pleasure: 11 … I have spoken it (*through My prophets*), I will also bring it to pass (*as a physical example*); I have purposed it (in **The Kingdom of**

Yahuah), I will also do it (*in the Spiritual Realm*).

Isaiah 42

> 9 Behold, the former things are come to pass, and new things do I declare: **before they spring forth I tell you of them**.

I am going to demonstrate clearly that Yahuah prophesied *The Abomination of Desolation* through the prophet Daniel, The Apostle Paul, and John the Revelator. Then that event was fulfilled as a physical shadow or example we are to study when Antiochus IV slaughtered a pig on the altar to Zeus on "Christmas". I am then going to prove that Jesus is the false image of Yahusha who we elevate in our heart as God and then slaughter a pig on His altar by keeping Easter. We must overcome the prevailing false doctrine of the Christian Church that a real man, some charismatic world leader, goes to a rebuilt temple in Jerusalem and proclaims himself to be God and sets up some kind of image of himself on the altar and stops the sacrifices. The physical event has already occurred, we are in the Spiritual covenant now and I will have to prove:

- The Temple will never be rebuilt again physically and exists now as the human body
- Antiochus IV fulfilled the physical aspect of the prophecy in Daniel
- The false messiah is not a real person but a "false image of Yahusha"
- There will not be another physical working alter, *The altar of Yahuah* now is the hearts/minds of man
- Jesus Christ is mention by name in Revelation 13 as the beast
- That Daniel foretold of two events, one physical event fulfilled by Antiochus and one spiritual event fulfilled at the end just before Yahusha returns

431

- Jesus Christ is the first beast and Christianity is the second beast of Revelation 13
- Elevating Jesus as God in our hearts, keeping Easter over Passover is The Abomination of Desolation.

The Third Temple of Yahuah is not a physical temple!

The false teachers in the Christian Church teach us to look for the construction of a third physical temple in Jerusalem and only then can **The Abomination of Desolation** occur. When we see this physical temple in Jerusalem we are taught to look for a charismatic world leader who conquers the Earth, brings peace to the Middle East, then goes to the temple in Jerusalem and proclaims himself to be God.

It isn't very hard to totally <u>disqualify</u> this false teaching because there will never be a third physical temple in Jerusalem. These false teachers show a total disconnect from **The Yahushaic Covenant**. Yahusha came to "fulfill" all previous covenants and transpose all things into The Spiritual Kingdom of Yahuah.

Scripture explicitly teaches that there will never be another physical temple and that the final **Temple of Yahuah** is already under construction.

Construction of the Third and Final Temple

We see in Revelation the physical Temple was not seen in the City of Yahuah Shammah, but rather that Temple is now spiritual:

Revelation 21
[22] I did <u>not see a temple in the city</u>, because the (*sons of*) Yahuah Almighty and the Lamb are its temple.

The reason there is no physical third temple ever built in Jerusalem is because we are **The Temple of Yahuah** in **The Yahushaic Covenant**. Like all aspects of **The Kingdom of Yahuah**; The Temple has been transposed from physical to spiritual. The final **Temple of Yahuah** is already under construction. It is the sum total of the sons of Yahuah. Construction of the final temple began with the resurrection (transposition of the body) of Yahusha who became the Chief Cornerstone:

Ephesians 2:19-22
So then you are no longer strangers and aliens, but you are fellow citizens with the saints, and are of Yahuah's household, having been built upon the foundation of the apostles and prophets, **the Messiah Yahusha Himself being the corner stone** (of *The Temple of Yahuah*), in whom the whole building, being fitted together is growing into a **Holy Temple of Yahuah**; in whom you also are being built together into a dwelling of Yahuah in the Spirit (*The Kingdom of Yahuah*).

Luke 20:17
17 But Yahusha looked at them and said, "What then is this that is written: 'THE STONE WHICH THE BUILDERS REJECTED, THIS BECAME THE CHIEF CORNER stone' (*of the third and final temple*)

1 Peter 2:6
6 For this is contained in Scripture: "BEHOLD, I LAY IN ZION (*The Kingdom of Yahuah*) A CHOICE STONE (*in the construction of the final Temple*), A PRECIOUS CORNER stone, AND HE WHO BELIEVES IN HIM WILL NOT BE DISAPPOINTED."

John 2
19 Yahusha answered and said unto them, Destroy this temple, and in three days I will raise it up.   20 Then said the Jews, Forty and six years was this temple in building,

and wilt thou rear it up in three days?   21 **But he spake of the temple of his body**.

The sons of Yahuah are the living stones built upon *The Chief Cornerstone* as *The Temple of Yahuah* is rebuilt.

I Peter 2:5
You also, <u>as living stones</u>, are being built up **as a spiritual house** (*Temple*)...

II Corinthians 6:16
What agreement has *The Temple of Yahuah* with idols? For **we are the temple of the living God**; just as Yahuah said, "I *will dwell in them* and walk among them; and I will be their God, and they shall be My people."

I Corinthians 6:19
Do you not know **that your body is a temple** of the Spirit of Yahuah who is in you, whom you have from Yahuah?

The Apostle Paul describes this "body Temple" below:

Ephesians 4:11-16
[11] So Yahusha himself gave the apostles, the prophets, the evangelists, the pastors and teachers, [12] to equip his people for works of service, so that the body of The Messiah may be built up [13] until we all reach unity in the faith and in the knowledge of the Son of Yahuah and become mature, attaining to the whole measure of the fullness of maturity in *The Yahushaic Covenant*.

[14] Then we will no longer be infants, tossed back and forth by the waves, and blown here and there by every wind of teaching and by the cunning and craftiness of people in their deceitful scheming. [15] Instead, speaking the truth in love, we will grow to become in every respect the mature body of him who is the head, that is, The Messiah. [16] From him the whole body, joined and held together by every

supporting ligament, grows and builds itself up in love, as each part does its work.

Yahusha returns, the sons of YHWH are resurrected and transposed (raptured) from the 4 corners of Earth and we all rebuilt the final Temple. In other words, as our bodies are transposed and each of the sons of Yahuah, being *living stones,* are assembled into **The Temple of Yahuah** which is an eternal living structure. Yahuah dwells in this eternal living Temple in the hearts of those living stones (our hearts are Altars to Yahuah not "Jesus"). The False messiah doesn't rebuild a physical temple and neither do the Jews. The final Temple of Yahuah is constructed when Yahuah gathers the living stones from the 4 corners of the Earth.

Zechariah 6:15
"Those WHO ARE FAR AWAY will come and help to build **The Temple of Yahuah**"

Haggai 2
[6] "This is what Yahuah Almighty says: 'In a little while I will once more shake the heavens and the earth, the sea and the dry land. (*speaking of The Great Tribulation*) [7] I will shake all nations, and what is desired by (*by Yahuah in*) all nations will come (*He gathers the elect from among the 4 corners*), and I will fill (*complete*) this house with glory (we are the glory of Yahuah),' says Yahuah Almighty. [8] 'The silver is mine and the gold is mine,' declares Yahuah Almighty. [9] 'The glory of this present house (*the Spiritual Temple of Yahuah*) will be greater than the glory of the former house,' says Yahuah Almighty. 'And in this place I will grant peace,' declares Yahuah Almighty."

What about Ezekiel's Temple Vision?

Ezekiel's Temple vision begins in Chapter 40 <u>AFTER</u> the tribulation is over and after the Millennial Kingdom begins. In the progression of Ezekiel's visions, he laid out the exact timeline as I understand it that is to unfold in the End Times prior to the final Temple being rebuilt:

- Chapter 34 - **Description of False Shepherds/True Shepherd** - Description of Christian Pastors that will be struck down, the sheep scattered to be re-gathered by The True Shepherd...
- Chapter 35 - **Judgment on Edom** for attacking Israel and dividing the land, they will be utterly destroyed
- Chapter 36 - **Judgment on all the nations** who participated in dividing the Land of Israel.
- Chapter 36:8-38 - **Israel returns to Yahuah** - The Seal is given out, the Elect are cultivated from Earth
- Chapter 37 - **THE FIRST RESURRECTION OF THE DEAD** and the Re-Unification of both Houses of Israel in preparation for the final conflict to liberate the Earth.
- Chapter 38 - **The Final Battle of Armageddon** as the armies of Earth attack Jerusalem at the 3rd Siege of Daniel and the sons of Yahuah defeat the armies of man
- Chapter 39 - **THE GREAT AND TERRIBLE DAY OF Yahuah**... The Earth is devastated, the armies of Earth destroyed, YHWH's Holy Name WILL NEVER BE PROFANED AGAIN... All nations will know and worship YHWH (vs. 7)... This is THE GREAT AND TERRIBLE DAY OF YHWH (vs. 8)... for 7-years (a Sabbath Week) where the Earth rests and regenerates (we don't burn trees) and the sons of YHWH gather the spoils of war. The first 7-months, we will be burying the dead after the Great and Terrible Day of YHWH. The massive slaughter of the unrighteous serves as a sacrifice to YHWH. YHWH again restores the fortunes of Jacob, and Remnant Israel and we live securely in the land for 1,000 years.

Now… after the sons of Yahuah are resurrected and transposed they begin the construction of *The Temple of Yahuah*. After the false teachers are struck down, Edomites are judged, nations of Earth are judged, the Shema is given out, the sons of Yahuah are resurrected, the armies of Yahuah, led by Yahusha, destroy the armies of Earth, and the great and terrible DAY of Yahuah occurs and we enter the Millennial Kingdom... **THEN** the third and final Temple is constructed.

- Chapter 40 - Measuring the Temple
- Chapter 41 - Building the Temple
- Chapter 42 - Chamber in the Outer Court
- Chapter 43 - YHWH's Glory returns to the Temple
- Chapter 44 - Duties of the Temple Priests
- Chapter 45 - Land of the Temple Priests
- Chapters 46-48 - The land is restored; living water flows from the Temple and turns the salt water oceans to fresh water etc. etc.

The false teachers in The Christian Church consistently demonstrate they have no spiritual understanding of the things of Yahuah. Teaching a physical temple will be rebuilt is just one example. By teaching these false doctrines they prove the Apostle Paul was correct when he said that those who elevate the image of man above Yahuah as God think they are wise but Yahuah has darkened their foolish hearts and they have no spiritual understanding (are fools):

Romans 1
[21] For although they knew Yahuah, they neither glorified him as Yahuah nor gave thanks to him, but their thinking became futile and their foolish hearts were darkened. [22] Although they claimed to be wise, they became fools.

Scripture stands as a clear witness against teaching that a physical man will enter a physical Temple in Jerusalem and commit *The Abomination of Desolation*. The physical shadow has already occurred in Antiochus IV.

There is no physical Temple ever rebuilt:

> **Revelation 21**
> [22] I did <u>not see a temple in the city</u>, because the (sons of)
> Yahuah Almighty and the Lamb are its temple.

Physical fulfillment of the Abomination of Desolation

The prophecies in Daniel are multifaceted finding fulfillment on multiple levels both physically and spiritually. They are the subject of much debate and it is outside of the scope of this chapter to go into all the various aspects of what Yahuah showed Daniel. For the purpose of this chapter I simply want to illustrate that Yahuah gave us a physical fulfillment of Daniels's prophecies that we are to study to understand the spiritual fulfillment.

> **Isaiah 48**
> [3] I foretold the former things long ago, my mouth
> announced them (*to my prophets*) and I made them known
> (*through physical shadows*); then suddenly I acted, and
> they came to pass (*Spiritually*).

The prophecies in Daniel were fulfilled literally in the physical realm by the Lucid King Antiochus IV. Antiochus fulfilled these prophecies to such a literal degree that many liberal scholars now believe that the book of Daniel was written <u>after</u> Antiochus IV invaded Jerusalem and committed *The Abomination of Desolation*. They believe these prophecies being so literally fulfilled by Antiochus could only mean they were written in *prophetic form* <u>after the fact</u> detailing a past event and then credited to Daniel. Of course, that is not true but that illustrates my point of how literally Antiochus IV fulfilled these prophecies. So literally it is hard to believe Daniel could have spoken of these events in such detail prior to the event occurring.

The school of thought that Antiochus IV fulfilled physically the prophecies concerning *The Abomination of Desolation* is known as '*the historical-critical interpretation of Daniel*'. This interpretation of Daniel became and is today the standard view of liberal scholars throughout the world. This view is supported by the Jewish Encyclopedia, the Jewish Publication Society study bible, the Catholic New American Bible commentary and some evangelical Christian scholars. There is no doubt when you look at Daniels prophecies *objectively* that they were fulfilled physically by Antiochus IV. So that is our "shadow-picture" to understand the spiritual event that we are to study.

The reason there are various views and interpretations of Daniel's vision is because, like I said, it is a <u>multifaceted</u> vision finding both physical and spiritual fulfillment. It is not the prophecies in Daniel that I will be focusing on in this chapter but those in the New Testament that speak directly of the False messiah. In this section I want to provide a quick explanation of Antiochus IV as the literal physical fulfillment of *The Abomination of Desolation* Daniel prophesied. We will then study that physical shadow in order to learn more and help identify the spiritual fulfillment of *The False messiah* and *The Abomination of Desolation* spoken of in The New Testament. That is what Yahusha meant when he pointed us back to the prophecy of Daniel and said "let the reader understand". Yahusha was indicating we are to study the physical to spiritual parallel.

Antiochus IV fulfilled Daniel's Vision in detail

Again this is only intended as an introduction to the physical fulfillment of *The Abomination of Desolation*. It is the spiritual fulfillment of this physical example that is within the scope of this chapter and relative to *The Kingdom of Yahuah*.

In Daniel's vision, the he-goat's first horn is broken, giving rise to four horns in its place. The "little horn" is sometimes understood to be one of the four horns that replaced the notable horn, who is accepted as Antiochus IV Epiphanes by historical-critical scholars. Daniel 8:10–14 is referenced to Antiochus' dealings with the Jewish people under his rule, which ended with the Maccabean Revolt and the rededication of The Altar. In addition, Daniel 11, with references to Persia and Greece and two kings, is thought to refer to the Seleucids, and specifically to Antiochus Epiphanes as "The King of the North".

The "prince who is to come" (Daniel 9:26) was Antiochus Epiphanes, whose armies partially invaded and destroyed Jerusalem and massacred many of its inhabitants. It was Antiochus IV Epiphanes who stopped sacrifice and grain offering in the middle of the week and offered a pig on *the altar of Yahuah* to Zeus (a shadow picture of Easter). This Abomination occurred on what we call Christmas around December 25th because Antiochus was a sun worshipper and Christmas is the annual rebirth of the Sun(god) Ba'al.

We read in the book of Maccabees

2 Maccabees 6:1–12
Not long after this the king (*Antiochus IV*) sent an Athenian senator to force the Jews to abandon the customs of their ancestors and live no longer by the laws of God; also to profane the temple in Jerusalem and dedicate it to Olympian Zeus, and that on Mount Gerizim to Zeus the Hospitable, as the inhabitants of the place requested...They also brought into the temple things that were forbidden, so that the altar was covered with (*the blood*) abominable offerings prohibited by the laws (*a pig*). A man could not keep the Sabbath or celebrate the traditional feasts (*of Yahuah*),

Sacking of Jerusalem and persecution of Jews

While Antiochus was busy in Egypt, a rumor spread that he had been killed. The deposed High Priest Jason gathered a force of 1,000 soldiers and made a surprise attack on the city of Jerusalem. The High Priest appointed by Antiochus, Menelaus, was forced to flee Jerusalem during a riot. On the King's return from Egypt in 167 BC enraged by his defeat, he attacked Jerusalem and restored Menelaus, then executed many Jews.

We again read in the book of Maccabees

> **2 Maccabees 5:11–14**
> When these happenings were reported to the king, he thought that Judea was in revolt. Raging like a wild animal, he set out from Egypt and took Jerusalem by storm. He ordered his soldiers to cut down without mercy those whom they met and to slay those who took refuge in their houses. There was a massacre of young and old, a killing of women and children, a slaughter of virgins and infants. In the space of three days, eighty thousand were lost, forty thousand meeting a violent death, and the same number being sold into slavery.

To consolidate his empire and strengthen his hold over the region, Antiochus IV decided to side with the Hellenized Jews (secular Jews) by outlawing Jewish religious rites and traditions kept by observant Jews and by ordering the worship of Zeus as the supreme god (what the Emperor Constantine would later do to create Christianity). This was an abomination to the Jews and when they refused, Antiochus sent an army to enforce his decree. Because of the resistance, the city was destroyed, many were slaughtered, and a military Greek citadel called the Acra was established (exactly what happened later when Rome destroyed Jerusalem and began executing the Jews and followers of Yahusha in coliseums and the Inquisition) .

2 Maccabees 6:1–12

Not long after this the king sent an Athenian senator to force the Jews to abandon the customs of their ancestors and live no longer by the laws of God; also to profane the temple in Jerusalem and dedicate it to Olympian Zeus, and that on Mount Gerizim to Zeus the Hospitable, as the inhabitants of the place requested...They also brought into the temple things that were forbidden, so that the altar was covered with abominable offerings prohibited by the laws. A man could not keep the Sabbath or celebrate the traditional feasts, nor even admit that he was a Jew. At the suggestion of the citizens of Ptolemais, a decree was issued ordering the neighboring Greek cities to act in the same way against the Jews: oblige them to partake of the sacrifices, and put to death those who would not consent to adopt the customs of the Greeks. It was obvious, therefore, that disaster impended.

Antiochus IV entered the Temple on Christmas Day in celebration of his son god, stopped the sacrifice and oblation, and slaughtered a pig on *the altar of Yahuah* to Zeus. He then ordered the changing of the Feasts of Yahuah to his pagan sun worship festivals, and changed The Sabbath to Sunday in honor of Dias Solis. Antiochus was a worshipper of Mithra the sungod. His original name before becoming king was Mithridates (Named after Mithra); he changed his name to Antiochus IV Epiphanes which means 'God Manifest' or "God in the flesh" or God Incarnate (just like Constantine).

This is exactly what Constantine did in the "image and name of Jesus H. Christ". Constantine too worshipped Mithra, believed himself to be the incantation of Zeus, changed the Feasts of Yahuah to pagan holidays, and changed The Sabbath to Sunday. Constantine then created a composite deity with all the same attributes (pagan holidays, Sunday worship, etc) called this new pagan demi-god **God Incarnate**. This false messiah was the composition of 3 pagan gods Hesus Horus and Krishna and was a

442

"false image" of Yahusha. Today that name has evolved over time into Jesus H. Christ who is The False messiah.

The False messiah is a false "image" of the True Messiah

Now that we have the physical example of *The Abomination of Desolation* fulfilled in Antiochus IV to study; we can recognize the true spiritual event at "the time of the end". The very one Yahusha told us that we must have "eyes to see with the spiritual understanding of our mind"!

While Antiochus IV was a real person just as Daniel prophesied, we see that in the final Spiritual fulfillment the False messiah is not a real person but an "image" or rather a false spiritual image of the true Messiah Yahusha. That is why the term False messiah is used of him. Everything about Jesus Christ is false! From his name… to him being the incarnation of God… to him changing the Sabbath to Sunday… to him changing Passover to Easter… to him abolishing The Law… and to him changing the Festival of Yahuah to pagan ones. We have literally accepted another Gospel in the name Jesus Christ than that which is found in The Bible.

> **2 Corinthians 11:4**
> For if someone comes to you and preaches a "Jesus" other than the Yahusha we preached, or if you receive a different spirit (*of abolishing The Law*) from the Spirit (*of loving obedience to The Law*) you received, or a different gospel (*The Trinity/Jesus/Sunday/Easter/Christmas*) from the one you accepted (*Yahuah/Yahusha/Sabbath/Passover*), you put up with it easily enough.

> **Galatians 1:6-8**
> [6] I marvel that you are turning away so soon (*to The LORD Ba'al*) from Yahuah who called you in the grace of Yahusha, to a different gospel (*The Cult of Sol Invictus which is the Trinity/Sunday/Easter*), [7] which is no gospel at

all; but there are some who trouble you and want to pervert the gospel of Yahusha the Messiah. ⁸ But even if we, or an angel from heaven, preach any other gospel to you than what we have preached to you, let him be accursed.

We see below that the False messiah is a spiritual <u>image</u> we are dealing with not a real person:

Rev. 14:9-12
"A third angel followed them and said in a loud voice: 'If ANYONE worships the beast and **his image** and receives his mark on the forehead or on the hand,

Rev. 19:20
With these signs he had deluded those who had received the mark of the beast and **worshiped his image**. The two of them were thrown alive into the fiery lake of burning sulfur".

Rev. 20:4-6
"I saw thrones on which were seated those who had been given authority to judge. And I saw the souls of those who had been beheaded because of their testimony for Yahusha and because of the word of Yahuah. They had not worshiped the beast or **his image** and had not received his mark on their foreheads or their hands.

Paul warns us **not to elevate this false "image of a man" in our hearts above Yahuah** as God. Paul warns us not to teach "unrighteousness as truth" or "that the Law is abolished is true". Those believing in The Pagan Trinity not having their minds Sealed by Yahuah and who have replaced Yahuah with this false image of Yahusha known as "Jesus" in their hearts will be given over to a *depraved mind.* That depraved mind is *The Spirit of Error* - Yahuah <u>will not permit</u> them to have any spiritual understanding whatsoever and they will be filled with unrighteousness (abolish His Law in their hearts):

Romans 1

[18] For the wrath of Yahuah is revealed from heaven against all ungodliness and unrighteousness (*Transgression of Desolation i.e. abolishing His Law*) of men **who suppress the truth in unrighteousness** (*teach unrighteousness or the Law was abolished as truth*), [19] because that which is known about Yahuah is evident within them (*The Law is written on our hearts*); for Yahuah made it evident to them… [21] For even though they knew Yahuah, they did not honor Him as God or give thanks, but they became futile in their speculations (*that* χ⛓ς *Jesus abolished The Law and that* χ⛓ς *is God*), and their foolish heart was darkened (*because The Torah is a light unto our path: Psalm 119:105*). [22] Professing to be wise, they became fools, [23] and exchanged the glory of the incorruptible Yahuah (*who cannot die*) for ***an image in the form of corruptible man*** (*χ⛓ς Jesus died their "god" was a corruptible man*)… [28] And just as they did not see fit to acknowledge Yahuah any longer (*pray to* χ⛓ς *Jesus, invite* χ⛓ς *Jesus to sit on the throne of Yahuah in their heart as God, have the mark of The Pagan Trinity on their mind*), Yahuah gave them over to a depraved mind, to do those things which are not proper (*iniquity or transgress The Law*), [29] being filled with all unrighteousness (*totally abolishing The Law*)

This is why the modern Christian scholars, preachers and teachers do not properly understand the prophecies in Daniel and teach the lie that a physical Antichrist is going to come and rebuild a physical Temple and stop a working altar and commit ***The Abomination of Desolation***. They themselves are guilty of committing ***The Abomination of Desolation*** already in their hearts and therefore have been given over to a depraved mind. This is also why our modern English translations are so poorly translated in error. Many of these errors totally change the meaning of the text. They simply do not have the spiritual eyes to see and ears to hear and they cannot comprehend with their Spiritual mind. Professing to the world how "wise" they are with all their human credentials they have no Wisdom and are but fools in the eyes of Spiritual Truth.

The Apostle Paul addresses this very fact again as we see this false image of The Messiah is setup in *The Temple of Yahuah* and exalted above Yahuah and proclaimed to be God incarnate. Keeping in context *The Yahushaic Covenant* and that Paul properly teaches that the altar is the heart of man and The Temple is the body of man we read:

2 Thessalonians 2
[3] Don't let anyone deceive you in any way, for that day will not come until the rebellion (*against The Law or Transgression of Desolation*) occurs

Isaiah 24 – the Transgression of Desolation, humanities rebellion

24 See, Yahuah is going to lay waste the earth and devastate it; he will ruin its face and scatter its inhabitants— [3] The earth will be completely laid waste and totally plundered. Yahuah has spoken this word… [5] **The earth is defiled by its people** (*they have committed The Transgression of Desolation*); **they have disobeyed the laws of Yahuah, violated the Festivals of Yahuah and broken the everlasting covenant of The Sabbath.** [6] Therefore a curse consumes the earth; its people must bear their guilt. Therefore earth's inhabitants are burned up, and very few are left.

and the <u>man of lawlessness</u> (*or image of a man in whom The Law is abolished*) is revealed (*to be The False messiah* ꭓＦＳ), the man doomed to destruction. [4] **He** ꭓＦＳ **will oppose and will exalt himself** (*in the hearts/minds of man*) **over everything that is called God or is worshiped,**

so that he sets himself up in Yahuah's temple (*the body of man*), **proclaiming himself to be God** (*incarnate*).

[5] Don't you remember that when I was with you I used to tell you these things? [6] And now you know what is holding him back so that he may be revealed at the proper time (*the time of the end*). [7] For the <u>secret</u> power of lawlessness (***Transgression of Desolation*** *i.e. abolishing The Law of Yahuah*) is already at work; but the one who now holds it back will continue to do so <u>till he is taken out of the way</u> (*Archangel Michael* ***Daniel 12:1*** *is taken away from providing our defense because of* ***The Transgression of Desolation*** *which is the transgression of The Law of Yahuah* ***Daniel 810-14***). [8] And then (*at the end when Michael is removed and* ***Yahuah*** *destroys the Earth because of* ***The Transgression of Desolation***) the lawless one (*the one* ꭓꙅꙅ *in whom The Law was abolished*) will be revealed (*as The False messiah by the word of Yahusha's testimony*), whom the Messiah Yahusha will overthrow with the breath of his mouth (*his testimony that he came in the name of* ***Yahuah*** *and his name is Yahusha, he is King of the Sabbath, he fulfilled The Law not abolished it*) and (*Yahusha will*) destroy (*the one* ꭓꙅꙅ *in whose image The Law was abolished*) by the splendor of his coming. [9] The coming of the lawless one (ꭓꙅꙅ) will be in accordance with how Satan works (*the spirit behind The False messiah is Dagon the dragon* ***Rev. 13***). He will use all sorts of displays of power through signs and wonders (*Christians are convinced by "miracles" not the words of The Prophets*) that serve the lie (*to convince them there is power in* ꭓꙅꙅ *Jesus Name*), [10] and all the ways that wickedness (*breaking The Law of* ***Yahuah***) deceives those who are perishing. They perish <u>because they refused to love the truth</u> (*of The Torah*) and so be saved (*eternal life is the promise of obedience to The Law*). [11] For this reason (*because they committed The Transgression of Desolation i.e. abolished His Law*) Yahuah sends them a powerful

delusion (*Christianity*) so that (*not having **The Seal of Yahuah** over their mind but the Mark of the Beast which is X on the forehead and belief in The Trinity*) they will believe the lie (*that* ⲭⲋⲋ *Jesus is God incarnate and he abolished The Law*) [12] and so that all will be condemned (*by the death decrees in The Law not being covered by the blood of The Passover Lamb because they put their faith in Easter* ⲭⲋⲋ *Jesus*) who have not believed the truth (*Yahusha did not abolish The Law and faith in Passover covers our sin*) but have delighted in wickedness (*transgression of His Law*).

Paul stresses this very same truth again in Romans:

Romans 1
21 Because that, when they knew Yahuah, they glorified Yahuah not as God, neither were thankful; but became vain in their imaginations, and their foolish heart was darkened (*to believe a lie*). 22 Professing themselves to be wise, <u>they became fools</u>, 23 And (*the foolish people who do not have **The Seal of Yahuah** but believe the Babylonian Trinity*) changed the glory of the incorruptible Yahuah into ***<u>an image</u>*** made like to ***corruptible man*** *(*ⲭⲋⲋ *<u>Jesus is an 'image' of a corruptible man, Yahusha, who died on the stake</u>*).

Peter called Rome Babylon

Keep in mind, Yahusha's disciples fully understood that the religion of Rome was a revived version of ***The Mystery Religion of Babylon***. Peter even called Rome... *Babylon*:

1 Peter 5
The church that is at Babylon (*speaking of the church in Rome*), elected together with you, saluteth you; and so doth Marcus my son

As I explained earlier in this book, the pagan Babylonian Priesthood was officially and formally transferred to Rome after Babylon fell. That priesthood was transferred over to the Roman Emperors who became Pontifus Maximus or "High Priest of Ba'al" a title now held by the office of Pope… Pontif.

Yahusha calls us out of Christianity

In Revelation one of the first things we see is Yahusha specifically calling humanity OUT of *The Mystery Religion of Babylon* which Peter identified as the religion of Rome. I demonstrated in this book series (*Mystery Babylon - the Religion of the Beast* and *Christianity – the Great Deception*) that the religion at the end time that leads the world astray is Christianity as it is a carbon copy of The Mystery Religion of Babylon.

> **Revelation 18**
> 18 And after these things I saw another angel come down from heaven, having great power; and the earth was lightened with his glory. [2] And he cried mightily with a strong voice, saying, **Babylon the great is fallen**, is fallen, and is become the habitation of devils, and the hold of every foul spirit, and a cage of every unclean and hateful bird. [3] For all nations have drunk of the wine of the wrath of her fornication, and the kings of the earth have committed fornication with her, and the merchants of the earth are waxed rich through the abundance of her delicacies. [4] And I heard another voice from heaven, saying, **Come out of her** (*Mystery Religion of Babylon i.e. Christianity*)**, my people, that ye be not partakers of her sins**, and that ye receive not of her plagues. [5] **For her sins** *(committing The Transgression and Abomination of Desolation)* **have reached unto heaven, and God hath remembered her iniquities** *('iniquities' is by definition transgressing His Law)*.

The reason why those who commit **The Transgression of Desolation** believing "Jesus Χ§Ϛ abolished The Law" is because that is what <u>by definition</u> The False messiah does. The False messiah is an "image" of Yahusha whose name and message is a lie, he is <u>The Lawless One</u> or the one in whose image The Law was abolished. This false image Χ§Ϛ is the abominable sacrifice of a pig on Easter on **The altar of Yahuah** (which is your heart) <u>stopping the sacrifice</u> of The Passover Lamb which destroys **The Temple of Yahuah** (which is your body).

The False messiah Χ§Ϛ is called "*the lawless one*" as it is he who ABOLISHES THE LAW and changes the ordained Feasts of Yahuah to pagan holidays:

> ### Daniel 7
> [25] He Χ§Ϛ (*the False messiah*) will speak out (*in our hearts because we "invited* Χ§Ϛ *into our hearts which are Altars to Yahuah*) against the Most High (*proclaiming himself God incarnate which is The Spirit of the False messiah*) and wear down the saints of the Highest One (*Christianity is the bloodiest 'religion' in history killing the Sabbath keeping sons for millinia*), and he will intend to make alterations in (*Yahuah's ordained*) times (*festivals*) and in The Law (*of Yahuah*).

We are living in the 6,000[th] year since Adam which means we are at the end of 6 days of The Sabbath Covenant and on the verge of the 7th prophetic day (Millennial Reign). In the history of humanity there is only one "image of <u>a man who died</u>" whose mark, monogram, Christogram, and pictogram is **XES** (what John saw in Revelation 13 Χ§Ϛ) that we have literally elevated as God incarnate in His Temple (our body, we invite Jesus into our hearts) and in whose name Χ§Ϛ the Feasts/Ordained Times of Yahuah were changed to pagan holidays. There will not be another "physical" man who pops up all of the sudden in some imaginary 7-year period, starts a world-wide religion that causes all humanity to worship him and then abolish The Law and change the Holy Days of Yahuah… they have already been abolished and changed! Only one man in history in whose image "causes the sacrifices made by the Eternal High Priest Yahusha to stop" changing Passover to Easter.

Daniel 9:27

He Χ§ς (*the false messiah*) will put an end to sacrifice and offering (*of The Passover Lamb, Yahusha only offers himself up as a "Lamb that has been slaughtered" for those who keep Passover in light of his sacrifice*). And at the temple (*your body*) he will set up an abomination (*the Ishtar Pig i.e. Easter. You spiritually slaughter a pig on the altar of your heart every Easter!*) that causes (*the*) desolation (*of your body, you will die dead in your sin because you did not put your faith in Passover and there is no sacrifice left for your sin*)

Only one man in whose image The Law was abolished therefore is **The Lawless One**…. Only one man whose monogram is **XS**. Only one man whose mark is the **X** on the forehead. Only one whose whose name is revealed by name Χ§ς **XES=IHS=JES**, only ONE whose name in English means Abominable Beast (**sus/pig**) of the Earth (**Je**) by definition of its Latin prefix and suffix! That is Hesus Horus Krishna a.k.a Jesus H. Christ the "god" created by Constantine at the Council of Nicea; the god of the False Religion of Christianity that is created in the "image" of all pagan god-men and pagan Trinities whose origin is BABYLON!

Physical to spiritual parallel of The Abomination of Desolation

Keeping this one very important fact in mind:

> ### Isaiah 48
> [3] I foretold the former things long ago, my mouth announced them (*to my prophets*) and I made them known (*through physical shadows*); then suddenly I acted, and they came to pass (*Spiritually*).

The "key" to understanding *The Word of Yahuah* is through *physical to spiritual parallel*s. We have established in scripture that in *The Yahushaic Covenant* (the covenant we are in) at the time of the end when the true Abomination of Desolation occurs; transposition has taken place:

- *The Temple of Yahuah* is the human body *1 Corinthians 6:19*
- *The altar of Yahuah* is the hearts/minds of man *Ex. 22:25 and 1 Peter 2:5*
- The Sacrifices to Yahuah are expressing faith through action *Psalm 40:6-8*
- The False messiah is a false image of Yahusha *Rev. 13:11-15*
- The Transgression of Desolation is the abolishment of The Law *Isaiah 24*
- The Abomination of Desolation is the sacrifice (expression of faith *Psalms 141:2*) in the most abominable animal a pig each Easter in honor of Tammuz the second member of the Babylonian Trinity in whose image ΧЅЅ was created on *The altar of Yahuah* our hearts that destroys *The Temple of Yahuah* our body

Let's examine what Yahusha said in the Gospels about the prophecy spoken by Daniel:

Matthew 24:15-16
"So when you see the abomination of desolation spoken of by the prophet Daniel, standing in the holy place (*let the reader understand*)

Notice Yahusha qualifies this statement with "*let the reader understand*". Yahusha used such phrases to indicate *physical to spiritual parallel*s.

Luke 8:8
"When he said this (*finished the parable of The Sower*), he called out, "***Whoever has ears to hear, let them hear***.""

Luke 8:10
10 He said, "The knowledge of the secrets of ***The Kingdom of Yahuah*** has been given to you, but to others I speak in parables, so that, 'though seeing, they may not see; though hearing, they may not understand.'

Yahusha is telling us that to understand the prophecy in Daniel you must have spiritual eyes to see and understand with your mind. He is telling us that the prophecy in Daniel conforms to Yahuah's standards of first foretelling the event, then giving us a physical shadow to study, then fulfills the event in The Spirit.

Isaiah 48
³ I foretold the former things long ago, my mouth announced them (*to my prophets*) and I made them known (*through physical shadows*); then suddenly I acted, and they came to pass (*Spiritually*).

We must employ the key of *physical to spiritual parallel*s to *"see the abomination of desolation spoken of by the prophet Daniel and only then can the reader understand"* with their Spiritual Mind.

Matthew 24:15-16
"So when you see the abomination of desolation spoken of by the prophet Daniel, standing in the holy place (**let the reader understand**)

As I stated earlier, Yahuah gave Daniel a vision of *The Abomination of Desolation* that was fulfilled by Antiochus IV as the physical shadow and later by ⲭⲉⲥ Jesus Christ in the realm of The Spirit. Yahusha is telling us to study Daniel from with a spiritual mind if we are ever to understand the spiritual parallel.

Let us now employ the key to understanding *The Kingdom of Yahuah* and define the true *Spiritual Abomination of Desolation* that occurs "at the time of the end" by the physical shadow picture of Antiochus IV.

The Physical Shadow

> Antiochus IV worshipped Mitha the sungod keeping the Babylonian religion of sun worship. The rituals of Babylonian sun worship are the rebirth of the sun on December 25th. The sacrifice is the pig of Ishtar celebrated on Easter by eating a ham. Antiochus believed himself to be the incarnation of God. Antiochus abolished *The Law of Yahuah*, outlawed keeping The Sabbath and by decree ordered the keeping of Sunday. Antiochus outlawed the Festivals of Yahuah and ordered the keeping of the pagan rituals of sun worship. Antiochus sacrificed the most abominable beast, a pig, on *the altar of Yahuah* to Zeus (the Roman version of Mithra). Antiochus ordered all in his realm to worship Zeus and killed all those true sons of Yahuah who would not bow down to the religion of sun worship.

When you look at the above physical shadow picture of *The Abomination of Desolation* fulfilled in Antiochus IV it would appear that the Roman Emperor Constantine used that as his

454

playbook in creating the false religion of Christianity. Constantine literally patterned the new composite deity of his new religion χξς Hesus Horus Krishna after Antiochus IV and Mithra. Constantine too converted to Mithra and it is simply a legend that he ever converted to Yahuah in *The Yahushaic Covenant*. Constantine remained until his death "committed to the invincible sun". I cover all of this in my book *Christianity – The Great Deception*.

Let us now look at the physical shadow of Antiochus IV and *understand* the spiritual parallel, I took the exact same physical parallel of Antiochus IV description above and I inserted the name "Jesus" for "Antiochus IV" below:

The Spiritual Parallel to Antiochus IV

> Jesus is a later incarnation of Mithra the sungod keeping the Babylonian religion of sun worship. Jesus represents the rituals of Babylonian sun worship which are the rebirth of the sun on December 25th; the sacrifice is the pig of Ishtar celebrated on Easter by eating a ham, etc. Jesus is said to be the incarnation of God. Jesus (by Papal Decree) abolished *The Law of Yahuah*, outlawed keeping The Sabbath, ordered the keeping of Sunday, outlawed the Festivals of Yahuah, and ordered the keeping of the pagan rituals of sun worship. Jesus is the sacrifice of the most abominable beast, a pig, on *the altar of Yahuah* to Zeus (the Roman version of Mithra). Jesus (through The Pope) ordered all in his realm (the Earth) to worship Zeus (Jesus means Hail Zeus in Latin) and killed all those true sons of Yahuah who would not bow down to the religion of sun worship (the inquisition, crusades, and countless wars in the name of Jesus).

χξς Hesus Horus Krishna is the composite deity created in the image of the Babylonian Tammuz the second member of the

Babylonian Trinity of Ishtar/Tammuz/Ba'al. $\chi\xi\varsigma$ Jesus H. Christ is a composite deity actually named after the later versions of Tammuz in other cultures to bring together all the religious factions of Rome under Constantine:

- **Mithra** is the Assyrian or Middle Eastern version of Tammuz and the second member of the trinity "ahuras"
- **Hesus** is the Celtic Druid version of the Babylonian Tammuz who is the second member of the Celtic Trinity.
- **Horus** is the Egyptian version of the Babylonian Tammuz and the second member of the Egyptian Trinity of Isis/Horus/Seb.
- **Krishna** is the Eastern Hindu version of the Babylonian Tammuz and the second member of the Hindu Trinity of Brahma/Krishna/Shiva

   NOTE: I cover all of this in detail in my book ***Christianity – The Great Deception***.

All of the above mentioned were pagan Christos or Christs and were all said to be demi-gods being the incarnation of the sun god. They were all worshipped on Sunday. They were all born on December 25th. Their sacrifice was on Easter it was a pig. Their followers dating back hundreds of years before Yahusha came were called **CHRISTIANS** notably those who followed Christos Mithras in Rome and later those who followed Christos Jesus or $\chi\xi\varsigma$ **XESus**.

The new "Christ" called $\chi\xi\varsigma$ Hesus Horus Krishna (which over time became known as Jesus H. Christ known by Greek Christogram $\chi\xi\varsigma$ and the associated pictogram **XES**) was said to be the real Messiah and through syncretism the lives of life of Yahusha was merged with the image of Jesus H. Christ. Yet everything "Jesus" stands for is polar opposite of the true Messiah Yahusha found in The Bible. The False messiah or false image of the true Messiah was born.

If perfect keeping with the physical shadow of Antiochus IV, this new Roman χξϛ False messiah is a spiritual carbon copy or fulfillment of the physical shadow. In the case of The Abomination of Desolation…

Isaiah 48 NOTE: below I insert the specific case of the Abomination of Desolation into this scripture to illustrate my point:

[3] I foretold *The Abomination of Desolation* long ago, my mouth announced it *to my prophet Daniel* and I made it known *through a physical shadow in Antiochus IV*. Then suddenly I acted, and *The Abomination of Desolation* came to pass *spiritually in* χξϛ *Jesus H. Christ as my mouth had announced to my prophet John in Rev. 13*.

The Abominable Sacrifice
The Sacrifice of a Pig to Tammuz (Easter)

Semaramis (The Queen of Babylon and mother of Tammuz) became known as the fertility goddess **Ishtar** (Easter in English) and called *The Queen of Heaven*. She took on many names in different cultures including Isis, Diana, Astarte, Ishtar, Aphrodite, Venus, and Easter. She was even identified with The Virgin Mary as Mary was falsely deified and took on the titles "Mother of God" and "Queen of Heaven". I cover all this in my book **Mystery Babylon: Religion of the Beast**.

Ishtar's son Tammuz took on many names as well such as Horus, Apollo, Sol, Krishna, Hercules, Mithra, **and finally Jesus**. The name Jesus H. Christ, in fact, originated by Constantine as Hesus Horus Krishna. "Hesus Horus Krishna" evolved into Jesus H. Christ over the years. All names of Tammuz put together by Constantine at the Council of Nicea into one demi-god. They are all pagan human *gods incarnate*, sons of the sungod and the second member of the Trinity worshipped on Sunday the day of the

Babylonian sungod… Ba'al which means **The LORD**. This is the
true god worshipped in The Christian Church as they literally
worship Tammuz and Ba'al on the day of the sungod. The names
have changed in our culture to Jesus and ***The LORD***. Calling
Yahuah by the pagan title of Ba'al which is "the LORD" is an
abomination and violation of the 2nd Commandment.

> ### Jeremiah 23
> [25] "I have heard what the prophets say who prophesy lies in
> my name. They say, 'I had a dream! I had a dream!' [26] How
> long will this continue in the hearts of these lying prophets,
> who prophesy the delusions of their own minds? [27] They
> think the dreams they tell one another will make my people
> forget my name, just as their ancestors forgot my name
> **through Baal worship**.

I cover all of this in GREAT detail in my books ***Mystery Babylon:
The Religion of the Beast*** and ***Christianity and The Great
Deception***.

In this section I want to demonstrate just how abominable the
sacrifice of the Easter pig "Jesus" really is. Semaramis instituted a
holy day in her Babylonian religion in honor of the supposed
"death/resurrection" of her son Tammuz.

Below is a picture of Semaramis and Tammuz, the
"Madonna/Child" then "Mary/Jesus"…

Notice the "child" in these images is not a baby but a small fully developed man. While protesting Catholics (called Protestants) deny worship of this pagan deity… they in deed contradict that denial in action as they openly do just that on Sunday, Christmas and Easter.

In the images above we see to the left the idol of Ishtar/Tammuz this idol was renamed Jesus/Mary by The Catholic Church. We see the painting of Jesus/Mary and they are all the exact same Babylonian deities. We need to begin admitting the obvious truth; these idols were not renamed because the pagans now believed in Yahusha the Messiah. No, Tammuz and Ishtar/Semaramis simply had their names changed in the false religion of Christianity which is a carbon copy of The Mystery Religion of Babylon!

An idol till remains in the Vatican of "Tammuz the great hunter" to this day… their (Christianity's) REAL messiah they renamed Jesus or Hesus or Iesous or I.H.S. or $\chi\xi\varsigma$ which means… Hail Zeus or Son of Zeus. The picture below is Tammuz the Great Hunter idol of Tammuz still standing in The Vatican today. How much more proof do we need? The second beast (Roman Christopaganism) has caused us unknowingly to worship the first beast $\chi\xi\varsigma$ Hesus Horus Krishna a.k.a Jesus H. Christ! We have literally elevated a false image of the true Messiah who died in our hearts above Yahuah who cannot die. We have been given over to The Spirit of Error as a result and fallen for The Spirit of the False messiah. We are all guilty of committing both The Transgression and Abomination of Desolation! We are offering our children on the altar of the Babylonian Moloch by teaching our children these abomination because after all "they are for the children".

We still "hunt Ishtar eggs" in honor of Tammuz the Great Hunter on Ishtar's day and eat ham in his honor we just call it Easter (the English transliterated name of Ishtar but every ritual remains the same as in ancient Babylon.

No longer do we keep Passover and eat Lamb as commanded by The Messiah (strengthening *The Law of Yahuah*) as he kept Passover on the 14th of Abib (eve of Passover) just before he gave his body as The Passover Lamb:

> ### Luke 22:19
> 19 And when he had taken some bread and given thanks (*on the eve of Passover*), He broke it and gave it to them, saying, "This (*Passover Dinner*) is My body (*Passover Lamb*) which is given (sacrificed) for you; do this (*keep Passover*) in remembrance of Me."

No longer do we "keep the memory of Yahusha's sacrifice alive on Passover each year". Instead we keep Easter which is the very definition of "doing it in an unworthy manner"!

> ### 1 Corinthians 1
> [23] For I received from Messiah Yahusha that which I also delivered to you: that the Messiah Yahusha on the *same* night in which He was betrayed took bread (*eve of Passover*); [24] and when He had given thanks, He broke *it*

and said, "Take, eat; this is My body which is broken (*on Passover the following day*) for you; do this (*keep Passover*) in remembrance of Me." [25] In the same manner *He* also *took* the cup after supper, saying, "This cup is the new covenant in My blood. This do (*keep Passover*), as often as you drink *it,* in remembrance of Me."

[26] For as often as you eat this bread and drink this cup (*every Passover and Sabbath*), you proclaim the Messiah's death (*as the Passover Lamb of God*) **till He comes**. *(it was never abolished it was changed in fulfillment of prophecy in the image of* $\chi\xi\varsigma$ *by the beast*)

[27] Therefore whoever eats this bread or drinks *this* cup of the Messiah in an unworthy manner (*on Ishtar/Easter Day*) **will be guilty of the body and blood of the Messiah**. [28] But let a man examine himself (*to see if he has the blood of the lamb on the Altar of Yahuah or the blood of the Ishtar pig on the altar of the Earthly (Je) Pig (sus)*), and so let him eat of the bread and drink of the cup (*on Passover NOT Easter*). [29] For he who eats and drinks in an unworthy manner eats and drinks judgment to himself (*for committing The Abomination of Desolation which sacrificing a PIG on the Altar of Yahuah which is your heart that destroys His Temple which is your body*), not discerning (*that the*) Messiah's body (*is the spotless Passover Lamb of Yahuah!*)

No… we have been lied to! We now keep Ishtar and eat HAM the most abominable "beast" in The Torah. $\chi\xi\varsigma$ Jesus Christ of the Christian Church is in reality the second member of the Babylonian Trinity Tammuz and we are celebrating his death on Easter not the true Messiah's. Tammuz/Jesus is the reincarnated Nimrod son of Ba'al (The LORD) to this day. Just like the Bible prophesied. This is denied by Christianity as **they have been given over by Yahuah to believe a lie**. They have literally fallen for Nimrod/Semaramis/Tammuz under another name as they

461

became Isis/Horus/Seb or **I.H.S** one of the many monograms for Hesus Horus Krishna $X\xi\varsigma$ all names for Tammuz. In Latin it remains I.H.S. in the middle of Sol Invictus, the same "invincible Sun" worshipped from Nimrod to Constantine!

This symbol of the sun with the pagan Babylonian Trinity of Isis Horus and Seb (I.H.S) with the elevated Cross of Tammuz is carried around by the High Priest of Christianity today with the cross of Tammuz blazoned on top, yes the PONTIF or "High Priest of Ba'al".

Summary - *the Spiritual Truth – the real Abomination of Desolation*

Antiochus IV, the so-called "incarnation of God/Zeus", entered *The Temple of Yahuah* on Christmas Day and sacrificed a pig to Zeus on *The altar of Yahuah*. This physical shadow was transposed into the spiritual parallel in the image χξϛ Jesus Christ as prophesied by John in Revelation 13. We were warned not to elevate the image of a man above Yahuah by the Apostle Paul. We were warned *The Spirit of the False messiah* would be the belief in the incarnation. We were warned *The Spirit of Error* would be the abolishment of The Law. We were warned the Earth would worship this beast and commit The Transgression of Desolation which would cause The Great Tribulation. We were warned to keep and put our faith in Passover and pour out the blood of The Passover Lamb on the Altar of Yahuah not invite "Jesus" into our hearts and slaughter the Ishtar Pig on the altar of χξϛ . **We have committed The Abomination of Desolation!**

We are commanded by Yahuah and Yahusha to keep Passover to express our faith in the sacrifice of The Lamb. In keeping Passover we express our faith (spiritual sacrifice to Yahuah) in Yahusha as the proper sacrifice for our sin. In doing so (keeping Passover in faith that Yahusha was that proper sacrifice) the blood of the Lamb is poured over the altar of our heart spiritually and the decrees in The Law that demand our death **are covered**. Being found in perfect obedience to The Law (through Grace which is only offered in light of our attempt to keep His Law and putting our faith in Passover) we receive the gift promised in The Law for obedience which is eternal life.

The true Abomination of Desolation that Yahusha spoke of that we must have spiritual eyes to see and understand with our spiritual mind is…

463

The Abomination of Desolation is inviting χ§ς JesUS (who comes in the name of Ze**us**, Hes**us**, Hor**us**, Krisha) into our hearts (*The Temple of Yahuah*). Declaring our belief in The Trinity; causing Yahuah to darken our foolish hearts to believe the lies of Christianity. We spiritually pour the blood of the pig of Ishtar over The altar of our hearts by keeping Easter over Passover. This causes Yahusha **to cease** offering himself up as The Passover Lamb on our behalf to cover our transgression of The Law. Not having the proper sacrifice for sin (which is the blood of The Passover Lamb poured out over *the altar of Yahuah* our hearts); we are found guilty of our transgression against His Law. The death decrees in The Law therefore demand our death for our transgression as they are not covered by the blood of the Earthly Pig Jesus. *The Temple of Yahuah* (our body) is therefore desolated or destroyed and we are not "Passed Over" from the second death. We die in the second death never to live again.

In short…

> *The Abomination of Desolation* is elevating Jesus as God in our mind and putting our faith in the Easter pig. By putting our faith in Easter we spiritually slaughter a pig on the altar of our hearts which desolates our Temple bodies.

The result…

> Christianity robs us of the Sign required, robs us of The Seal required, and robs us of our Deliverance through the blood of The Passover Lamb. Christianity leaves us without the 3 witness in *The Lambs Book of Life* and not having those witnesses our names are blotted out and we are then robbed of our eternal life.

Christianity is the Great Deception foretold in The Bible that has deceived the Earth. Those who have ears let them hear, those who have eyes let them see and understand so that they may be saved.

Acts 28:27

27 For the heart of this people is waxed gross, and their ears are dull of hearing, and their eyes have they closed; lest they should see with their eyes, and hear with their ears, and understand with their heart, and should be converted, and I should heal them.

It is never too late as long as you live this life. Yahuah will heal those who fallen for this lie if they turn from it. You must declare His Shema, keep His Sabbath, keep His Laws and Festivals, and put your faith in Yahusha the Passover Lamb of Yahuah by keeping Passover before it is too late. Yahuah/Yahusha promise that if we "endure until the end" or rather it is not over until you die, and overcome

Revelation 2:11

'He who has an (*Spiritual*) ear, let him hear what the Spirit of Yahuah (*Mystery Language Alert!*) says to the churches He who overcomes (*this false image of the true Messiah*) will not be hurt by the second death.'

Revelation 12:11

"And they overcame him χ ξ ς **because of the blood of the Lamb** (*they did not slaughter the Easter Pig of Ishtar on the Altar of Yahuah*) and because of the word of their testimony (*the put their faith in Passover not Easter*), and they did not love their life (*were willing to face persecution from the Beast i.e. Christianity and their friends*

and family for denying ⲬⳄⳄ *) even when faced*
with death (*Mystery Language Alert!..*
excommunication… you will be dead to them if you
give your life to Yahuah not 'The LORD' i.e. Ba'al
and rededicate the Altar of your heart back to
Yahuah with the blood of the Lamb and dethrone
Jesus and cleanse the Altar from the blood of a
pig. Stop sacrificing your children to Moloch!
You will face more persecution that you ever
imagined when you no longer keep Sungod Day,
no longer bow down to a pagan Idol/Christmas
Tree and accept gifts from Nimrod, no longer hunt
Ishtar Eggs in honor of Tammuz).

It really isn't that hard. Just replace the pagan rituals with the true
Festivals of Yahuah; the ones actually ***IN*** The Bible. Keep
Sabbath not Sunday. Celebrate Passover not Easter. Call on the
name of Yahusha not Jesus. And proclaim with a loud voice …
Hear O Israel… Yahuah is the one and only God and there is no
other beside Him which is the greatest commandment in the entire
Bible! Declare as Yahusha did that Yahuah is the ONE and ONLY
TRUE GOD! And enter into covenant with Yahuah through the
blood of the true Messiah Yahusha, and live!

> **John 17:3**
> Now this is eternal life: that they know you (*Yahuah*), **the**
> **only true God**, and (*enter into covenant with Him through*)
> Yahusha the Messiah, whom you have sent (*as a substitute*
> *for our sin ON PASSOVER*).

Stop calling on a pagan name and call on the one name under
heaven that expresses the truth that Yahuah is our savior! You are
already doing the same amount of things! Just trade in the "way of
the pagan gentiles" and stand up and be counted as one of ***The***
Lost Sheep of the House of Israel. As you do, Yahuah will

personally write as a witness on your behalf 3 entries in *The Lambs Book of Life* and you will become Signed, Sealed, and Delivered into *The Kingdom of Yahuah*.

Just think about that... long and hard.

Chapter 22

The Mark of the Beast

The Cross of Tammuz

Revelation 13

16 It (*the beast Mystery Babylon/Christianity*) also forced all people, great and small, rich and poor, free and slave, to receive a mark ($\mathcal{X}$) on their right hands or on their foreheads, [17] so that they could not buy or sell unless they had the mark ($\mathcal{X}$),

Tammuz, the second member of the pagan Babylonian Trinity, the incarnation of God in the flesh, is the false messiah of the religion created by Semaramis (the Whore mentioned in Revelation). Yahuah has commanded us (His people) to "come out of her" and cease prostituting out the worship of the ONE true God to others.

The symbol of "the son of The LORD god Baal" in the pagan religion of Babylon was a cross. It is called *The Cross of Tammuz*.

This cross was worn on the head dresses of the Babylonians and breastplates of priests and warriors alike in honor of Tammuz. The cross was a representation of "T" in Tammuz and his symbol "x".

The cross is a tradition of the Church which our fathers have inherited was the adoption of the words "cross" and "crucify". These words are nowhere to be found in the Greek versions of the New Testament.

These words are mistranslations, a "later rendering", of the Greek words stauros and stauroo.

Vine's Expository Dictionary of New Testament Words says,

> "STAUROS denotes, primarily, an upright pole or stake ... Both the noun and the verb stauroo, to fasten to a stake or pole, *__are originally to be distinguished from__* the ecclesiastical form of a two-beamed cross. The shape of the latter had its origin in ancient Chaldea (Babylon), and was used as the symbol of the god Tammuz (being in the shape of the mystic Tau, *__the initial of his name__*) ... By the middle of the 3rd century A.D. at the Council of Nicea the churches had either departed from, or had travestied, certain doctrines of The Faith found in The Bible.

In order to increase the prestige of the apostate ecclesiastical system (known as Christianity) pagans were received into the churches **apart from regeneration by faith**, and were permitted largely to retain their pagan signs and symbols. Hence the Tau or T, in its most frequent form, with the cross piece lowered, was adopted and to this day remains the "symbol" of Jesus (Tammuz) or the X.

http://en.wikipedia.org/wiki/Christogram

> The most commonly encountered Christogram in English-speaking countries in modern times is the **X** (or more accurately, Greek letter chi) in the abbreviation **X**mas (for **"Christ**mas"), which represents the first letter of the word Christ Χ ζ ς .

We see that the "cross" is not in the Bible at all, but rather predates the New Testament in all pagan religions.

Dr. Bullinger, in the Companion Bible, appx. 162, states,

"crosses were used as symbols of the Babylonian Sun-god (Tammuz)... Constantine was a Sun-god worshipper ... The evidence is complete, that Yahusha was put to death upon an upright stake, not on two pieces of timber"

Rev. Alexander Hislop, The Two Babylons, pp. 197-205,

frankly calls the cross "this Pagan symbol ... the Tau, the sign of the cross, the indisputable sign of Tammuz, the false messiah ... the mystic Tau of the Cladeans (Babylonians) and Egyptians - the true original form of the letter T the initial of the name of Tammuz ... the Babylonian cross was ***the recognized emblem of Tammuz.***"

In the Encyclopaedia Britannica, 11th edition, vol. 14, p. 273,

we read, "In the Egyption churches the cross was a pagan symbol of life borrowed by the pagan-Christians and interpreted in the pagan manner." Jacob Grimm, in his Deutsche Mythologie, says that the Teutonic (Germanic) tribes had their idol Thor, symbolized by a hammer, while the Roman Pagans had their crux (cross). It was thus somewhat easier for the Teutons to accept the Roman Cross.

Greek dictionaries, lexicons and other study books also declare the primary meaning of stauros to be an upright pale, pole or stake. The secondary meaning of "cross" is admitted by them to be a "later" rendering to accommodate Rome. At least two of them do not even mention "cross", and only render the meaning as "pole or stake".

In spite of this strong evidence and proof that the word stauros should have been translated "stake", and the verb stauroo to have been translated "impale", almost all the common modern versions of the Scriptures persist with the Latin Vulgate's crux (cross), a fallacious "later" rendering of the Greek stauros. Why then was the "cross" (crux) brought into the Faith? And why are our modern English Bibles implicit in this lie?

Again, historical evidence points to Constantine as the one who had the major share in uniting Sun-worship and the Messianic Faith into a modern day version of ***The Mystery Religion of Babylon***. We will look in depth at the history and evolution of Christianity in my next book **Christianity:** *The Great Deception* and see exactly what happened.

Constantine's famous vision of "the cross superimposed on the sun", in the year 312, is usually cited. Writers, ignorant of the fact that the cross was not to be found in the New Testament Scriptures, put much emphasis on this vision as the onset of the so-called "conversion" of Constantine. But, unless Constantine had been misguided by the Gnostic Manichean half-Christians, who indeed used the cross in their hybrid religion, this vision of the cross superimposed on the sun could only be the same old cosmic religion, **the astrological religion of Babylon**. The fact remains: that which Constantine saw, is nowhere to be found in Scripture. But rather was a common symbol of his god... the Sungod. Constantine had just a few years prior converted to The Cult of Sol Invictus! Constantine worshipped Chistos Mithras and the followers of Mithra were called Christians. I prove this too in this book series. So looking up to his "sungod" seeing the cross of Tammuz should have been expected and understood for what it really was. There was a REASON why he was bowing down to the "sun" in the first place. Constantine did not convert to the Jewish High Priest and Messiah Yahusha. He converted the world to his existing religion that was known at that time as Christians.

We read in the book of Johannes Geffcken, The Last Days of Greco-Roman Paganism, p.319, "that even after 314 A.D. the coins of Constantine show an even-armed cross as a symbol for the Sungod." This is the symbol of all sun worshipping religion as I have stated. This equidistant cross is the cut-out of the center of The Zodiac. Many scholars have doubted the "conversion" of Constantine because of the wicked deeds that he did afterwards, and because of the fact that he only requested to be baptized on his death-bed many years later, in the year 337. His coins to the day he died read "Sol Invictus Committi" or "committed to the invincible sun". The Catholic Encyclopedia even admits Constantine's conversion was a legend and should be stricken from our literature entirely.

Catholic Encyclopedia, **Farley ed., vol. xiv, pp. 370-1**

The smooth generalisation, which so many historians are content to repeat, that Constantine "embraced the Christian religion" and subsequently granted "official toleration", is "contrary to historical fact" and should be erased from our literature forever (Catholic Encyclopedia, Pecci ed., vol. iii, p. 299, passim).

Simply put, Constantine was already a 'Christian' a follower of Christos Mithras and the Church acknowledges that the tale of his "conversion" and "baptism" are "entirely legendary". So, if the vision of the cross impressed him, and was used as a rallying symbol, it could not have been in honor of Yahusha, because Constantine continued paying homage to the Sun-deity and to one of the Sun-deity's symbols, **the cross** until the day he died. This continuation of Sun-worship by Constantine is demonstrated by the images of the Sun-deity on his coins that were issued by him up to the year 323. Secondly, the fact of his motivation to issue his Sunday-keeping edict in the year 321, which was not done in honour of Yahshúa, but was done because of the "venerable day of the Invicible Sun", as the edict read, is proof of this continued allegiance to Sol Invictus. I'll cover this in detail in this book series.

Where did the cross come from, then? J.C. Cooper, **An Illustrated Encyclopaedia of Traditional Symbols**, p. 45, aptly summarises it,

> "*Cross - A universal symbol from the most remote times; it is the cosmic symbol par excellence.*" Yes, the cross is THE mark or cosmic symbol of The Zodiac of all pagan sun worshipping religions "par excellence". Other authorities also call it a sun-symbol, a Babylonian sun-symbol, an astrological Babylonian-Assyrian and heathen sun-symbol, also in the form of an encircled cross referred to as a "solar wheel", and many other varieties of crosses. The cross with the sun in the background is taken directly from the center of The Zodiac:

This symbol of the Sun from the center part of The Zodiac is the exact symbol of Christianity:

Also, "the cross represents the Tree of Life", the age-old fertility symbol, combining the vertical male and horizontal female principles, especially in Egypt, either as an ordinary cross, or better known in the form of the crux ansata, the Egyptian ankh (sometimes called the Tau cross), which had been carried over into our modern-day symbol of the female, well known in biology.

As stated above, the indisputable sign of Tammuz, the mystic Tau of the Babylonians and Egyptians, was brought into the Church chiefly because of Constantine, and has since been adored with all the homage due only to the Most High.

The Protestants have for many years refrained from undue adoration of, or homage to the cross, especially in England at the

475

time of the Puritans in the 16th - 17th centuries. But lately this un-Scriptural symbol has been increasingly accepted in Protestantism and now widely believed to be a symbol of the Messiah.

We have previously discussed "the weeping for Tammuz", and the similarity between the Easter resurrection and the return or rising of Tammuz. Tammuz was the young incarnate Sun, the Sun-divinity incarnate. This same Sun-deity, known amongst the Babylonians as Tammuz, was identified with the Greek Adonis and with the Phoenician Adoni, and the Roman Mithras all of them Sun-deities, being slain in winter, then being "wept for", and their return being celebrated by a festivity in spring, while some had it in summer - according to the myths of pagan idolatry.

The evidence for its pagan origin is so convincing that The Catholic Encyclopedia admits that "*the sign of the cross, represented in its simplest form by a crossing of two lines at right angles, greatly antedates, in both East and the West, the introduction of Christianity. It goes back to a very remote period of human civilization.*" That remote "period" they fail to identify is Babylon!

The Catholic Encyclopedia then continues reverence to the Tau cross of the pagan Egyptians, "*In later times the Egyptian Christians (Copts), attracted by its form, and perhaps by its symbolism, adopted it as the emblem of the cross.*" That is because the Egyptian god Horus was another incarnation of Tammus. Further proof of its pagan origin is the recorded evidence of the Vestal Virgins of pagan Rome having the cross hanging on a necklace, and the Egyptians doing it too, as early as the 15th century B.C.E. The Buddhists, and numerous other sects of India, also used the sign of the cross as a mark on their followers' heads. The cross thus widely worshipped, or regarded as a 'sacred emblem', was the unequivocal symbol of Bacchus (Tammuz), the Babylonian Messiah, for he was represented with a head-band covered with crosses. It was also the symbol of Jupiter Foederis in Rome. Furthermore, we read of the cross on top of the temple of Serapis, the Sun-deity of Alexandria. This is Tammuz, whom the

476

Greeks called Bacchus, with the crosses on his head-band.

After Constantine had the "vision of the cross", he and his army promoted another variety of the cross, the Chi-Rho or Labarum. The identical symbols were found as inscriptions on a rock, dating from the year ca. 2500 B.C. the time of Babylon the Great, being interpreted as "a combination of two Sun-symbols", as the Ax or Hammer-symbol of the Sun- or Sky-deity, and the or as the ancient symbol of the Sun, both of these signs having a sensual or fertility meaning as well.

Another proof of its pagan origin is the identical found on a coin of Ptolemeus III from the year 247 - 222 B.C. A well-known encyclopedia describes the Labarum (Chi-Rho) as, "The labarum was also an emblem of the Chaldean (Babylonian) sky-god and in Christianity it was adopted..."Emperor Constantine adopted this Labarum as the imperial ensign and thereby succeeded in "uniting both divisions of his troops, pagans and Christians, in a common worship ... according to Suicer the word (labarum) came into use in the reign of Hadrian, and was probably adopted from one of the nations conquered by the Romans. "It must be remembered that Hadrian reigned in the years 76 - 138, that he was a pagan emperor, worshipped the Sun-deity Serapis when he visited Alexandria, and was vehemently anti-Judaistic, being responsible for the final near-destruction of Jerusalem in the year 130.

The "Cross of Tammuz" and The Mark of the Beast ⲭⳍⳋ

I go great detail on The Mark of the Beast in my book *The Christianity and the Great Deception*. But I will cover some of that book here because this mark of The Cross of Tammuz which represents the Babylonian Trinity was the mark of that religion on their foreheads! This mark of Tammuz was depicted on the forehead of Aphrodite (Semaramis the mother of Tammuz) above We see the mark of the Cross of Tammuz on the forehead of the goddess Ishtar dating back to Babylon! What is the "mark of the beast" of which we read in Rev 13:16-17, Rev 14:9-11, Rev 15:2, Rev 16:2, Rev 19:20 and Rev 20:4 - a mark on people's foreheads and on their right hands? Rev 14:11 reveals the mark to be "the mark of his (the beast's) name." Have we not read about the mystic Tau, the T, the initial of Tammuz's name, his mark? This same letter T (Tau) was written in Egyptian hieroglyphics and in the old Wemitic languages as, representing the CROSS.

This is the "mark" literally made on the foreheads of Christians in the Catholic Church. We are led as sheep to the slaughter into Babylonian worship of Tammuz in the image and name of "Jesus". Many protesting Catholic (Protestant) Churches across the world on "Ash" Wednesday!

Following in the Babylonian tradition each year as they "mark" their followers with this same mark on their forehead:

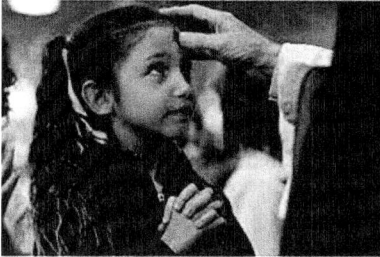

Let us rather use the true rendering of the Scriptural words stauros and stauro, namely "stake" and "impale" and eliminate the un-Scriptural "cross" and "crucify". The early Church Fathers attested to the use of the sign of the cross and that it is the Seal or Mark of Christianity; the mark that opposes The Shema.

Tertullian (d. ca. 250) described the commonness of the sign of the cross:

> "In all our travels and movements, in all our coming in and going out, in putting on our shoes, at the bath, at the table, in lighting our candles, in lying down, in sitting down, whatever employment occupies us, **we mark our foreheads with <u>the sign</u> of the cross**" (De corona, 30).

St. Cyril of Jerusalem (d. 386) in his Catechetical Lectures stated,

> "Let us then not be ashamed to confess the Crucified. **Be the cross <u>our seal</u>**, made with boldness by our fingers on our brow and in everything; over the bread we eat and the cups we drink, in our comings and in our goings out; before our sleep, when we lie down and when we awake; when we are traveling, and when we are at rest" (Catecheses, 13).

Gradually, the sign of the cross was incorporated in different acts of the Mass, such as the three-fold signing of the forehead, lips, and heart. Ash Wednesday is the first day of Lent which is the Babylonian ritual of "Weeping for Tammuz". Occurring 46 days before Easter which is the sacrifice of a pig in honor of the death of Tammuz. At Masses and services of worship on Ash Wednesday, ashes are imposed on the foreheads of the faithful.

They who don't have the mark (X) could not buy or sell

In Revelation 13:17 we see that those who do not take the mark of Jesus Christ (X) are prohibited from commerce within his realm. Is this referring to some futuristic physical "mark" or biochip in our forehead and hand as is being taught today? Or have we simply overlooked the obvious because we are unwilling to acknowledge the Jesus Christ is the beast and Christianity is the second beast? If we simply take an honest look throughout history, we see that Christianity has outlawed "buying and selling" specifically for all those who do not bow down to the authority of The Pope and accept the specific mark on their forehead X.

The Book of Revelation is misunderstood by many as applying only to the last 7 years of "Tribulation" when in fact is was given 2000 years ago and covers a 2000 year span of Christian dominance. We see below the Mark of the Beast is the sign of the Cross X and those who do not have that mark were forbidden to "buy or sell" throughout history and that the mark of the X is the "seal on the forehead":

Jamieson-Fausset-Brown Bible Commentary

> *the mark, or the name—Greek, "the mark (namely), the name of the beast." The mark may be, as in the case of **the sealing of the saints in the forehead**, not a visible mark, but symbolical of allegiance. So the sign of the cross in Popery. The Pope's interdict has often shut out the excommunicate from social and commercial intercourse.*

Clarke's Commentary on the Bible

And that no man might buy or sell, save he that had the mark – "If any," <u>observes Bishop Newton,</u>

*"dissent from the stated and authorized forms (of Christianity); they are condemned and excommunicated as heretics; and in consequence of that they are no longer suffered **to buy or sell**; they are interdicted from traffic and commerce, and all the benefits of civil society.*

Roger Hoveden relates of William the Conqueror,

*that he was so dutiful to the pope that he would not permit any one in his power **to buy or sell** any thing whom he found disobedient to the apostolic see (The Pope).*

The canon of the council of Lateran, under Pope Alexander III.,

*made against the Waldenses and Albigenses, enjoins, upon pain of anathema, that no man presume to entertain or cherish them in his house or land, **or exercise traffic with them** (that do not follow Papal authority).*

The synod of Tours, in France, under the same pope, orders,

*"under the like intermination, that no man should presume to receive or assist them, no, not so much as hold any communion with them, **in selling or buying**; that, being deprived of the comfort of humanity they may be compelled to repent of the error of their way."*

It was ordered by a bull of Pope Martin the Fifth,

> *"that no contract should be made with such, and* ***that they should not follow any business and merchandise****: **save he that had the mark***; took the oath to be true to the pope, or made a public profession of the Popish religion: or the name of the beast; Papists, so called from the pope"*

> *"In the tenth and eleventh centuries the severity against the excommunicated was carried to so high a pitch, that nobody might come near them, not even their own wives, children, or servants; they forfeited all their natural legal rights and privileges, and were excluded from all kinds of offices."*

Again the false teacher and prophecy "experts" who are filled with the Spirit of Error are totally blind to the fact that the mark of the cross of Tammuz is identified by John in Revelation 13 as the χ! And Christianity has already fulfilled this prophecy of "buy/sell" in detail over the exact period prophesied.

Revelation 13
16 It (*Christianity*) also forced all people, great and small, rich and poor, free and slave, to receive a mark (χ) on their right hands or on their foreheads, [17] so that they could not buy or sell unless they had the mark (χ),

This was fulfilled by the ordered of Pope Martin the Fifth,

Gill's Exposition of the Entire Bible

And that no man might buy or sell,.... Either in an ecclesiastical sense, as to, be in any church office, or perform any such service, to say Mass, hear confession, give absolution, sell pardons and indulgences, &c. or in a

482

civil sense, as to trade, and exercise merchandise, and this was forbidden by several Popish councils and synods; the Lateran council, under Pope Alexander, decreed against the Waldenses and Albigenses, that no one should presume to retain or encourage them in their houses or countries, or "trade" with them; and the synod of Tours in France forbid any reception of heretics, or protection, and that any communion should be had with them "in buying and selling", as Mr. Mede has observed; and it was ordered by a bull of Pope Martin the Fifth, that no contract should be made with such, and that they should not follow any business and merchandise:

save he that had the mark; took the oath to be true to the pope, or made a public profession of the Popish religion:

or the name of the beast; Papists, so called from the pope; thus the antichristians are called from antichrist, as the Christians from Christ:

The Mark of Jesus is "X" as in X-mas which is drawn on the forehead of Christians while reciting "in the name of the Father, the Son, and the Holy Ghost" and sealing the mind with Trinity:

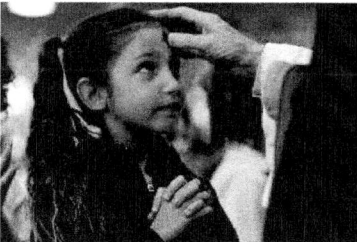

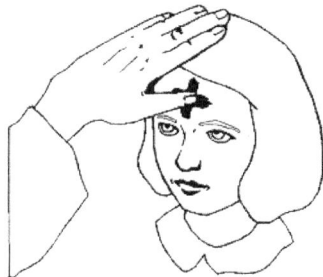

Bishop Newton,

> *"dissent from the stated and authorized forms (of Christianity); they are condemned and excommunicated as heretics; and in consequence of*

483

that they are no longer suffered <u>to buy or sell</u>; they are interdicted from traffic and commerce, and all the benefits of civil society.

The Cross is the opposite of the Mark/Seal of Yahuah

The Seal of Yahuah or the protective shield over the minds of His servants is known as ***The Shema***. Shema is the Hebrew word for "hear" and comes from the definition of ***The Seal of Yahuah*** in The Torah "Hear O Israel". That seal is the knowledge of Yahuah, the declaration that He alone is God and there is no other. A claim Yahuah is very clear about making... *He alone is God and there is no other. He alone is Creator and He did it alone all by Himself. He alone is our savior, our redeemer*:

Isaiah 44
24 "This is what Yahuah says— your Redeemer, who formed you in the womb: I am Yahuah, who has made all things, **who alone** stretched out the heavens, who spread out the earth **by myself**,

Isaiah 24
15 Therefore in the east give glory to Yahuah; exalt the name of Yahuah, the God of Israel! 8 "I am Yahuah; that is my name (not Yahusha, not LORD, and certainly not Jesus)! I will **not give my glory to another** or my praise to idols (no other, not even to His first born son! The name Yahusha even cries out *"Yahuah is our savoir"*).

Jude 1:25
25 to **Yahuah Our Savior**, who alone is wise, be glory and majesty, dominion and power, both now and forever.

Isaiah 42

5 This is what Yahuah says— **he who created** the heavens and stretched them out, who spread out the earth and all that comes out of it, who gives breath to its people, and life to those who walk on it:

Isaiah 45

5 <u>**I am Yahuah, and there is no other; apart from me there is no God**</u>. …

> 18 For this is what Yahuah says— **he who created the heavens, he is God**; he who fashioned and made the earth, he founded it; he did not create it to be empty, but formed it to be inhabited— he says: "**I am Yahuah, and there is no other**."

Isaiah 46

5 "To whom will you compare me or count me equal? To whom will you liken me that we may be compared (not even His messiah)? 8 "Remember this, fix it in mind (seal your mind with it), take it to heart (write it on your heart), you rebels. 9 Remember the former things, those of long ago; <u>**I am God, and there is no other; I am God, and there is none like me.**</u> 10 I make known the end from the beginning, from ancient times, what is still to come. I say: My purpose will stand, and I will do all that I please.

The Seal of Yahuah is very well defined as **His Name** written on our foreheads. That is a metaphor for those who know His Name and **understand** that He alone is God and there is no other. He is not a trinity nor is He a bi-entity. To fully understand *The Seal of Yahuah* we must understand and employ the intended *physical to spiritual parallel*s given to us and how they were explained over time through progressive revelation and then transposed into His Kingdom. I will explain these in detail.

The Seal of *The Kingdom of Yahuah* is clearly defined both in The Torah and *The Yahushaic Covenant*. Let us first define exactly what that seal is. *The Seal of Yahuah is quite literally **His***

Name and ***the knowledge that He alone is God*** and it is "written" on the foreheads as a SEAL over the minds of those who will inhabit His Kingdom:

Revelation 3
12 ***Him who overcomes I will make a pillar in the temple of my God*** (those sealed will become ***The Temple of Yahuah***). Never again will he (Yahuah) leave it (that Spiritual Temple). I will write on him (who overcomes) **the name of my God** (Yahuah)

Revelation 7:3
3 "Do not harm the land or the sea or the trees until we put ***a seal on the foreheads*** of the servants of our God (Yahuah)."

Revelation 9
4 They were told not to harm the grass of the earth or any plant or tree, but only those people who did not have ***the seal of God*** (Yahuah) ***on their foreheads***.

Revelation 22
4 They will see his face, and **his name** (Yahuah) **will be** (written/sealed) **on their foreheads**.

This seal is defined in detail in The Torah in Deuteronomy Chapter 6 below, in keeping with progressive revelation, ***physical to spiritual parallel***s, and transposition I will explain the meaning of these physical metaphors in (blue parenthesis):

Deuteronomy 6
6 "Now this is the commandment, the statutes and the judgments which Yahuah your God has commanded *me* to teach you, that you might do *them* in the land where you are going over to possess it (*the future Kingdom of Yahuah*), ² so that you and your son and your grandson might fear Yahuah your God, to keep all His statutes and His commandments (*the governing constitution in The*

Kingdom of Yahuah) which I command you, all the days of your life, and that your days may be prolonged (*the promise for obedience found in The Law is Eternal Life*). [3] O Israel, you should listen and be careful to do *it*, that it may be well with you and that you may multiply greatly, just as Yahuah, the God of your fathers, has promised you, *in* a land flowing with milk and honey (*the future Kingdom of Yahuah*).

[4] "**Hear (***Shema***), O Israel! Yahuah is our God, Yahuah is one (***God***)!** [5] **You shall love Yahuah your God with all your heart and with all your soul and with all your might.** [6] These words, which I am commanding you today, shall be (*written*) on your heart (*in **The Yahushaic Covenant** see Jeremiah 31:33*). [7] You shall teach them diligently to your sons and shall talk of them when you sit in your house and when you walk by the way and when you lie down and when you rise up. [8] You shall bind them as a sign on your hand (*the works of your hand*) and they (*His Law*) shall be as frontals (*or spiritual seal*) on your forehead (*over your mind*).

Yahusha also proclaimed ***The Seal of Yahuah*** to be essential to eternal life, just as it was defined in Deuteronomy 6 and confirmed in Revelation:

John 17:3
[3] And this is eternal life, that they may know You (*Yahuah*), **the only true God (*The Shema*), AND** (*be in covenant with*) Yahusha (*the*) Messiah whom You (*Yahuah*) have sent (*as the Passover Lamb to purchase that eternal life by covering the decrees in The Law that demand our death for transgressing His commandments and ordinances*).

The Meaning of Frontals

We see that Yahuah's Law and specifically the declaration and knowledge *that Yahuah is ONE God* (not a trinity or bi-entity) *and there is no other God* is said to be as **_frontals or protective shield on our foreheads_**:

> ### Deuteronomy 6:8
>
> "they (*His Law*) **shall be as frontals** (*or spiritual seal*) **on your forehead**(*Spiritual Mind*).

The Frontal Bone is literally the protective shield in the cranium (physical metaphor) that protects the Frontal Lobe of the brain:

This *physical to spiritual parallel* employed by Yahuah in Deuteronomy can only now be understood in the context it was meant. Science has defined the purpose of the Frontal Lobe of the human brain and we can see why that lobe MUST be sealed by Yahuah.

The Frontal Lobe has been identified and described as follows, according to Dr. Donald Stuss of The Rotman Research Institute:

> **The frontal lobe is a critical center and it controls the "essence" of our humanity.** The frontal lobes, which are also called the cerebral cortex, are the seat of **emotions** and **judgments** related to **sympathy**, which is the ability to feel sorrow for someone else's suffering, and **empathy**, which

the ability to understand another's feelings and problems. They are also the seat of understanding humor, including subtle witticisms and word plays. The frontal lobes also recognizes sarcasm and irony. **And they are where recognition of deception occurs guiding our judgment between right and wrong.** The cerebral cortex, or frontal lobes, is indeed the seat of our essence and nature.

We need to always keep in the foremost of our mind that Yahuah's purpose is to govern the Universe with His sons. The Frontal Lobe is critical in all aspects of judgment, empathy, knowing right from wrong. Yahuah literally provides a "protective shield" called *The Seal of Yahuah* which protects that very part of our mind that enables us to have empathy toward others, recognize deceptive philosophies, and determines our essence and nature.

In effect those who have this seal have in the foremost of their mind the truth that Yahuah is ONE God and that His Law defines what is right and wrong and that it is love (empathy) for others that are the foundation of that Law. This is exactly what was declared by Yahusha when asked.

When questioned by the Pharisees (teachers of The Law) about what is the single greatest commandment, Yahusha declared The Shema, *The Seal of Yahuah* by literally quoting Deuteronomy

Chapter 6:

> ### <u>Mark 12:28-34 (NIV)</u>
>
> 28 One of the teachers of the law (*Torah*) came and heard them debating. Noticing that Yahusha had given them a good answer, he asked him, "Of all the commandments, which is the most important?" 29 "**<u>The most important one</u>**," answered Yahusha (*then he quoted Deuteronomy 6*), "is this: *'Hear, O Israel, Yahuah our God, Yahuah is one. 30 Love Yahuah your God with all your heart and with all your soul and with all your mind and with all your strength.'* 31 The second is this: 'Love your neighbor as yourself.' There is no commandment greater than these." 32"Well said, teacher," the man replied. "You are right in saying that Yahuah is one and there is no other but Him. 33 To love him with all your heart, with all your understanding and with all your strength, and to love your neighbor as yourself is more important than all burnt offerings and sacrifices."

We see Yahusha confirm that *The Seal of Yahuah* is the Greatest Commandment of all. He went on to explain that in that understanding that *Yahuah is the ONE and ONLY God* our minds are sealed with the Love required to enter His Kingdom: Love Yahuah and your neighbor.

Yahusha was not giving us two new commandments here that the "Church would be built upon" as the "Old Laws" were abolished. Not at all, Yahusha was simply summarizing the 10 Commandments which were themselves a summary of the full set of 613 Laws. The Pharisees understood that and declared Yahusha a "true teacher of The Law".

The first 5 Commandments instruct us in detail how to express our love toward Yahuah. The last 5 Commandments instruct us in detail how to express our love toward our neighbor.

We see below that both the Seal and Sign of *The Kingdom of Yahuah* are expressed in the 10 Commandments:

How to love Yahuah	How to love your neighbor
1.You shall have no other gods before me (The Seal of *The Kingdom of Yahuah*) 2.You shall not make for yourself an image in the form of anything in heaven above or on the earth beneath or in the waters below. You shall not bow down to them or worship them; for I, Yahuah your God showing love to a thousand generations of those **who love me and keep my commandments**. (The Seal of *The Kingdom of Yahuah*) 3.You shall not misuse the name of Yahuah your God, for Yahuah will not hold anyone guiltless who misuses his name. (The Seal of *The Kingdom of Yahuah*) 4.Remember the Sabbath day by keeping it holy. the seventh day is a Sabbath to Yahuah your God. (The Sign of *The Kingdom of Yahuah*) 5.Honor your father and your mother, so that you may live long in the land Yahuah your God is giving you (because your parents are given as proxies in Yahuah's stead so loving them is loving Him.)	6.You shall not murder (your neighbor). 7.You shall not commit adultery (with your neighbor's wife). 8.You shall not steal (from your neighbor). 9.You shall not give false testimony against your neighbor. 10.You shall not covet your neighbor's house. You shall not covet your neighbor's wife, or his male or female servant, his ox or donkey, or anything that belongs to your neighbor.

The Pharisees understood that Yahusha was summing up The Law which was summed up into the 10 Commandments then further summarized into "love" by The Messiah. Yahusha was a "sealed servant of Yahuah".

Conclusion

I realize this book has been quite a study and covers a lot of ground in many areas. I felt it necessary to cover every angle because it is that important and I do not come out and say "Jesus Christ is the Antichrist" lightly. There was a time in my life when I would rather have had my tongue cut out of my mouth than to ever deny that name. But then I grew up!

In this book, we have proven that:

χξϛ Jesus Christ is not the name of the true Messiah and fails the test to come in the 'name of Yahuah' but rather comes in the name of 3 pagan gods.

χξϛ Jesus Christ's name was identified by name, mark, monogram, Christogram, and pictogram by John in the book of Revelation.

χξϛ Jesus Christ is the first beast and Christianity is the second beast that John saw in Revelation Chapter 13.

χξϛ Jesus Christ is The Lawless One who represents the Spirit of Error leading to Transgression of Desolation.

χξϛ Jesus Christ represents the Spirit of the False messiah/Antichrist that leads those who follow this false image to commit the Abomination of Desolation.

χξϛ Jesus Christ represents the cross of Tammuz which is the spiritual mark of the Trinity and is the Mark of the Beast that contradicts the Mark of Yahuah which is His name 𐤉𐤄𐤅𐤄

χξϛ Jesus Christ represents the Pig sacrifice of Ishtar Day on the Altar of Yahuah to Zeus... Hesus! Both in name Je (earthly) sus (pig) and in the ritual of Easter.

493

𝙭𝙨𝙨 Jesus Christ enters the Temple of Yahuah every Easter and desecrates the Altar thereby stopping the daily sacrifice Yahusha offers of himself on your behalf as Passover Lamb before Yahuah.

𝙭𝙨𝙨 Jesus Christ represents the gods, rituals, and sacrifices of Mystery Babylon the Harlot.

𝙭𝙨𝙨 Jesus Christ is the prophesied Antichrist that Christianity has caused all humanity to worship in the image of a man who died as God over Yahuah.

As I pointed out the word 'sacrifices' were added to scripture in the book of Daniel placing a seal one of the many "seals" over that book that has hidden the identity of the Antichrist/False image of the Messiah. However there is one place where the word sacrifices was not added and that is in Daniel chapter 9. I wanted to address this passage quickly:

Daniel 9
[25] "Know and understand this: From the time the word goes out to restore and rebuild Jerusalem until the Anointed One (*Yahusha*), the King (*of Kings*), comes, there will be seven 'sevens,' and sixty-two 'sevens.' It (*Jerusalem*) will be rebuilt with streets and a trench, but in times of trouble (*Israel would go from Babylon to Persian to Roman captivity*). [26] After the sixty-two 'sevens,' the Anointed One (*Yahusha*) will be put to death (*as The Passover Lamb on Passover*) and will have nothing. The (*Roman*) people of the ruler who will come (*later, the false messiah* 𝙭𝙨𝙨 *Jesus Christ, he is a Roman invention i.e. an image*) will destroy the city and the sanctuary (*in 70 AD*). The end (*of the city and sanctuary*) will come like a flood (*of War*): War will continue until the end (𝙭𝙨𝙨 *brings war in his name until the very end*), and **desolations** (*plural not one*) have been decreed (*until the very end*). [27] He will confirm a

494

covenant with many for one 'seven.' In the middle of the 'seven' he will put an end to sacrifice and offering (*of Yahusha who offers himself as The Passover Lamb on the Altar/hearts of man*). And in the temple (*the body of man*) he χ§ς will set up an abomination (*of the Ishtar Pig sacrifice on that altar in that temple*) that causes desolation (*the destruction of those who follow The Lawless One as the Ishtar Pig is not the proper sacrifice for sin*), until the end (*when the Testimony of Yahusha destroys this false image*) that is decreed (*in The Law for abolishing it*) is poured out on him (*and* χ§ς *is revealed to be Jesus Christ the image of a man who died in whom the Law was abolished that we have elevated in our hearts as God above Yahuah is destroyed*).

We are at that time of the end and Jesus Christ has been revealed to be… The Antichrist χ§ς or False image of the true Messiah. Unfortunately we, most of us reading this book, have invited Jesus Christ into our hearts and by keeping Easter have slaughtered the Beast of the Earth or Earthly Pig over Yahuah's altar. We have believed the Spirit of Error that The Torah/Law was abolished by χ§ς .

I want to leave you all with this encouragement. It is never too late until you die to reverse this abomination and rededicate the altar of your heart properly back to Yahuah your Creator. We must dethrone this false image of the Messiah known as χ§ς Jesus Christ who has elevated himself above all that is called God and seated himself on the altar of Yahuah proclaiming himself to be God incarnate. We must then STOP keeping and putting our faith in Easter, clean the blood of that Earthly Pig χ§ς off the altar of our hearts. Then we must begin putting our faith in and keeping Passover in light of Yahusha thereby pouring out his blood on the altar of Yahuah and proclaim the greatest commandment of all… Hear O Israel, Yahuah is ONE God, the only true God, and there is no other. Then we in the example of Yahusha must give our lives as living sacrificial lambs to Yahuah.

𐤗𐤔𐤎 Jesus Christ destroys all those whose names are not written
in the LAMBS Book of Life. Because Yahuah has given us a sign
(the Sabbath), and seal over our minds (the Shema), and a
deliverance through Passover (Salvation of Yahuah which is what
Yahusha means). Yes the entries in The Lambs Book of Life you
must have are that you have been signed/sealed/delivered into His
Kingdom by keeping His Commandments not falling for this lie.

𐤗𐤔𐤎 Jesus Christ robs you of all three witnesses in The Lambs
Book of Life. If you follow this false messiah you will not display
the sign of the Sabbath but the sign of Babylon which is Sunday.
You will not have the seal of the name of 𐤉𐤄𐤅𐤄 on your forehead
but rather the seal of Babylon which is Trinity/Cross. You will not
be delivered by the Passover Lamb because you have put your
faith in the JE(earthly) SUS(pig) of Ishtar and there will be no
sacrifice to cover your sin.

But, like I said we can overcome this and be forgiven for
making this abominable sacrifice of a pig on His altar
(The Abomination of Desolation)... but YOU have to
overcome this false messiah, this other gospel, this lying
spirit of Babylon called Mystery Babylon... but it can be
done. This book was your first step; now it is up to you to
overcome it, but if you do...

Revelation 2:11
'He who has an ear, let him hear what the Spirit
says to the churches He who overcomes (𐤗𐤔𐤎)
will not be hurt by the second death.'

1 John 5:4-5
For whatever is born of Yahuah overcomes the

(*pagan*) world; and this is the victory that has overcome the (*pagan*) world--our faith *(in The Passover Lamb sacrifice of Yahusha)*. Who is the one who overcomes the (*pagan*) world, but he who believes Yahusha is the (*first born*) son of Yahuah (*not God incarnate*)?

Revelation 12:11

"And they overcame χξϛ (*this Ishtar Pig*) **because of the blood of the Passover Lamb** (*they stopped keeping Easter and overturned The Abomination of Desolation by properly being covered by The Passover*) and because of the word of their testimony (*that Yahuah alone is the only true God*), and they did not love their (*pagan*) life (*and all the holidays*) even when faced with death (*to themselves i.e. gave their life to Yahuah as a living sacrifice*).

Revelation 3:21

'He who overcomes (*the Beast* χξϛ), I will grant to him to sit down with Me on My throne, as I also overcame (*this pagan world*) and sat down with My Father on His throne.

Revelation 3:12

'He who overcomes (χξϛ), I will make him a pillar (*living stone*) in the temple of My God, and he will not go out from it anymore; and I will write on him the name of My God 𐤉𐤄𐤅𐤄

Revelation 3:5

'He who overcomes (*The Trinity/Sunday/Easter* Ⲭ§Ϛ) will thus be clothed in white garments; and I will not erase his name from the book of life (*because you will have the Sign/Seal/Deliverance needed*), and I will confess his name before My Father and before His angels.

Revelation 2:26

'He who overcomes Ⲭ§Ϛ , and he who keeps My deeds *(follows in the footsteps of Yahusha)* until the end, TO HIM I WILL GIVE AUTHORITY OVER THE NATIONS;

Revelation 2:17

'He who has an ear, let him hear what the Spirit says to the churches To him who overcomes Ⲭ§Ϛ , to him I will give some of the hidden manna (*The Spirit of Holiness*), and I will give him a white stone, and a new name written on the stone which no one knows but he who receives it.'

Revelation 2:7

'He who has an ear, let him hear what the Spirit of Holiness says to the churches To him who overcomes Ⲭ§Ϛ , I will grant to eat of the tree of life which is in the Paradise of God.'

1 John 4:4

You are from Yahuah, little children, and have overcome them (*that follow* Ⲭ§Ϛ); because greater is He 𐤉𐤄𐤅𐤄 who is in you than he Ⲭ§Ϛ who is in the world.

1 John 2:13
I am writing to you, fathers, because you know Him 𝔶𝔥𝔴𝔷 (*Yahuah*) who has been from the beginning I am writing to you, young men, because you have overcome the evil one 𝔵𝔰𝔰 I have written to you, children, because you know the Father.

Romans 8:37
But in all these things we overwhelmingly conquer 𝔵𝔰𝔰 (*the Earthly Pig of Ishtar/Easter*) through Him (*Yahusha The Passover Lamb*) who loved us (*enough to die for us*).

May Yahuah bless and keep us all and seal our minds with His Holy Name and guard our frontal lobes from this Great Deception.

This is book 4 of The Original Revelation Series. In book 5 I will now properly introduce us all to the REAL Messiah of Israel in my book *Melchizedek and The Passover Lamb*. Yahusha was the royal prince from the Davidian Dynasty and Zadokian son heir to the office of High Priest. Join me as I begin to relay our foundation in Truth as I define The Kingdom of Yahuah, The New (Yahushaic) Covenant, and The Passover Gate whereby we enter into eternal life…

Bondservant of Yahuah, disciple and apostle of Yahusha
....*Rav Sha'ul*.

Printed in Great Britain
by Amazon

18236024R10302